ENTREPRENEURIAL BEHAVIOR

BARBARA J. BIRD
Case Western Reserve University

SCOTT, FORESMAN AND COMPANY
Glenview, Illinois   London, England

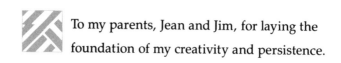 To my parents, Jean and Jim, for laying the foundation of my creativity and persistence.

Acknowledgments are listed in the References section beginning on p. 383. This is to be considered a legal extension of the copyright page.

Cover photo: Radio Light, 1984 by Paul Seide/Courtesy of Heller Gallery.

Library of Congress Cataloging-in-Publication Data

Bird, Barbara J. (Barbara Jean)
    Entrepreneurial Behavior / Barbara J. Bird.

    Includes bibliography and index.
    1. Entrepreneurship. 2. Organizational behavior. 3. New business enterprises—Management. 4. Creative ability in business.
    I. Title.
    HB615.B57 1989
    338'.04—dc19   88-38218
    ISBN 0-673-39791-2   CIP

    1 2 3 4 5 6—MVN—94 93 92 91 90 89

PREFACE

Small and growing businesses provide much of the fuel for today's global economy, and entrepreneurship gives rise to healthy, innovative, and competitive small businesses. Such businesses created more than two-thirds of the net new jobs between 1980 and 1985, and account for a surprising number of exports important to altering the U.S. trade deficit. Entrepreneurship attracts media attention and is increasingly perceived as a valued career alternative to corporate management.

Entrepreneurs do more than create new ideas, write business plans, arrange financing, sell their products or services, and make profits. They add value through organizing resources and assuming risks. To understand who will try to launch a new venture—and how well that venture may fare—we can look at the ways in which entrepreneurs perceive opportunity, accept risk, and intentionally organize resources to add value. This book examines the behavior of entrepreneurs by focusing on the characteristics, relationships, and competencies that influence successful entrepreneurial behavior, drawing from relevant literature and original research. Concepts developed in the book apply to entrepreneurial start-ups and acquisitions, and can be extended to corporate entrepreneurship and other forms of organizational creativity such as innovation. The book offers insights to potential entrepreneurs, as well as to their families, friends, employees, and professional advisors.

Implications sections throughout the book highlight the importance of specific behaviors to venture initiation (distinguishing who will become an entrepreneur and how to help create more entrepreneurs) and to venture success—that is, survival and growth. Most chapters include vignettes that illustrate the behavior of entrepreneurs and the personal challenges they face in pursuit of their goals.

To distinguish among different forms of entrepreneurship, the book establishes a four-dimensional typology comprising the entrepreneur's goals, entry process, technological context, and chosen ownership structure. The issues of temporal tension, strategic focus, and strategic posture are repeatedly highlighted to emphasize the intentional nature of entrepreneurial behavior.

The material compiled and discussed in the book will provide readers with an appreciation of the personalities, backgrounds, lifestyles, relationships, and dilemmas faced by today's entrepreneurs. It might also give you an opportunity to diagnose your own entrepreneurial competencies and begin developmental efforts if you so desire.

This book can be used in courses on Entrepreneurial Behavior, such as the one taught at Case Western Reserve University, which appeals to (1) students interested in becoming entrepreneurs but not ready to write a business plan; (2) students interested in working for or with entrepreneurs; and (3) students who have entrepreneurial friends or relatives. The book can also be used as collateral reading in a range of entrepreneurship courses such as Business Planning, Small Business Management, and New Venture Development. As a supplement, the book builds a bridge from the functional responsibilities of financing, product development, and marketing to individual competencies and helps to explain "how they do it." Finally, the book can also supplement other courses such as Innovation and Corporate Entrepreneurship, Leadership, Careers, Management, and Organizational Behavior.

This work began with my dissertation under the mentorship of Warren Bennis, and I am grateful for the creative support that has always characterized our relationship. I thank the MBA students in my Entrepreneurial Behavior class and my teaching assistant, Leo Dumdum, for their use of comments on early versions of the book. For their reviews of early drafts of chapters, I thank my colleagues at Case Western Reserve University, specifically Richard Boyatzis, Bill Pasmore, Huggy Rao, and Don Wolfe. For their patient, informed, and "blind" reviews of the book, I thank Jim Burrow, Alan Carsrud, Bill Gartner, Carol Haag, Jerome Katz, Robert Ronstadt, and Karl Vesper. I am particularly grateful to Alex Greene for his patience and persistence and kind words of support. I thank my family and friends for their patience and support during the three years this project absorbed me. Of course, the book rests solidly on the entrepreneurs whose adventures provide the "grist," and I thank all those whose stories are reported here.

B.J.B.

TABLE OF CONTENTS

Chapter 1
DEFINING ENTREPRENEURIAL BEHAVIOR
1

Chapter 2
ENTREPRENEURSHIP: CREATIVE VISION
35

Chapter 3
IDENTIFYING AND DEVELOPING THE RIGHT STUFF:
EXPERIENCE AND BACKGROUND
57

Chapter 4
IDENTIFYING AND DEVELOPING THE RIGHT STUFF:
MOTIVATION
77

Chapter 5
THE IMPACT OF PERSONAL HISTORY: BEYOND FEAR
AND GUILT
113

Chapter 6
THE PLACE: SITUATIONS THAT CATALYZE
ENTREPRENEURSHIP
137

Chapter 7
THE PATH: CAREERS AND LIFESTYLES OF
ENTREPRENEURS
169

Chapter 8
INTERNAL TEAMS: PARTNERS
205

Chapter 9
INTERNAL TEAMS: EMPLOYEES
233

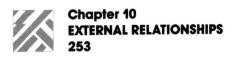

Chapter 10
EXTERNAL RELATIONSHIPS
253

Chapter 11
**THE ENTREPRENEURIAL ROLE: THE EVOLUTION
OF A LEADER
299**

Chapter 12
**LEARNING, SELF-MANAGEMENT, AND OTHER
COMPETENCIES OF SUCCESSFUL ENTREPRENEURS
349**

CHAPTER 1

DEFINING ENTREPRENEURIAL BEHAVIOR

INTRODUCTION

Entrepreneurship is one of the "sexy" business terms of this decade. Current popular images such as Steven Jobs, founder of Apple Computer and Next, Inc.; Frederick Smith, founder of Federal Express; Ted Turner, founder of Turner Broadcasting; An Wang of Wang Laboratories; and Paul Hawkin of Smith & Hawkin show the great rewards of entrepreneurship. Fame and fortune, the dreams of Horatio Alger success, political importance in terms of the generation of new jobs and taxes, and a heroic charisma attach themselves to the notion of entrepreneurship. This chapter defines entrepreneurial behavior and its relationship to new venture creation, innovation, and social and economic values. The intentional nature of entrepreneurial behavior will be described and different types of entrepreneurs discussed.

FOUR DIMENSIONS OF ENTREPRENEURIAL BEHAVIOR

When we think of entrepreneurship, we think of the *individuals*—the entrepreneurs—who set the process in motion and who direct the early stages of new ventures. We ask questions such as "Who becomes an entrepreneur?" and "Why?", "What is the 'right stuff' of entrepreneurship?", "What characteristics and motivations determine success?"

We also think of the *organizational outcomes* of that process—the new organization, career, jobs, wealth, products, etc. Often these outcomes so impress us that we seek to find ways to achieve them for ourselves or our communities—they motivate the reading of this book. However, we will see that highly valued outcomes take on different meanings for entrepreneurs. For many, money and organizational size are more a way of keeping score than ends in themselves.

After we recognize our fascination with entrepreneurs and their success, we begin to consider the *process* of entrepreneurship itself—the conceiving, creating, organizing, promoting, and implementing of new organizations. Here we ask questions about how the process works, what entrepreneurs do, who they interact with and how, and what changes occur as entrepreneurs and their organizations grow.

There is a fourth factor: *The environment* of venturing. This refers to the larger social, economic, and political forces that support or restrict entrepreneurship. Contexts include factors such as property rights, the presence of venture capital, society-wide beliefs in free trade, and technology as well as more "local" resources such as incubators, networks, friends, partners, and family support.

These four elements together shape entrepreneurial behavior. See Figure 1.1. They predict whether or not a new venture is started and how it develops. Each of the four elements influences or conditions the others. Throughout this book, the various relationships among the elements will be described.

FIGURE 1.1   A Theoretical Framework for Understanding New Venture Creation

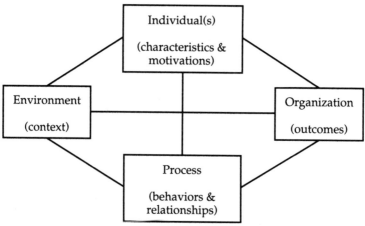

Source: Data from W.B. Gartner, *Academy of Management Review*, 10:696-706 (Mississippi State, MS: Mississippi State University, 1985).

Let us begin with a simple definition of entrepreneurship.[1]

DEFINITION 1: Entrepreneurship is the creation of value through the creation of organization.

At the most general level, entrepreneurship is the creation of value through the creation of organization. Entrepreneurs discover, invent, reveal, enact, and in other ways make manifest some new product, service, transaction, resource, technology, and/or market that has value to some community or marketplace. For the purposes of this book, the process of creating value operates through the creation of a multiperson system (organization) that transforms input such as materials, money, and time into output such as products and services. Excluded are the activities of the solely self-interested (the clever thief and the con artist) and those who create without deliberate and choiceful organizing of human resources (e.g., artists, inventors, and solo-self-employed professionals). Included are those who start a business or nonprofit agency and those who transform (acquire, redirect, restructure, and "turn around") existing organizations so they add new values to the community or marketplace.

OPERATIONAL DEFINITIONS

Being able to define entrepreneurship conceptually, as we did above, and being able to point out concrete examples (cases such as Steven Jobs, Frederick Smith, Ted Turner, etc.) are the minimum required to study entrepreneurial behavior. However, in order to study entrepreneurs in a systematic way that will allow comparison and generalization, we need to be much more precise and operational in our definitions. For example, the owner of the local dry cleaner may operate in ways similar to or different from the engineer who starts a high-technology production process or the corporate executive who buys an existing business. Researchers and consultants have devised a wide range of more specific definitions, and because different

---

[1] The word *entrepreneur* comes from the French language (*entre* + *prendre*) and means, literally, to undertake or to take between. Among the earliest economic uses (16th and 17th centuries), it referred to *government contractors* for military or public works projects. Later a Scottish economist, Richard Cantillon, specified the important function of entrepreneurship—that of bearing economic risk. At this time the classic entrepreneur was the *farmer* who plants and tends to crops without any certainty of whether or not they will survive to harvest or the price they will bring (Hebert & Link, 1982). The term has come to be applied to any risk taker, any independent merchant, or any promoter. It has been defined by economists, sociologists, politicians, bankers, and entrepreneurs themselves, with each definition flavored to serve the definer's purposes.

definitions result in different people and organizations being studied, it behooves us to attend to the issues of who is studied.

DEFINITION 2: Entrepreneurship is the process of starting and/or growing a new profit-making business.

This is probably the most common definition of entrepreneurship. The operation, starting a new profit-making business, is more narrow and specified than our first definition. Here the type of value (profit) and organization (business) have been specified and the process has been limited (to starting the business). Furthermore, the definition implies a standard of success (e.g., profits are indeed made). However, partnerships, sole proprietorships, and corporations as well as stable, small firms and fast-growth firms (which may differ considerably) are included.

We can take this specification one step further. In order to study business start-ups, we need some concrete indicators for determining when a new business exists. Some researchers have used indicators such as a new listing in the local telephone directory (those that are not number changes) (Shapero & Giglierano, 1982); the clients of the Small Business Administration or related government agencies designed for new venture start-up assistance (Chrisman & Hoy, 1985); the clients of venture capitalists and underwriters; Dun and Bradstreet files; and unemployment insurance data (Birley; 1984). Finally, studies often select firms that have a certain longevity (e.g., three months, one to three years, more than five years, etc.) or size (e.g., more than five employees but fewer than 50, fewer than 100 employees, sales less than $5 million, etc.). Such criteria specify a sample of entrepreneurs that may differ markedly from other samples. This makes comparisons among entrepreneurs possible, provided variables are measured in similar ways across studies. However, the generalization of each study is restricted.

DEFINITION 3: Entrepreneurship is the process of providing a new product or service.

This alternative definition focuses on the values of innovation and creativity, the creation of *new* values. That is, innovative firms introduce one or more of the following "new combinations" (Schumpeter, 1961):

1. New goods [and we would add services]
2. New methods of production (e.g., advanced manufacturing technology)
3. New markets
4. New sources of supply
5. New organization of the industry [as with a cartel or monopoly]

This definition extends entrepreneurship to processes that do not necessarily involve the creation of a new organization (new products/services are produced through existing organizations). It raises questions about what is "new" and might be further specified in terms of patents, copyrights, and other proprietary rights. Such criteria exclude "copycat" enterprises that replicate existing products/services.

The power of these definitions is found in the narrowing of our vision by finding concrete, objective criteria. This enables empirical studies, the results of which will be presented in this text. As suggested, there are myriad definitions and no reason to believe that all types of entrepreneurs are alike. Thus generalizations must be questioned and remain tentative (see Appendix A).

Implications
If different definitions of entrepreneurship result in different people and different organizations being studied, then we may have myriad formulas for success. Just as there is no "one best way" to organize or mobilize an existing large organization such as General Motors, IBM, or Harvard University, there is no one way to venture survival, growth, and stability.

ENTREPRENEURIAL BEHAVIOR
The study of entrepreneurial behavior looks at the activities, interactions, competencies, feelings, and relationships of the entrepreneur and the entrepreneurial team. We will begin with a description of what entrepreneurs do. The remainder of the book will look at how that behavior comes about as an interaction between individuals with certain characteristics and social contexts that support or inhibit entrepreneurial behavior.

> DEFINITION 4: Entrepreneurial behavior is opportunistic, value-driven, value-adding, risk-

accepting, creative activity where ideas take the form of organizational birth, growth, or transformation.

This definition forms the focus for the remainder of the book.

ACTIVITIES

Entrepreneurs do many things that distinguish them from managers and others in organizations. Indeed, their activities may help us recognize just who *is* an entrepreneur.

> I don't think you can tell a guy's an entrepreneur just by having a conversation with him, you'd have to see where he's fitting into the world and what he's doing—it's his action. . . .
>
> Irv Robbins of Baskin-Robbins

One set of consultants who had worked with a number of entrepreneurs developed a flow chart of no less than 57 separate activities, which begins with evaluating personal goals and includes such specific actions as defining sales goals, evaluating locations, and finding sources of supply. The activity culminates in making and delivering the first sale (Swayne & Tucker, 1973).

Almost every version of "how to start a business" books and seminars includes a checklist of things to do and the order in which to do them. The multitude of specific activities is too cumbersome and detailed for consideration in this book. We turn instead to more abstract and general types of activity.

Several entrepreneurship researchers have offered their versions of the start-up activities of successful entrepreneurs. Table 1.1 shows several of these lists.

The entrepreneurial activities listed in Table 1.1 show that entrepreneurial behavior requires competency in many different areas such as marketing, finance, information gathering, decision making, team building, etc. Successful entrepreneurs are those who are able to juggle many activities and roles at the same time (that is, they are generalists). Based on these descriptions of entrepreneurial activities we can conclude that entrepreneurial behavior is *complex*, requiring a wide range of competencies. It is also *intentional* since no one is forced by others or by luck into becoming an entrepreneur (the career is voluntary). Although these lists do not show the emotional tone of entrepreneurial behavior, it is also *passionate*, full of

TABLE 1.1 Entrepreneurial Activities

Steinhoff (1978)	Determine desired profit, complete projected income statement
	Survey the market for probable sales volume
	List assets to be used
	Prepare opening day balance sheet
	Study the location
	Prepare layout for store/office/work space
	Choose legal form for the business
	Review merchandising plan
	Analyze estimated expenses: fixed and variable
	Determine break-even point
	Establish credit policy
	Review risks and plans for managing them
	Establish personnel policy
	Establish adequate accounting records
Tate, Megginson, Scott, & Trueblood (1978)	Develop a timetable
	Establish business objectives
	Set up organizational structure
	Determine personnel requirements
	Determine physical plant requirements
	Plan marketing approach
	Prepare budget
	Locate financial resources
	Implement plans
Meredith, Nelson, & Neck (1982)	Decide to go into business
	Analyze individual strengths and weaknesses
	Select a product or service
	Conduct market research
	Assess potential share of the market
	Select a location for the business
	Prepare a financial plan

TABLE 1.1   Entrepreneurial Activities (*continued*)

	Prepare a production plan
	Prepare a management plan
	Prepare a marketing plan
	Borrow funds to begin
Silver (1983)	Identify the opportunity
	Create the solution
	Plan the business
	Select the entrepreneurial team
	Produce and test-market the product
	Raise venture capital
Gartner (1986)	Locate a business opportunity
	Accumulate resources
	Market products or services
	Make the product/provide the services
	Build an organization
	Respond to government and society

emotional energy, drive, and spirit. The passion can best be seen over time, in the persistence, tenacity, and long hours in the start-up and growth phases and in the tendency for entrepreneurs to experience their venture's successes and difficulties as personal events. The focus of the following discussion is the intentional, complex, and passionate nature of entrepreneurial behavior.

INTENTIONAL QUALITY OF ENTREPRENEURIAL BEHAVIOR

Intentionality is a conscious state of mind that directs attention (and therefore experience and action) toward a specific object (goal) or pathway to achieve it (means). Entrepreneurial intentions aim toward the creation of a new venture or new values in existing ventures. Intentions have at least two dimensions: (1) location—e.g., whose intentions are operative, those of the entrepreneur (internal locus) and/or those of other stakeholders, markets, etc. (external locus) (Katz & Gartner, 1986)—and (2) the relative rationality versus intuition of the person(s) with entrepreneurial intentions at any given moment in the process.

This latter dimension involves mental or intrapsychic activity that varies along a continuum from a *rational, analytic, and cause-and-effect-orientation* found in formal business plans, opportunity analysis, resource acquisition, goal setting, and most observable goal-directed behavior to an *intuitive, holistic, and contextual orientation* found in the networking, focus, persistence, and vision of the entrepreneurial act. Figure 1.2 shows how these two forms of thought interact in the entrepreneurial process.

The intrapsychic process begins in service of the entrepreneur's personal needs, values, wants, habits, and beliefs, which have their own precursors and which will be discussed in Chapters 3 and 4. The process operates from perceptions (ideally these are accurate) of the situation or context (covered in more depth in Chapter 5).

FIGURE 1.2   The Rational and Intuitive Origins of Entrepreneurial Behavior

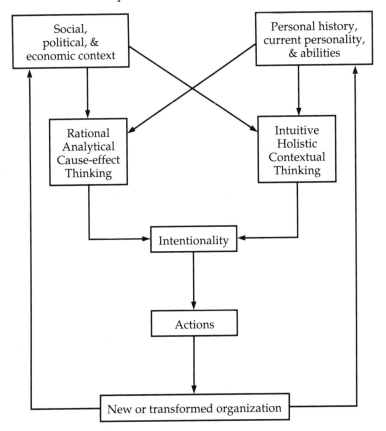

The process appears to involve four intrapsychic actions: (1) creating and maintaining a temporal tension (based on a gap between "what is" here and now and "what will be" in the desired future); (2) sustaining strategic focus while moving between the details of operations and the "big picture" of strategy and planning; (3) choosing a path toward a chosen goal or using a chosen means; and (4) choosing the posture or alignment between the self and the outer world. The results of intentional direction include actions, statements, relationships, and experiences that change the context and ultimately combine to form a new organization. Finally, the actions and organization change existing needs, values, etc. of the entrepreneur and may fuel continued intentional drive or diffuse it. (See Figure 1.3)

Sustaining temporal tension. In the Western world, time is conceived as irreversible movement along a straight line whereby "the moving finger writes, and having writ, moves on" (Omar Khayyam). The most obvious dimension of temporal tension among Western entrepreneurs involves linking the known present (the "way it is," the "way it is always done," the "way we do it around here") to the future, which is not yet manifest or realized. "To carry him through . . . he needs a 'tomorrow' toward which he moves . . . the entrepreneur

FIGURE 1.3 Intention-Direction

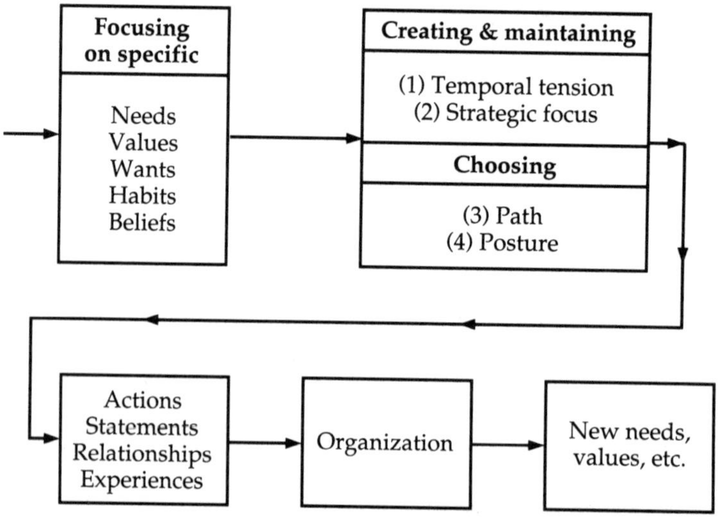

continually trades away his present for his anticipation of the future" (Collins et al., 1964, p. 162) and the further into the future the vision, the greater the uncertainty and the greater the temporal tension as one draws that future into the present.

The future time horizon is most important and the tension greatest for the innovative entrepreneur. "Time horizons for radical innovations make them essentially 'irrational' from a present value viewpoint" (Quinn, 1985, p. 74). In his study, Quinn found that the lag between invention and marketing a product ranged from 3 to 25 years (average 19.2 years). This time lag translates into behavioral and tactical "incrementalism," a more day-to-day orientation, and less planning.

Yet to succeed, the entrepreneur *must sustain some vision*, if not plan, for the future. The vision hooks in to his or her passion, sustains optimism in the face of setbacks, and allows the mobilization of others' beliefs and energies. Indeed, one study reveals that future time orientation relates positively to success factors such as organizational growth. In their study of applicants for National Science Foundation seed capital grants, Smith and Miner (1985) found those with faster- compared to slower-growing firms tend to have a stronger future orientation, a more pronounced need for feedback, as well as other aspects of task motivation.

Time span of intention. In his general history of organizations, Jacques (1976) argues that "work has to do with bringing an idea of the future into present reality—or of continuously shaping the present to realize this idea" (p. 118). Furthermore, work capacity is a characteristic of individuals that "enables the person to organize the moving present so as to work through into the future" (p. 122). In other words, the structuring of the present to bring about desired future states is the nature of most work and a central and defining aspect of entrepreneurial work. "The entrepreneur begins to set in motion a series of events he intends will lead to a future state of affairs" (Collins, et al., 1964, p. 151).

The time span of intention or discretion is the timeframe in which one is comfortable working without structure or feedback from someone else (Jacques, 1976). Jacques argues that time span of intention/discretion is a positive correlate of individual work capacity and feelings of work importance (weight). The longer into the future one is working without structure or feedback (i.e., longer time span of intention), the more complex the path to the goal, the greater the number of things to be done and managed, the greater the number of potential obstacles and opportunities, and the more information that needs to be assimilated and used.

Jacques also argues that there are discontinuities among individuals in the distribution of work capacity and the future timeframe of comfort. That is, some individuals are more comfortable than others with long, ambiguous, and complex tasks. Some are more comfortable than others with shorter-term, more clearly structured tasks.

From these observations we can conclude that entrepreneurs with longer time spans of intention will be better able to see through to completion venture ideas that have longer incubation periods. Entrepreneurs with shorter time spans of intention will be more likely to succeed in ventures that have short-term milestones and payoffs. Thus we would look for a longer time span in successful entrepreneurs in R & D-driven ventures or ventures that need several yearly cycles to prove themselves. Those with shorter-term time spans would more likely meet with failure in such ventures.

Entrepreneurial versus managerial time spans. Entrepreneurs tend to be generalists whereas managers are specialists, with more narrow timeframes of intention and action. Support for this assertion comes from two sources.

First, Jacques' (1976) theory suggests that individual differences in time span comfort relate to organizational level. Table 1.2 shows six layers of organization; there are observable differences in time span of discretion/intention among the layers. As can be seen, longer timeframes are associated with greater responsibility, rank, prestige, and power, and—not surprisingly—time span of discretion is positively related to perceptions of job size and felt fair pay (Richardson, 1971). The theory suggests that managers with specific hierarchic positions bring with them or tend to develop specialized future timeframes, extending from several weeks to over ten years as one moves up the hierarchy (Jacques, 1976). Second, another theory based on management functions proposes (and research confirms) that individuals specialized by function (e.g., marketing, research and development, production), tend to develop specific future timeframes, with R & D longer than marketing, which is longer than production (Lawrence & Lorsch, 1969).

In contrast, entrepreneurs are "generalists," involved with all aspects of their organizations from selling to manufactur-

TABLE 1.2   Relation of Time Span of Discretion to
Organizational Roles

Time span	Description of time span Type of job/role
< 3 months	Perceptual motor, concrete operations "The quality of capacity at this level is . . . one of concreteness in the sense of needing to be in immediate perceptual contact with the physical output . . . and to be able to manipulate it motorically as work progresses and the task is carried out" (p. 144). Typists, manual labor, sales clerks, some first-line supervisors
3–12 months	Imaginal concrete "The quality of the capacity . . . is that of being able to hold the concrete problem firmly in imagination and to work with it mentally, without the support of being able continuously to test judgment and imagination by tactile manipulation of a physical thing" (p. 146). Floor nurse, social worker, short-term research, foreman
1–2 years	Imaginal scanning "The person must be able to sense the interplay of the various parts without the support of being able physically to perceive at one time the various parts making up the whole" (p. 147). Owner of small business (fewer than 150 employees), sales manager with eight reporting sales assistants, battalion commander
2–5 years	Conceptual modeling, design, creativity where neither output nor project can be foreseen concretely "The task requires the individual to retain mental contact with what exists, but then at the same time to achieve a detachment from this experience and to work with ideas of things which are different from what exists—which look different, function differently, do different things" (p. 148). "The central quality is that of detachment; of abstraction in the sense of being

TABLE 1.2   Relation of Time Span of Discretion to
                     Organizational Roles (*continued*)

	able to work at specific and concrete problems without dependence upon mental contact with existing things, and with the ability to contact things without becoming mentally fixed on them" (p. 150). Designers, proposals for new methods, procedures, policies
5–10 years	Intuitive theory "Based on the mental possession of intuitive theories built up from experience. . . . The construction of the project has now become a matter of unconscious intuition, with a complex of apparently disconnected facts and figures [which are] intuitively sorted over" (p. 151). Chief executives, managers of businesses, and army units employing 5,000–10,000 people.
10–20 years	Institution creating "If technology allows, there is a shift towards managing in terms of policy setting and away from directing and coordinating the activities of subordinates with collateral relations" (p. 152). Head of diversified organization, multinationals, governmental agencies employing (responsible for) tens to hundreds of thousands of people.

Source: Data from Jacques, 1976.

ing, from stuffing envelopes to meeting with venture partners. They have a wide range of responsibilities, each with a different future time span (Bird & Neiswander, 1987). Likewise, entrepreneurs as "doers" and CEOs tend to operate at all levels, often violating the chain of command that they have set up and "second guessing" managers. In the early stages, this is necessary and entrepreneurs need multiple and flexible future horizons. Thus entrepreneurs operate both in the here-and-now and the long-term future, and as a result *experience greater temporal tension and develop greater time complexity and time agility than most mangers.*

Entrepreneurial behavior is also characterized by the *ability to make quick, incremental decisions in adjustment to the timing of the environment* (markets, government, labor, etc.):

> Because of familiarity with their chosen field, [entrepreneurs] . . . have the ability to recognize patterns as they develop and the confidence to assume that missing elements of the pattern will take the shape they foresee. This early recognition enables them to get a jump on others in commitment to action.
>
> Stevenson, 1985, p. 40

In any organizational decision process there are four time lags: (1) time between environmental change and when information about that change is received by the entrepreneurial team; (2) time between the receipt of that information and when a decision is made; (3) time between decision and action; and (4) time between action and results such as increased productivity, increased value of the firm, and better quality. Entrepreneurs apparently shorten the first three segments. The fourth seems out of control in that it requires environmental response. (See Figure 1.4.)

As the total time lag between environmental awareness and action increases, we expect the environment to change in ways not anticipated by the action. This is especially true in turbulent environments (Emory & Trist, 1965/1969), such as recently deregulated industries, which are particularly well suited to new ventures ("Valentine," 1985). As the context changes, actions "miss their mark." It appears that sustained vigilance, updated expertise, and an ability to see beyond the present result in faster responses by entrepreneurs compared to others who remain unaware and/or uncertain.

Sustaining strategic focus. Strategic focus, or clarity about mission, purpose, and goals, is generally important to leadership effectiveness (Bennis & Nanus, 1985) just as goal clarity is important to individual achievement (Locke, 1968). Since entrepreneurship combines organizational leadership with opportunities to demonstrate individual contributions, focus is a particularly important quality of entrepreneurial behavior. Sustaining a central focus for a new venture requires a steady hand, unwavering commitment, and persistence in reiterating and reinforcing the goals.

FIGURE 1.4   Action Time Lags

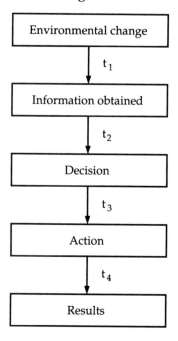

Like effective executives in other studies, successful entrepreneurs demonstrate a willingness to make simple, clear statements about what is valued and where they are headed, and to follow through with resources. For example Don Oberg, founder of Oberg Industries, a tool-and-die business in Pennsylvania, dots his plant with signs such as "If it's almost right, it's wrong" and "The biggest room in our company is the room for improvement" and other simple aphorisms that display his philosophy. His follow-through is widely acknowledged within the organization (Fenn, 1985b).

However, entrepreneurs also have a reputation for being "tentative, uncommitted, or temporarily dedicated," making commitments quickly and decommitting quickly (Stevenson, 1985, p. 45), often branching onto tangential opportunities (Ronstadt, 1984). While opportunistic and having certain tactical advantages (Stevenson, 1985; Quinn, 1982, 1985), this style results in uncertainty about the duration of an entrepreneur's commitment to a project, vision, or venture.

We can resolve the apparent equivocality of entrepreneurs by postulating *perceptual skill akin to the zoom lens,* which allows flexibility and rapid, fluid change in focus. Such perceptual skill enables the entrepreneur to move from operations, where details are important, to strategy, where the "big picture"/ vision and new opportunities are important—from an inside view of the enterprise to an outside view.

A related dilemma, that of delegation, is social and interpersonal and not very amenable to change. Entrepreneurs *prefer hands-on work and want to be "where the action" is, doing it;* in contrast, managers with a "bias for action" help others to do it (Peters & Waterman, 1982). An excellent example rests with Steven Jobs, whose hands-on involvement with publicly held Apple Computer (which he co-founded) resulted in his ouster from leadership of that firm by his CEO, John Sculley. In contrast with Jobs, Sculley is a career manager who has learned to work through others.

> 'Hands on' accomplishment generates . . . a qualitatively different effect from accomplishment by indirection. . . . Inability to delegate . . . is usually attributed to feelings of responsibility for the results and unwillingness to depend on others for the discharge of that responsibility. But it may also be due to the diminished satisfactions some managers [and entrepreneurs] feel when delegation deprives them of the opportunity to participate directly in the problem-solving process.
>
> Simon, undated

The hands-on orientation results in the entrepreneur's involvement everywhere, with everything, bypassing existing management structure, ignoring corporate politics and individual egos, and violating bureaucratic procedures (Welsh & White, 1983). As a result subordinate managers may come to feel overcontrolled, untrusted, underchallenged, and incompetent. However, *if* the entrepreneur chooses to build a growth-oriented venture, delegation and empowerment of others seem essential. This requires a *hands-off attitude, letting go of details, and less involvement* with operations and some decision making. Wider focus is especially important if organizational growth is a goal, since new products, markets, resources, acquisitions, and possible partners must be identified and the entrepreneur's time is limited. These issues will be discussed again in Chapter 9.

Choosing the path. As suggested, the path into entrepreneurship is one that is primarily goal-directed or ends-oriented (e.g., owning a profitable firm, having increasing personal wealth.) Occasionally, individuals begin and build organizations to practice their craft or profession and may be process-directed or means-oriented. These two approaches reflect different forms of opportunism. The first is tactical (seizing unanticipated means for goal achievement). The second is strategic (adopting unanticipated goals in response to new events or new interpretations of old circumstances) (Miner, 1986). These approaches will be discussed further in Chapter 6.

Goal-directed entrepreneurs tend to be *opportunistic* about how they reach their goals. They have a reputation for being instrumental and transactional in their relationships with objects and people, where these relationships are valued for what they can give the venture rather than valued in themselves. "When it comes to the control of resources, the . . . [entrepreneurial] mentality says, 'all I need from a resource is the ability to use it' " (Stevenson, 1985, p. 49). Thus entrepreneurs prefer to rent resources and subcontract work rather than buy resources or hire full-time workers, and prefer employees to partners (Collins & Moore, 1964). This opportunistic behavior may be a necessary part of having chosen goals.

> Goal setting is what you want, not how you're going to get it. People want to dictate . . . [both what they want and] "how". . . [they're going to get it]. "I want a beautiful relationship and I want it with this person, in this house, with these kinds of cars, and two kids . . . and now." All that does is frustrate them and create negative energy.
>
> SB, Microcomputer Training Entrepreneur;
> Bird, 1983, p. 111

Research suggests that successful entrepreneurs are indeed opportunistic in perceptions and behaviors, engaging in more opportunistic (compared with social) questioning (Bailey, 1986) and being actively involved with finding opportunities (Long & McMullan, 1984).

Means-oriented entrepreneurs—those who begin an organization to practice their craft, trade, or profession—tend to have slower growing, less innovative, stable, small businesses (Richman, 1985b; Smith, 1967). Others who set up business to support an ideal image (e.g., looking rich and acting powerful) stand to lose their credibility and organizational good will.

Ethical considerations. Do ends justify means? Can the creation of jobs, wealth, or tax dollars justify any method of accomplishment? We think not. Indeed, we do not include the blatantly illegal activities (organized crime) nor the immoral exploitation of others in the category of entrepreneurship. The value added by such activities needs to be questioned by all concerned.

Can means justify ends? Is "how you play the game" more important than the winning or losing? We think not. By sticking to a favorite method or means of conducting business, the entrepreneur may create an organization that reflects his or her values but may have difficulty surviving without his or her involvement. The ethics of creating such temporary organizations also need to be examined.

There seems to be a Heisenberg effect here.[2] To the extent that the entrepreneur chooses an end goal (profits, an organization, a product), he or she must be more or less opportunistic about how he or she gets there. To the extent that a person chooses a means of behaving, a code of conduct, he or she must be more or less accepting of where that path leads. It seems that we cannot simultaneously choose or equally control both means and ends. Becoming insistent about both what you want *and* how you will get it boxes you in. The result is frustration.

Choosing the posture. An intentional posture involves the position of the entrepreneur in relation to his or her values, needs, etc., and in relation to the outer world. Two postural variables are considered here, alignment and attunement.

Alignment can be understood as a configuration of parts, such that all parts are contributing to a single purpose and direction. Intrapsychically, in terms of intention, this means that the entrepreneur's many inner "voices"— which reflect different and conflicting needs, values, memories, wishes, etc.—need to agree on one direction. One microcomputer training entrepreneur described her internal dialogue.

> The inner voices do a little work with me. It's like having a committee of people that you have a dialog with, bat around ideas and brainstorm with. . . . It's like me talking to me, but it's not me.

> Bird, 1983, p. 106

[2] The Heisenberg principle of uncertainty is derived from high-energy physics and says essentially that we cannot know with certainty both the position and the velocity of a particle. In observing one aspect, we cannot observe the other.

A lack of psychological alignment prevents focused intention. A conflict in values such as work versus family or control versus growth can slow, stop, and even divert intended action. Perhaps this is what happens to potential entrepreneurs who are serious about venturing but never take appropriate action (Ronstadt, 1984a). This is discussed again in Chapter 5.

Attunement can be conceived as a readiness to send and receive information, influence, or meaning to and from other sources. At the simplest level, this means rational adjustment to economic pressures and opportunities. It also refers to noneconomic missions and higher purposes, which some entrepreneurs serve. Such attunement involves the personal values and beliefs of the founder/owner and the impact of these on organizing (Guth & Tagiuri, 1965) and on creating high performance (Garfield, 1986). Thus entrepreneurs use their organizations and resources for social purposes such as peacemaking (Rhodes, 1984a; Willens, 1984), philanthropy (Buchsbaum, 1984; Wojahn, 1976) or promoting a certain ideology (Critser, 1986). Examples of entrepreneurs with noneconomic missions will be found throughout this book.

Implications

Successful entrepreneurs operate within a zone of future time perspective. The match between the entrepreneur's time span of comfort and the time span demands of the endeavor will contribute to the potential success or failure of the endeavor, as well as indicate when measures of success should be taken. This future time span allows the entrepreneur the advantage of spending time in decision making and action. Failure to properly frame new venture projects will result in missing the mark, poor timing, and missed opportunities.

Entrepreneurs with clear vision, perceptual flexibility, and vigilance will be better equipped to launch a new venture. These qualities contribute to success in terms of survival, making break even, and taking off on a growth path. Clear vision paired with commitment to either a goal or a method of doing business indicates that the entrepreneur has chosen a particular path for his or her venture. Specific and articulate venture goals allow others to join the venture process, thereby making success more likely.

TYPES OF ENTREPRENEURSHIP

Many of those who work with entrepreneurs and who study the creation of new ventures recognize that there are different types of entrepreneurs. Being able to see the similarities and important differences among entrepreneurs has value to members of the business community and to those who study entrepreneurs and their processes.

Those who aspire to the entrepreneurial career are well advised to look at how the small business owner differs from the leader of the fast-growth, high-potential business. They might also ask how those who acquire a going concern differ from those who start from nothing. Those with family businesses want to know how they are similar to and different from other entrepreneurs. The list goes on.

The larger economic community is interested in the frequency and type of firms that emerge in geographic regions. Some constituents such as bankers and venture capitalists would like to find out how successful entrepreneurs differ from the unsuccessful and how to recognize income-substitution firms (created as an alternative to working for someone else and which provide employment and income to the entrepreneur and his or her family), which are seen as "marginal firms," and those of high potential. Regional planners are interested in the employment potentials in different sectors (e.g., manufacturing and service).

Scholars of entrepreneurship need to make these and other distinctions among the rather large and ill-defined category of entrepreneurs. We also need to make comparisons between entrepreneurs of different types and between entrepreneurs and managers based on a theoretical framework.

ARCHETYPES OF ENTREPRENEURIAL WORK

Gartner (1986) offers a look at how various entrepreneurial activities cluster, and suggests there are eight distinct types of entrepreneurship.

1. *Escaping to something new,* where the business is started part time, funded through friends and family, is low on innovation, and in a highly competitive market of the "average" consumer. Examples include pet stores and boutiques.

2. *Networking or "putting the deal together,"* by linking different aspects of the business (e.g., suppliers, distributors, producers) into a "deal" where everyone "wins." Knowing the right people is important. Two subtypes include the real-estate developer and the "novelty" firm (i.e., building a good idea into a firm).

3. *Rolling over skills and/or contacts* from previous work situations. The individual has no long-term interest in starting a business, which is perceived as risky, but does so because employment offers limited career advancement. The individual quits and starts full time, with little capital beyond personal savings, spending little time in venture analysis or sales, relying on previous contacts and experience. Firms offer generic services such as law and advertising.

4. *Purchasing a firm* based on previous experience and a long-term goal to own a business, where the venture is perceived as low risk. Time is spent finding the business and planning the turnaround from previous owners. Two subtypes seem possible: the leveraged buyout from a manager's parent company and the purchase of an unfamiliar firm.

5. *Leveraging expertise* when the current employer is unwilling to pursue a new product idea even though there seems to be low risk of failure. The new firm usually involves partners and offers an innovative product or service. Much time is spent developing sales.

6. *Aggressively providing service* through a consulting firm in a specialized area, related to previous employment or training. The individual has had a long-range goal to own a business and spends a great deal of time developing sales and scanning for new opportunities. Networking is important.

7. *Pursuing the unique idea* that is not technically sophisticated or difficult to manufacture but high in quality. Uncertainties exist about resource adequacy and ability to deliver. In the new venture, tasks require expertise different from that developed in previous jobs, resulting in perceived high risk. The individual has had a long-range desire to own a business.

8. *Organizing methodically* in an area that differs from previous work experience (with resulting perceptions of high risk). The individual uses planning in acquiring the skills and performing the tasks, actualizing a long-range desire to own a business. The product/service is in a competitive en-

vironment with some slightly different angle. The venture starts part time, with another job as the source of income used to keep the venture afloat.

A TYPOLOGY OF ENTREPRENEURIAL EVENTS

Another way to see some of the distinctions is to categorize the entrepreneurial event by the four factors presented and diagrammed by Gartner (1985) in Figure 1.1. Of specific interest are (1) the goals of the entrepreneur (e.g., income substitution, freedom, growing an organization, tax advantages), (2) the entry process or how an entrepreneur begins—slow/part-time versus fast/full-time, start-up versus acquisition/franchise, (3) the industrial and technological context (e.g., high versus low technology, service, etc.), and (4) the organizational structure and ownership (e.g., partnerships, teams, sole proprietorships, etc.). Table 1.3 outlines this categorization of entrepreneurs and Table 1.4 (on page 30) shows alternatives proposed by others.

Goals. Entrepreneurs tend to have an initial and two sustaining or strategic types of monetary goals. The initial or start-up goal is to obtain enough cash to make it to the first sale or to

TABLE 1.3 Types of Entrepreneurship

Goals	Monetary: Income substitution Profits Tax and legal advantages Non-Monetary: Personal values Grow a firm
Entry process	Speed: Slow Fast Style: Independent Acquired Corporate Franchised
Industrial and technological context	High-low technology Industrial category (e.g., Service, Manufacturing, other industry)
Structure/ownership	Solo Partnership Team Corporate Franchise

break even. The sustaining goals are income and profit. These goals reveal the motive for organizational growth. Income goals result in organizations of sufficient size and financial health to generate an adequate income for the entrepreneur and his or her family. In this case, entrepreneurship is a substitute for salaried work. The ventures are created to support a certain lifestyle and tend to be internally financed, with manufacturing contracted out and size kept small.

Profit goals are more open ended—once adequate income has been achieved, there are still more profits to attend to. Thus a profit motive may result in considerable organizational growth and ventures of any size. For these entrepreneurs, profits and organizational size are important as ways of keeping score (Timmons, 1978).

A less common monetary goal involves sheltering income from taxation and liability. Thus some individuals get involved in self-employment and incorporate for economic protection. However, we could debate whether or not such conservative and probably risk-averse individuals are true entrepreneurs.

Besides monetary goals, entrepreneurs may or may not have a mission. There is a common assumption that nonprofit (i.e., tax-exempt) organizations are primarily "mission oriented." Among nonprofit organizations, the type of mission— health care, education, arts, professional organizations, membership-benefit—is an important determinant of what kind of value is added by the organization. One writer has suggested that the source of funds might help us distinguish among nonprofit missions—those that depend on charitable contributions, which are deductible from personal income taxes, and those mutual-benefit organizations where contributions are not deductible (Young, 1983).

Missions are not restricted to nonprofit organizations nor to service organizations. Entrepreneurs may build organizations to develop themselves, enact a humanitarian need (see the Case of BP at the end of this chapter), or create large-scale social change (Flower, 1984).

THE EXAMPLE OF MEL ALLERHAND

Mel Allerhand, whose health-care partnerships are his latest enterprise, talked about how his effectiveness in building an organization with survival potential rested on a switch in his priorities or goals. Earlier in his career as a child psychologist, Allerhand had started several short-lived organizations with a humanistic mission, such as setting up a school for children with problem behaviors. These organizations quickly ended because they never became self-supporting.

After several such beginnings and endings, Allerhand became motivated to make money. He wanted to overcome his worrying about where money would come from to fund the current mission.

> "I didn't know how much I wanted. I knew that I wanted to feel very comfortable about doing whatever I wanted to do. Up to this point, I had always worried about the shoelaces and I let my guilt about money stand in the way."

In his opinion, his guilt about earning money stemmed from his father, who had made it clear that those who go into helping professions such as psychology were not supposed to be money oriented. "My father said that when you are a professional, you don't go into business to make money. Unfortunately, I listened to him too well."

It took some therapy to work through this guilt and his negative feelings about how his father limited his ability to make money. When he was free from his guilt, Allerhand switched his priorities from mission first to money first. The mission remained, but became second in importance. By putting money first, Allerhand learned about the financial operations of his organization and began to feel comfortable talking to money experts. He got a much better sense of what he had thought was a "big sandbox" (finance, banking, accounting) where he couldn't play. He said, "Now I find that it's more a sandbox than I thought it was," and he's playing in it quite successfully.

In moving beyond his fears and putting money first, Allerhand was able to send out clear signals to others about his intentions. He became more selective of those who wanted to join him and has built an organization of partnerships with people very different from those in his earlier organizations.

> "Before I would hook up with people too quickly . . . because they offered to help, because they offered some money. Very often they were not right for the project. Now I am clear about my money-mission priorities. I look twice at people who seem right and I have been very successful at finding people with the right resources and expertise."

The example of Mel Allerhand, an entrepreneur who consciously switched his money and mission goal priorities, shows how important such goals are to entrepreneurial behavior and the process of building an organization. The goals an entrepreneur sets—concerning money and mission—determine the range of activities and resources that are sought and become available, and thus determine the substance and structure of the organization that is developed. (See Chapter 3 for further discussion of goals.)

Entry process. There are two important aspects of the process of beginning an entrepreneurial career—the timing of commitment and the origins of the business concept. *Entry into entrepreneurial roles can occur relatively slowly or quickly, with vague or clear boundaries between previous work and entrepreneurial work.* The slow process, probably related to risk aversion, favors incrementalism and typically involves a period of moonlighting—working for someone else while starting a business in one's spare time (Vesper, 1980). There is some evidence that slow starters do not finish first, or at least do not endure as long as those following the fast, direct path (Ronstadt, 1984a). Fast-pathers make a total commitment to the venture, although perhaps only after extended study and planning. The personal investment of the entrepreneur in terms of his or her source of income differentiates "hobbyists" from serious starters.

Entry begins with a business concept that can arise from various sources. Independent new start-ups arise from the vision and ideas of the founding entrepreneur(s). It is in these ventures that the entrepreneur plays the strongest role as founder. Other business concepts are acquired through the purchase of an existing business, a going concern with existing equipment, personnel, and organizational systems. In these ventures the entrepreneur transforms the existing organization, adding value. If no new values are added by the new owner, he or she would be excluded from our definition of an entrepreneur.

Another way of acquiring a business concept is through franchising. Traditionally, the franchisor has exerted more control over business practice than the franchisee. The franchisor licenses his or her business concepts and, for a fee, helps set up independent franchises. The franchisor usually sets policy and frequently determines sources of supply, technology, marketing approaches, and even business appearance. The franchisee usually pays for the franchise and the privilege of learning business from the franchisor. The franchisee has considerably less, if any, influence on policy, strategy, and business practice. Indeed, the relationship is as much one of employer-employee as it is one of partners in entrepreneurship. Most franchise owners would therefore be excluded from discussions in this text.

Finally, a business concept can be developed within a larger corporate body. In this case, entrepreneurial behavior is found in corporate employees or "intrapreneurs" whose role is to develop new businesses within the existing business (and not through acquisition). Ownership is discussed further later in this chapter.

Industrial and technological context. As with larger organizations, the technological or industrial niche where new ventures begin will help determine the structure and culture of the emerging organization. In addition, specific technologies attract specific kinds of individuals to begin new ventures (e.g., high technology attracts individuals with engineering backgrounds). Furthermore, an individual's background experience with a specific industry or technology, and his or her experience with previous start-ups, are important predictors of success in a current or future new venture. (See Chapter 3 for more on the personal background of entrepreneurs.)

A high-technology organization is by definition in a rapidly changing technological environment, facing stiff competition, requiring state-of-the-art expertise, and needing to adjust rapidly to the changing environment. Often expertise of widely different sorts is needed (e.g., computer hardware and software) and the new venture must develop teamwork as an organizational structure to manage interpersonal differences as well as the need for frequent change. Thus, along with technological skills, high-technology entrepreneurs need good interpersonal skills, in order to coordinate with others without bureaucracy, as well as perceptual and behavioral flexibility.

Businesses whose technology is changing less rapidly are in less turbulent technological environments (however, there may be considerable financial and market turbulence) and are in need of fewer experts. Such low-technology organizations would attract different kinds of entrepreneurs and may evolve different structures and cultures. Likewise, a service-based organization such as health care or banking will require different kinds of expertise in the founder/leader than either high- or low-technology production firms.

Ownership and structure. The fourth dimension offered here has to do with the way ownership of the organization is structured. An organization that involves only one entrepreneur (sole proprietorship) differs from a partnership. Whereas the sole proprietor is legally and financially personally responsible for the new venture, partners share this responsibility. Whereas the sole proprietor reaps all of the benefits of his or her business, partners share these benefits. Both individuals and partnerships can incorporate for legal and tax purposes, but each continues to operate as a sole proprietorship or partnership until it is publicly held or passed on to second-generation family members.

The structure of partnerships may vary in important ways—the distribution of ownership, responsibility, and control are all negotiable between partners be they general partners who are actively involved and personally liable for business debts, limited partners who are "silent" and whose liability is limited, venture partners, or franchise partners. Small and large partnerships might also differ significantly. (Chapter 7 includes more on partnerships.)

Finally we note the operation of entrepreneurship within an existing, stable corporation where the new venture is owned by the parent. For large organizations there is strategic value in developing *corporate entrepreneurship or "intrapreneurship"* (Miles & Snow, 1978; Pinchot, 1985). Those who operate entrepreneurially within a larger organization have a context different from those who independently start or acquire a new business. Intrapreneurs operate under some form of corporate accounting system, with reporting relationships to hierarchical superiors; entrepreneurs stand alone. Intrapreneurs do not personally face the financial risks that entrepreneurs do, nor do they foresee the same rewards. As a result, their experiences and behaviors differ somewhat from those of the entrepreneurial sole proprietor or partner. Differences in perceptions of risk, resource availability, and autonomy might be expected to influence decision making, relationships, commitment, and other behavior. Likewise, the individuals who choose the career of corporate entrepreneur over that of an independent entrepreneur might need different competencies to succeed. For example, corporate entrepreneurs need to be fairly skilled at corporate politics (MacMillan, 1983), something most independent entrepreneurs find reprehensible and that motivates some to resist working for anyone but themselves (Collins & Moore, 1964).

Implications

A four-dimensional typology of entrepreneurs suggests that the criteria for success may also differ for different types of entrepreneurs. The entrepreneur's goals and entry process, and the industry and structure chosen for venturing, act to focus the entrepreneur's intentions and resources in *qualitatively* different ways. It is likely that *success criteria developed for one type of venture will not apply in the same way, with the same weight or importance, to other types of ventures.* If this is so, then different measures of success need to be developed and applied. For example, a partnership based on personal values that is begun part time in the service sector is considerably different from a franchise in high-technology retail service or a solo venture begun to substitute for income in low-technology manufacturing. Likewise, what it takes to succeed may vary considerably across different types of ventures. "Tailored" assessments of entrepreneurial characteristics and competencies would need to be developed, and very different strategic proscriptions might follow.

CASE OF BP

BP projects a sense of weight and power, although he is not extraordinarily tall or heavy. His eyes are shrewd and often gleeful as he reveals his own agendas and "moves" in the enterprise game.

He begins to tell of his entrepreneurial venture with stories of his youth as a shoeshine boy in Brooklyn. There he learned about competition—about being first (to find a position where traffic in the subway station was good), being "bad" enough to hold his spot when someone came along and tried to dislodge him, being good (so that customers would wait to have him shine their shoes), and being "bad" enough to keep the money he made when someone came to rob him.

After high school he joined the military; his military technical training allowed him to take advantage of opportunities in aerospace companies, where he worked for 17 years as an engineer and manager. During this time he completed a university education, worked hard in middle management, and met the man who later became his partner.

BP had three incentives to own his own business: (1) a limited growth potential in big-industry middle management; (2) a racial ceiling to his progress, since he is black; (3) a belief that he could make better decisions than most of his superiors. Thus, with a partner he purchased Solo, a technology-based firm with poor sales, in 1970.

TABLE 1.4 Alternative Ways to Type Entrepreneurs

Smith (1967)	*Craftsman entrepreneur*: Blue-collar origins, narrow low-technology work experience, "mechanical genius," most business contacts are on plant floor, reputation in the industry; a "marginal" person who identifies neither with management nor with labor unions.
	Opportunistic entrepreneur: Middle-class origins, well-rounded education, variety of work experience, "chief executive," most contacts with top management, reputation across industries, identifies with management.
Kets de Vries (1977)	Above categories plus: *R and D technical entrepreneur*: Work experience in high technology, more formal education, greater use of teams.
Liles (1974)	*Marginal firms*: Designed to provide income, but not as an alternative to management or engineering careers. Examples include a dry-cleaning establishment or a small steel-service business.
	High-potential firms: Intended to grow rapidly in sales and profits.
	Attractive small firm: Not intended to grow but can provide income equivalents to professional and managerial careers with flexibility in work, lifestyle, and geography.
Vesper (1980)	*Solo self-employed*: Includes Mom 'n Pop stores and professionals and tradespeople who work alone or with very few other people, and who do most of the work personally.
	Team builders: People who build an organization through incremental hiring.
	Independent innovators: Inventors who build an organization to produce and sell an invention; includes high technology.
	Pattern multipliers: People who expand a business concept through franchises or chains of similar stores.

TABLE 1.4 Alternative Ways to Type Entrepreneurs
(*continued*)

Vesper (1980)	*Economy of scale exploiters*: People who increase volume and lower price by larger-scale production or sales.
	Capital aggregators: Includes banks, savings and loan institutions, insurance companies, and venture capital organizations.
	Acquirers: Involves purchase or inheritance of a going concern.
	Buy-sell artists: Those who buy companies to later resell them at a profit; turnaround artists; corporate raiders and takeover experts.
	Conglomerators: Variation of acquirers; those who use the assets of one company to buy control of others not necessarily related to the first business.
	Speculators: The purchase of an asset such as land is used to leverage the purchase of other assets (more land, construction); resold later at a profit.
	Apparent value manipulators: This is the "buy low-sell high entrepreneur," the classic "arbitrageur"; those who repackage, redefine, or restructure to add apparent value.

Solo, which supplies parts and equipment to corporate and military customers, was transformed from a no-growth firm to one that eventually ended up on the *Inc. 100* list of fastest-growing privately held firms for two consecutive years. However, at first the growth was slow, based on an unwritten partnership agreement that profits would be put into real estate until there was sufficient liquidity for BP to buy out the partner. After seven years, he did so, making a generous deal that "people who were close enough to the situation thought was terrible for me."

I have a personal requirement that when I'm involved in a business situation with someone else, like a partnership or

> joint venture . . . the ideal situation to me is that we both prosper. For my partner to be more prosperous than I was at the time we separated the business . . . more prosperous in the balance sheet . . . was preferable to me. It's the only way I can be sure to see it's fair. If I see it elsewhere, great. Wildflowers. If I really want to make sure there's flowers, I want to cultivate them.

BP initiated new projects and built staff rapidly. He uses a formal strategic planning process and has been able to move quickly to seize opportunities. He has also tried to develop an entrepreneurial top-management team while making important tough decisions himself.

> Feedback from internal observation and external observation is that I move directly in a situation too late, later than I should. Which is the side of it I prefer, because I want the maximum amount of delegation and the minimum amount of dependence on me. If the perception is that BP is not going to move as soon as he should, they [the top managers] have to depend more on each other and themselves to do things.

While doing well in growing a profitable organization, BP is also implementing a personal mission and a set of values. His agendas attempt to demonstrate that the so-called unemployable are employable, that depressed neighborhoods can flourish, that women can wield power, and that blacks can achieve standing through entrepreneurship.

> There are certain myths, women can and cannot do certain things, people in certain communities, certain colors can and cannot do certain things. Part of me has a very practical, economic, natural interest and human purpose to dispel all of that . . . by modeling what can be done. Every time you make a decision, you make a statement.

He enacts this mission by making the strategic choice to locate the business in a "problem" community in Southeast Los Angeles. He employs people from the economically depressed neighborhood and has suffered no more vandalism, theft, or absenteeism than businesses in other areas. He enacts this mission by hiring and supporting two women vice-presidents. He says, "Anyone who cannot work for a female can work somewhere else."

He implements his personal and business values in daily decisions and actions.

> My approach to that is just do it because every time you make a decision, you make a statement. Every decision a

manager makes, especially an owner-manager, makes a statement. My statement to the employees, the lowest paid to the highest paid, is that you are going to have an opportunity to do your job based on your ability to do the job. Notwithstanding anything else. Every decision I make either makes that statement or refutes that statement. That statement being consistent across the company is the most powerful statement we have in the company.

One of the personal values he implements is "fairness."

"Fair" is only a concept that you can understand and practice yourself. It is a wonderful concept for those of us who feel it and see the value of it within the framework of our control and our power. You have to actually exercise it. That's the only way you can have any certainty about it. There is nothing indigenous to any culture, any society, anywhere that provides "fair."

In addition, he plans to turn the ownership of Solo over to senior managers and employees.

Ownership is important to me now for control and the ability to give direction and set the dictum and the things in motion. You don't have to negotiate with everybody. But at the point that you have an institution that essentially belongs, operationally, to the people who make it up, then you have to transfer that ownership to them so that decisions have that level of depth and credibility.

CHAPTER 2

ENTREPRENEURSHIP: CREATIVE VISION

INTRODUCTION

Entrepreneurs are among the more creative of organizational players. It is their business to generate or add value as they venture, introducing new forms, new organizations, new products, and new language to the world at large. Entrepreneurship, centered on novelty and the generation of variety in the marketplace, means that the processes of innovation, discovery, and invention are at work. Of course, not all ventures are equally creative—some copy others' ideas, and some are intended to simply substitute for jobs and income that would be earned as an employee. In this chapter we look at the more creative side of entrepreneurship—the value-adding, innovative, and organization-creating aspects, recognizing that creativity requires an audience to add value.[1]

In some economic theories, innovation is a key, defining aspect of entrepreneurship. Schumpeter (1934) was first to point out the importance of the new values created by entrepreneurs. More recently, Carland, Hoy, Boulton, and Carland (1984) extend and specify Schumpeter's idea, saying that entrepreneurs:

- introduce new *goods*
- introduce new *methods* of production
- open new *markets*
- open new *sources of supply*
- *reorganize industry* (this would include buying a firm or acting as a "turnaround" CEO).

[1] Thanks to Tojo Thachankery and the ORBH 520 class in fall, 1987 at Case Western Reserve University for helping clarify this point.

To this list, I would add

• introduce *new services.*

Peter Drucker (1984), a well-known management professor and business consultant, defines entrepreneurship in terms of the generation of new jobs and the production of new flows of income (Drucker, 1984). The creation of jobs through entrepreneurship is now so well documented that regional leaders have turned to considering how the local government and community can stimulate or foster new business, a topic covered again in Chapter 5.

> A society or community with a high level of entrepreneurship ultimately incurs less risk than one that relies upon the illusory security of large-scale enterprise. For only a large number of company formations, occurring continually over time, can help ensure the creativity and resilience that a community needs to respond to change and capitalize quickly on new opportunities.
>
> Shapero, 1981, p. 23

Both innovation and job creation involve the creation of new organizations of interdependent activities carried out by several people to accomplish a goal. Says Alfred Chandler of Harvard Business School,

> Historically, the key entrepreneurial act has been creating an organization. . . . Technological innovations are no good until you exploit them organizationally. . . . Historically, the person who really cleaned up was the one who picked up the innovation and created a team.
>
> "The Valley," 1985

As organization makers, entrepreneurs are economic and cultural "Johnny Appleseeds," planting new institutions in our economy, our political process, and our educational process and seeding economic, cultural, social, and political variety. They also precede and create the context for management: They develop organizations that are subsequently in need of strategy, structure, performance, culture, and change.

Implications

Future management requirements are being "seeded" by today's entrepreneurs. There is considerable evidence that the entrepreneurs of the late 1980s are beginning organizations that include novel management philosophies. If these organizations survive and grow, they will require some very different management competencies. You'll read more on this when entrepreneurial cultures are discussed later in this chapter, and when we address entrepreneurial values in Chapter 11.

THE CREATIVE PROCESS

DEFINING TERMS

Expanding the definitions offered in Chapter 1, we consider the following:

> DEFINITION 5: Entrepreneurship is the intentional creation of value through organization, by an individual contributor or a small group of partners.

This definition reflects the purposive nature of entrepreneurship highlighted in Chapter 1 (i.e., entrepreneurs are not "forced" into venturing against their will) and the creative function of entrepreneurial behavior.

Creativity. Creativity is a fairly abstract and general process of bringing something new into existence, often through imaginative skills. Much of what we know about the creative process stems from studies of artists and those involved in creative problem solving. For the purposes of this text, we focus on three specific types of creativity involved in many entrepreneurial ventures: discovery, invention, and innovation.

Discovery. The process of discovery refers to finding something that already exists but is not yet perceived, just as the Vikings, and later Columbus, discovered North America. Discovery involves making the unknown known, pointing to previously ignored or imperceptible facts, opportunities, and combinations. When discoveries are consciously intended, the process is considered "exploration" and "experimentation." For example, hours of biological experiments may result in the discovery of disease viruses, which enables the development of vaccines, and experiments in chemistry labs result in new polymers that ultimately lead to the development of new materials.

Other discoveries are unintended, serendipitous or accidental. These might be called "lucky breaks." For example, Irv
Robbins located his first ice cream store in Los Angeles as the
result of a "fork in the road"; he got lost and found a hard-to-
find empty store front. This serendipity resulted in the establishment of the first store and later resulted in the construction
of a new headquarters building for Baskin–Robbins ice cream.

Invention.   Inventions differ from discoveries. Invention

> is the act of creating or producing by exercise of the imagi-
> nation. . . . [Inventions] have no prior existence. Their con-
> ceptions are each original acts.
>
> Davis, 1982, p. 78

Instead of uncovering and naming what already exists, the
inventor finds novel uses for things already discovered. Applying known principles and available resources, the inventor
makes "a better mousetrap," develops a welding robot, or uses
a computer to provide more information, thereby adding value
to a product or service.

Invention is often (but not necessarily) linked with technology in the creation of new tools (products, physical equipment) and techniques (processes, methods) that extend human
capability (Schon, 1967). Some good examples include the invention of the first user-oriented personal computer by Steven
Wozniak and Steven Jobs (Apple Computer), the development
of a small-package overnight delivery system by Fred Smith
(Federal Express), and the extension of franchising to food
services by Irv Robbins (Baskin-Robbins) and Ray Kroc
(McDonald's).

Considered broadly, invention is not restricted to laboratories or scientists/engineers. Says Shapero (1982a):

> Everyone invents [e]very day. . . . The great mass of inven-
> tive activity is personal, local and unique. We begin to hear
> of some of this mass of activity, when through the medium
> of a newspaper column by Heloise we learn about house-
> keeping inventions that would otherwise be lost (p. 2).

Our concern in this book is with inventions that result in
entrepreneurial ventures and new organizations. Most likely
these are designs and concepts amenable to patent or copyright
or that result in "proprietary" rights. Such inventions are an

entrepreneurial resource and not necessarily the entrepreneur's "brain child." That is, entrepreneurs know how to commercialize others' inventions. It is important to note that many new ventures begin without a core invention (e.g., those who exploit special "niches," pattern replicators) and that most inventions are never commercialized. Finally, we note that "big business" and government are the sources of many inventions and commercializations.

Innovation.   Frequently people use the terms *invention* and *innovation* interchangeably although there are important differences. To some people innovation refers to an end product, "an idea, practice or product perceived as new by the individual" (Rogers & Shoemaker, 1971, p. 19), very similar to our definition of invention. However, innovation also implies commercialization of ideas and/or the implementation and change of existing systems, products, and resources. To at least one important thinker, Peter Drucker (1985), innovation is the specific function of entrepreneurship and defines what is entrepreneurial and what is managerial. In this book it refers to the process of "bringing inventions into use" (Schon, 1967, p. 1) through engineering, organizing, and marketing.

Other observers and writers focus on innovations embedded in larger organizations, innovations thought to be necessary for change and long-term survival of these organizations (Kanter, 1983). They see an innovative process as one that is recognized as new by the adopting system and/or results in a major restructuring of the adopting system (Kimberly, 1981).

Invention and discovery compared.   The *moods* of discovery and invention are considerably different. Davis (1982) argues that scarcity/necessity is the "mother of invention" and that abundance is the "mother of discovery"—thus scarce resources and time pressures feed into invention, while discovery requires adequate physical and temporal resources. Thus we expect inventions to come from engineers facing real problems and constraints, and discoveries to come from scientists doing more or less "pure" research.

The *questions asked* by these processes also differ. Invention is a process that answers "How to?" (i.e., how to use a resource, solve a problem) and involves finding novel solutions to problems. Discovery is a process that answers "What is?" (i.e., What is the nature of this polymer? What are my current resources, opportunities, alternatives?). Whatever the differences between the processes of discovery and invention, each results in something new becoming available to the world at large. They are equally creative acts and of great value in the entrepreneurial process.

CREATIVITY IN PROBLEM SOLVING

In business settings, the way to understand creativity and vision is as part of an intentional decision-making or intentional problem-solving process. The problem-solving process most often discussed in management schools is shown in Figure 2.1. It starts with a problem and follows a logical progression. The creative process (Figure 2.2) starts before problems are defined and involves more intrapsychic and irrational work such as incubation, which might involve mulling over why a particular product or service does not already exist. Both processes (problem solving and creativity) are intentional and involve temporal tension, flexible focus, and attunement.

The process of creativity is thought to begin with *experiences of doubt, uneasiness, and wonder* (Henle, in Getzels & Csikszentmihalyi, 1976, p. 5), "a diffuse feeling about things not fitting into place" (p. 84). For the entrepreneur, this might mean recognizing an unexploited opportunity because a need is not being met, a resource is not well used, or a product is poorly marketed. The experience might include being uncertain about the veracity or truthfulness of a personal perception and wondering why no one else has seized the opportunity. This is represented in Figure 2.2 as *vague feelings* that arise when some discrepancy or opportunity is first recognized.

Problem finding. From the vague feeling, the creative challenge is to *find or formulate a problem* that can be solved. For the entrepreneur, the problem is finding a good way to exploit opportunity: How can this need be met, this resource more profitably used, or this product presented to the market? Entrepreneurs are noted for asking themselves the question "How can I gain control over the resources to make this deal happen?" in contrast with managers, who tend to ask themselves questions such as "How can I best use the resources within my control?"

Finding a problem involves perceptual and thinking skills different from those used to solve a presented problem—the kind of skills most often used in business school courses and the kind of problems most managers solve. *When a problem is presented* by a teacher, textbook, or a superior, there is the expectation that solving this problem is the best use of one's time and talent and that a "right," "best," or "satisfying" solution

FIGURE 2.1　The Problem-Solving Process

FIGURE 2.2　The Process of Creativity

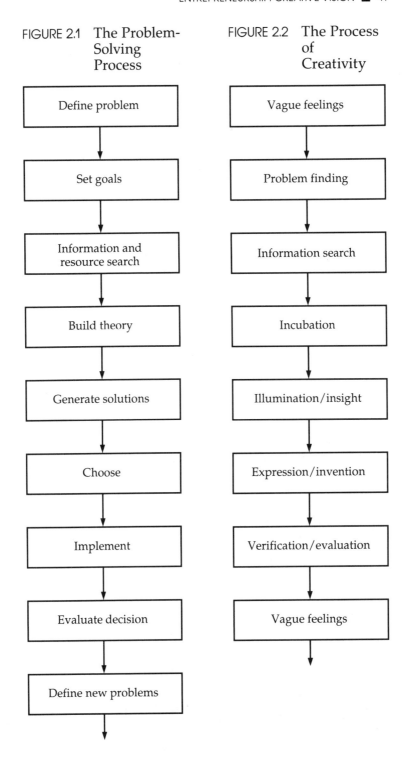

can be found, given careful application of one's analytic tools. For example, we assume there is an optimal or satisfactory portfolio of investments for a given firm, an acceptable accounting and information system, or effective recruitment and selection system. In contrast, *when a problem is discovered*, we may not be sure if it's the right problem or when a solution is at hand. That is, if we find a business opportunity (the problem is whether or not or how to start the venture) we cannot be sure that this is the brightest opportunity facing us. There may be better ways to spend our time and energy. Likewise we cannot be sure if our solution, business concept, or plan will work.

For the entrepreneur, problem finding means making a series of judgment calls in the opportunity analysis. Is this the right combination of resources and opportunity? Is this the right place? the right time? For some entrepreneurs these judgments derive from systematic information search and rational analysis; for others the decision seems more intuitive.

There is some research to suggest that taking time to *explore many different problems* (*not* solutions) pays off in the value of the final solution. In their research on artistic creativity, Getzels & Csikszentmihalyi (1976) found that the quality of artistic product (as judged by other artists, art teachers, and non-art students) was positively related to the *time spent finding the problem to solve* and *problem finding behaviors* such as contacting many objects, manipulation of the objects, delay of problem definition and keeping open to problem reformulation during execution. Extended to entrepreneurs, this suggests that taking time to explore different business ideas in a concrete way—by contacting customers, suppliers, and competitors, keeping open to different opportunities, can help entrepreneurs identify problems that may expose potential business opportunities. An example of such a process is presented in the laser technology example.

EXAMPLE: HOW TO USE LASER TECHNOLOGY?

One of George Foster's latest businesses involved the manufacture and sale of laser-based measurement equipment, designed for "real-time" correction of production processes. When he began the firm, his idea was to sell this equipment to tire manufacturers who would use it to ensure a uniform depth of tread on tires.

When tire manufacturers began to slow their growth and even shrink in capacity after the oil crisis in the late 1970s, Foster faced a dilemma. The value of the laser measurement technology in tire manufacturing diminished. His intended market shrank to the point where it was not worthwhile to tailor equipment prototypes to that industry's needs.

It was only by contacting potential customers in a wide range of areas that Foster was able to find other uses for his machinery and two new markets opened up. One involved the uniform application of insulation to electrical wire (variations in thickness result in headaches and lost time among electricians) and the other involved the control materials used in the manufacture of cookies (e.g., cookie dough thickness, one of the variable costs of production). These two industries are insulated from the cycles of the automobile industry, and Foster's ability to see his equipment operating for other purposes helped to save his firm by adapting his equipment and selling it to wire manufacturers and bakeries.

In terms of the creative process, Foster found the right problems at the right time. He obtained information from sources outside his original formulation of the problem, and was able to visualize his invention operating in different situations.

Information search. As in more traditional problem solving, creativity requires the *gathering of information* pertaining to the problem. The study cited earlier by Getzels & Csikszentmihalyi (1976) suggests that, as more information is gathered, the creative problem goes through reformulation. There is an iterative and possibly discontinuous, erratic, and dialectic (i.e., paradoxical and conflict-producing) process in which problem definition (what business?) directs attention to information (resources, markets, competition, etc.) and the information obtained changes the definition of the problem (Perkins, 1981). This stage may begin the business-planning process, which is likewise iterative and influenced by new information and may address products and markets that differ considerably from the original problem or idea.

Incubation. The creative process seems to require a process of incubation, when rational, conscious activity is stopped and the unconscious is allowed to work on the problem. Other terms for this process include gestation, mulling over, "cooking on the back burner," and "sleeping on it." The important feature is that problems are being addressed without our conscious involvement. Driver (1979) proposes two types, fast and slow incubation. The fast process works rapidly to integrate information with the problem definition and results in a relatively immediate insight or hunch. The slow process is characterized by seemingly unproductive mulling that can be transformed into insight by (1) overload (taking in more information than you can absorb), (2) imbalance (taking in conflicting information), and (3) interruption.

It is important to note that the faster process aids the "fast dancing" of the entrepreneur and shortens initial time lags. A good example of a fast process is found with Tecmar, an advanced technology firm started by Dr. Martin Alpert and his wife Carolyn.

EXAMPLE: TECMAR

Begun in the early 1970s and incorporated in 1974, Tecmar was intended to produce and sell a Pulmonary Diagnostic Instrument for diagnosing lung problems. However, in the process of building the PDI, Tecmar designed microcomputer components that were not available in the market. These computer products quickly became the mainstay of the firm, and the PDI was never marketed.

Alpert quickly seized an opportunity that made his firm the fast-growth superstar of Northeast Ohio. When in August 1981, IBM first announced it would market a personal computer, Alpert recognized that he had the advanced technology to manufacture add-on devices. "We thought about it . . . for a microsecond." In the three months before the IBM-PC was unveiled and sold, Tecmar designed products for the new machine.

Alpert was so prepared for the IBM unveiling that early on the morning of October 7 [1981], when the personal computer went on sale, a Tecmar executive flew to Chicago and waited outside a Sears Business Center. When the store opened, he rushed in and purchased two new-model computers. These were the first IBM personal computers sold anywhere.

In a process of reverse engineering, Tecmar engineers disassembled the computer and put it back

together. 'Within a few days we discovered exactly
how to build interfaces for the personal computer,'
Alpert says.

Whelan, 1983, p. 67

In contrast, the slower process is characterized by time
uncertainties (i.e., Will this problem ever be resolved?) and
psychological tensions (i.e., Do I really want to do this? What
will happen if I do start a business?). The tensions associated
with slow incubation may account for differences among individuals in the time they take to implement an idea, where slow
starters incubate their ideas longer. The slow process may not
be present once implementation begins and the venture is
underway, or if present, it is not well suited to the rapid-
fire decision making frequently associated with the start-up
process.

The slower process can be found in the formation of a retail
store selling clocks in Northeast Ohio. The business concept
was thoroughly researched by a husband-wife team over approximately six years before the suppliers, site, and sales
processes were understood well enough for the business to
begin.

The incubation process may also relate to when an entrepreneur begins his or her career—after schooling, out
of management, or in retirement, depending on how condu-
cive these environments are to mulling over ideas. Finally, the
incubation process may be interrupted and thereby
slowed or even stopped by social or economic crises such as
changes in one's family (e.g., a new baby), changes in one's
health (e.g., a heart attack), economic downturns and layoffs,
and new government restrictions. Paradoxically, these same
interruptions serve as displacements (see Chapter 6) and
can "pop" the problem into more immediate solution and
action.

Illumination or insight. Breakthroughs in the creative problem-solving process result from earlier stages of problem finding, information search, and incubation and can be delayed if
these stages are bypassed or hastened. The experience of a
breakthrough or "aha" involves an often sudden, usually complete picture of a solution that "comes to us," sometimes even

in dreams. Frequently, we cannot explain the cause of the insight, nor explain how we derived it. This numinous or magical quality of the experience results from unconscious work that has gone on.

The classic examples here are the invention of the sewing machine (the problem was the needle) by Elias Howe and the discovery of the benzene ring by Kekule (Faraday, 1974). More recently, a professor of microbiology began consulting to industry on applications of microbiology and genetics. These contacts exposed him to promising new genetic engineering firms. His "aha" came in 1976. "It dawned on me that I should start my own genetic engineering company," which he did in 1980. By 1982 the company was involved in eight projects and had $5 million in revenues (Long & McMullan, 1984).

Expression/invention. In order for the breakthrough to add value to anyone else, there must be some expression of the insight. There is an output—a proposal, a plan, a prototype—that can be experienced by important stakeholders (e.g., customers, bankers, suppliers, employees). The expressed solution is concrete, objectively perceived, and no longer in the entrepreneur's head. This expression of the idea may have been selected from several alternatives and types of output (e.g., which prototype to display, which way to present the business plan), or it may be the first and only solution derived.

For example, entrepreneurs faced with unused capacity in a plastic-extrusion facility sought to develop a product that would exploit this capacity. They designed and made prototypes of several garden chairs made of plastic tubing and fabric. They continued to explore their potential product by literally living with the products themselves for several months—the garden chairs were found in the dining room, living room, or on the porch of the entrepreneurs. In all that contact, they refined their product, its market, and its price.

Verification or evaluation. Prototypes and plans are evaluated by others. The prototype is tested by other engineers, subjected to marketing and production criteria, and its commercial potential is evaluated. The business plan is scrutinized by bankers, consultants, venture capitalists, suppliers, customers, and/or potential employees, and their evaluation and actions help or hinder the implementation of the idea. In this stage, others seek to support or refute the idea. Eventually, markets either support or fail to support the new product or service. These tests and feedback from them may or may not result in other vague feelings about some potential or better way . . . and the cycle may repeat.

Implications

The problem-finding competency of entrepreneurs would predict not only product or service innovations but also the creativity, innovativeness or cleverness of the strategies chosen by the entrepreneurs. We can also predict that entrepreneurs who use the slow incubation process will not be creative in running their new ventures—decisions need to be made too quickly. If creativity and innovation are the keys to competitive advantage, then the long-run success of firms led by such entrepreneurs needs to be monitored. On the other hand, those with predominately fast incubation may not be able to solve the truly complex problems that advanced technology, global economies, and human potential present. Entrepreneurs with long incubation processes (and longer future time perspectives) might produce more cutting-edge and standard-setting products, services, and management practices. Finally, the incubation process may be correlated with the entry into entrepreneurship, with slow incubation associated with "wading in" and the fast process with "the plunge."

BARRIERS TO CREATIVITY

Creativity is limited by fear and negative emotion, intellectualizing, being closed- versus open-minded, and basing decisions on experience and memory ("the way I/we have always done this in the past"; Driver, 1979). Entrepreneurs tend to overcome the specific barriers to creativity, which include (Adams, 1980, p. 164):

1. *Fear of making a mistake or failing.* Although potential entrepreneurs might experience fear of failure, it is not strong in those who proceed. (See Chapter 10 for more on entrepreneurs' attitudes toward failure and mistakes.)

2. *Inability to tolerate ambiguity; overriding desires for security, order, "no appetite for chaos."* Entrepreneurs who proceed from their ideas into a concrete venture tend to have higher than average tolerance for ambiguity, and many find their greatest opportunities in chaotic environments.

3. *Preference for judging ideas, rather than generating them.* Little is known about how entrepreneurs stack up on the

generativity versus judgment dimension. We do know that once begun, the venturing process itself brings more new business ideas than most entrepreneurs can implement.

4. *Inability to relax, incubate, and "sleep on it."* Although we do not know much about the incubative process of entrepreneurs, we do know that they tend to be "type A" individuals (impatient, hurried, competitive, etc.). This suggests short incubation periods.

5. *Lack of challenge; problem fails to engage interest.* Although potential entrepreneurs might find the problems of new ventures uninteresting, those who proceed and persist have, by definition, overcome this obstacle. Entrepreneurs tend to find their venture so interesting that it becomes the primary focus of attention, often to the neglect of families, friends, and hobbies.

6. *Excessive zeal; excessive motivation to succeed quickly.* While this obstacle does not necessarily interfere with the start-up phase of a new business, it often creates concern in potential investors. Most investors have a five-to-seven-year timeframe for harvesting their investments, and "get-rich-quick" entrepreneurs are considered unqualified to grow a solid venture. Finally, while visionary zeal is important in some ventures, it does not guarantee success or endurance.

7. *Lack of access to areas of imagination.* There is little known about the imagination of entrepreneurs. One study found that only 12 percent of the entrepreneurs surveyed reported using visualization in the process of starting a business, and many of these began consulting firms (Rockey, 1986).

8. *Lack of imaginative control as in daydreaming; inability to focus on one idea.* Little is known about how or when entrepreneurs focus in on a winning business concept. However, entrepreneurs are known as "dreamers who do," so this does not appear to be a problem for those who proceed with their ideas.

9. *Inability to distinguish reality from fantasy.* Little is known about this in entrepreneurs; however, psychologists Donald Levine and Gregory Kuhlman (1984) consider entrepreneurs to have adequate reality-testing competencies.

> Every entrepreneur must deal with his environment and internal states. He must assess whether any particular information he processes is derived from external or internal sources. Judging the extent to which internal issues distort perception of the environment is one of the key concerns of the entrepreneur (p. 3).

Implications

Entrepreneurs who experience none or few of these barriers will be more innovative than others. Entrepreneurs with fewer obstacles and more creativity should be more successful in the long run. Conversely, entrepreneurs who experience more of these barriers (or bigger barriers) are likely to be less innovative than they could be. Increasing creativity involves removing these barriers, and good coaching and counseling may help (although change may take many years). However, these barriers are often manifestations of deeply rooted habits and characteristics that are often difficult to identify. Perhaps more easy to identify are the positive qualities of the creative personality.

THE CREATIVE PERSONALITY

Listed in Table 2.1 are characteristics found by various researchers to be associated with creative individuals. Compare this list of characteristics to that in Table 2.2, which lists research on personality characteristics thought to be important

TABLE 2.1   Personality Characteristics of Creative
Individuals

| Getzels &
Csikszentmihalyi
(1976) | Sensitivity and open to experience
Not stereotyped as extremely masculine
  or feminine |
|---|---|
| Maddi (1980) | Transcendent
Uninterested in socializing
Unconcerned with acceptance by others
Less predictable, repetitive, and
  conforming
More imaginative, intense, and original
Assertive
Self-sufficient
Personal integration
Casualness
Bohemian tendencies
Low superego strength
Suspicious
Prone to guilt, tension and emotional
  instability
Tolerant of ambiguity
Impulsive
Craving for novelty, autonomy and self-
  assertiveness |

TABLE 2.2   Personality Characteristics Frequently Found
in Entrepreneurs

Sexton & Bowman (1984)	Energetic Dominant Less nurturant Socially adroit Broad interests Less responsibility Less interpersonal affect Autonomous High self-esteem Less affiliative Lower conformity Endurance Less participation Less succorance
Hornaday & Aboud (1971)	Less need for social support More need for independence
Welsh & White (1983)	Sense of urgency Low need for status Self-confidence Comprehensive awareness Objective
Swayne & Tucker (1973)	Self-confidence Empathy without sympathy Goal- (rather than task-) oriented Intelligent Action-oriented Thick-skinned Selectively curious Competitive, aggressive
Timmons (1978)	Self-confidence
Miller (1963)	Ambitious Robust (physically, mentally, morally) Controlled vitality Courageous Optimistic Intelligence Articulate Integrity
Begley & Boyd (1986)	Need for achievement Risk-taking propensity Tolerance for ambiguity Type A behavior

to the entrepreneurial personality (a more thorough treatment of motivations and abilities appears in Chapter 3).

As can be seen, entrepreneurs tend to have some of the characteristics of creative personalities. They tend to be less nurturant and require less social support, which, along with self-confidence, enables them to proceed with ideas that others may question. They tend to be more tolerant of ambiguity and more action-oriented, with a sense of urgency (not necessarily impulsive). In contrast with the profile of the creative personality, entrepreneurs have not been shown to be casual, Bohemian, or excessively suspicious (psychoanalytic studies notwithstanding; see Chapter 4). Finally, many of the characteristics of creative personalities have never been measured in entrepreneurs for comparison with the general population or other organizational players.

ENTREPRENEURIAL CREATIVITY

In general, we are fascinated by the lives and personalities of creative individuals and our fascination with the entrepreneur is no exception. Indeed, entrepreneurs who add value through organization are creative almost by definition. In general, the results of several studies confirm the picture of the entrepreneur as creator.

Studies of entrepreneurs' needs and values demonstrate that *entrepreneurs tend to need and value creative expression.* In his study of 44 college graduates before graduation and three-to-five years later, Schein (1977) found five basic career needs, one of which is creativity. Based on his interview data, the creative need is most characteristic of those in "entrepreneurial" careers (not all were self-employed or organization builders), who wish to "create something new which can be clearly identified with the individual" (p. 55). A different study confirms this notion, finding that high-technology entrepreneurs have a high value for aesthetics, and that over 25 percent had a high value for variety, using paper and pencil measures of individual differences (Komives, 1972).

Other research suggests that entrepreneurs may *have personality characteristics* more like those of the highly creative individual outlined previously. One study looked at personality differences among college graduates and found that those with some ownership in a business were more creative than those with no ownership (this scale did not discriminate those who had taken part in starting the business from those who did not; Hull et al., 1980). Another study compared entrepreneurship majors with business and nonbusiness majors, finding that potential entrepreneurs had broader interests and more innovativeness than nonbusiness majors, and were less conforming than either group (Sexton & Bowman, 1984).

Entrepreneurs who are especially creative *tend to behave differently* than their less-creative siblings or managerial cousins. When Silver (1983) surveyed wealthy entrepreneurs, he found that noncreative entrepreneurs were unable to identify a problem or a solution (creative ones were able to do this). Less-creative entrepreneurs ended up in leveraged buy-outs (taking a publicly held unit private with borrowed funds) and in real estate. More creative entrepreneurs were involved in start-ups in more diverse areas.

Entrepreneurs can and do *use mental rehearsal and imagination* in the design and implementation of their projects, as Rockey's (1986) research suggests. He found that about 12 percent of entrepreneurs used some form of visualization in solving business problems such as planning facilities, developing confidence, structuring, and staffing. The visionary aspects of entrepreneurial leadership are discussed again in Chapter 8.

Finally, one study suggests that creative entrepreneurs may *be more disorganized and have more difficulty with organizing and expanding a business* than less-creative and more action-oriented individuals. In her comparison of creative thinkers and activist entrepreneurs, Sinetar (1985) suggests that the creative thinker has a "stylized, unpredictable, and often disorganized" method of working. She concludes that the creative style often works against the process of organization, since it is both very individualistic and creates uncertainties through these characteristics:

1. Easily bored by familiar territory
2. Comfortable with ambiguity at work
3. May be uninterested in social matters
4. Experience their work as a calling or dedicated vocation (especially among those with "healthier" personalities)

EXAMPLE: SCHOLASTIC BOOKS

The formation of Scholastic Books demonstrates many of the creative processes that distinguish creative entrepreneurs. The venture, aimed at publications in the professional-academic niche, was begun by SA and her husband, MA. Twenty years later, the firm is prospering in a slow but steady growth pattern. MA was the visionary, who from his years in the publishing industry and his scholarly network saw the need for scholarly publications. His ideas and intellect guided the firm for over 20 years.

The firm was predicated on forming quality relationships with research-productive scholars in a variety of disciplines. Scholastic Books offered faculty new vehicles for publishing their ideas as well as products (other people's ideas) needed to advance their own work. The firm published ideas that would not have been published elsewhere, and has become part of the infrastructure of several emerging disciplines. Thus the values that guided the birth and development of Scholastic Books were some combination of economic and aesthetic, political, and moral values.

Although personality measures were not administered to SA and MA, we can assume that their early career choices to enter the publishing industry signal some creative predispositions. We do find that their preferences for staying personally involved with the creative juices of the firm (e.g., contact with the authors) had a limiting effect on how well they organized, motivated, and developed others to fill decision-making roles and became a bigger problem as the firm grew.

Implications

If creative entrepreneurs are responsible for organizational births, creative products, and ingenious strategies for survival and growth, then it behooves us to find ways to recognize and assess the creative potential of entrepreneurs and would-be entrepreneurs. We have suggested four ways to do this: (1) investigate the individual's values and needs; (2) assess the individual's personality, using any one of several measures of creativity; (3) observe the behavior of the individual for problem finding, incubation processes, and creative expressions; and (4) observe or test for the ability to visualize or imagine.

Can creativity be taught or learned? Because personality is considered relatively stable and difficult to change, personality-based approaches to creativity leave little hope for training or improving individual creativity. However, the more behavioral approaches suggest ways individuals may become more creative—by contacting more objects, problems, customers, employees, etc., and by learning and practicing visualization.

CREATION OF CULTURE

As suggested in Chapter 1, entrepreneurs create their organizations intentionally and the values added by the organization tend to be consciously chosen. In addition to the generation of new ideas and solutions to product and market problems, entrepreneurs create organizations that can very well outlive them. First, by selecting certain individuals to become members of the start-up or growth team and later by reinforcing and reiterating certain principles, assumptions, values, and "rules," the entrepreneur shapes the emerging organizational strategy, structure, and culture. Organizational culture can be defined as

> the pattern of basic assumptions that a given group has invented, discovered, or developed in learning to cope with its problems of external adaptation and internal integration—a pattern of assumptions that has worked well enough to be considered valid and, therefore, to be taught to new members as the correct way to perceive, think, and feel in relation to those problems.
>
> Schein, 1983, p. 14

Founders and founding teams begin with their individual or shared theories of business, often based on previous work experience. Based on these theories, they make strategic choices in their "tactical" behavior. That is, the founder's day-to-day decisions, activities, and relationships form the initial strategic template of the organization and therefore the initial structure and culture.

> . . . entrepreneurs are very strong-minded about what to do and how to do it. Typically they already have strong assumptions about the nature of the world, the role their organization will play in that world, the nature of human nature, truth, relationships, time, and space.
>
> Schein, 1983, p. 17

Sometimes the theories and values of the founder(s) are conscious and articulated and other times they are unconscious. A good example of a new venture whose leadership is culture-conscious is that of Sequent Computer Systems Inc., manufacturer of a flexible, high-powered office computer. Founder Karl C. "Casey" Powell and his team of three vice-presidents and the human resource director have "made culture a deliberate priority, and they have nurtured Sequent's values, heroes, and rituals as carefully as a parent nurtures a child" (Benner, 1985, p. 76). For example, the team set six corporate objectives in 1983: (1) profitability; (2) customer satisfaction; (3) market domination; (4) "a culture that rewards our employees for their contributions"; (5) "an organization that provides individuals with the means to accept the maximum responsibility for the overall success of their company"; and (6) community responsibility (Benner, 1985, p. 78). In addition, the company consciously, purposefully uses rituals (e.g., the telling of jokes, passing of symbols of work) and creates artifacts (e.g., yearbooks, buttons).

The entrepreneur's original theories, values, and assumptions, many of which have little to do with the fiscal health of the organization, are subsequently refined by early-stage learning in the new venture. (Later chapters will offer other examples of how founders have embedded noneconomic values into their organizations.) It is through the interaction of founding values and theories and new experiences and subsequent learning in the new venture that organizational culture begins to take shape and perpetuate itself.

Perhaps organizational culture is easiest to "manage" and influence when organizations are small and new. However, the payoff or penalty for strong or weak cultures may not show up in the early stages. It is, however, a major concern in stable and larger organizations seeking to remain competitive through innovation, employee commitment, etc. (Deal & Kennedy, 1982). Thus entrepreneurs caught in pressing short-term decisions face an often overlooked creative opportunity to consciously and intentionally build an organization with specific cultural qualities.

Implications

If long-term values are held, then the creation of culture by the entrepreneurial team may be a good predictor of the future of the firm. While organizational culture may not contribute to the values harvested by early-stage investors, it is important to those who eventually buy out these investors—underwriters, stockholders, and banks.

IMPORTANCE OF CREATIVITY

Entrepreneurs can be and often are very creative individuals. In the business world, there are few individuals who appear to demonstrate as much generativity—creating new products, new processes, new markets, and new organizations. A complete understanding of entrepreneurship cannot be had without considering its creative aspects, centering on the individual (or team) that intends this outcome.

While not all entrepreneurs invent new products or services or discover new resources, each founder who builds an organization that adds value and who intends to continue in business (thereby creating jobs) is involved in an act of economic generativity. The process by which entrepreneurial ideas are refined, problems chosen, and solutions expressed and evaluated is one that is fundamentally creative. Also important to the entrepreneurial process is how barriers to creativity are overcome (through self-selection of those psychologically equipped, through mental rehearsal, through supportive relationships, etc.).

While personality seems important to the creative potential—after all, not all of us are as imaginative, resourceful, persistent, and self-confident as the innovative entrepreneur—it seems more useful to look at behaviors involved in creating new ventures. Research suggests that creative approaches to problem finding and evaluation relate to the kind of business begun (start-up versus acquisition) and that creativity may have some negative consequences related to later-stage needs for stability and organizing.

We have shown that entrepreneurs, in the process of creatively solving problems and introducing new goods and services, spawn organizations that embody and enact their values and beliefs. Like children, these organizations contain and reflect the "father" or "mother" founder. This suggests that the generative potentials of entrepreneurs have a deeper meaning and a longer life than a surface look at inventions, discoveries, and innovations leads us to believe.

In conclusion, it is the creative potential in the entrepreneurial act that attracts our attention and, increasingly, the attention of the media. However, we must recognize that mythologizing the creative potential, which results in notions of "overnight millionaires" and "whiz kids," leaves us with inflated and unrealistic stereotypes of entrepreneurs. In the remaining chapters, these stereotypes are disassembled. Creativity, however, remains.

CHAPTER 3

IDENTIFYING AND DEVELOPING THE RIGHT STUFF: EXPERIENCE AND BACKGROUND

INTRODUCTION

This chapter and the next address those here-and-now qualities of the individual that can be used to assess the likelihood of someone becoming an entrepreneur and the likelihood of that entrepreneur succeeding. These chapters are based on a common model of performance, in which *performance* (choosing an entrepreneurial career, profitability) is the result of *abilities* and *motivation* as shown:

$$P = A \times M$$

Abilities and motivations are assessed through measures of personality (Chapter 4) and through review of prior experiences and background. If either is lacking, performance will also be lacking.

Experiences, such as those that might appear on a resume or in a biography, contribute to the development of skills, abilities, and competencies important in entrepreneurship as well as to the values, needs, incentives, and drives that energize the entrepreneurial idea. It is possible that some individuals learn from their experiences more effectively than others. In general, learning from one's experience requires an ability on the part of each learner to (1) recognize an important learning experience—"failures" and "successes," (2) reflect on that experience to see through his or her ego, emotions, and assumptions to what was really going on, (3) abstract from that experience and relate it to other experiences and his or her theory or picture of what is going on, and (4) based on these, to try something new next time (Kolb, 1984).

Entrepreneurs in general learn from their experience as well as anyone else (few make it to adulthood without this ability). There is some suggestion, however, that entrepreneurs tend to be biased toward action (experiments) and away from reflection. Very few of the entrepreneurs interviewed in 1983 (Bird, 1983) and later spent much time reflecting on their previous experiences. For most, the interviews were the first time they had tried to put the pieces of their venture experience together into a coherent story.

Experiences that contribute to the entrepreneurial "right stuff" can come through work, education, maturation, and social-biological "givens" such as race and gender. Each of these is discussed below.

WORK EXPERIENCES

There is a widely held, but untested, consensus that past work experience is a better predictor of decisions, performance, and behavior than education. The popular opinion is based on a common-sense notion that the "school of hard knocks" prepares one better than colleges, universities, seminars, and books. Thus we will look first at work experience and then at education.

Among those who invest in entrepreneurs, the entrepreneur's track record of "thorough and proven operating knowledge of the business they intend to launch" is considered very important (Timmons, 1976, p. 13). Three types of experience are considered important in determining this track record: (1) industrial (technical or market) expertise; (2) management expertise; and (3) entrepreneurial experience. The role of each of these, and the impact of previous work satisfaction, are discussed below.

INDUSTRIAL EXPERIENCE

It is considered risky to begin business without specialized knowledge of the industry—either technology or market. Many examples can be given about businesses that struggle and fail because the lead entrepreneur is unaware of industry norms regarding pricing, employment, and supplier relations.

Vesper (1980) tells of a young man who, after his father's death, entered the fish brokerage business, having very little industry experience. He ended up with net losses and fewer gross sales than in previous years in part because he paid more for poorer-quality fish than his competition.

> It was several months before the young entrepreneur found out that the "old hands" he was buying from were charging him higher than usual prices while at the same time mis-representing quality in the fish he bought. . . . It seemed to him that his suppliers would not take him seriously, as they had his father, in business deals (p. 38).

Other studies suggest that lack of experience relates to a shorter career as an entrepreneur (Ronstadt, 1984a). The explanation for this seems to involve the lack of synergy between past experience and new endeavors, whereas successful start-up entrepreneurs seem to be able to capitalize on their own experience as well as other resources.

However, many entrepreneurs do succeed in unfamiliar territory. Those who enter into businesses in areas where they lack previous experience usually do so through acquisition of a going concern (including knowledgeable managers and workers) rather than through starting up a new business (Vesper, 1980). These entries are usually well-researched and rational considerations made without the urgency that often comes with an economic displacement.

Thus there are two groups of entrepreneurs—those with considerable decision-making experience and those with little experience in the industry. In an empirical study of success and failure in small manufacturing ventures, Hoad and Rosko (1964) found that 32 percent of the successes and 24 percent of the failures had ten or more years of experience as an owner or manager in a similar business; 35 percent of the successes and 51 percent of the failures had no such previous experience. Thus previous industrial experience seems to be important but is not the only contributor to success.

Perhaps previous experience with technology and/or the marketplace may be more important for certain types of industry than for others. For areas where scientific processes form the core technology (biochemistry, genetic engineering), previous education may be more important than work experience in running a laboratory and designing production (Vesper, 1980). In contrast, work experience may be more important in businesses that rely on industrial inside information (e.g., tool-and-die shops, Vesper, 1980), management expertise (financial services), and those with considerable competition (restaurants and fast foods).

In some cases work experience in a certain industry results in key technical skills. Collins and Moore (1964) developed a model of work experience based on an early study of low-technology manufacturing entrepreneurs in Michigan. "The school for entrepreneurs" involves three phases.

1. There is a period of *drifting* in which the future entrepreneur is driven by a diffuse restlessness and in which he picks up critical technical know-how from different jobs.

2. Basic dealing or deal making is learned. The basic problem is "bringing a variety of resources together into a combination that makes possible establishing an ongoing enterprise" (p. 108). It requires strong character and sacrifice.

3. Protégéship involves finding a sponsor and working for and with that sponsor. The experience is either one of emotional highs and lows with generally positive learning or one of fear, distrust, and aggression on the part of the entrepreneur. Important to this lesson is ending the relationship, with the entrepreneur breaking away. "It is precisely his fear of superordinates, his distrust of peers, and his tendency to cut intolerable situations rather than stay and solve them, which causes the entrepreneur sooner or later to dissolve the protégé-sponsor [*sic*] relationship" (p. 116).

Implications

Experience with an industry provides the entrepreneur with certain key competencies and inside information needed to recognize opportunities and evaluate and manage risk. Successful entrepreneurs might be recognized by their ability to make sense of their prior experiences with an industry and to assess the strategic issues facing firms in the industry. Those lacking industrial experience (e.g., high-school and college graduates) may compensate for the unproven and possibly undeveloped skills with technical training and extraordinary zeal and energy.

MANAGEMENT EXPERIENCE

The importance of managerial experience to entrepreneurship is debatable. Indeed, some people clarify the notion of entrepreneurial behavior by contrasting it with managerial behavior (see Chapter 10). However, once initiated most organizations do require some form of management. How important to success is the managerial experience, relative to the technical or market experience of the entrepreneur?

Ronstadt (1984a) argues that for most entrepreneurs, "managerial know-how may be the least important form of experience" (p. 105). He reasons that most new ventures stay small and require more self-management than organizational management. However, it may be that organizations stay small because they lack appropriate management systems. Certainly, to the faster-growing firms, managerial experience is more important to success. On most lists of "causes of business failure," lack of management is near the top.

Another important factor in the relative worth of managerial experience depends on who is evaluating the situation. Venture capitalists frequently value the ability to assemble, motivate, and manage entrepreneurial teams (Timmons, 1976). The importance of these internal teams, which may include partners as well as employees, is discussed in a later chapter. For now we conclude that management experience has important benefits to organizational growth and development.

PREVIOUS JOB SATISFACTION AND MOBILITY

There is some strong evidence that before starting their ventures, entrepreneurs were dissatisfied with their jobs. Brockhaus (1980a) found that in general, entrepreneurs are most dissatisfied with previous work, supervision, opportunity for promotion, and coworkers (and more satisfied with pay) than the general population of workers. Dissatisfaction is thought to "push" one into entrepreneurship. More will be said about such displacements in Chapter 6.

Dissatisfaction with previous work experiences also seems to contribute to the success of the new venture. Brockhaus (1980b, cited in Brockhaus, 1982) found that successful entrepreneurs were more dissatisfied with their previous jobs than unsuccessful entrepreneurs. He suggests that this dissatisfaction motivated them into extra efforts to avoid returning to the workplace as an employee.

A related aspect of previous work experience is the sheer number and variety of jobs held. One would expect a dissatisfied employee to look for another job, provided labor-market conditions support the move. Empirical research, however, does not consistently support the image of the restless entrepreneur suggested by Collins and Moore (1964) and Sexton and Kent (1981), who found that women entrepreneurs tended to have had more jobs than women executives. Entrepreneurial stability was found by Brockhaus and Nord (1979); entrepreneurs had worked at an average of three organizations, whereas managers had had an average of four previous employers. Similarly, successful entrepreneurs may have significantly fewer previous positions than unsuccessful entrepreneurs (Sexton & Van Auken, 1982).

These results make sense when we consider *career dissatisfaction* (compared with job dissatisfaction). Careers are cumulative across jobs, education, vocations, and hobbies. Career dissatisfaction results not from a particularly dissatisfying job, but from the range of experiences, challenges, and opportunities one faces in that career. Career dissatisfaction is slow to grow and may not involve many job changes. However, once dissatisfied with one's career, the individual looks for new paths—and starting a new venture or acquiring a going concern is one way to switch careers. For example, a teacher in a junior college in Canada grew bored and dissatisfied with his career as teacher. He left academe and started a business manufacturing redwood hand mirrors. Finding the rewards of this career dissatisfying, he left again to take up the career of self-employed contractor and carpenter.

Implications

Experience as a manager can contribute certain competencies to the new venture—team building, control, and the ability to grow to significant size. Dissatisfaction with a managerial career also provides the motivation to "take the plunge." Satisfied managers are the least likely to choose to venture and have needs, values, and motivations very different from—and perhaps inimical to—those of entrepreneurs. As a result, it is possible that entrepreneurs may not be recognized, appreciated, or accurately valued by those with managerial frameworks; this has implications for the venture capital and investment industries, which need to make such assessments. Finally, those lacking extensive management experience (e.g., high-school and college students) may be less likely to grow their initial or early ventures.

ENTREPRENEURIAL EXPERIENCE

Previous experience with entrepreneurship is an important factor in looking at current or future performance of specific entrepreneurs. Some of this experience is vicarious, coming from working for or with an entrepreneur who becomes a role model. Another form of vicarious experience is growing up with an entrepreneurial parent or watching a friend develop a business.

Some experience is hands-on, from having started previous ventures. Apparently, venture creation becomes easier with experience, and presumably from learning from that experience (Ronstadt, 1984a). Typically, one out of five entrepreneurs has had direct venture experience prior to their current enterprise (Hornaday & Aboud, 1971). This experience contributes to objective measures of success as viewed by entrepreneurial advisors (bankers, etc.; Woodworth et al., 1969, cited in Vesper, 1980).

One of the important outcomes of having prior experience in new venture development is that once on an entrepreneurial path, new opportunities for other ventures become clear. Ronstadt (1984a) calls this the "corridor principle." "An intriguing and vital aspect of this phenomenon is that often one or more of the corridors leads ultimately to the venture success that the entrepreneur sought, but did not find with his/her original venture" (Ronstadt, 1984a, p. 60). Ronstadt goes on to report that 57 percent of all the Babson entrepreneurs surveyed in 1981 had been involved in either sequential (21 percent) or overlapping (36 percent) ventures. Ronstadt reports that among those entrepreneurs practicing for more than six and one-half years, 65 percent had been involved in multiple ventures. Apparently, the longer one is an entrepreneur, the more likely one is to get involved in multiple ventures.

Whether or not these prior ventures were successful was not reported. However, Cooper (1971, cited in Shapero, 1982b) found that previous failure was not an impediment to starting again. "Failures apparently do not shake the credibility of the company-formation act, but may even appear to reinforce the credibility of the act to the entrepreneur (as well as serving as a learning experience)" (Shapero, 1982b, p. 16). There will be more about the entrepreneurial career path in Chapter 7.

Implications

Prior experience as an entrepreneur is a good predictor of venturing again. Prior ventures add to the competencies needed to succeed—as long as the entrepreneur is willing and even eager to learn from his or her experiences (painful or pleasurable). Prior ventures also provide considerable motivation to venture again—a taste of independence, control, creativity, and leadership can become "addicting" and few alternative jobs can provide the same stimulation.

WORK EXPERIENCE: Implications

Prior work experiences can provide advantages to the entrepreneur and his or her venture, *contingent on how well and what he or she learns from those experiences.* Slow learners do not do well in the highly competitive and chaotic early days of a start-up or turnaround. It is also conceivable that would-be entrepreneurs might learn the wrong lessons from their experiences. For example, most adults have had a trust betrayed. Does the would-be entrepreneur become increasingly distrustful or even paranoid (see Chapter 5 on Freudian approaches to the entrepreneurial personality)? Does he or she become more discriminating or build a cadre and network of reliable and ethical counterparts? It is what one does with the lessons from the school of life that makes the difference—whether the school is as employee, manager, or entrepreneur.

Those with limited work experience are handicapped by unproven or undeveloped skills and the lack of credibility perceived by seasoned managers, customers, and lenders. They also lack the extra motivations that derive from job dissatisfaction and the taste of financial independence. Thus students, homemakers, and others lacking experience must work extra hard and learn quickly and vicariously to compensate.

EDUCATION

Some observers hold that formal education impedes the entrepreneurial process or drive by reducing curiosity, vision, and willingness to take risks (Fallows, 1985; Shapero, 1980). Others contend that formal education helps entrepreneurs to succeed (Robinett, 1985b; Ronstadt, 1985b).

Several studies suggest that *entrepreneurs are well educated, but not as well educated as managers.* In an early study of owner-managers of midwestern manufacturers, Hoad and Rosko (1964) found that 25 percent of their sample (92 firms) had at least one owner-manager with a baccalaureate degree. Another early study of manufacturing entrepreneurs in Michigan showed that entrepreneurs tend to have less education than business leaders, although the entrepreneurs were better educated than the general population of Michigan (Collins & Moore, 1964). A more recent study showed entrepreneurs with an average of 13.6 years of education and managers with an average of 15.5 years (Brockhaus & Nord, 1979). In their study of the founders and employee members of the National Federation of Independent Business, Kent and his colleagues (Kent, Sexton, & Van Auken, 1982) found that more managers than entrepreneurs had one-to-four years of college, with more management courses such as accounting, economics, finance, management, and statistics. However, they also found that more entrepreneurs than managers had more than four years of college. The authors suggest that this finding may be due to the inclusion of solo self-employed professionals.

Another explanation has to do with the technical requirements of certain types of enterprises. In their study of high-technology entrepreneurs, Roberts and Wainer (1966) found that 86 percent of the entrepreneurs had a college degree compared to 55 percent of business leaders and 5 percent of the general population. This study revealed with the median level of education was an M.S. degree, with 17 percent attaining a Ph.D. or greater. These results might also extend to biotechnology and health care.

Education may also separate the more successful entrepreneurs from those who are less successful. A 1964 study of success and failure of new business (Hoad & Rosko) showed that successful firms had more college-educated owner-managers than did failures. A survey of the perceptions of professional advisors to entrepreneurs (e.g., lawyers, accountants, and management consultants) found "more successful" entrepreneurs slightly better educated than "typical" entrepreneurs (Woodworth et al., 1969, cited in Vesper, 1980). These results are supported by a more recent study of 40 successful (significant enterprise growth for four years) and 40 unsuccessful (former) entrepreneurs in which successful entrepreneurs had more formal education than the unsuccessful group (Sexton & Van Auken, 1982).

EDUCATION: WHAT IMPACT?

Ronstadt (1984a) and others argue that formal education can as frequently operate as an impediment to entrepreneurship as an asset in the entrepreneurial process. He claims that, rather than develop creative free thinkers (who would be prone toward innovation and entrepreneurship), the traditional liberal arts education fosters conformity and low tolerance for ambiguity.

> The end result is thought and behavior processes that re-
> fuse to admit ignorance, and social values that preclude
> "getting one's hands dirty" with entrepreneurial pursuits
> (p. 104).

As previously discussed, entrepreneurs entering into certain industries require specialized and advanced training to
design and market products and services. In these cases the
importance of technical degrees (engineering, medicine, science) is obvious. More questionable is the value of a general
business education, and particularly the acquisition of an
MBA. Ronstadt feels that business education may work against
entrepreneurial tendencies. Shapero (1980) agrees, suggesting
that only bureaucratic and professional-staff concepts and values are taught in the typical MBA program. This bias may be
changing as more schools design and deliver entrepreneurship
programs.

Despite these criticisms, there is evidence and argument
that formal education, especially management education, has
a positive impact on entrepreneurship. There are indications
that MBA curricula, and especially entrepreneurship courses,
majors, and programs, actually help entrepreneurs get started
and succeed.

> Recent graduates of programs who became entrepreneurs
> owe something critical to their education: either practical
> skills—how to approach financiers, develop training pro-
> grams, or develop the business—or a role model who en-
> couraged their incipient interest in entrepreneurship and
> spurred them to turn their ideas into businesses.
>
> Robinett, 1985, p. 50

Entrepreneurship programs in colleges and universities
offer undergraduate and graduate students a range of courses
(usually three or more) that particularly focus on entrepreneurship. These courses usually include one that involves the
writing of a business plan. Other courses may deal with entrepreneurial behavior, strategy, markets, and technology. Other
elements of formal educational programs include opportunities to meet successful local entrepreneurs, to work with entrepreneurs (as consultants or interns), and to start a student-run
venture.

Entrepreneurship programs may attract those who have
the "right stuff" for entrepreneurial careers. Alternatively, the
courses and programs may move students toward an entrepre-

neurial archetype by challenging assumptions and encouraging the development of certain competencies (such as risk acceptance, promotional skills, independence, control, temporal agility, temporal complexity, attention to operational detail, customer orientation) not usually fostered in traditional business degree programs.

Students who take entrepreneurship majors differ in important ways from regular business majors and nonbusiness majors. They tend to be less conforming, more impersonal, more risk-taking, more welcoming of change, and have a higher energy level, greater social adroitness, greater need for autonomy, and less need for reassurance than other students, a profile similar to that of successful entrepreneurs (Sexton & Bowman, 1984). Those who take an undergraduate course in entrepreneurship are more likely to be full-time self-employed or part-time self-employed several years later, compared to those who do not take such a course (Hornaday & Vesper, 1981). Whether programs attract "budding entrepreneurs" or develop them, the importance of concentrating the entrepreneurial energies of young people and providing a broad base of entrepreneurial networking cannot be underestimated.

Of course there is debate among educators and entrepreneurs on just how much of entrepreneurship can be taught (or learned in a formal setting). Basic to this debate are assumptions one makes about whether entrepreneurs are born or made. Debates also exist about how to provide appropriate learning experiences beyond case studies and the new venture business/marketing plan.

ALTERNATIVE CLASSROOMS

There is an expectation among those who hope to foster new venture proposals and to assist others in finding ways to be successful that some information and training are important. In their study of members of the National Federation of Independent Business, Kent et al. (1982) found that, in terms of alternative post-secondary learning experiences, only seminar attendance distinguished owners from managers. In this case, managers attended more seminars (topics were not specified in the report) than entrepreneurs. Unfortunately, not much more is known about the type and frequency of workshops, seminars, and conferences that entrepreneurs attend, or what the impact of such attendance might be.

Implications

The cumulative evidence suggests that education is important to many entrepreneurial ventures, through the development of competencies important to success in many careers. For example, undergraduate education aimed at fostering creativity, curiosity, open-mindedness, and good interpersonal skills contributes to innovativeness and the ability to marshall resources later in life. Beyond that, technical training is important to careers and ventures using or creating advanced-technology products.

Education can also influence the motivation toward entrepreneurship, often with a dampening effect. Risk-averse faculty in generally conservative institutions may be ill-equipped to inspire entrepreneurship in students. Furthermore, professional training tends to foster values and steady-state careers (Driver, 1979) that differ considerably from those of entrepreneurs (Bird & Allen, 1987).

Entrepreneurs operating from less education may have difficulty obtaining important advanced educational resources. It is often difficult (from fear of loss of control and not knowing appropriate performance criteria) to hire someone more well educated, more experienced, and smarter than you are (Jacknis, 1987). Thus education obtained while young (most entrepreneurs have no inclination to go back to school) is an important contributor to the entrepreneur's ability to hire and retain educated workers, who are critical to success in the "information age."

AGE EFFECTS

The chronological age when one begins a new venture relates to both education and work experience. The longer one studies or works for someone else, the older one is at the beginning of the entrepreneurial career. However, the age at which one begins an entrepreneurial career seems less important than other "facts" about the person. None of the major books on new venture development index the concept of age or even timing of entrepreneurial events.

A study of Babson College alumni (from certificate programs and those with baccalaureate degrees and MBAs) compared entrepreneurs with "serious nonstarters" (who considered but did not implement a venture; Ronstadt, 1984a,b). The study produced several findings with regard to the entrepreneur's age. First, most entrepreneurs begin their career as entrepreneur between 22 and 55 years of age. This suggests very different entry points into entrepreneurship, ranging from out of school to retirement (see Chapter 6 for more on career paths). Ronstadt suggests (but does not confirm) that there is more variation in chronological ages when the entrepreneurial career begins than when other careers begin. However, another study of members of the National Federation of Independent Business revealed no significant age differences between entrepreneurs (owners) and managers (employees) (Kent et al., 1982). Ronstadt (1984a,b) also suggests that chronological *age of beginning an entrepreneurial career (one's first new venture) contributes to differences in long-term success,* with younger entrepreneurs having longer careers as entrepreneurs.

Second, there are *"milestone years . . . when individual[s] are more inclined to consider and start an entrepreneurial career"* (p. 93). Ronstadt suggests that these years occur every five years at ages 20, 25, 30, and 35, as shown in Figure 3.1. Entrepreneurs reported feeling "it's now or never" as these birthdays occurred, which may contribute to the motivation needed to actually begin a venture.

Third, *the earlier people start an entrepreneurial career, the longer they are likely to remain in it* (despite venture failures). Tenure as an entrepreneur is a measure of entrepreneurial success, compared to becoming an ex-entrepreneur and working for someone else. Ronstadt found that those who started before 31 stayed with the entrepreneurial career an average of 7.4 years. In contrast, those who started after 31 years of age held the entrepreneurial career for 5.5 years. He explains the shorter careers of those who were chronologically older when they began in terms of individual risk aversion, which increases with age, and resilience in recovering from financial losses, which decreases with age.

Finally, there are *three types of entrepreneurial careers, each associated with a different age at inception* (measured in years since baccalaureate graduation from college): early starters who begin within one year of graduation (early 20s); those who work for someone else in anticipation of eventually becoming an entrepreneur (eight years after graduation, late 20s to early 30s); and those who did not anticipate becoming entrepreneurs who do so later (eleven years after graduation, mid 30s— the most frequent pattern).

In an empirical study of successful (significant growth of business over four years) and unsuccessful (former) entrepreneurs, Sexton and Van Auken (1982) found that successful en-

FIGURE 3.1   Milestone Years for Beginning an
Entrepreneurial Career (Ronstadt, 1984b)

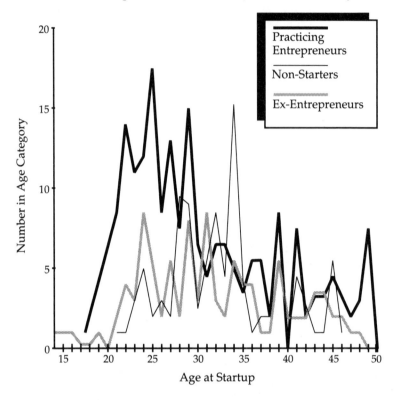

Source: "Ages of Entrepreneurs at Startup" from *Entrepreneurship: Text,
Cases & Notes*, by R. Ronstadt, p. 94. Copyright © 1984 by Lord Publishing,
Inc. (Dover, MA).

trepreneurs tend to be younger, with 35 percent of successful
and 20 percent of unsuccessful entrepreneurs under 40 years
of age. Most entrepreneurs in this study (successful and unsuccessful) were 41 to 50 years old.

Implications

The net result of research on age is that younger is better,
mostly due to the personal energy level (i.e., high motivation)
available to youth. However, previously cited findings of the
importance of education and industrial experience suggest

some lower limit. Of course teenagers can and do start businesses. Rarely are these successful by normal standards of sales, profits, and market share.

Older entrepreneurs may not last as long as younger ones, but that may be because they succeed faster and retire sooner. We might expect older entrepreneurs, with more experience, to enter entrepreneurship through acquiring an existing business more often than younger ones. Likewise, there are differences according to age in the future time span that is conceived and frames one's venture activities (Bird & Jordan, 1987). Because of these differences and differences in personality (risk aversion, need for achievement, need for control) and ability, we need to assess younger and older entrepreneurs differently.

RACE, GENDER, AND ETHNIC BACKGROUND

Differences in race, gender, and ethnic background, operating through family dynamics and social conditioning, might be expected to affect individual abilities and motivations. Thus we predict that these factors have an indirect, although important, impact on the decision to become an entrepreneur and on entrepreneurial performance.

GENDER

Most of the research summarized in this volume has focused on male entrepreneurs. The virtual absence, until recently, of research on female entrepreneurs is probably due to their lack of visibility as entrepreneurs. There tend to be far fewer female entrepreneurs, and these tend to operate smaller businesses than their male peers (The Bottom Line, 1978). Hisrich and Brush (1985) report that only 4.6 percent of all firms in the United States are owned by women. However, the number of self-employed women (not necessarily organization creators) has increased—by 35 percent between 1977 and 1982 (Hisrich & Brush, 1985), with women owning three million firms and entering into business at a rate five times faster than men (Female Owners, 1985).

Interestingly, research suggests that male and female entrepreneurs are more similar than different in many core attributes. For example, both men and women cite a desire for autonomy and control and a desire to achieve or "make things happen" as important motivations. Both men and women point to frustrations with current employment as another important impetus to take action (Hisrich & Brush, 1986). Like men, women entrepreneurs tend to place higher emphasis on their jobs, and have less job stability than their managerial peers (Sexton & Kent, 1981). Another study suggests that, like men, women entrepreneurs tend to be lower in conformity, interpersonal affect, harm avoidance, and succorance than women managers and higher in energy level, risk taking, social adroitness, autonomy, and change (Sexton & Bowman, 1986). Both men and women tend to value self-respect, freedom, a sense of accomplishment, family security, honesty, ambition, and responsibility (Fagenson, 1986). Finally, there are few differences between the sexes in the role of past experience or the proportion of start-up costs that are borrowed (Birley, Moss, & Saunders, 1986).

In comparing women in general to those who become entrepreneurs, we find results similar to those for men. That is, women entrepreneurs (despite racial differences) tend to be more oriented toward achievement, autonomy, aggression, recognition, independence, and leadership and less oriented toward support, conformity, and benevolence than the general population of women (DeCarlo & Lyons, 1979). Like her male counterpart,

> The typical woman entrepreneur: is the first born; from a middle or upper class family; has a self-employed father; has a college degree; is married with children; starts their [sic] significant entrepreneurial career between the ages of 40–45; has previous experience in the venture; and independence, achievement and job satisfaction are the strongest motivations to starting their [sic] own enterprises.
>
> Hisrich & Brush, 1985, p. 575

However, some gender differences do occur. Women entrepreneurs are more concentrated in retail and service sectors compared to men, and work fewer hours per week (45–50) than do men (Ronstadt, 1984a). Female entrepreneurs are also more concentrated in small enterprises in terms of sales and employees (Binder, 1978). One study reports that women entrepreneurs tend to be younger than males who began their ventures at approximately the same time. The same study showed women to have more female customers, employ more labor, use their families less as employees, start up more slowly, and subsequently incorporate more frequently than men (Birley et al., 1986). Although the home-based business is considered to have unique value to women (who want to combine business with child rearing), the Birley et al. (1986) study showed more men than women having home-based ventures.

Men and women entrepreneurs experience different problems and obstacles in assembling the resources for new ventures, with women usually facing extra barriers. Chief among these is finding financial support and credit in the face of overt and covert sex discrimination (Hisrich & Brush, 1985). This obstacle may limit women to start-ups with low overhead and capitalization requirements (i.e., sales and service instead of production). Although networking for resource access is important to men and women entrepreneurs, there is some suggestion that women go about this more formally (joining clubs and networking organizations) than men, who tend to rely on specific interpersonal relationships (Black, 1986).

There is some suggestion that women entrepreneurs may take on a particular style of leadership once the venture has been created. They tend to employ more labor than men (Birley et al., 1986) and may pay more attention to employee relations. Women tend to place higher value on equality and forgiveness than do men, who place higher value on family security and self-control (Fagenson, 1986). *The Wall Street Journal* reported that women entrepreneurs tend to treat employees idealistically and liberally, with some important and problematic business repercussions (Female Owners, 1985). However, the generalizability of these and other findings is in question, based on the paucity of research.

In general, we conclude that women entrepreneurs tend to have backgrounds, abilities, and motivations very similar to those of men who are entrepreneurs. The differences that do arise have more to do with access to resources, the type of business established (more likely to be income-substitution, independent start-up, in the service industries), and the type of employee relations that emerge in the new organization. However, women entrepreneurs are considerably different from women in general, having more of the competencies and drive needed to initiate and persist in a venture.

RACE

In terms of personality, demographics, and previous experience, there are few differences between white and black entrepreneurs. The differences that were found by Hornaday and

Aboud (1971) were attributed to socioeconomic factors (a higher divorce rate among blacks, fewer years in the current business, and the number of college graduates) or to different distribution across industries (more whites were in manufacturing and more blacks were in sales and service). The only personality difference in this study was that blacks tended to be more benevolent than whites. On all other scales—achievement, autonomy, aggression, support, conformity, recognition, independence, and leadership—there were no significant differences.

Like white entrepreneurs, minority entrepreneurs choose entrepreneurship out of previous job frustration. However, minorities and women, more often than white males, perceive a ceiling to their upward mobility in larger organizations (Hymowitz, 1984) that motivates independent action.

One such entrepreneur left a *Fortune 500* firm to begin an aerospace contracting firm because of promotional and racial barriers. He was able to demonstrate to top management that he could operate in the capacity of a vice-president of operations. This he did by effectively troubleshooting and problem solving in a newly acquired business. However, in his words "they were not ready to have a black vice-president" (Bird, 1983).

Like women entrepreneurs, minority entrepreneurs face additional obstacles to venturing. Ronstadt (1984a) suggests that both groups have difficulty in dealing with sources of finance and find smaller businesses less risky. He also suggests that moving from income substitution into a growth enterprise is particularly difficult for minority entrepreneurs. There is some indication that both women and minority entrepreneurs use formal rather than informal resources to solve problems; that is, they tend to use government agencies, small business centers, and network-oriented clubs more than the "old-boy" network and personal referrals (Hisrich & Brush, 1986; Young, Welsch, & Triana, 1984).

Minority entrepreneurs have "profiles" similar to those of white entrepreneurs; that is, they tend to have similar competencies and motivations. Minorities may be additionally motivated by perceived and real limitations to upward mobility, which make business ownership more valued. To the extent that work, education, and prior venture opportunities are limited, minorities may be less likely to develop the "right stuff" for current ventures.

RELIGIOUS AND ETHNIC BACKGROUND

Most studies of minority entrepreneurs have focused on black entrepreneurs. The results of these studies might apply to other minorities—Hispanics and Orientals, for example. Further research is needed to test this hypothesis. However, there is some indication that, along with cultural differences, language differences create obstacles to be overcome (in the United States, for those whose first language is other than English) (Young et al., 1984).

Ethnic minorities (and to some extent blacks and women) may feel more "displacement" than the white males who are the subjects of most studies. Displacement refers to events and circumstances that break old patterns and inertia—immigrating, being fired, etc. Shapero (1982b) argues that ethnic groups that have produced high numbers of entrepreneurs are also displaced groups (e.g., "Jews, Lebanese, Ibos in Nigeria, Jains and Parsis in India, Gujeratis in East Africa" and Chinese located off the mainland, p. 17).

Only one recent study specifically addressed differences between Jewish and non-Jewish entrepreneurs. Roberts and Wainer (1966) found that among high-technology entrepreneurs, those with a Jewish background were more likely than non-Jews to have a father who was self-employed (and thus a role model). Jewish entrepreneurs also tended to be more well educated than those of other religious backgrounds.

Implications

The results of these studies suggest that it is the choice of the entrepreneurial path that distinguishes entrepreneurs from management and the general population. The research suggests that entrepreneurs are more like other entrepreneurs than they are like their peers in the general population, and that other differences (such as gender, race, and ethnicity) do not differentiate entrepreneurial types. These individual differences (which are virtually impossible to change) do appear to influence the opportunity structure of the entrepreneur (his or her context and resources) and thus influence the type of industry entered, the size of the venture, and possibly the success of the venture. These factors also influence the experiences a person has and thus the development of competencies and motivations, which in turn affect performance.

Thus the lower performance (in terms of sheer numbers of business owners and size of businesses owned) of women and minority entrepreneurs can be attributed to *experience handicaps* and a *constrained opportunity environment*. However, in the increasingly segmented marketplace, with increasing demands for "tailored" goods and services and high information, the unique nonwork experiences of women and minorities (i.e., cultural and lifestyle differences) may be an important entrepreneurial resource.

CHAPTER 4

IDENTIFYING AND DEVELOPING THE RIGHT STUFF: MOTIVATION

INTRODUCTION

So far we have described some of the factors related to the ability to enter into new ventures and succeed—experience, education, and age. However, as suggested earlier, actual performance involves motivation—the needs, drives, and values that add energy to and direct one's abilities. Stated another way, given the same set of abilities, why do some individuals take up the "call to adventure" while others do not? This chapter looks at the important motivations found among entrepreneurs.

ACHIEVEMENT MOTIVATION

Achievement motivation is an underlying behavioral tendency to choose and persist at activities that involve a *standard of excellence, a challenging task* (one with moderate probability of success), and require *personal skill and responsibility for success* (McClelland, 1961). The motivation is thought to contribute to the vigor, intensity, and persistence of action in *achievement-oriented situations,* which are chosen because of a value placed on achieving as well as other directing values (McClelland, 1985).

Lying behind the motive to achieve are *needs* of individuals to achieve or *"do things better"* (compared to their own past performance, the performance of others, or relative

to some goal). Some researchers also consider the dampening effect of *fears,* such as the fear of failure or the fear of
success.

Thus the individual's need to achieve contributes to his or
her overall motive to achieve as well as to the value he or she
places on doing well. These needs and motives have been
found to predict *preferences for moderately risky or challenging
tasks,* whether this be driving behavior, classroom behavior, or
career choice. For example, businessmen have been found to
have higher need-for-achievement scores than other professionals across cultures, and salespeople have been found
to score higher than managers (research summarized in
McClelland, 1985).

The motive to achieve has been found to predict a *preference for personal responsibility* in these challenging situations.
The motive is not aroused by situations that are mostly determined by chance, such as gambling. This personal responsibility results in personal involvement in the task and a related
outcome of being less sensitive to interpersonal dynamics (research summarized in McClelland, 1985). In entrepreneurs,
this preference relates to their need for control, autonomy, and
independence.

Those who have high achievement motivation have *greater
value or need for performance feedback.* They get this feedback
from tasks that have obvious completion or progress points
(such as building a house or starting a business) and through
symbolic "scoring" systems, like money (McClelland, 1985).
Others verify that entrepreneurs, and especially those who
succeed, do not see money as an incentive, but rather as a
means to an end (financial security) or as a measure of performance (see the section on values below).

McClelland (1985) also argues that those high on achievement motivation are *more innovative.* They seek to "do things
better," and that this manifests itself in two questions the individual asks: (1) "How can I get the same result with less
work?" and (2) "How can the same amount of work produce a
bigger result?" (p. 249). McClelland reviews two decades of
research showing that achievement-motivated individuals
tend to move on to ever more challenging work, are quicker to
adopt new ideas, seek more information about opportunities,
are more restless and prone to migration. They are also more
likely to cheat.

> This is why entrepreneurial groups high in *n* Achievement
> tend to acquire the reputation of being dishonest or tricky;

it appears that they are so fixated on finding a short cut to the goal that they may not be too particular about the means they use to reach it.

McClelland, 1985, p. 250

ACHIEVEMENT MOTIVATION IN ENTREPRENEURS

McClelland has demonstrated a linkage between collective levels of achievement motivation and economic development in many different cultures and countries, including an historic look at the achievements of Greece and Rome (McClelland, 1961).

It turned out that the achievement motive has been a major factor in the economic rise and fall of ancient and modern civilizations. In fact, since efficient business activity is a key element in the economic success of individuals and nations, it is not stretching the evidence too far to suggest that the achievement motive has a lot to do with wealth and poverty or the standards of living people enjoy.

McClelland, 1985, p. 595

Other studies link achievement motivation to entrepreneurs as individuals. Some have studied entrepreneurs to see how they score on achievement measures. Results vary because the measurement tools differ and the definitions of entrepreneurs differ. For example, McClelland (1965) studied different types of jobs. He found that more of those who were "business entrepreneurs" (e.g., employees in "sales, real estate, fund raising, founder, management consultant, etc.," p. 391) scored higher in achievement motivation than "business nonentrepreneurs" (e.g., employees in credit, traffic, and personnel) and professionals. Another early study compared managers of shop operations (considered "entrepreneurial") to staff specialists. Managers scored significantly higher than staff in ranking by superiors in terms of achievement motivation. These results are confirmed in other studies comparing founders and nonfounder managers in small businesses (Begley & Boyd, 1986) and high-technology entrepreneurs (Komives, 1972).

Other studies link important organizational outcomes such as profits and growth to the achievement motivation of entrepreneurs. One such study used McClelland's Thematic Apperception Test and found that those with a high need for achievement led companies with the highest rate of growth

(Wainer & Rubin, 1969). Another study by Kock (1965, reported in McClelland & Winter, 1971) found that achievement-motivation scores of owner-managers predicted the growth of the organization (in terms of number of employees, gross value of output, gross investments, and turnover) at a later time. In this study, achievement motivation of leaders did not predict organizational profitability. McClelland & Winter (1971) explain this in two ways: (1) profit is a derived measure and not a direct and timely piece of feedback on performance; and (2),

> It can be argued that a too narrow concern with profits and returns may interfere with expansion and growth. In a certain sense *n* Ach leads to irrational concern with expansion, sometimes at the cost of self-interest (p. 14).

Another set of studies looks at the impact of achievement-motivation training. Results of these studies suggest that the training does increase the number of business activities of individuals (McClelland, 1965; Miron & McClelland, 1979; Timmons, 1971).

> The improvement seems to be due to a shift from the fear of failure to the hope of success aspect of achievement motivation, and also to strengthening the other determinants of an action outcome—namely, the perceived probability of success and the value placed on business improvement.
>
> McClelland, 1985, p. 606

Implications

These studies show entrepreneurs to be highly achievement motivated, perhaps even archetypal achievers. Starting a venture involves work where personal skills make a difference, tasks are challenging and moderately risky, and feedback on performance is timely. The studies also show that the entrepreneur's achievement motivation relates to important organizational outcomes such as *growth and culture* (Litwin & Stringer, 1968). However, *achievement motivation is also high among managers, and not all high scorers are achievers in the business sector.* Thus, while achievement motivation tells us about what drives entrepreneurs, it says little about who will become one, what type of career or venture they will create for themselves, or how profitable their ventures will be.

We suspect that achievement motivation helps the entrepreneur sustain temporal tension, because he or she feels responsible for achieving a moderately risky outcome that has short-term benchmarks. We suspect that higher achievement motivation will be found in entrepreneurs who take "the plunge," whereas those who "wade" into business ventures have lower achievement motivation due to higher fear of failure or fear of success.

Achievement motivation, if accurately assessed along each of the defining dimensions, can be used to predict entrepreneurial proclivity and venture success. Of course, other variables moderate this aspect of personality. These are discussed below and in the following chapters.

NEED FOR CONTROL

The expectancy of being able to make something happen is a defining behavioral competency of entrepreneurs. Research suggests that entrepreneurs have unflagging optimism and a "can-do" attitude. Some call this trait self-confidence (Timmons, 1978); others see it as veridical perception (honest self-appraisal, Schrage, 1965), as perceptions of venture feasibility (Shapero, 1982b), and as personal efficacy (McClelland & Winter, 1969). Beyond the objective "facts" of the entrepreneurial situation and event, the entrepreneur's perceptions play a leading role, because perceptions precede and inform decisions and actions. The expectancy of being able to make something specific and intended *happen* is important to creativity, strategic implementation, and developing the confidence of others who have a stake in the enterprise (e.g., partners, investors, customers).

The "can-do" belief is related to other beliefs—namely beliefs about control. One of the earliest theories of personal control beliefs was done by Rotter (1966), who defined internal and external control.

> When a reinforcement is perceived by the subject as following some action of his own but not being entirely contingent upon his action, then in our culture, it is typically perceived as the result of luck, chance, fate, as under the control of powerful others, or as unpredictable because of the great complexity of the forces surrounding him. When the event is interpreted in this way by an individual, we have labeled this a belief in *external control*. If the person perceives that the event is contingent upon his own behavior or his own relatively permanent characteristics, we have termed this a belief in *internal control* (p. 1).

Rotter (1966) hypothesized and others (McGhee & Crandall, 1968; Gurin, Gurin, Lao, & Beattie; 1969) substantiated that those with internal control beliefs have a greater need for achievement, which has been determined to be an important motivation for entrepreneurs. Indeed, entrepreneurs tend to score higher on measures of internal control than the average person (Shapero, 1975), and higher than nonfounders in small businesses (Begley & Boyd, 1986). Brockhaus (1980a, cited in Brockhaus, 1982) found that owners of businesses that survived over a three-year period held more internal control beliefs than those whose businesses had ended.

Control beliefs are energized by a *need for control* over important life and business situations. Taking personal responsibility for venture outcomes results in greater activity and creativity. Founders and managers who believe that they exert some control over outcomes tend to be more active and persistent (Durand & Shea, 1974). While executives, in general, tend to believe in their own (internal) control, those with greater internal beliefs were more innovative and probably more entrepreneurial (Miller, Kets de Vries, & Toulouse, 1982).

However, not all studies report positive findings. For example, Brockhaus and Nord (1979) found that entrepreneurs did not hold more or stronger beliefs about their ability to control events than managers who had changed organizations or been promoted. Brockhaus (1982) concludes:

> An internal locus-of-control belief may . . . be associated with a more active effort to affect the outcome of events. This internal belief and the associated greater effort would seem to hold true for both successful entrepreneurs and successful managers. Therefore, *it fails to uniquely distinguish entrepreneurs, but holds promise for distinguishing successful entrepreneurs from the unsuccessful* (p. 45; emphasis added).

Our personal control is, however, limited, and other dimensions of control need to be considered. Our common-sense experience suggests that both self-control and outer control are possible and important in determining outcomes. Accordingly, an alternative scale was devised by Levenson (1974) in which three dimensions of control were independently measured (using six-point Likert scales instead of the forced-choice format of Rotter's scale). The three dimensions are (1) internal control, (2) powerful-others control, and (3) chance control. This is the scale shown in Appendix B.

Using this scale Borland (1975) found that among students internal control beliefs predict entrepreneurial intentions (expectations of and desire for starting a company within three years of leaving school) better than achievement motivation. In another recent study of entrepreneurial predispositions, Sexton and Bowman (1984) found that entrepreneurship majors and business majors (whose scores were very similar) score higher on the internal control scale than nonbusiness majors.

IMPORTANCE OF CHANCE AND POWERFUL OTHERS

A variety of other hypotheses remain to be tested. For example, do entrepreneurs who successfully use networking to start and build their organizations score higher on both internal control and powerful-others control than other entrepreneurs and those unsuccessful in networking? Under what conditions could a successful entrepreneur believe both in his or her own control and in chance, luck, and serendipity?

Politics and powerful others enter as important keys to success when we recognize that no enterprise is a one-person show. There are important and powerful outsiders, such as venture capitalists, bankers, stockholders, politicians, lobbyists, judges, and competition, who exert considerable influence over entrepreneurial events. There are also powerful insiders—partners and key employees. For now it is worth noting that while entrepreneurs *need to feel in control of their enterprise,* they also *need to develop interpersonal skills including the perception of when another is objectively and legitimately exercising control* (e.g., partners have the right to make decisions that commit organizational resources, and investors share the rights, privileges, and responsibilities of ownership). Another key interpersonal skill needed to grow an organization is the *ability to accept and extend influence* (e.g., share control) so that all key parties are moving together in the same direction (e.g., toward higher quality or greater market share).

Opportunism, luck, chance, and serendipity are also important to entrepreneurship. These are discussed in greater detail in Chapter 11.

> Chance—or luck, as the superstitious call it—has a hand in every undertaking, and in none is its role a subject of greater curiosity than in that of the business entrepreneur, whose progress offers a succession of hostages to fortune.
>
> Miller, 1963, p. 153

Implications

Entrepreneurs tend to have a high need to control their destinies. Despite some evidence to the contrary, entrepreneurs tend to have a higher need for control than managers. It is this need to control one's worklife and economic destiny that leads many into entrepreneurial careers. We expect a higher need for control from the sole proprietor and among those who start new ventures than among those who acquire a going concern or franchise, because independent start-ups require more decisions and activities to be controlled and have fewer people to take that control. We would expect individuals with somewhat less need for control to begin with partners (who must share control) or to buy a going concern (where controls have already been distributed within the organization).

We expect that control is related to the behavioral tendency to keep hands-on involvement with operational details. This hands-on orientation provides a sense of control and opportunities to make quick adjustments (e.g., "fast dancing"). However, the same need for control that helps initiate a new venture might interfere with the venture's subsequent growth and development. Those who need to control have difficulty letting go of control and delegating work and decisions to others, and such delegation is necessary as the organization grows.

RISK ACCEPTANCE

Entrepreneurs tend to be risk accepters and are often perceived by others who are more risk averse as being risk oriented or risk seeking. However, research suggests that entrepreneurs make calculated risk assessments, based on information not available to or not appreciated by others.

Risk enters into entrepreneurship because many resources and opportunities are uncertain when a commitment of money and time is made. The entrepreneur risks not being able to assess opportunities, to garner appropriate resources, and to use these effectively. While the financial and insurance communities have tried and succeeded to some extent to find "objective" measures of certain business risks, the psychology of risk is equally if not more important to entrepreneurial behavior. For our purposes in this book, risk involves a psychological assessment of the probabilities of success or failure for any given action or action plan.

A MODEL OF RISK BEHAVIOR

"Risky situations . . . involve two or more alternatives where at least one alternative exposes a person to a chance of loss" (MacCrimmon & Wehrung, 1986, pp. 20–21). Theoretically, risk has three components: the magnitude of potential loss (i.e., the size or value of the loss); the chances of potential loss; and the exposure to potential loss (i.e., one's vulnerability). Furthermore, risk has three determinants or sources:

1. lack of control due to natural forces, other people, and insufficient resources, information, and time;
2. lack of information, where information is incomplete, unreliable, unfamiliar, or unpredictable;
3. lack of time, when one must decide before sufficient information or control is at hand (MacCrimmon & Wehrung, 1986).

What's at risk? Entrepreneurs face uncertainty and possible loss in five areas: (1) financial, (2) social and familial, (3) emotional and physical (health and well-being), (4) career or future employability, and (5) organizational (whether or not their organization will grow and prosper). Financial risks include "putting it all on the line," investing one's savings and pensions, mortgaging one's house and the future education of children, and down-scaling the family's lifestyle. Many entrepreneurs also risk other people's money, and in the early stages this means the savings of family members and friends. For many observers, financial risk taking is the core competency of entrepreneurs.

Social and familial risks follow. A new venture often requires 60 or more hours of work a week, and many times as much as 100 hours. In essence, the new venture takes time away from traditional lifestyle activities (entertainment, political involvement, family activities) and from the maintenance and development of personal relationships. Family and friends can feel neglected or deserted. If, in addition, family and friends have significant financial investment in the venture, relationships can be stretched beyond tolerance. Important emotional and social support can erode, leaving the entrepreneur increasingly alone, lonely, and stressed (weary, vulnerable to disease and accident). (There will be more on the lifestyle of entrepreneurs in Chapter 7.)

Career risks come in the form of missed opportunities for career advancement in more traditional work roles. The entrepreneur foregoes the corporate ladder (another way of measuring one's achievement) and the relative security of corporate life for the venture. In doing so, the entrepreneur engages in experiences and develops a resume that may have little market value should he or she decide to return to the ranks of the employed.

The organizational risks involve making decisions about who to hire, how to organize, how to maintain quality and stay flexible as the organization grows, and how to protect one's assets without losing the innovative edge. Early decisions by entrepreneurial leaders have lasting impact on the organization's future. In addition to personal and organizational risks, entrepreneurial ventures face uncertain, even chaotic, environments including technological change (how can we best use new technologies available to us and our competitors?), market uncertainties (what changes in competition are likely? how are customers changing?), and changes in government regulations.

These uncertainties seem magnified by the quick decisions and actions typical of the entrepreneur (and part of his or her strategic advantage). However, risk taking, at least in the form of making quick decisions without complete information, is often the rational choice.

> The increasing uncertainty of the nation and world economies pushes us in the direction of accepting risk as a given and developing shorter time frames for decision making in response.
>
> Stevenson, 1985, p. 40

Risk across all of these dimensions can be understood as a result of the entrepreneur's orientations toward risk. His or her risk behaviors include his or her choices and methods of managing the risks he or she faces. Figure 4.1 presents a model of risk behavior. The chief determinants of perceptions of risk, of attitudes toward risk, and ultimately of risk management are the individual's personality and background and his or her social context.

Personality and background. Personality characteristics that predispose people to positive orientations toward risk include "risk taking propensity," (a generalized tendency to choose more risky alternatives), optimism, tolerance of ambiguity, high need to achieve, fearlessness (especially low fear of failure), impulsiveness, a decisive cognitive style, beliefs about

FIGURE 4.1   Model of Risk Behavior

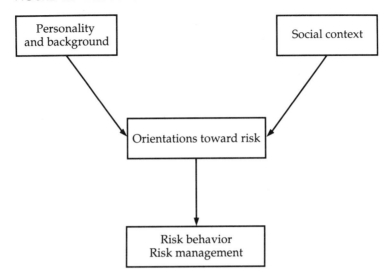

one's personal control, and personal values (e.g., for an exciting life). Background factors that predispose people to a positive orientation toward risk include a personal history in which risk taking was rewarded (e.g., a family member succeeded in a risky venture or early career risks were rewarded), being younger—since people tend to become more risk-averse as they age, and having family conditions that support or at least do not detract from risk taking (people with working spouses might be willing to risk their own career, whereas those with dependent children tend to be more risk-averse than others without dependents).

Social context.   The entrepreneur who assumes the risk inherent in the opportunities he or she faces is likely to be surrounded by a supportive social system (family and friends who encourage rather than discourage his or her efforts). This entrepreneur is also likely to have a network of instrumental relationships that provides access to key resources (see Chapter 9 on external teams). The business location can decrease the risks involved (i.e., locating the business in one's hometown adds to the probability of the venture succeeding, since the entrepreneur will know key customers and suppliers). Locating the venture in a business incubator with lower rents, shared services, and management assistance can lower financial, social, emotional, and organization risks.

Risk orientations. Entrepreneurs generally do not see themselves as taking excessive risks. Ultimately, the perception of risk is subjective and not derived from actuarial tables or from calculators. The subjective nature of risk explains the very real differences between entrepreneurs and managers in the assessment of new venture risks.

It is important to keep in mind that for the entrepreneur, the acceptance of new venture risks may be an avoidance of other risks (e.g., the risk of failure in the corporate climb). Keyes (1985) points out that because we are especially aware of the risks we avoid, it is easy to assume that others are taking bigger risks, especially if these are the risks we avoid. When we dub someone a risk taker, we are actually applying our fears to their actions. So for risk-averse managers, bankers, and investors, new ventures are extremely risky, and for the entrepreneur, working for a corporation with subsequent loss of independence and autonomy as an employee is likewise risky.

However, there is some suggestion that the entrepreneur's perceptions of new venture risk are less accurate than outside views (Shapero, 1975). Other research suggests that entrepreneurs put on "blinders" to factors they cannot control and that these blinders contribute to persistence and determination and sometimes to venture failure (Aspaklaria, 1986a).

The entrepreneur's orientation toward risk, as well as his or her attitudes, perceptions, and preferences about risk, security, certainty, ambiguity, and opportunity determine his or her behavior. Risk preferences range from risk seeking to risk avoidance. Despite the swashbuckling image of entrepreneurs, most are not risk seekers (some are, and can be quickly identified by their preferences for leisure-time activities such as hang gliding, rock climbing, gambling, etc.) Nor are entrepreneurs risk averse. Most entrepreneurs are *risk accepters*, seeing situations differently than nonentrepreneurs and accepting and managing the risk inherent in a given opportunity.

Risk management. Risk management involves at least five dimensions suggested by economist Frank Knight (1921): (1) the ability to form correct judgments about the future course of events and, especially, to read human nature; (2) the ability to judge means and plan adjustments called for in the future; (3) the ability to execute plans; (4) the confidence in one's judgments and execution; and (5) a willingness to fit luck with one's purpose.

Furthermore, behavior in risky situations varies along a continuum from passive acceptance to active adjustment. More passive risk management means choosing from existing alternatives without attempting to change them. In contrast, active risk managers (entrepreneurs) attempt to structure the risky situation by gaining time, information, and control (MacCrimmon & Wehrung, 1986).

Entrepreneurs actively manage the risk of their ventures by assuming control, being hands-on and involved in the nitty-gritty of the business. They gain control by gaining access to information, often feeling as if they had hedged their bets. They reduce their exposure to financial loss by including investors, but often with the risk of losing control. Finally, they gain time (and often reduce risk from competition) by shortening the time span between having ideas and taking products and services to the market. However, quickness may also have its liabilities—information and incubation of ideas may be inadequate and timing may be off.

Implications

We would expect some types of entrepreneurs to take more risks, bigger risks, or more frequent risks than others. Those whose money goal is income substitution are more likely to become more risk-averse when an acceptable income is achieved. Those who use profits as a way of keeping score will continue to make calculated risks. Likewise, we would expect the fast starters who "plunge" (with full commitment and personal investment) to accept more risk than slow starters who wade in (e.g., part-time while moonlighting).

RESEARCH ON ENTREPRENEURIAL RISK TAKING

Risk and achievement motivation. McClelland (1961) suggests that moderate risks bring out the most achievement motivation in people. Tasks where the chance of success is very certain (very easy tasks) or very uncertain (very difficult tasks) do not arouse expectations that skill is a great determiner of outcomes, and those who need to feel personal responsibility and control are not highly motivated. Of course ventures are never very easy or very certain, but for many nonentrepreneurs they can appear very risky.

Just what constitutes moderate risk? Atkinson (1957), following McClelland, proposed that a subjective probability of success of 50 percent is moderate and would generate most achievement motivation. In practice, chances are rarely specified and probably vary from 40 to 60 percent in the moderate range. Interestingly, timeframes can be used to adjust risk. That is, a task with a short timeframe for completion is more difficult and the risk of completion greater than the same task with a longer timeframe.

Even though we might have high achievement motivation, we might still avoid moderate risks if our fear of failure is greater than our need to achieve (Atkinson, 1957). If our fears are great we will tend to prefer very risky or very certain situations where we know what the outcomes will be and can avoid taking personal responsibility for them.

Risk preferences. One of the ways of assessing risk taking in entrepreneurs is to look at individual differences in the willingness to take a risk. Brockhaus (1980a) defines this as

> . . . the perceived probability of receiving the rewards associated with success of a proposed situation which is required by an individual before he will subject himself to the consequences associated with failure, the alternative situation providing less reward as well as less severe consequences than the proposed situation (p. 513).

Although there is considerable debate about whether one's risk-taking propensity generalizes across situations (e.g., work, personal health, family) (MacCrimmon & Wehrung, 1986), several methods of measuring this characteristic have been introduced. One of the widely used instruments is the Choice Dilemmas Questionnaire (CDQ, Kogan & Wallach, 1964). The questionnaire poses hypothetical situations and asks the respondent to indicate the chances he or she needs (out of ten) that the risky choice will prove successful in order to make the risky choice. This instrument has been severely criticized for its psychometric properties (individual items tend to measure different types of risk rather than a unitary predisposition) (Cartwright, 1971).

Using this instrument, Brockhaus (1980a) compared new start-up entrepreneurs with managers and found no significant differences in risk preferences between the groups and no difference from the general population. In another report, Brockhaus (1982) compared the risk-taking propensity of entrepreneurs who failed three years later to that of entrepreneurs who were still in business. Again, no significant differences were found. Apparently, generalized risk taking does not distinguish entrepreneurs from managers, from the general population, or successes from failures.

However, these results may be due to the CDQ instrument. It may not measure the appropriate dimensions or qualities of risk taking. Entrepreneurs deal with very real, personally relevant and emotionally charged business and financial events, not hypothetical situations in a variety of contexts. Sexton and Bowman (1984) used the CDQ, the Jackson Personality Inventory (JPI, risk taking scale), the Personality Research Form–E (PRF–E, harm avoidance scale) and the Tolerance–Intolerance of Ambiguity scale (AT). They found that entrepreneurship majors were no different from other students (general business majors and nonbusiness majors) using the CDQ but were more risk-taking than other students when using the JPI. Harm avoidance was significantly lower for entrepreneurship majors than other students, and tolerance for ambiguity was greater than for nonbusiness majors. These results are supported by other studies using the JPI (Begely & Boyd, 1986) and other measures of risk propensity (Hull, Bosley, & Udell, 1980).

These findings suggest that risk taking may indeed separate entrepreneurs from others. However, recall that most entrepreneurs do not seek risk. Instead most successful entrepreneurs *accept* the risk inherent in the opportunities they seize. A recent survey of *Venture* magazine readers showed that only 29 percent liked "the thrill of going for it all," whereas 72 percent liked taking some risks or calculated risks (Are you a risk taker?, 1986). Most entrepreneurs who take risks also act to manage and minimize the risk, as described earlier.

Tolerance of ambiguity. Another way to look at risk involves assessing how individuals tolerate ambiguous situations without a structure, a procedure, or even guideposts. Timmons (1976) reviewed the literature and the views of venture capitalists and concluded that entrepreneurs tend to have great tolerance for ambiguity. Research has found entrepreneurs more tolerant of ambiguity and more comfortable with complexity and novelty than managers (Begley & Boyd, 1986) and "budding entrepreneurs" (Schere, 1982). Another study of prospective entrepreneurs showed they were more tolerant of ambiguity than those with other career intentions (Sexton & Bowman, 1984).

Clearly the new venture process is one where very little can be predicted ahead of time. The environment of the venture is uncertain at best, and is often changing rapidly, as competition increases and technology advances. To enter into a new venture, notwithstanding the preparation involved in developing a business plan, requires considerable tolerance of ambiguity and flexibility.

Changing risk perceptions. Perceptions of risk change over time, and Liles (1974) proposes that risk becomes important to entrepreneurial intentions only when the new venture becomes a serious career alternative. Work with potential entrepreneurs in an evening MBA program shows that most feel their risk aversion is the greatest obstacle to behaving in an entrepreneurial way. There seems to be an approach-avoidance gradient; the closer one comes to "taking the plunge"—the colder the water looks and the more seriously one considers the entrepreneurial career from the vantage point of a secure and well-paying job, the riskier the entrepreneurial path appears.

The risk involved in a specific venture seems to be a function of the individual's age, the financial condition of the family, opportunity, and resource availability. As we grow older, take on dependents, and achieve in our existing careers, we become more conservative, less open to the risks of venturing, *unless a displacement upsets our inertia.*

Once the venture is launched, the real areas of uncertainty include the *length of time that the entrepreneur will remain committed* (Stevenson, 1985; based on his understanding that entrepreneurs who succeed quickly move in and out of opportunities) and the *adequacy of resources* (e.g., capital and technical expertise).

> There is a constant tension between the adequacy of commitment and the potential for return. . . . Many entrepreneurs, when looking back on their careers, say that the high point came when they placed their last chip on the table, still knowing it may not be enough (p. 43).

I would suggest that there is another important area of risk: *knowing when and whom to trust.* Rotter (1980) defines interpersonal trust as the "generalized expectancy held by an individual that the word, promise, oral or written statement of another individual or group can be relied on" (p. 1). He reviews psychological studies and concludes that people who trust others are more trustworthy (important to financial partners), more respectful of others (important to internal teams), and more satisfied and liked by others. Other studies reviewed by Rotter suggest that predisposition to trust goes along with discrimination about whom to trust.

Implications

Entrepreneurs are risk accepters, preferring and being energized by moderate risk situations and actively managing the risks inherent in the opportunities they pursue. They manage these risks by psychological processes, such as conceiving of timeframes that produce a moderate level of difficulty, and by talking about their venture in terms of opportunities or challenges instead of risks and problems. See the Case of SB at the end of this chapter for an example of an entrepreneur who carefully manages language. Entrepreneurs also use social processes to manage risk. They network, draw on many different resources, and involve others in the venture.

Although research on risk taking has been confounded by measurement problems, evidence suggests that entrepreneurs are less risk-averse than their managerial cousins. However, because risk is subjectively perceived and evaluated, we must be careful when attributing risk taking to ourselves and to others. It seems that we see our own choices as relatively safe, and see those of others who do what we avoid as relatively risky. The truth of the entrepreneur's risk lies somewhere between.

More important to the success of a new venture than generalized risk preference is the entrepreneur's tolerance of ambiguity. Is he or she comfortable with uncertainty or even energized by not knowing how, when, or where a solution to a critical concern will come? Equally important is the entrepreneur's commitment and access to resources. How resources are portrayed and communicated is very important to the risk-reward perceptions and decisions of investors, employees, and customers. Finally, trust is a fundamental building block for risk assessment and management.

Those who invest in entrepreneurs financially or in terms of time and expertise (as *pro bono* consultants or employees) need to assess the risks of the venture. Bear in mind that the true risk is probably smaller than that seen by a banker and greater than that seen by the entrepreneur. Assessment might usefully tap into tolerance of ambiguity, commitment time horizons, resource networks, and the proclivity to trust and trustworthiness.

VALUES

Expanding on the model of entrepreneurial behavior introduced in Chapter 3, we conceive of entrepreneurial action as the outcome of three psychological states—expectations that one "can do" (one's abilities), expectations that an outcome will follow action (a sense of control over outcomes and resulting sense of achievement, moderated by risk), and the value of that outcome.

A recent theory of values distinguishes terminal values (preferred end states of existence, such as inner harmony or a sense of accomplishment) from instrumental values (preferred ways of conduct, such as honest or ambitious) (Rokeach, 1973). Although there is little research on entrepreneurial values, the distinction between valued ends and valued means is important for understanding entrepreneurs.

Frequently we cannot control both ends and means and some trade-off is involved. To try to control both results (ends) and how we get results (means) may box us in—put blinders on our ability to see opportunity, limit our behavior, and frustrate us. To the extent that one selects ends (a profitable business), he or she must be relatively opportunistic about means. To the extent that one values means (a life without stress, an adventurous life), he or she must be willing to end up anywhere. Of course, most often we select both means and ends, allowing ends to constrain means and means to constrain ends.

Rokeach (1973) also suggests that both sets of values are best understood as a hierarchical system where some values are more important than other values. Other than the study by Fagenson (1986), who looked at value differences between male and female entrepreneurs using a modified Rokeach Value Survey, there is no empirical research on the value system (ranking and interrelation of values) of entrepreneurs.

However, we can infer something about entrepreneurial values from other studies. Instrumental values that are frequently associated with entrepreneurs include a value for excitement (Bird, 1983), independence and freedom of action, and creativity (Kao, 1985). Terminal values of entrepreneurship include traditional rewards such as wealth and financial security, fame, and "new-age" outcomes such as community, transcendence, charity, and social justice (Kao, 1985). Each of these sets of values will be discussed in turn.

ENTREPRENEURSHIP: A VALUED LIFESTYLE

Entrepreneurship is valued as a way of life and a means to make a living. Just living the life of an entrepreneur is important to some entrepreneurs. The most frequently cited reason for undertaking this career is the desire to be independent—to be one's own boss and have the self-satisfaction of being solely or primarily responsible for outcomes. Prospective entrepreneurs (entrepreneurship majors in college) tend to be more autonomous than other students, including regular business majors (Sexton & Bowman, 1984). However, results must be interpreted carefully with regard to the scales used; in another study entrepreneurs were no different from the general population in their value for autonomy, but were less in need of social support with more desire for independence than the general population (Hornaday & Aboud, 1971).

Other operational or life-style values of entrepreneurs include the nature of the work and "fun" (Duffy & Stevenson, 1984), preferences for leadership, benevolence, order, and aesthetics. In a study of high-technology entrepreneurs, Komives (1972) found that they had higher values for aesthetics and theory than for religion and economics. These entrepreneurs also tended to score high on interpersonal values of independence, benevolence, and leadership and high on personal values of achievement, decisiveness, practical mindedness, variety, and goal orientation.

Some entrepreneurs use their position in their organization to implement personally important operating values. Some implement professional values (Richman, 1985); others implement social values. Some implement a desire to work in an orderly and disciplined way, as did Don Oberg.

THE EXAMPLE OF DON OBERG

Word has it that the company president will fire you if he finds fingerprints on your machinery. Once, the story goes, he saw a stray match on his spotless shop floor and, like Sherlock Holmes, relentlessly followed every clue until he found the matchbook it had come from. Pennsylvania's Allegheny-Kiski Valley is dotted with tool-and-die shops started by employees who just plain got fed up with the "prison camp" atmosphere and who left to start their own companies. In the midst of union country, it is the largest nonunion company in Western Pennsylvania.

Still, every year applicants show up by the hundreds, hoping for a chance to work at Oberg Industries Inc. Last year, 1,600 applied; 30 were hired. And those 30 had a taste of what was to come not only by the rumors, but by the very selection process.

"We had to draw circles with both hands," recalls Keith Schultz. "And you had two circles, one inside the other, and you had to draw a line in between them without touching both lines—at seven o'clock in the morning!" Schultz is describing the beginning of a long, stressful day of psychological testing at Oberg's Freeport, Pa., headquarters, a day patterned after Oberg's own workday: Start at seven a.m., quit at five, 15 minutes for lunch. No chitchat. Twenty years ago, there was even a dress code—no T-shirts, no blue jeans, no beards or mustaches, no long hair. Veteran journeymen say the company is less strict today, but the legend of Don Oberg the authoritarian lives on.

Oberg, the 69-year-old president and founder of Oberg Industries, believes passionately that precision products require a disciplined work environment. And that the ideal tool-and-die worker is one with unflagging patience for meticulous, often monotonous, detail who, at the same time, is creative enough to be always on the lookout for better, more efficient ways of getting the job done. A special breed.

When he started his company in 1948, Oberg was among the first in the tool-and-die industry to see the potential of tungsten-carbide, a material more costly than steel, but one that lasts 15 times as long. Thirty-seven years later, Oberg Industries still makes tungsten-carbide dies. But in an industry immediately hit by any downturns in manufacturing and one that is increasingly vulnerable to foreign competition and overseas manufacturing, Oberg Industries has diversified both its products and its markets. A typical tool-and-die company has about $2 million in annual sales; last year, Oberg racked up $27 million. On the average, employees in tool-and-die shops number 30; Oberg has 320 workers in its main plant and four wholly owned subsidiaries. The company also shines in sales per employee: $84,000 in 1984 compared with the industry average of $67,000.

While Oberg, along with the rest of the tool-and-die industry, is wary of Japanese competition, the company manages to compete successfully with the Japanese in the Hong Kong market. "The Japanese know that quality is the way you solve problems. When you strive for quality, all the other things fall in line. Oberg instinctively understood this from the beginning and made it his practice," says Myron Tribus, director of the Center for Advanced Engineering Study, at Massachusetts Institute of Technology. The company gets away with charging premium prices,

5% to 10% above the industry average. But to people looking for quality, the price is right because the product is right.

The Oberg philosophy is apparent to visitors even before they enter the main plant. To the left of the entrance is an iron bucket filled with sand—a subtle suggestion to douse cigarettes and a reminder to all of Oberg's personal anti-smoking crusade. Before entering the main plant, a sign requests: "Please clean your feet, dirt is our biggest enemy."

That is just the beginning. Inside, Don Oberg's strategically placed small green signs are ubiquitous—"If it's almost right, it's wrong," "We should strive for progressive improvement rather than postponed perfection," "Let's do the job right the first time," and the one closest to his heart, "The biggest room in our company is the room for improvement." The signs are everywhere—in the offices of managers, on secretaries' desks, in the waiting room, on the plant walls. Never missing an opportunity to convert a visitor, Oberg has extras stored in a cabinet in his office.

Bad housekeeping is one of Oberg's chief pet peeves, and he makes sure his employees know it. All new hires spend one to two months on the skeleton maintenance staff, a stint that not only gives them a lesson in cleanliness, but also familiarizes them with the entire plant before they are assigned to specific sections. Every day at 4:55, the machines stop, and the housekeeping starts—each person is responsible for cleaning his or her own work area.

What seems like an obsession with cleanliness to an outsider is just plain smart in the precision tool-and-die business. Oberg makes parts that are cut and ground to tolerances of up to .00005 of an inch—1/150 the width of a human hair—and a speck of dirt can create havoc by skewing a measurement. It makes good marketing sense, too: "Our plant is our biggest selling point," says vice-president of marketing and sales Phil Dolan. When the company flies customers in to see the plant, "they assume that because it's so meticulously clean, attention to detail of the product must be the same."

In the tool-and-die business, it can take 2,000 to 3,000 hours to build just one precision die. Oberg's 76 surface grinders, among the most skilled employees in the plant, work in small, glass-enclosed, fully equipped, carpeted rooms, complete with piped-in music. Oberg was one of the first in the industry to build such rooms, at a cost of $40,000 each. They cut down noise, increase productivity, and have the added benefit of inhibiting conversation among employees. With 15 minutes for lunch in the course of their 10-hour workday (plus 5 hours on Saturday), there is little time for socializing anyway.

From the time they are hired, Oberg employees are given the subtle message that they are, indeed, the best. Only a fraction of those who apply for the apprentice program in the course of a year have good enough high school math and science grades to be called in for the day of testing. Of those who take the test, only 10% are hired. The rigorous selection process gives employees a feeling of camaraderie, and they often speak of it with the fervor of someone who has just completed an Outward Bound weekend. But they are definitely among the survivors. "The first question your friends ask when you're hired here is, 'Who did you know?' " says Dan Felack, who applied to the Oberg apprenticeship program after he was laid off by a local steel mill. But the question is irrelevant. "That's one thing about this company that I really like," Greg Chambers adds. "It doesn't help to have any pull, it really doesn't." Don Oberg would be pleased to hear that. When asked how he thought employees view him, he answered, "That I'm tough, stubborn. I hope more than anything else that they realize I'm fair. I lean over backward to be fair." Chambers, a college graduate, recalls that many prospective employers refused to hire him, because he was overqualified. "Oberg didn't take that into consideration," he says. "They don't care what your background is—they're really taking you from scratch. They accept you as you walk through that door, and they're going to mold and make you into what they want you to be."

The molding begins with the four-year apprentice training, standard in the industry. Oberg's program has "a certain eliteness" about it, according to Bill Di Pietro, of the Pittsburgh-area office of the Labor Department's Bureau of Apprenticeship & Training. The classroom portion, about 10% of the overall training, is taught by Oberg's engineering department. "Most companies," Di Pietro says, "send their apprentices to vocational-technical schools or to community colleges; the fact that Oberg does in-house training is rather unique."

Oberg Industries is a meritocracy from day one. Everyone's work, from the new hires to the veterans, is evaluated every six months by a supervisor, but the spirit isn't punitive. "I feel I'm learning, I'm being watched," says apprentice Felack. "Not like Big Brother looking over my shoulder—it's a helpful type of watch." Most apprentices receive merit pay increases every six months until they earn their journeyman papers. Journeymen, whose pay averages $36,000 to $42,000, also get raises on a merit basis—their seniority gives them no added clout even when it comes to layoffs, infrequent though they may be.

In a county where unemployment is 10.3%—nearly 3% higher than the national average—Oberg stands out. In a cyclical industry, Oberg not only keeps its people working, it has kept them working overtime during most years. "Since I've been here," says journeyman John Arthur, "I've only had a few months in 20 years when I didn't work 50 hours a week."

When times are hard, many tool-and-die companies drop their apprenticeship programs, a practice Oberg Industries finds shortsighted. In recessionary 1982 and '83, especially tough years, Oberg hired eight new apprentices. "We continued to hire, to train people," explains David Shondeck, 41, executive vice-president. "We knew we were going to come out of the recession, and we wanted to be in a position to take advantage of that." Still, the company had to cut back somewhere. "We asked for voluntary layoffs among the journeymen," says Shondeck. The company assured its employees, nonunion as is 95% of the industry, that all the volunteers would eventually be recalled. Over a five-month period, more than 20 journeymen stood in unemployment lines, confident that the company would keep its word. It did. As apprentice Chambers says, "You can afford to put your trust in a company if you know everyone is giving 100%."

Everyone knows the man at the top is giving 100%—and then some. Apprentices boast that Don Oberg's car is in the parking lot when they arrive in the morning and after they leave at night. By his own reckoning, Oberg has visited thousands of companies all over the world to see what ideas he can bring back to Freeport. His endless quest for better ways of doing things is how he discovered psychological testing so early in the game. Within six months of founding his company, Oberg had to fire one of his cousins, a painful family affair, and decided then and there to find a way to avoid hiring the wrong people in the first place.

What Don Oberg has been most caught up in, however, are new technologies, direct ways to improve production at his company. He thrives on change. In 1975, he says, Oberg Industries was the first tool-and-die maker to bring in a computer-aided design and manufacturing system, now a $4-million investment. Oberg is certain that the system has improved productivity, but ask him for hard numbers and he will stare incredulously, as if you have missed the point entirely—to him, it represents the best in new technology, and if it is new and the best, then there is no question that his company will benefit.

Over the past few years, changes of all sorts have occurred at Oberg Industries at an even faster clip than usual. In 1979, Oberg hired back as assistant plant manager Dave Shondeck, a mechanical engineer who, a few years earlier, had left the company, deciding there was not enough room at the top. This time around, Oberg assured him, he could go as high as he wanted, except for the presidency, which was reserved for his son Rick.

The company was on a roll at the time, Shondeck recalls, faced with a "myriad of opportunities." To make any decisions at all, some long-range plans had to be made. As usual, it so happened that Don Oberg had talked to someone who had had a good experience at the American Management Associations' Center for Planning & Implementation, in Hamilton, N.Y. So, in 1980, Shondeck, Oberg, and members of the board signed up. Over the next six months, they developed a plan to diversify products and markets and to create a new management team.

"Take any one aspect of Oberg Industries today," says Phil Dolan, vice-president of marketing and sales, "and you can't accurately call it unique; what's unique is that Oberg is now a multimarket, multiproduct company." The company's diversification plans are on schedule, and today, it manufactures products as diverse as dies for flip-top cans and lead frames to parts for nuclear-reactor fuel cells. Oberg's customers include Gillette, IBM, Eastman Kodak, and the U.S. government.

His company may have changed, but Don Oberg has remained pretty much the same. In his office, he surrounds himself with memorabilia of the old West, including a collection of flintlocks and at least five powder horns. "I'm an old cowboy at heart," he confesses, and whether it is his uncanny resemblance to Ronald Reagan or the restless way he sits, you see it immediately—Don Oberg is a cowboy and, like his heroes, he has done most of his pioneering alone.

That has been a mixed blessing. If Don Oberg's biggest strength has been his consistent ability to keep ahead by putting new ideas into practice, his biggest weakness over the years has been a failure to communicate with key employees, primarily supervisors, during that process. "About 10 years after starting the company, I just announced to our department managers that as of next Monday, we were going to start making form dies," Oberg recalls. At the time, the company's major business was in laminations for electric motors. "My chief engineer said, 'Form dies! We don't know enough about form dies to do it.' I said, 'I know you don't know much about it, but I do.' " His decision appeared so precipitous to the engineer that the man left the company. Ten years ago, Oberg made the same type of announcement, only this time it was that the company was going to start making its own diamond wheels. "It creates problems," says Rick Oberg. "He doesn't say it, but you almost hear the unspoken words, 'You're doing it that way because I told you so.' Your first reaction is a little anxiety."

Don Oberg sees it differently, of course. Next to bad housekeeping, his major complaint has been with supervisors who are resistant to change. The only way to get anything done, he concludes, is to do it himself. "If he sees someone doing something wrong, and there are four layers of management between him and that person, he'll just complete the loop himself and zip right down to the shop floor to rectify the situation," says Rick. That may give shop-floor workers instant access to the president, but it does little to build the confidence of managers.

In the late 1960s and early '70s, increasing dissatisfaction among supervisors, both about the strict work environment and their lack of authority, resulted in several key people leaving. It all started when a golf buddy, described by Oberg now as an "ex-friend," lured away six employees, most of them managers, in an effort to duplicate Oberg's successful business. After about a year, most of the six left their new employer to start their own companies, and over the next few years others from Oberg Industries followed suit. Today, many of the newcomers compete directly with Oberg, and, since they make fewer capital expenditures, they have significant cost advantages. Bob Grafton, 56, president of Ultra Precision Inc. and one of the original six, has applied to his own business what he considers the best of the Oberg philosophy—the emphasis on quality and cleanliness.

Still, Grafton and his contemporaries are more than willing to acknowledge their debt to their mentor. Last December, after 16 years of not speaking to Grafton, Oberg finally agreed to let his ex-employee organize a testimonial dinner, sponsored by the 22 companies Oberg Industries has spawned. "It wasn't held to toss bouquets and sing 'Auld Lang Syne,' " says Grafton, "but in recognition of the fact that if it weren't for Don Oberg, none of us would be in the business today. . . . Anywhere in the country, wherever people think of carbide dies, they think of Oberg."

It won't be long now, however, before bouquets are tossed and "Auld Lang Syne" is sung in earnest in Freeport. Don Oberg will be 70 years old in February. While he insists that he has 20 good years of work left in him, he is thinking seriously of naming Rick president at that time. It is not surprising that the question at Oberg Industries these days is: What will happen to the company then?

By his own admission, Don Oberg won't ever fully retire. Indeed, it is difficult to imagine Oberg Industries without him. Even though he has mellowed a bit over the past few years, his vision, values, and decisive leadership permeate the corridors and cubicles of Oberg Industries just as surely as do the little green signs urging "progressive improvement."

As Shondeck, now executive vice-president, admits, Oberg's physical presence has made a big difference in the plant. "A lot of the supervisors depended on him . . . which meant that if Don was in the plant, we had one degree of motivation, and if he was out of the plant, we had another. We now emphasize to the supervisors that it's up to them. . . . They're expected to recommend new equipment, machines, new techniques."

Perhaps the biggest source of speculation is how Rick Oberg will make out as president. In a company that has succeeded in large part through Don Oberg's deep belief in rewards based on fairness and merit, passing the torch to Rick, when Shondeck is, for all practical purposes, ex officio keeper of the flame, seems to fly in the face of reason. Since the trust that Oberg has in Shondeck is no secret, it is no wonder that many, particularly some of the veterans, feel he is the natural heir to the throne. What's more, they know Shondeck better. Rick has spent most of his time in Arizona and will continue to live there, commuting to Freeport when he takes over.

Don Oberg, with his strong sense of family loyalty, sees it differently, however. To him, it is only fair that a son should have the chance to follow in his father's footsteps—if, that is, he can pass muster. Oberg says, "When Rick becomes president, I'm going to stay on as CEO and chairman, and if he doesn't do his job, he won't stay on as president. We have 275 employees here [in Freeport]. It's not fair for somebody to get that job just because he's related to me. I want this company to continue to grow."

Rick is in many ways the antithesis of his father. His cigarettes and constant companion—a standard poodle named Willi—belie his strict upbringing. Even a casual observer can detect tension between the two. But curiously, Rick is less concerned about how his father will view his performance than about the employees' expectations. "It bothers me from the standpoint of their anticipation, the perception of my filling my father's shoes," he says quietly. "I can't do that. I'm not built the same way. He's zooming here and there; I'm more of a plodder." And, as he says, he will rely heavily on the management team headed by Shondeck.

In the final analysis, the future of Oberg Industries may depend less on Rick Oberg or Dave Shondeck than on Don Oberg's ability to let them run the business, whatever their titles. And, single-minded about his company as he is, the man who fervently believes that "resistance to change is what's killing our country" shouldn't be underestimated. In his seventieth year, he may well be ready to endorse the biggest change yet in the history of Oberg Industries.

One characteristic that seems to reflect a set of operational values is the entrepreneur's "never-ending sense of urgency" (Welsh & White, 1983, p. 43). My own research suggests that *entrepreneurs value the excitement of their jobs.* During open-ended interviews with 20 entrepreneurs, I found several who offered metaphors of teeter-totters, roller coasters, and poker tables. These metaphors convey an attitude toward venturing that is playful and exhilarating. A woman who founded a computer-training organization described it:

> I prefer to be extremely out there at the end of the teeter-totter, very vulnerable, and really make it large. You could go a little more towards the center of the teeter-totter, be a little more secure and take a market share . . . or we can come to the direct center . . . and play by ourselves. . . . I'm hanging out here [at the end] all the time. Out here's a whole lot of fun because out here is a lot of excitement.

A male founder of a low-technology production organization used the same analogy:

> The teeter-totter swings back and forth kind of like this. We got the order but now we can't make it. Now we can make it but we're being threatened by a new competitor.

For some, the excitement is all in the present; for others the ill-defined future is what generates energy and optimism:

> [There's an] old Arabic quote that says he who looks back only sees shadows. I have the excitement of tomorrow. I've got that green sign, I've gotta get going.

Excitement along with urgency, a bias for action, and fast dancing in terms of time all suggest the energizing potential of the new venture process. The entrepreneur lends his or her energy (i.e., his or her libido, for it is a love, a mistress, or child for many) to the venture. In turn the venture provides a nearly endless series of challenges, changes, new people, and new opportunities. The entrepreneur becomes re-energized (usually), adds again to the venture, and the symbiotic relationship continues.

VALUED ENTREPRENEURIAL RESULTS

Entrepreneurship is also valued for what it produces for the entrepreneur. Most of those who consider undertaking an entrepreneurial career think about the results of that career. Entrepreneurs are rewarded by equity or ownership and a salary (equity is the most important economic value for self-employed entrepreneurs; for non-self-employed entrepreneurs, current income is more important) (Duffy & Stevenson, 1984). For many this results in financial security or personal wealth and the freedom that brings.

There are other valued outcomes. For some the fame and recognition that go with successful entrepreneurship are the most valued ends. For others they are freedom, independence, and autonomy. Still others value the opportunity to implement some "new-age" values in organizations they build.

Money. Whether as personal wealth, cash flow, or financial security, money is clearly important to those who undertake the risks and hard work of entrepreneurship. However, research on the value of money tends to show that entrepreneurs, and especially successful entrepreneurs, have less personal greed than many might think. One study of college graduates showed that those who later had some ownership in a business were no different from those who had never been business owners in their values for money and fame (Hull et al., 1980). For many entrepreneurs money is a way of keeping score, rather than a goal.

> The entrepreneur is involved in a continuous process of making money, going out and investing it in another company, and then starting all over again. This cycle never seems to end and the money is a way of measuring performance.
>
> Timmons, 1978, p. 4

In interviews done in 1985, entrepreneurs were asked to define wealth and success. A man with a successful mail-order business replied, "Success means putting points on the scoreboard and this scoreboard is money." Other entrepreneurs defined wealth more philosophically. "Wealth is a short period of time when I'm content with what I've done and content with the rewards of my labor" (real-estate developer). "Wealth is a feeling of well-being, of being satisfied with what you are doing with your life" (retail shop owner). Another responded this way:

Q: So you started the business for monetary reasons?

A: Yes and no. Everyone in the architectural business wants to have their own business, therefore we extended our ego and started a business. We wanted to make money and to be artists. When we started our company we could put our philosophy of design into practice and attack it in the way we wanted (founding partner in an architectural firm).

Fame. Some entrepreneurs seem most interested in *fame, recognition, status, and power* (Kets de Vries, 1984). In describing restaurant entrepreneur Philip Romano (Fuddruckers, Stix Eating Spa), Tom Richman writes, "Romano wants approval, approbation of which profit, like praise, is just a measure" (1986b, p. 130).

However, other research suggests that fame and visibility are of little importance to many entrepreneurs. One study found that entrepreneurs were no different from the general public in their desire for recognition and were less in need of social support, suggesting that esteem needs are not what drives entrepreneurs (Hornaday & Aboud, 1980). This finding is confirmed in reports by Welsh and White (1983) that entrepreneurs have little need for status, and by a recent *Inc.* magazine article suggesting that entrepreneurs prefer less rather than more visibility. "Privacy is a passion in business, and secrecy is often a key to success; it is no wonder that so many businesspeople abhor the glare of public life" (Brownstein, 1985).

Idealism. While limited in scope, there is some indication that entrepreneurs engage in organizational creation and organizational development for the purpose of some *ideal social value.* Kao (1985) argues that as young people of the 1960s become the entrepreneurs of today, they will bring to their enterprises important values including a desire to keep organizations human in scale, participative, nonhierarchic, and fluid. He expects the new wave of entrepreneurs to be more interested in creativity, transcendence, and social justice.

Support for this contention comes from business leaders who have begun to take active roles in social issues such as making peace (Rhodes, 1984a; Willens, 1985) or by focusing their business on charitable contributions, such as Ron Schulz's Medicine for Children, Inc. which donates 100 percent of its profits to charity (Buchsbaum, 1984). Other entrepreneurs use their organization to demonstrate a point, such as BP (in the case at the end of Chapter 1), who decided to debunk myths with his company. Other exemplars include Paul Hawken, who moved from being an entrepreneur to being a statesman of a new economic philosophy (Hawken, 1983; Whitehead, 1984) and Marilyn Ferguson, who turned her notions of the "Aquarian Conspiracy" into a profitable new-age newsletter, *The Brain/Mind Bulletin.*

ORGANIZATIONAL IMPACT OF ENTREPRENEURIAL VALUES

The founder's values, assumptions and beliefs, along with his or her early market, product, and technology decisions, form the strategic template for the emerging organization. Because the founder is chief decision maker, his or her values influence organizational strategy and structure (which is also influenced by contextual variables such as organizational size, technology, environment, current structure, and organizational composition) (Bobbitt & Ford, 1980; Mintzberg & Waters, 1982). In looking at the impact of top managers, Hambrick and Mason (1984) theorize that the CEO's (and by extension, the entrepreneur's) values and beliefs limit the field of vision and interpretation of data by the organization's managers. These narrowed perceptions in turn influence strategic choices and ultimately organizational outcomes such as culture, structure, performance, and profits. Thus the impact of values seems to work through the focusing of attention and energy in organizational members and thus through emerging organizational culture. Of course, entrepreneurial values also operate on the context, attracting interest, resources, and competition from external parties.

The impact of entrepreneurial values on organizational outcomes should be even greater than the impact of corporate top managers, since the organization's structure, culture, systems, and procedures have yet to be laid down. Thus instead of changing organizations incrementally, most entrepreneurs (at least those who start new firms) create new organizations that correspond in some direct way with their personal vision and values.

The most central organizational outcomes are survival and success (positive cash flow, profits, growth). Success seems to follow from entrepreneurs who value financial independence and self-satisfaction that are rather long-term, involving extended commitment. In contrast, unsuccessful entrepreneurs tend to value making money and being one's own boss (shorter-term) (Sexton & Van Auken, 1982). Thus being "in it" for the money is not a mark of success. Nor is being "in it" for power or influence (Wainer & Rubin, 1969).

Other research suggests that *the operational values of entrepreneurs also predict relative success.* A priority placed on family affiliation (long-term support) has been correlated with success (Sexton & Van Auken, 1982). Other process values such as open-mindedness, or the ability to consider other perspectives and values, has been shown to relate to organizational variables such as innovation and growth. In a study on entrepreneurial belief structures, Gasse (1977; 1979, cited in Brockhaus, 1982) found that open-minded entrepreneurs tend to hold a managerial orientation, using abstract concepts and rational systems in solving business problems.

Integrity and reliability are considered important values for entrepreneurs to hold, especially as seen by important stakeholders. Timmons (1978) suggests that an entrepreneur's credibility to the financial networks relies on candor.

> An early eliminator of a venture proposal is the discovery by a venture capitalist that the entrepreneur has not been straightforward and honest in revealing past dealings or even failures (p. 6).

These attributes clearly pertain to an entrepreneur's reputation (ability to do handshake "deals"), ethics, and employee relations, all important to the organization's long-term survival and growth.

Implications

Entrepreneurs can be recognized by their value systems. Most of those we call successful—those with growth-oriented and profitable ventures—value outcomes such as sales, profits, market share, and personal wealth (as a means of keeping score). They are accordingly opportunistic about how these ends are achieved, often operating in ethical grey areas. Income-substitution entrepreneurs and those with nonmonetary missions will be more willing to accept organizational stability, small niche markets, and income sufficient for one's lifestyle as long as the quality of life is acceptable and/or other social values are being advanced.

Values inform and underlie much of what the entrepreneur intends. These values help the entrepreneur tie the present to the future, and are fundamental to the processes of alignment and attunement that define intentional action.

THE ROLE OF ABILITIES AND MOTIVATION: A SUMMARY

The abilities (seen best in terms of prior experiences and education) and motivations (need for achievement, need for control, risk acceptance, etc.) of potential entrepreneurs determine if they will act to form a new venture or acquire an existing business. Prospective entrepreneurs usually assess abilities and motivations for themselves (most often informally) in terms of what is feasible (Do they have the ability to put the deal together? Do they have access to resources? Is the timing right?) and what is desirable (Is this what they want to do with their time and energy? Is the risk worth taking? How do others feel about it?). Existing entrepreneurs make decisions and act to implement them based on similar considerations—their abilities and motivations (or their perceptions of these).

Together, ability and motivation predict (1) the decision to start a new venture, (2) the ability to implement that decision, and (3) the results of that venture. Other factors moderate or influence the impact of abilities and motivations. Factors such as the circumstances and environment of the venture, the team that gets built, and the network of external relations also determine these outcomes. These factors are discussed in later chapters.

EXAMPLE OF SB

For an educator/trainer, SB's career has been nontraditional. She graduated from high school, one senses, with relief—learning there had been far too slow for her. She didn't enjoy it and never considered continuing in a traditional university education.

A few months after high-school graduation, when computer engineering and programming courses opened up to women, SB joined the army. She excelled in the training program, which is fast-paced and "more concerned that you get what you get and that you understand it for today's sake and not carry it with you tomorrow." She graduated first in her class, and in her second year with the army she taught the program to others. This is when she learned state-of-the-art teaching techniques using the right and left brain and began her career as an educator.

She left the army to work directly in computer applications rather than continuing in education. She says that, at the time, industrial education was not ready to include computer courses or technology. Over the next six years she worked as an engineer for a manufacturer of instant teller machines, as a trainer in microcomputer applications for a nuclear medicine firm, and as a national trainer for engineers using computers for design.

At this point she realized that a major application for microcomputer technology would be in business. Since she had no business experience she faced a choice: To go back for formal schooling in management (this was so far from her preferences that she didn't even consider it), to assume a line management job in an organization (which she considered "dreadful"), or to start her own business. So she started Micro in 1981 as a vehicle for learning. "I got a very very quick, fast-paced learning experience on what it's like to talk to the IRS and fill out tax forms, and do payroll, and do projections, and do cash flow analysis, and break even, and so forth."

Micro provided in-house training to microcomputer end users, produced training materials, and provided public seminars and lectures. The company was incorporated and held by an investor group, with SB as a major stockholder. Within its first four years it grew to employ 17 people and had developed excellent press, stemming from the November 1983 COMDEX show, where Micro was seen as one of the only solid training firms in an industry that was beginning to see the need for education in product use.

SB used intentionality (that is, temporal tension, strategic focus, and posture) in a conscious way, articulating purposes, clearing up intrapsychic and interpersonal barriers, taking considerable care with the language that was used by her people, etc. For SB, purpose involves some alignment with a mission or a bigger-than-SB purpose.

> The purpose statement for Micro is basically the company is organized to ease the transition into the computer age through education for all people who need it. A big charter. Bigger than me. I like having charters bigger than me. I always have something to work on.

When problems would arise, such as slow sales or financial stress, SB went through several self-analytic processes to find ways to work on the problem. First, she would ask herself if she hadn't already achieved the intended goal, but simply failed to recognize that what she had was what she had intended. She gave the example of setting the goal of experiencing business as a fast-paced learning experience and nearly going bankrupt.

That was not my expectation. I expected to be doing phenomenally well and playing with the big guys and learning. Here I was going bankrupt. Exactly where I was was what I had asked for. The things I learned I could not have learned any other way. At that point in that situation I got what I was looking for. That teaches you how clear you have to be when you're setting your goals.

She would ask herself questions about the appropriateness of the goal and found that inappropriate goals result in struggle, "when every time I turn around something seems to smack me in the head." Other internal questions involved whether she was holding on to things and relationships while aiming at changes, thereby creating a state of unconscious conflict. With both inappropriate goals and "holding on" she used a technique of "letting go," a subjective state of willingness to detach from where she was and what she had. She reports that once she let go of her desire to keep her house, her cars, and her relationships unchanged while she created Micro, progress toward Micro happened quickly.

After asking herself an internal question, she would watch for answers.

I try to be conscious all day long, looking for answers to that question. The answer comes up anywhere. You might say a line to me right now, a sign on a billboard . . . all of a sudden there's an answer. So I'll ask a question and wait, sometimes three days, sometimes a week. Inevitably I'll get key physical signs . . . I'll hear a song and two words strike me.

She also used imagery or visualization. First, in a quiet place without interruptions, she would clear her mind of negative or limiting thoughts, making explicit any reasons she has for not attaining a desired goal. For example, does one of her beliefs prevent her from selling Micro's services to a Fortune 500 company? After allowing these beliefs to surface, and countering each with an affirmation that she will achieve her goal, she would form a visual image of having already attained the goal (e.g., seeing the customer signing a contract).

A similar process was used to maintain positive beliefs in her staff, who received handouts on why beliefs were important to Micro and how to create and maintain positive attitudes. She told of several recent incidents where an employee was unable to live by these rules and who said to SB, "I know we haven't got the check in yet from ABC, Inc., so

I haven't given you my expense report yet because I know you can't pay it." SB found such incidents to be both irritating and very real barriers to her business. Her response was to coach both employees and board members to hold positive rather than limiting beliefs.

Micro came to an end in 1984 when SB apparently lost her energy to make the business work. She claims to have learned what she set out to learn and had no use for a long-term commitment to a business.

CHAPTER 5

THE IMPACT OF PERSONAL HISTORY: BEYOND FEAR AND GUILT

INTRODUCTION

The entrepreneurial abilities and motivation that are so crucial in determining whether one will venture or how successful one will be in venturing derive from previous experiences. In Chapter 3 we identified some of these experiences (e.g., education, prior work). However, since personality and motivational drives begin to develop very early in life—with one's family—a closer look at the entrepreneur's family is warranted. The link between childhood experiences and adult behavior is made using two conceptual models, psychoanalytic and social-learning or role modeling. Each of these tools is used in this chapter to understand how childhood experiences may affect entrepreneurial behavior.

Psychoanalysis—the attempt to delve into early development and unconscious motivations—has been used by a handful of distinguished scholars to shed light on entrepreneurs. In general, psychoanalysis attempts to see through the behaviors, problems, and rationalizations of adults to *underlying tensions, drives, and emotions.* Observers who have applied psychoanalytic insight to entrepreneurs base their interpretations mostly on Freudian psychology, with its emphasis on neurotic adult behavior stemming from childhood development and family dynamics. This model will be used extensively in this chapter, although the author does not share the fairly negative views put forth by the Freudian researchers.

An alternative model is that of social learning, which emphasizes conscious and unconscious *learning of behavior through imitation, vicarious satisfactions, and relationships* between role model and learner. More specifically, parental role models provide exemplars for personality development (through identification, whereby the child identifies with the parent) and, later, for adult role expectations (e.g., how to be a good spouse, parent, employee, or entrepreneur). Parental and other adult role models also provide opportunities for the child to learn vicariously. While not extensively used in entrepreneurship research, some implications of this theory are presented in this chapter.

The personal backgrounds of entrepreneurs show some intriguing patterns. Entrepreneurs are frequently first-born children of distant, sometimes self-employed fathers and supportive mothers. Studies of early family dynamics of entrepreneurs reveal a frequent (though by no means universal) pattern: one of struggle, deprivation, lack of strong male role models with a personal connection to the child, and resulting insecurity, guilt, and obsessive need for control. Such family relationships are thought to result in the drive to become self-employed, the need for control, and the preference for interpersonal distance that characterizes many entrepreneurs.

In a frequently cited study, Collins and Moore (1964) interviewed 110 entrepreneurs who founded manufacturing firms in Michigan between 1945 and 1958. All were men; all were interviewed about their business, their history, and their plans. Most reported unhappy or deprived childhoods. Four themes were found in the stories of childhood told by these men:

1. Escape from poverty
2. Escape from insecurity (lack of stable and reliable adult figures)
3. Death (especially sudden death) of a parent
4. Inversion of the father-son role (e.g., with son employing father in his business)

While perceptions about childhood deprivations and struggles may differ from the objective facts (if these facts could be determined), psychologically the difference is very slim. What one believes or remembers to be true has the impact of an objective fact in the development of personality and in current conduct. In other words, whether or not childhood was deprived, entrepreneurs (especially those who were starting as young men in the post-depression years) experienced deprivation. That deprivation set up a chain of drives and motivations that resulted in entrepreneurial behavior.

PSYCHOANALYTIC MODEL OF ENTREPRENEURSHIP

Table 5.1 shows an overall picture of the psychoanalytic approach to entrepreneurship. Because psychoanalytic theory is complex, the overall model will be explained before going further into research findings.

Children are conceived, born, and raised in a certain country during a certain period of history. These larger system qualities have an impact on the type of childrearing practices used by parents and family and on the social expectations about the conduct of children. Thus children born to immigrant parents during the depression in the United States entered into a different context than children conceived and raised by parents in the post-WWII boom or more recently by the yuppies of the 1980s. Collins and Moore (1964) and others whose data derive from entrepreneurs active in the 1950s focus on men born into the poverty of immigration and the Great Depression as well as into European social systems that supported the development of authoritarian personalities (Adorno et al., 1950).

With a parental configuration of an absent, distant, authoritarian father and a nurturant, nonworking mother who took charge of family affairs, the child can experience uncertainty and problems in identifying with appropriate role models. Children from these types of families are also likely to develop "closed mindedness" and dogmatism (Rokeach, 1960), a tendency to see the world in categorical and value-laden terms (e.g., black and white, good and bad). Also likely is the development of low self-esteem, distrust, powerlessness, dissatisfaction, and even pessimism.

Collins and Moore (1964) and others (research summarized below) found that family origins like this result in adulthood tendencies shown in Table 5.1. When adults with this type of background become entrepreneurs, creators of value through organization, distinctive problems emerge. These are discussed below.

TABLE 5.1 Psychoanalytic Model of Entrepreneurship

Social, cultural, historic, economic context

Society that supports the development of authoritarian
  personality
Family poverty

AND

Childhood family dynamics

Father's: absence   Mother's: dominance
  remoteness   nurturance
  villainy
  role model

RESULT IN

Disrupted, deprived childhood
Conflicts in identification (love-hate)
Splitting the good and bad (either-or thinking, closed
  mindedness)
Persistent feelings of dissatisfaction, rejection, powerlessness,
  low self-esteem, distrust

THAT DEVELOP INTO

Young adulthood characterized by

Disorientation, goal-lessness, testing
Non-conformity, rebelliousness
Enjoying setbacks (martyrdom, masochism)
High need for control
Suspicious thinking
Fear of being victimized
Scanning the environment

THROUGH A SERIES OF CONSCIOUS CHOICES A PERSON ENDS UP AS AN ENTREPRENEUR

Adulthood creation of an organization that is

Authoritarian
Centralized
Lacking trust and delegation
Lacking planning, impulsive
A work environment of high dependency and power that is a
  function of centrality or closeness to the entrepreneur
Unresolved regarding
  succession: Rivalry with sons
               Coping with loss or losing control

THE ENTREPRENEUR'S FAMILY

NEGATIVE FATHER

The work done by Collins and Moore (1964) and Kets de Vries (1977; Kets de Vries & Zaleznik, 1975) reveals that some entrepreneurs experience their fathers as villains and the source of considerable childhood insecurity. This villainy may involve distance by the father through work or more active abuse or abandonment (through desertion or death).

Sometimes, entrepreneurs have fathers who are entrepreneurs or otherwise self-employed (Roberts & Wainer, 1966). As for most entrepreneurs, the father's job comes first—he works long hours and as a result is distant and not involved in family life. The child in turn feels rejected and ambivalent (i.e., both proud and indebted, angry and sad) about the father.

Another form of the negative father occurs if the father deserts, manipulates, or abuses the family—or is perceived this way. One frequent pattern in the Collins and Moore (1964) study was the early death of the entrepreneur's father, and "death may be interpreted by a child as the ultimate form of desertion or rejection" (Kets de Vries, 1977, p. 45). We can also speculate that very authoritarian fathers were also perceived with a love-hate ambivalence and spawned a child's need for control (Adorno et al., 1950).

Either through desertion, death, or a father's absorption in his own business, the potential entrepreneur often grows up with a distant and uninvolved male role model. The child whose culture says fathers are loving, good providers, and doing their best as caretakers experiences ambivalent feelings of attraction and resentment, love and hate. Says Kets de Vries (1977, p. 46),

> The lack of familiarity and unpredictability of a remote father image makes the process of growing up not a very happy or harmonious one. It may leave the child and later the adult troubled by a burdensome psychological inheritance centered around problems of self-esteem, insecurity and lack of confidence. Repressed aggressive wishes towards persons in control are not strange to these individuals and the resulting sense of impotence and helplessness contributes to these feelings of rage, insecurity, and low self-esteem.

Although society has changed since the 1940s, a recent survey by *Venture* magazine suggests that families of entrepreneurs may not have changed greatly. The study reported a small but suggestive difference between company founders and nonfounders in their readership survey. Founders tended to describe their fathers in negative terms such as "intimidating" and "preoccupied with work." Nonfounders tended to use more positive terms such as "instructive," "nurturing," and "a role model" ("Just Like Dear Old Dad," November, 1985). Says Eva Thompson in that article:

> There's usually some kind of deprivation—financial, physical, or emotional—in [a founder's] . . . childhood relationship with their father. The child learns to make up for that, to be more creative in fulfilling his needs, to be more self-reliant and manipulative in trying to control the situation.

FATHER AS A ROLE MODEL: SOCIAL LEARNING

Of course some aspects of this pattern also produce a role model for the future entrepreneur. Several studies suggest that having a self-employed father is important to the potential entrepreneur. For example, Roberts and Wainer (1966) found high-technology entrepreneurs more likely to have self-employed fathers than the general population, and Ronstadt (1984a) found that practicing entrepreneurs were more likely to have entrepreneurial fathers than ex-entrepreneurs and "serious nonstarters."

As a role model the father (uncle, cousin, friend) teaches values and attitudes toward independence, tolerance of risk, and achievement. The son (or daughter) observes the father's responses to the ups and downs, the stresses and turmoil of self-employment, and this has a profound impact. In this way the pitfalls of self-employment are seen, making the future entrepreneur's business concepts likely to be more realistic. Finally, incentives to succeed in ways the father failed are developed.

IMPACT OF FATHER

Whether negative or more positive, the father is seen as the source of motivation and drive for the entrepreneur—not only in starting a business but throughout an entrepreneurial career. "Even when he is in his thirties, and his dad is retired, the approval and praise of his father still provides a basis for his drive" (Mancuso, 1974).

We might also expect this relationship to take on different value for the *woman entrepreneur*. Girls have different types of relationships with and learn different things from their fathers. If the father is absent or distant, the girl (and later woman) may develop unusually strong attractions to men along with fear of men (Hetherington, 1973). A wounded relationship with one's father or with the larger patriarchical society we live in can result in adult women who feel despair, loneliness, isolation, fear of abandonment, and considerable rage (Leonard, 1983), which are qualities that work against entrepreneurial careers (Carsrud, Olm, & Ahlgreen, 1986). Finally, we know that the father-daughter relationship is important in the development of women who learn to work with men, network, and succeed in middle- and top-management positions (Hennig & Jardim, 1977). Unfortunately, little is known about the family dynamics of women entrepreneurs and how this might differ from that of men.

POSITIVE AND NEGATIVE MOTHER

While possessed of (and later obsessed with) a negative father, the men in the Collins and Moore (1964) study reported nurturing yet strong, decisive, controlling, ambitious, and domineering mothers. "Since there is no one else to take responsibility, the mother often has no choice. She will give the child his sense of direction" (Kets de Vries & Zaleznik, 1975, p. 223). Silver (1983), who surveyed wealthy entrepreneurs (with personal wealth of more than $20 million and publicly held organizations), likens the mother of the entrepreneur to the "frontier woman," someone clearly to be admired (i.e., positive).

What these women do is provide their sons (and often their daughters) with early opportunities for independent action, moderate risks, and timely feedback. These are the conditions that develop achievement motivation, especially in first-born children who have no competing siblings and no sibling supervision.[1] Support for this contention derives from other studies showing that leaders in business (Andrew Carnegie, George Eastman, Thomas Edison), politics (Lyndon Johnson, Douglas MacArthur, Franklin Roosevelt), and the arts (Frank Lloyd Wright) had positive, supportive, and strong mothers (Fenn, 1985a; McCullough, 1982; Kets de Vries & Zaleznik, 1975).

Unfortunately, masculine models have long dominated both psychoanalytic thought and research into entrepreneur-

---

[1] While mothers provide this, especially in the absence of the father, it is important to note that fathers can provide conditions that foster achievement.

ship. As a result little is known about the mother's impact on women entrepreneurs. We can speculate, however, that role modeling occurs and that daughters of women business owners will be more likely to see self-employment and entrepreneurship as potential careers for themselves.

We can question, however, just how positive this image of the mother is. Masculinity is highly valued in business, commerce, politics, and perhaps all forms of instrumental activity where competition occurs. Qualities of decisiveness, "take-charge" aggressiveness, and single-minded focus on organizational growth and profits are highly valued.

Although perceptions and experiences are changing, the feminine has been unvalued or at least undervalued for generations if not for centuries. Both men and women have contributed to and continue to sustain the devaluation of feminine qualities such as compassion, cooperation, relationship, intuition, sensitivity, and receptivity. Generally, these qualities are less appreciated, less rewarded, and considered less important in the "school of hard knocks" or for business decision making and leadership.

When mothers have lost contact with and appreciation for their biological heritage and gender, they may become "negative mothers." For men, this means mothers who undermine their masculinity through overprotection and dominance. For women, the negative mother creates ambiguity in values (e.g., "I am feminine but masculine is rewarded and valued") and a rejection of biology seen symptomatically in eating disorders (e.g., anorexia, obesity, and bulimia; Woodman, 1980).

The negative mother gives up her own dreams, and in her disappointment projects her possibilities onto her children. Her unspoken wishes, dreams, and feelings of sacrifice pass unconsciously to the child, who feels responsible and guilty.

> In order to achieve the money, cleanliness, beauty and brains necessary to live the affluent middle-class life, the household had to run like clockwork. All members were expected to take responsibility and to perform according to their collective roles. . . . Mom, likewise bewitched by appearances, was typically a highly intelligent, ambitious woman who sacrificed her own career for her children, and then more or less unconsciously expected them to achieve what she did not. Her energy went into making her body, her brain, her life, her children into works of art.

Woodman, 1985, p. 101

The problem is compounded by the mother's apparent ability to exercise control and make all things right.

> That is power masquerading as love. When she cannot control her world, she falls into the dark side of the mother. She moves from abundance to deprivation, from symbiotic intimacy to rejection, from love to hate.
>
> Woodman, 1985, p. 118

The result of negative mothers and societal rejection of the feminine is a mutilated feeling function in adult men and women. To succeed, women accept the masculine standpoint, and thereby betray their own souls (Woodman, 1985, p. 156).

> The same is true for a man. If he habitually ignores his feeling in favor of a rational standpoint, he too is betraying his own soul. . . . The "mother's son," for example, so vulnerable to feeling guilty that he is not "better," or "more manly" or "more capable," thinks automatically of pleasing the women in his life. He may believe that is how he feels, but it is not true feeling. It is thinking contaminated by the mother complex. It is sheer sentimentality. . . . If he can contact and express his real feeling, he can stop seeing women as negative mothers whose demands he is constantly trying to live up to.
>
> Woodman, 1985, p. 157

Observers of the negative mother have not extended their thinking to entrepreneurs. However, we can speculate that men and women who lack positive feminine influences may be well developed rationally and politically, capable of making dispassionate decisions involving the lives of others (e.g., bankrupting a competitor, firing obsolete employees, disbanding a partnership). However, these men and women may also lack confidence in their intuition and timing of decisions (aspects that cannot be rationally determined) and the compassion, human relations skills, and sensitivity necessary to build a strong venture team and subsequent organization involving many people. Thus the negative mother contributes to but also limits the venture's potential.

IMPACT OF FAMILY ON PERSONALITY

Positively or negatively, the parents instill an early sense of *independence and desire for control* in the future entrepreneur. Reflecting on common aspects of entrepreneurs' early family dynamics, Silver (1983) says, "The entrepreneur, it seems, did the high wire act without the net below. Courage and no fear of failure are predictable outcomes" (p. 34).

Polarized thinking. A deeper analysis of male entrepreneurs suggests that the combination of a dominant, supportive mother and a remote, ambivalent father may result in identity confusion. The boy may reject his father (and then confuse his own and his father's rejection—who rejected whom?) and may fantasize about powerful male figures since there is no powerful male close by. He grows up perceiving high control by others (positive control by mother; negative by father) and rejection (by the distant father or busy mother). All of these responses result in a *polarized world view.* Things and people are either good, strong, and tough or bad, weak, and powerless. There is no middle ground (Kets de Vries & Zaleznik, 1975).

This dynamic is thought to contribute to the adult entrepreneur's value system and his decisive and sometimes arbitrary and authoritarian decision-making style. It contributes to the entrepreneur's social and emotional distance from others, his strong desire/need to control his enterprise, and his attempts to enact the persona of a "powerful man."

Revenge, rebellion, and control. Kets de Vries (1977) suggests another developmental dynamic, that of *revenge and rebellion.* In this case desertion by the father and control by the mother are resented, resulting in fantasies of revenge.

> A state of anger may be the legacy of this particular type of family dynamics, anger which may be directed toward the self or projected to others contributing to a sense of guilt and undermining self-confidence. In a later state of personality development this tendency toward hostility and anger may injure relationships with peers (p. 47).

Without therapeutic intervention, the resentment, ambivalence, and hostility are maintained in adolescence, resulting in an inability to make interpersonal commitments and persistent feelings of rejection, powerlessness, and low self-esteem (Kets de Vries, 1977; Kets de Vries & Zaleznik, 1975). Rebellion is one response to these feelings. This behavior pattern is one of impulsivity, low tolerance for frustration and tension, short attention span, and a demand for immediate satisfaction (short-term gain). "A lack of analytical thinking, an absence of active search procedures and self-critical reflections becomes a predominant mode" (Kets de Vries, 1977, p. 49). As a result, the adolescent often does poorly in school. Socially, the rebel resists authority and isolates himself. He sees himself and is seen by others as the misfit, the man who cannot take orders, who prefers to go it alone.

Another response to this history transforms feelings of helplessness and rejection into a *strong need for personal control.* The need for control, common in studies of entrepreneurial personality, drives the entrepreneur to create and dominate his organization. Frequently entrepreneurs report their motivation for beginning an entrepreneurial career is the desires for autonomy, independence, and "being one's own boss."

Sources of fear and guilt. In his study of wealthy entrepreneurs, Silver (1983) found entrepreneurs frequently reporting feelings of guilt, "in merely existing as an entrepreneur" (p. 39). He explains this in terms of (1) society's historical ambivalence about entrepreneurs—we seem to love them and hate them—and (2) the individual's guilt from childhood, lack of peer support, and unwillingness to talk about feelings. These combine with long hours and frequent travel to make entrepreneurs good candidates for interpersonal problems in adulthood, especially divorce. Divorce, when it occurs, exacerbates the guilt and drives the entrepreneur to compensate by succeeding in his enterprise ("I'll show her"). The business also becomes a place where feelings of love, commitment, fatherhood, and "family" can be sublimated and enacted. Silver, based on his experience as a venture capitalist, says that venture capitalists are "high on divorced entrepreneurs and 'guilty marrieds'; but they loathe to back the never-married bachelor" (p. 42) because of his apparent lack of commitment and guilt.

IMPACT OF PSYCHODYNAMICS ON ORGANIZATION
While guilt may be a positive incentive to develop an organization, the relationship between the individual's guilt, fear, suspicion, and need for recognition and organizational outcomes needs to be more carefully examined. Neurotic individuals build neurotic organizations that tend to have productivity and morale problems (Kets de Vries & Miller, 1984).

Uneven or stunted growth. Fearful leadership, and especially fearful entrepreneurs, can produce organizations with unnecessary cycles of growth and decline. In their study Collins and Moore (1964) found entrepreneurs feel most free from their guilt and fears only when business is at its worst. A downturn is experienced as penance. "With the alleviation of anxiety, a base is created to start anew. The release of new energy renews their enthusiasm and sense of purpose" (Kets de Vries, 1984, p. 5).

Environmental relations. The fearful and guilty personality may also result in *extensive vigilance* on behalf of the organization. Fear of loss of control and fear of being at the mercy of others can be managed by careful and continuous scanning of the environment. The organization benefits by early awareness of changes in government, competition, and industry. However, the same personality is suspicious of authority, and the individual is *unable to accept the influence of others.* He or she may remain "closely held," avoiding external encumbrances from venture capital and other financing and failing to take advantage of the "rented expertise" of consultants.

Organizational dynamics. Paranoid thinking in entrepreneurs has some important internal organizational costs. Small things get blown out of proportion, conflicts are taken personally, and important areas of poor performance can go unnoticed. Distrust of others, avoidance of structure (which is experienced as stifling by the entrepreneur), and inability to cooperate and delegate can permeate the organization's culture and limit the organization at all levels. "Frequently [cooperation by the entrepreneur] seems possible only in those instances when the entrepreneur created the structure; if the work is done on his or her terms" (Kets de Vries, 1984, p. 4). This results in idiosyncratic work rules and low potential for organizational learning and innovation.

Distrust and need for control result in an authoritarian or paternalistic leadership style with rewards based on loyalty. This can result in a homogeneous top-management team, with a concomitant lack of variety, high potential for misperceiving changes in the business environment, and low innovation. There is an unwillingness to delegate (trust) key employees, so employees are not allowed to participate in decisions. As a result, satisfaction and productivity can be expected to be low and innovation difficult.

Finally, the need for control and the failure to delegate and develop others result in a flat organizational structure with everyone reporting to the CEO entrepreneur. This in turn limits growth and engenders a crisis when the issue of leadership succession arises.

Building monuments. Deprived of it in childhood, entrepreneurs frequently have a strong need for recognition, "a strong urge to show others that they amount to something" (Kets de Vries, 1984, p. 6). This often shows up in the "monuments" they build—decisions about office location, new products, and other publicly visible symbols of their success (such as membership in a country club). If based on a neurotic need for recognition, these decisions may not be well informed and may signal trouble ahead. For example, venture capitalists and other investors are leery of ventures in which office furnishings and the entrepreneur's lifestyle (e.g., house, car, first-class travel) are excessive or conspicuous. If it appears that personal aggrandizement takes priority over bottom-line, growth, or quality concerns, investors, customers, and employees fail to make the commitments needed to ensure long-term success.

COMMON PSYCHOLOGICAL TENSIONS
Whether or not one's family of origin had some or all of these disturbing features, psychoanalytic theory predicts that there will be some emotional and unconscious residue from childhood. No one's parents are perfect and all children pass through separation anxiety (fear of rejection and fear of loss of love); all face ego-boundary issues (what and who do I control? when? how?); and all face evaluation by those they love (and resultant pride, hubris, guilt, shame, fear, etc.). Entrepreneurs, like the rest of us, have to make peace with family legacies.

In addition to fathers and mothers, entrepreneurs frequently have brothers and sisters (although the entrepreneur is frequently the first born) and experience resulting rivalry. These relationships undoubtedly have an effect on adult abilities to form friendships, partnerships, and employment contracts.

Entrepreneurial organizations can also become family businesses. Sometimes the husband and wife are business partners as well as marriage partners, and this produces unique opportunities and problems. (See Fooner, 1983; Helm, 1986; and Nelton, 1986 for further information on married partners.) Other times the father and son or daughter are the stars in the family business drama, with leadership succession being a primary concern. (See Beckhard & Dyer, 1983; Kepner, 1983; Landsberg, 1983; Levinson, 1971; Rosenblatt, Mik, Anderson & Johnson, 1985; and Ward, 1986 for more information on family business concerns.) The family business, while fraught with deep, historical tension, is also a context for social learning—through role models and vicarious experience of rewards and setbacks.

SUMMARY

The family dynamics portrayed in this chapter can influence entrepreneurs in two ways—unconsciously and often negatively as the psychodynamic model suggests, or more positively through social learning/role modeling. The psychoanalytic model proposes that unresolved feelings from childhood motivate entrepreneurs to venture, and then influence their leadership behavior in the developing enterprise. The social learning model proposes that entrepreneurs learn the "ups and downs" of self-employment and organization building from their entrepreneurial parents, often (but not necessarily) becoming second-generation entrepreneurs in the family firm.

It is important to note that entrepreneurship is just one solution to the insecurity, fear, need for control, and guilt that have childhood origins. Many individuals grow up in families with problems like these; very few become entrepreneurs. Others release tension in corporate work-aholism, neurosis, disease, other acts of rebellion, dedication, and art. When the solution (creating autonomy and control through self-employment) is perceived as successful, tension may be released and satisfaction found. When the solution is unsuccessful (e.g., even though the business survives, it does not rid the founder of his or her feelings), the entrepreneur continues to fight ghosts, seeing authority as unreliable, unable to move from reaction to action, and thereby possibly disabling his or her enterprise.

It is also important to note that while the psychoanalytic model helps explain entrepreneurial personalities and motivations, it does not explain all entrepreneurs. Many entrepreneurs come from family backgrounds considerably more balanced, nurturing, and supportive than those found by psychoanalysts. Other factors must contribute to the drive, persistence, and focus of entrepreneurs.

IMPLICATIONS OF THE AUTHORITARIAN ENTREPRENEUR

The psychoanalytic model helps explain why entrepreneurs tend to be "rugged individualists" with a high need for control and a low need for social support. Knowing why entrepreneurs are as they are takes some of their heroic aura away. The swashbuckling entrepreneur who must make all decisions himself is a man with wounds and problems.

Knowing why entrepreneurs have these personality dynamics may enable others—investors, partners, employees, and even spouses—to better deal with the "strong man," the authoritarian. However, the authoritarian entrepreneur profiled here is not likely to grow a new venture beyond the size he can control. This entrepreneur, with his short-term focus and defensive perceptions, will lack the ability to sustain temporal tension, the flexibility to adjust his strategic focus, and the sensitivity and maturity to align and attune his venture for healthy growth. The authoritarian personality does not make for a good manager, leader, or team builder—roles that are necessary for venture growth.

Investors may be advised to either avoid such characters or anticipate hostilities when the entrepreneur fails to expand the venture beyond his control and the investors begin to insist. Potential employees, too, may want to take care in making decisions to work for the authoritarian entrepreneur. He or she is likely to be less trusting, have more difficulty delegating, and be less willing to listen to others or encourage innovation and participation.

Finally, the psychoanalytic explanation of entrepreneurial character results in a fairly pessimistic view of the possibilities of change in adulthood. Personality is deeply rooted, and it is difficult, if not impossible, to change. Change, if it occurs, requires years of painful self-analysis guided by a professional healer (psychoanalytic or other).

BEYOND FEAR AND GUILT: THE CALL TO ADVENTURE

Although little attention has been paid to entrepreneurship by those who follow the psychology of Carl Jung, some of his thinking can usefully be applied. Jung's theories provide a model of motivation that is considerably more positive, involving the development of human potential. Jung did not dwell on the childhood and dysfunctional family dynamics of the individual. He was rather more impressed with themes that emerge in all societies in all ages—themes such as "the good mother," "the bad mother," birth, death, initiation, etc. He felt that these themes carry a transpersonal energy related to instincts because they occur in every society across history in some form. He felt that the energy behind these themes was more than personal; he called this energy "archetypal."

We might consider the recurrence of entrepreneurship throughout history as an expression of archetypal energy. The work done by McClelland and his associates (summarized in McClelland, 1985) over the past two decades on the relationship between achievement motivation and social events, from the golden ages of Greece and Rome to modern times, suggests that the archetype of the entrepreneur may be theoretically sound. In recent history we see this in the "rugged individualist" of the United States, the self-made man personified by Horatio Alger stories. More work on the symbols, energies, and meanings of entrepreneurial events across cultures and history is needed to substantiate the archetypal quality.

An alternative Jungian approach, and the one taken here, looks in depth at the entrepreneurial event for archetypal energy. Is there more to entrepreneurship than the start of a business, the creation of jobs, and the generation of taxes? Is the career of an entrepreneur more than a job or a way of making money? Does the entrepreneurial event have an overarching theme that ties person, process, and outcome together in some way that extends the significance, meaning, or value of the event?

The Jungian method for looking at archetypes includes studying myths, ceremonies, symbols, and stories. For example, considerable insight into the psychology of women (and the feminine aspects of men) comes from analysis of the myth of Psyche and Eros (Johnson, 1977), the story of Helen of Troy (Leonard, 1983), the myth of Inanna-Ishtar (Perera, 1981), or the symbol of the marriage basket (Andrews, 1981). To better understand the psychology of the entrepreneur, we look at the stories and myths of heroes.

THE HERO'S JOURNEY

Consider for a moment that an entrepreneur is a type of hero, in search of adventure and treasure. Although entrepreneurs have been glamorized in the U.S. of the 1980s by exemplars such as Steven Jobs (Apple Computer), they have not always been models of virtue (e.g., the "robber barons") and although virtuous, they have not always been respected by society. Nor are heroes always appreciated or rewarded by their own social groups. The call to adventure takes the hero away from his or her group and may require activities that deviate from the norms of the group. Heroes are rarely legends in their own time.

To look at entrepreneurship as a heroic journey is one way to expand its function (e.g., see it more broadly as a behavioral pattern) and to examine its significance. We begin with an overview of the hero's archetypal life by synthesizing many heroic tales, which are not mere stories but "a reality lived . . . believed to have once happened in primeval times, and continuing ever since to influence the world and human destinies" (Raglan, 1956, p. 126). Raglan describes twenty-two features or incidents that are found in the various tales of heroes. These are listed in Table 5.2.

TABLE 5.2   The Hero's Life

1. The hero's mother is a royal virgin;
2. His father is a king, and
3. Often a near relative of his mother, but
4. The circumstances of his conception are unusual, and
5. He is also reputed to be the son of a god.
6. At birth an attempt is made, usually by his father or his maternal grandfather, to kill him, but
7. He is spirited away, and
8. Reared by foster-parents in a far country.
9. We are told nothing of his childhood, but
10. On reaching manhood he returns or goes to his future kingdom.
11. After a victory over the king and/or giant, dragon, or wild beast,
12. He marries a princess, often the daughter of his predecessor, and
13. Becomes king.
14. For a time he reigns uneventfully, and
15. Prescribes laws, but
16. Later he loses favour with the gods and/or his subjects, and
17. Is driven from the throne and city, after which
18. He meets with a mysterious death
19. Often at the top of a hill.
20. His children, if any, do not succeed him.
21. His body is not buried, but nevertheless
22. He has one or more holy sepulchers.

Source: from Reglan, *The Hero: A Study in Tradition, Myth, and Drama,* Franklin Watts 1949, reproduced by permission of Pitman Publishing, London, England (Westport, CT: Greenwood Press, 1956).

While entrepreneurial heroes may indeed have lives like this, we are most interested in the adult years of the hero, steps 10–17 in the table—the journey to the kingdom and fighting battles to achieve success, winning the spoils of victory, and managing the kingdom. Seen as the entrepreneurial event it might look like this:

1. The entrepreneur, reaching a plateau or experiencing a displacement, finds a need to prove him- or herself.
2. In venturing, he or she finds that competition, bankers, suppliers, and customers present serious, venture-threatening problems, which he or she solves.
3. The entrepreneur establishes a business, which is often experienced as "mistress," "child," or "family."
4. The entrepreneur becomes CEO.
5. For a time the entrepreneur runs the business smoothly.
6. The entrepreneur designs the organization, establishes procedures, hires and trains managers and other employees, and builds organizational momentum.
7. The entrepreneur loses the favor of outside investors who want return on their investments or of employees who want more pay, respect, or control.
8. The entrepreneur is forced to change the organization (e.g., through public offering, acquisition, or unionizing) or leave.

As we look more closely at these stages, we find personal and social transformations that help explain more about entrepreneurs. Figure 5.1 depicts this journey.

The figure depicts an individual journey and represents both outer activity and inner development. In the story the transformation of the person/hero is as important as the acquisition of treasure or the conquest of a kingdom. The journey is an allegory for becoming conscious and whole or self-actualized as a person. Since their journey is personal, the hero and heroine are not group-oriented, although they will assemble the resources, crews, or teams necessary to accomplish their goals.

Research on entrepreneurs suggests that personal development is very important, and that the goals of money or power are not the most important objectives in undertaking the risks and responsibilities of a new venture (see Chapter 3). What seems important is the opportunity to test one's limits, to explore, and to learn. Also important to entrepreneurial success is the ability to see oneself and one's context or envi-

FIGURE 5.1   The Entrepreneur as Hero: The Journey

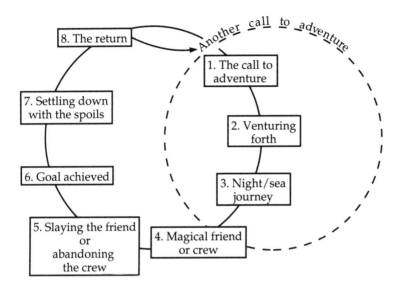

ronment (including opportunities and resources) as clearly as possible. Finally, the individualism of entrepreneurs seems obvious in many cases where the entrepreneur wants or needs to act as sole author, having objective, utilitarian, and exchange-oriented relationships rather than subjective, personal, and co-authoring relationships (e.g., preferring an employee to a partner).

The call to adventure.   The journey begins with the call to adventure. The hero, inspired by some sacred or secular vision of the outcome, takes up the call to adventure. The quest is both external (to market a product, build an organization, find a treasure) and internal (to test his or her limits; self-discovery); failing to find inspiration or failing to act, he or she falls into stasis (inertia or status quo positions in organizations and society). Staying on the hero's path requires accepting and managing the tension between the vision (the call) and what is (the status quo)—what we call temporal tension.

Entrepreneurs experience the "call" in different ways and at different times. Many decide in youth that they will be self-employed. Others generate a winning business concept later in life. For some the journey resolves the inertia of a plateaued career or unemployment. Whenever and however opportunity knocks, we know that entrepreneurs are volunteers, freely and consciously deciding to take the risk involved in finding the treasure. Most will not see this career decision as a path of personal transformation. However, if archetypal energies infuse it, the decision will transform the entrepreneur.

Venturing forth. Once called to the venture, the hero goes forth into the unknown. Because no one has taken *this* journey before, first steps are uncertain and risk seems great. For the entrepreneur, this stage of the journey means *action*. He or she makes commitments, changes his or her lifestyle, refocuses support systems, and proceeds to set up business. Without the movement from idea to implementation, inertia sets in. This explains why so many business concepts are never implemented and why some serious potential entrepreneurs never fulfill their potential.

Night/sea journey. Taking up the call to adventure, the hero must undergo a series of "tests," here called the night/sea journey. The path is dark, uncertain, and full of unanticipated obstacles, some of which are genuinely frightening and stressful—objective barriers in the real world and self-limiting unconscious beliefs. The path is wet, possibly oceanic, symbolizing emotionality and the feminine unconscious in most men.[2] This represents a possibly prolonged period of self-questioning, anxiety over resources, fear of competition, anger at regulations, uncertainty, stress, and loneliness. The entrepreneur must surmount obstacles and face personal limitations without losing sight of the goal. Said an aerospace entrepreneur:

> You're driving down the road to go someplace. There's a detour sign, a hole in the road, a traffic jam. You've got to go off course to keep moving. You've got to remember where you want to end up. So you say to yourself, "I'll go down so many blocks. As soon as I can I'm going to make a left turn and then another turn and get back on course." A

[2] The hero's journey is a fairly masculine one. The feminine version is slightly different. The cycle of taking the call to adventure (or awareness) is much the same although the adventure is more one of healing; lessons involve dealing with inertia, patience, and interpersonal relations more than with conquest, treasure hunting, and colonization. In a woman the masculine is unconscious and her journey might be more one of desert survival than a night/sea journey. See de Castillejo (1973), Johnson (1977), Perera (1981), and Woodman (1985) for insights into the feminine journey.

lot of people can't do that. Faced with a detour, they get lost. They say, "I know if I stay on this road I'll get there. You make me turn off it, I'm finished."

Magical helpers. To pass safely through the obstacles, including the limits of personal abilities, talents, and stamina, heroes need a "magical friend" and/or a "crew." The magical friend could be a spouse, friend, mentor, role model, key employee, financial advisor, or imagined figure who helps the entrepreneur overcome obstacles and maintain a sense of purpose and direction. The friend is a "true believer" who helps the entrepreneur remain conscious of his or her vision and personal power in the darkest hours. The crew or team is any group of such friends. The friends, family, crew, or team represent the necessary resources (including money) and talents to surmount the barriers, find the treasure, and reach the goal. The inner lesson here is one of *trust* and, in the entrepreneur's case, delegation.

A good example of the magical crew is the collaboration that John P. Stack has implemented in his leveraged buy-out and turnaround of a division of International Harvester, now Springfield Remanufacturing Center Corporation. To make every employee a member of his team, Stack teaches people the "game of business," shares key financial data, and rewards performance. As a result of employee involvement, Stack has shown impressive results including sales growth of 40 percent per year and a reduction of the debt-to-equity ratio from 89:1 to 5.1:1 in three years (Rhodes & Amend, 1986).

Remaining independent. Toward the end of the hero's story, the magical friend or crew cannot or will not do what the hero alone must do. The last obstacle is the hero's personal test, and he or she must go ahead alone, moving beyond the friend's influence ("slay the friend" or abandon the crew). Once again the inner developmental issue is trust—this time self-trust and knowing when to be independent and when to consult with others.

This suggests that entrepreneurs need to return to autonomous decision making and personal responsibility. Although delegation works in most circumstances, a timely use of centralized decision making results in the flexibility and speed that are the strategic advantages of the entrepreneurial firm.

The aerospace entrepreneur previously mentioned provides a good example. His style of management is to leave the team/organization to work out most problems and to intervene and be personally involved in key decisions only when progress stops.

> When slowed down you have to resist temptation to get in. When things stop, that's when you get in. Everybody should know that. When you're a manager and people have seen you resist [going in directly to solve the problem] when things are slow [and instead] work through the delegated people. . . . when they see you exercise that kind of discipline on the one hand and when they have seen you, and they have seen me in this company, go shoot the jackass when the column has stopped. . . . [Here he refers to the scene from the movie, *Patton*, where the general shoots the donkeys who stop his column on a bridge]. . . . then what happens is they develop an atmosphere in the company: "Don't ever let the column stop."

Enjoying goal achievement.   The treasure finally in hand, the hero is invited to enjoy the fruits of his adventure. He is offered the keys to the city, a house on the hill, a princess to marry, and numerous inducements to settle down. For the entrepreneur, the goal is the immediate and short-term rewards that come with venture success (profits). This might include leadership in the business community, membership in the country club, and other things that money and recognition can produce.

Continuing adventures.   If the hero is to complete his learning and personal transformation (and not fall into inertia), he must return to the place where the call to adventure began— back "home," back to the source of inspiration. Inner development is completed here with the realization that the goal and the rewards are not what the adventure was all about. Once back to the source, on another level of the spiral path, the hero is again open to the call to adventure and the cycle is repeated.

If the entrepreneur is not to fall into organizationally prescribed roles or submit to the control of the enterprise he has created, he must go back to the creative process and remain open to opportunities and willing to risk. For many this means another business venture. For others it begins a political career or a calling to "do good." (More will be said about this and sequential and parallel ventures in Chapter 6.)

Implications

The archetypal approach to the entrepreneurial personality focuses attention on the potential relationship between outer activity and inner development that occurs during the process of creating or transforming organizations. Instead of predicting what "causes" an entrepreneur or predicting the financial outcomes of entrepreneurship, this model asks questions about how the project serves to develop the person.

Here the project or venture is an outward manifestation of inner visions and development. Although there is little research on how ventures might mirror the entrepreneur, providing him or her with important personal insights, the model suggests this might be so. Anecdotal evidence from the mainstream of organizational behavior research suggests this relationship might exist. For example, I have observed a student low on self-confidence write a dissertation on self-confidence, and another who needs the support of others studies networking.

The metaphor of the hero's journey and its linkage of personal and outer transformations (value-adding) suggest that there is value for the entrepreneurial players (including advisors and employees) in becoming aware of this correspondence. For the entrepreneur, consciousness of inner states, personal lessons, and self-development are important to intentions and the concrete outcomes of intentional action (i.e., organizations; Bird, 1986). These insights are also important to learning from one's experiences (see Chapter 12).

One interesting aspect of the Jungian model involves the inherent tension between the uncertainties of adventure and leaving or avoiding a relatively certain and comfortable status quo. Many overcome inertia through being "pulled" into venturing by opportunities. Others are "pushed" by uncontrolled changes in the status quo such as unemployment, being out of school, being released from the army, and being plateaued or passed over in their organizations. In other cases, the entrepreneurial career is the preferred and planned-for choice. Future research might examine the differences between displaced and voluntary entrepreneurs in the meaning, significance, and value of the venture.

We would expect entrepreneurs with clear nonmonetary goals based on personal values to experience a different form of psychic involvement with and personal growth from their firm. As long as the firm is self-sustaining economically, the venture is an opportunity to experience values in action, perhaps more clearly a call to adventure than firms begun for other purposes. Of course, even firms that fail to become self-sustaining offer opportunities (most often short-lived) for this type of experience and learning.

We expect the journey of the entrepreneur to differ depending on the entry process—slow versus fast start and whether it is a start up, acquisition, franchise, or corporate venture. The journey will also vary depending on the industrial and technological context and the way ownership is structured.

Other questions remain. What happens to the person, in terms of developmental issues, when the organization becomes successful? What are the differences between the first venture and subsequent ones in terms of personal development? What kinds of entrepreneurs are aware of the correspondence between inner and outer work? I hope that future research into entrepreneurship will include examination of the meaning and significance of the work to entrepreneurs and their teams.

CHAPTER 6

THE PLACE: SITUATIONS THAT CATALYZE ENTREPRENEURSHIP

INTRODUCTION

Thus far we have looked at the make-up of the individual entrepreneur in terms of background, personality, and creativity. Individual characteristics help us predict entrepreneurial behavior—who will become an entrepreneur and how successful that effort will be. However, there is considerable "error" in predictions based solely on the individual. People with similar characteristics make very different choices; only some potential entrepreneurs become entrepreneurs, and only some entrepreneurs succeed (survive and grow). Likewise, entrepreneurs vary considerably in terms of personal characteristics, and for every generalization about the "right stuff" of entrepreneurship, important exceptions can be found.

To aid in our understanding and predictions of entrepreneurship, we need to look at the situations and conditions that predispose people to entrepreneurial behavior. The context that precedes an entrepreneurial event is important to understanding why, of all the people whose personalities predispose them to entrepreneurship, some actually act as entrepreneurs. The situations surrounding entrepreneurial events also help explain why some people succeed where others fail, and how the organizations created by entrepreneurs are likely to develop.

THE NATURE AND IMPORTANCE OF CONTEXT

Context refers to the tapestry of events, circumstances, situations, settings, environments, and niches that surround the entrepreneurial event. This chapter will look at antecedent or catalytic contexts that predispose or enable a person to engage in entrepreneurship and the economic, social, and political impact of entrepreneurial activity. Implications for strategy (governmental policy aimed at entrepreneurship and organizational strategy aimed at firm survival and advantage) will be addressed briefly.

The *context of entrepreneurship* is the larger framework of events and circumstances within which the entrepreneurial event occurs. At a societal or general level, context includes the (1) economic, (2) political, and (3) technical "givens" of any moment of time in any location, (4) the *Zeitgeist* or spirit of the times, and (5) the cultural milieu. Thus the availability of equity capital, human resources, a public stock market, and large markets for products or services, as well as the opportunity to make and keep money, are important general contextual variables in the entrepreneurial event (Johnson, 1985). At a more operational level, important contextual variables include perceptions of stock-market conditions, the degree of risk aversion among large holders of capital (individuals, institutions, pension funds, foundations, and banks), the presence of research universities, the unemployment rate, taxation, real estate and transportation costs and availability, technical networks, and the regional quality of life. Market size is a variable related to the industry the new venture enters, and includes market structure, "the number of buyers and sellers, barriers to entry, product differentiation, cost structures, and the degree of vertical integration" (Sandberg, 1986, p. 44) and the growth rate of the market.

These societal context variables usually do not change quickly and are the subject of most policy interventions by governments and social activists such as Chambers of Commerce and small-business lobbying groups. Along with other market variables, these determine the relative support and nurturance available to new ventures (and thus the survival and growth of some).

At a specific level (i.e., in a new venture or the rate of firm births in a given region), context includes the displacement, through immigration and unemployment, of specific individuals or groups within a region. Other aspects of the specific context include localized intentional and formal efforts to nurture and promote entrepreneurship (usually called incubators) and the intended and unintended creation of new organizations by parent organizations (in the form of organizational spinoffs). Each of these aspects of context will soon be discussed in turn.

Figure 6.1 shows these variables and how they affect entrepreneurship. The general or societal context affects the individual through his or her background and history. The specific context is contemporaneous and directly affects the entrepreneurial event. The entrepreneurial event, in turn, affects the context, changing resources and opportunity structures and making economic, social, and political contributions at local, state, and national levels (e.g., jobs, products, and exports).

THE ECOLOGY OF ENTREPRENEURSHIP

A number of observers have addressed the aggregate view of new ventures and have found an ecological model to be appropriate and useful. Essentially, this model looks at populations of organizations and is concerned with the aggregate birth and death rates of firms in given economic regions. Thus issues of organizational foundings (e.g., which ideas get funding), organizational failure and conversely survival, and organizational persistence and transformation should be considered from this perspective.

One model is analogous to natural selection in biology. It posits that populations of organizations compete within their species (e.g., industrial type), and that those most equipped with useful innovations (akin to genetic variations) are more likely to survive both competition for scarce resources and changing environmental conditions. In this model, the environment (markets, financial conditions, political conditions, etc.) selects certain organizations for survival and potential growth and selects against others (which dissolve through bankruptcy, acquisition, or merger). An extension of the model considers "communities" of organizations of different "species" and the synergy or competition among organizations of different industrial classifications in given regions.

An alternative model of the same reality (venture entry, survival or death, and growth) is strategic. Dealing with new ventures at the firm or organizational level, strategy approaches aim at helping particular organizations achieve com-

FIGURE 6.1   The Context of Entrepreneurship

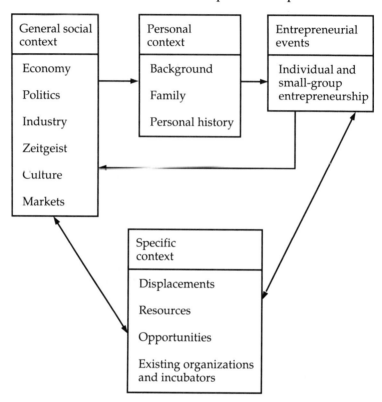

petitive advantage. Thus, rather than being selected by ecological or environmental "forces" outside the control of individual entrepreneurs (or their teams), successful ventures are thought to act intelligently and proactively.

SURVIVAL: SELECTION BY "NATURE"

Like the food chain in biological niches, entrepreneurial ventures compete with and form support relationships with larger, established firms and other new ventures. This occurs with an economic niche or community of organizations. The relative advantages and liabilities of large established and small new firms merit consideration.

Liabilities of newness and smallness.   Entrepreneurial firms, at least at the outset, face two inherent liabilities that work against favorable selection—being new when other organizations are older, and being small when other organizations are larger. The liability of newness includes the new venture's internal need to learn new roles, negotiate and organize different roles, and form trusting relationships with strangers (Stinchcombe, 1965). This liability also includes external conditions and relations such as the need to develop linkages to customers (Stinchcombe, 1965) and other barriers to entry such as "(1) product differentiation, (2) technological barriers, (3) licensing and regulatory barriers, (4) barriers of entry due to vertical integration [of competitors], and (5) illegitimate acts of competitors" (Aldrich & Auster, 1986).

Thus the start-up venture faces many obstacles just because it is new. Although many of these obstacles are not present if the entrepreneur acquires a going concern, some may still affect the firm's success since the focal entrepreneurs are new to being entrepreneurs or to leading these particular ventures.

A good example of an acquisition that eliminated some of the liabilities of newness and capitalized on the many years of industrial management experience of the founders is Solo, a high-technology firm contracting to the defense industry. Says the founder about the decision to buy a going concern:

> If you want to buy a business, you buy an existing business that has operations already established even if they're not the best. They have instant credibility. However, you go down the checklist of qualities of the firm you want, checking off everything on the list except sales. Buy one that doesn't have sales. That means, buy a business in an area where you feel you have market access where the existing firm's market situation is the pits.
>
> We found a business where sales were poor because the original owner had retired, left an employee-manager to just take orders off the phone, and didn't allow any market development. He had written off the assets of the business. So we offered him a fraction of the value of the assets, a ridiculous offer, and he accepted it.

The liability of smallness is conceptually independent from the liability of newness (although most ventures start out both new and small). Most organizations remain small as they age; a small minority of firms reach substantial size in terms of sales or employment (Birely, 1986; Reynolds, 1987). The liability of smallness includes: (1) more problems in raising capital (trouble getting it, paying higher interest rates and facing greater threats to entrepreneurial control by investors than larger firms); (2) a tradition of fewer tax advantages compared to larger firms; (3) proportionally greater costs from government regulations (where larger firms can streamline ways to meet governmental demands and proactively gain favorable treatment); and (4) competitive problems in finding and retaining skilled workers and managers (Aldrich & Auster, 1986). Thus the start-up venture faces certain obstacles just because it is small. We would expect acquisitions and growth-oriented ventures to face fewer of these obstacles.

Advantages of smallness and newness. Entrepreneurs can and do obtain distinctive advantages over larger organizations in their ability to introduce value-adding innovations. Large organizations tend to be characterized by excessive bureaucracy and its correlates—rationalism, inappropriate incentives, short-term horizons, intolerance of fanatics, and isolation of top management. In contrast, entrepreneurial organizations have fewer sunk costs, longer time horizons, an ability to exercise trial-and-error learning, managers and workers with personal motivations linked directly to tangible organizational outcomes, and flexibility and quickness (Quinn, 1985).

> A new enterprise [compared to established firms] . . . does not have to change an internal culture that has successfully supported doing things another way. . . . Organized groups like labor unions, consumer advocates, and government bureaucracies rarely monitor and resist a small company's moves as they might a big company's.
>
> Quinn, 1985, p. 74

Implications

The liabilities of newness and smallness operate with other environmental factors (considered below) to select against many new ventures. Theorists use these factors to predict the aggregate death rate and the selective retention of some organizational forms over others. The limitation of this approach is that it is difficult to see how an individual entrepreneur can predict his or her chances of success or anticipate what he or she can do to militate against failure. The strategy recommendations following from this approach are to acquire a firm instead of starting up, to form tight links (through franchising or long-term contracts) to larger and older organizations that can shield the new venture from some of these liabilities, and/or to plan to later merge with or be acquired by a larger, older firm (Aldrich & Auster, 1986).

SURVIVAL: STRATEGIC "NURTURE"

Just as agronomists can intervene in certain biological niches to produce greater crop yields and plants and animals with greater resistance to disease and harsh conditions, so too can entrepreneurs and policy makers intervene to aid the new venture. Some researchers have looked at how new ventures have adapted or adjusted their structures, policies, market orientations, leadership, and other internal factors to better compete and thus survive and grow. New ventures can and do adjust their innovativeness, legitimacy, network, size and growth, and niche within which they compete and perform. While nature selects, individual firms can intentionally change to survive and grow—which is the essence of new venture strategy and planning.

Innovation: The introduction of variation. New ventures tend to have advantages over larger, older firms in terms of innovation, introducing disproportionately more product innovation and process innovation (Aldrich & Auster, 1986). New ventures have the advantages of: (1) new leadership with less concern for retained earnings, payout of profits, or conservation of capital; (2) less formalization and specialization (e.g., less bureaucracy with intrinsic red tape and slow response times); (3) employees and managers with less vested interest in how things are done or how resources are allocated (e.g., less resistant to change); and (4) employees and managers of considerable diversity who are informally socialized or trained for their jobs, leaving considerable role ambiguity and also freedom to innovate and create their jobs. New venture strategies that take advantage of the firm's variety, novelty, and ability to change quickly should contribute to the firm's survival and growth.

Legitimacy. Organizational legitimacy refers to perceptions of outsiders and insiders that this venture can and will perform well and over time. "Organizations with high reliability, a low variance in performance, and high accountability, the ability to account rationally for organizational actions, are favored by selection processes in organizational populations" (Singh et al., 1986). Although simple passage of time (i.e., age of the firm and organizational learning) and experience of the entrepreneur (his or her prior understanding of management and leadership) result in much of the reliability and accountability of the venture, one variable that can be strategically manipulated is the perception of venture legitimacy. A study of nonprofit organizations shows that the greater the external legitimacy of the venture (in terms of endorsement by powerful external agencies and the development of strong relationships with external constituencies through a board of directors), the greater its chance of survival (Singh et al., 1986). Thus new ventures that create the perception of size and legitimacy enhance their chances of success.

Dan Moore, founder of Moore Plastics, a plastics extrusion company, applied this principle in his early start-up. In contract negotiations to supply parts to one of the major automobile firms, representatives from Detroit wanted assurance that Moore could supply the volume they would require. In essence, he needed to overcome the liability of smallness as his manufacturing set-up was very limited. To create confidence, he created the image of size by using storage space containing unrelated pieces of equipment and boxes he covered with canvas tarps. When the visitors arrived, they were shown "top secret" equipment that could not be uncovered for proprietary reasons. Moore got the contract and gained increased legitimacy in the financial community. Later, to meet demand and to ensure his control over operations, he bought property and substantially expanded his operation. While questions of ethics can be raised with this example, it does point to the importance of legitimacy, or perceived market presence and ability to follow through with products and services.

Networking. As suggested earlier, new ventures can form strategic relationships with larger established firms. Additionally, ventures may link themselves with other entrepreneurial firms and other entrepreneurs. These other ventures offer entrepreneurs a peer group for shared learning and support, and offer ventures advantageous trade relationships through networking. These relationships are discussed in greater detail in Chapter 10.

Start big and grow fast. Another strategy for long-term survival and growth is to start with volume sales and planned growth. A one-year longitudinal study of firms in Minnesota found that survival was predicted by "being an older firm; not being in the retail sector; a strong pattern of initial sales and sales growth; lower job growth rate; and an emphasis by management [the year before] on financial issues and on the implementation of strategy" (Reynolds, 1987, p. 239). Of particular interest is the development pattern of the high-potential firms—those with high initial sales and high sales growth over one to five years. These firms represented only 31 percent of the sample but accounted for over two thirds of the sales, exports to other states, and new jobs of the total sample (Reynolds, 1987). Because they start bigger and grow faster, they overcome the liabilities of smallness faster than low- or slow-growth firms, they are at risk for fewer years, and they subsequently have survival advantages over other firms.

Nichemanship. One strategy for the survival of new ventures is to find a market segment, a tailored and high-value-added product, or another "niche" that is protected from large firm competition. Large firms may be uninterested in small market segments or may find the cost of entry prohibitive. The ecological concept of a niche refers to combinations of resources in the environment necessary to survive and grow (Hannan & Freeman, 1977). For organizations, a niche refers to an industrial classification and a geographic position, and includes the labor supply, financial resources, governmental policies, the technology available for the production of goods and services, and the structure of the marketplace.

Most frequently, new ventures are advised to compete by becoming specialized in a niche too small to be of interest to larger, older firms.

> The extant literature generally advises small firms not to meet larger competitors head-on. They should concentrate on specialized products, localize business operations, and provide products which require a high degree of craftsmanship. . . . [They should provide] customer service, product customization, and other factors which are inimical to large-scale production.
>
> Cooper, Willard, & Woo, 1986, p. 248

However, the authors of this study find that direct competition with industry leaders is a viable strategy under certain conditions. (1) When the industry is changing as a result of "deregulation, new technology, organizational and management innovations and changing consumer preferences," (p. 251) new ventures can find competitive advantages. (2) When there are opportunities for product or service differentiation through adding value or subtracting (simplifying) value to meet consumer preferences, small, agile firms have advantages. (3) New ventures also benefit from introducing a new production technology that can lower price and allow direct competition with industry leaders (Cooper et al., 1986, p. 251).

Thus new ventures can choose strategies that focus on niches, tailored products, and small segments of the market or strategies that take advantage of the liabilities faced by larger, older industrial leaders. Whichever strategy is used, the assumption behind it is adapting the new venture to enhance its chances for survival and growth.

Implications

Entrepreneurs and their teams can and often do act to control the venture's innovativeness, legitimacy, size, growth rate, and market niche. To the extent that these variables are chosen, premeditated, and planned, a new venture strategy has been formed. If the entrepreneur and his or her team respond reactively or impulsively, strategy is nonexistent, unconscious, or emergent.

We would expect entrepreneurs with the goal of venture growth to behave more strategically, and to use more strategic planning in the organizing process, than entrepreneurs with lifestyle goals. Likewise, entrepreneurs with technology backgrounds and products would need to pay more attention to strategic innovativeness than those in low-technology domains.

GENERAL CONTEXT: ECONOMIC, SOCIAL, AND POLITICAL CONDITIONS

While new ventures operate in specific industrial and market niches and are affected most by direct competitors, suppliers, and customers, new ventures also operate in larger contexts. Entrepreneurs and their ventures operate in certain economic regions, societies, and cultures—and not in others. They begin at certain historical times and not at others. This larger context and its cycles affect the new venture process from inception through survival to growth and maturity.

ECONOMIC, TECHNOLOGY, AND MARKET CONDITIONS

Economic, technological, and market conditions are expansions of the particular niche within which an organization operates. These variables cover more time and territory than the niche, and cross industry and market boundaries.

Economic conditions. The economic conditions that seem important to the emergence of new ventures include capital available for high-risk investment. Most ventures are financed initially from the savings and borrowings of the lead entrepreneur(s), family members, and friends (Birley, 1985a). Recently financial industries have turned some resources to the provision of "seed" capital that is needed to fund initial product development and preliminary market research. Often this is provided by private, informal, and local investors called "angels" (Logan, 1986; Neiswander, 1985). Later-stage high-risk capital is provided by venture capital firms that finance a small number of companies (for one to three percent of the business plans reviewed each year), usually those with balanced management and track records of product and market development. Other sources of later-stage financing include bank loans (Churchill & Lewis, 1985) and loans and equity investments made through Small Business Investment Corporations (SBICs) (Feigen & Arrington, 1986).

Another economic condition that correlates positively with the birth of local new ventures is high unemployment (more will be said about this in the section on displacements). Paradoxically, low unemployment—along with social conditions such as high percentages of well-educated mid-life adults—correlates with the birth of new firms likely to participate in larger markets (i.e., more likely to export out of state) (Reynolds, 1987).

Technological and market conditions. Economists Michael Piore and Charles Sabel (1985) argue that the marketplace for mass-produced goods is nearly saturated (i.e., such goods have become commodities) and that consumers (households and other businesses) demand more specialized and tailored products with higher quality. This market force, combined with the flexible technologies made possible by microcomputers, results in a competitive advantage for innovative small businesses. The long-term trend from mass production to craft (small-batch) production could result in small business becoming "the dynamic leading edge of the economy" (p. 36).

Other visionaries also see a competitive advantage in small business ventures. Paul Hawken (formerly of Erewhon Trading Co. and now with Smith & Hawken) suggests that a reshaped world economy is emerging. One important aspect of this macroeconomic change is the changing ratio of product mass (size and energy) to product information (design, utility, durability), with size decreasing and the complexity of products increasing. For example, adding information to products such as "smart" houses, cars with displays of approximate miles that can be traveled before running out of fuel, and even bags of mesquite wood for barbeques that include history or recipes, adds value to the mass of these products. Smaller businesses are better able to capitalize on this trend "because small businesses can change more quickly, have better internal communication, and can tailor their products more specifically to smaller markets" (Hawken, 1983, pp. 88–89).

Peter Drucker (1984) agrees that technology-based and knowledge-based new ventures are important, making up one third of all new ventures. Drucker also declares "with high confidence that we are no more than midway into this period of renewed technology-based entrepreneurship" (p. 61). Besides technology-based firms, Drucker sees one third of new ventures in the service area and one third in the "so-called primary activities that create wealth-producing capacity (education and training, health care, and information)" (p. 60).

The supply and demand for entrepreneurs have also changed. On the supply side, more entrepreneurs bring management experience and training to their first ventures; many bring previous venture experience; and some bring considerable start-up capital from personal savings and severance pay. On the demand side, entrepreneurship figures importantly in the creation of jobs, taxes, and exports (in products and services) for a region or state and also in the "Third Sector" (nonprofit but nongovernment) and "Fourth Sector" (public-private partnerships) (Drucker, 1984).

TURBULENCE AND CHAOS

The entrepreneurial context is one of turbulence and change. Entrepreneurial organizations tend to fare better than more stable firms in rapidly changing environments (e.g., high technology) and new organizations tend to bring about "the most ambitious advance[s]" in an industry (Klein, 1977, p. 77) and thus induce change and uncertainty. In this context of uncertainty and change, as many new ventures fail as are just starting up—at least in the United States.

> The entrepreneurial environment is constantly changing, and at an accelerating rate, and in all directions at once. And what counts is your ability to sense what's going on in that confusion, make sense out of it, and turn it into some

form of corporate activity that is profitable. It's very very difficult—like walking a multidimensional tightrope every minute of the day.

Birch, 1985, p. 32

This chaos is particularly apparent in emerging industries such as voice-activated computing, expert systems, organ transplantation, and AIDS treatments. In such industries there are no established rules of the game. Barriers to entering an emerging industry include: (1) proprietary technology, (2) access to distribution channels, (3) access to raw materials and labor at competitive cost and quality, (4) cost advantages to early entrants from trial-and-error experience, and (5) risk due to technological and marketplace uncertainties (Porter, 1980). Such barriers are usually more easily transcended by entrepreneurs than by managers of larger, established firms.

Opportunities from confusion. The very confusion and volatility of the environment creates an opportunity for entrepreneurship. Says Don Valentine (of Sequoia Capital, a venture capital firm serving Silicon Valley and other areas),

> One of our theories is to seek out opportunities where there is major change going on, a major dislocation in the way things are done. Wherever there's turmoil, there's indecision; and wherever there's indecision, there's opportunity. When it becomes obvious to anybody who reads *Time* magazine . . . it's already too late in the cycle to invest. . . . So we look for the confusion phase, when the big companies are confused, when other venture groups are confused. That's the time to start companies. The opportunities are there, if you're early and have good ideas.

Valentine, 1985, pp. 30, 32

Ongoing fluctuations. Not only are organizations born out of turbulence, they continue to fluctuate in size and "health" as a result of debt/equity problems that occur with rapid growth, cash flow problems, people problems, market changes, new competition, and internal debate over the strategic uses of resources. As a result of both "slings and arrows of outrageous fortune" and conscious choice, entrepreneurial organizations develop unevenly (and thus with more internal turbulence), with periods of progress followed by slow growth and/or setbacks. In their study of the strategy of a retail chain over 60 years, Mintzberg and Waters (1982) found a series of "sprints and pauses" in the expansion of the organization. In this case, the organization exploited short-lived opportunities by stretching human and capital resources, followed by periods of slowdown and recuperation. These ups and downs or "pulsations" describe how organizations do in fact grow (Birch, 1985). Furthermore, these pulsations may be necessary for growth and therefore strategically chosen (Mintzberg & Waters, 1982).

Creating a disturbance. Through their fits and starts, aggregate "births" and "deaths," and the resulting variety, novelty, and turnover of organizations in the larger social system, entrepreneurs *create chaos*. First conceived of by Schumpeter (1934/1961) as "creative destruction," the disturbance created by entrepreneurs has been more recently described by Gilder (1984) as a rebellious and revolutionary act, one likely to produce fear in business elites and politicians. Perhaps this explains how the entrepreneurial efforts in a small rural town provoked political behavior as reported by Gatewood, Hoy, & Spindler (1984).

> Public sector inducements led to entrepreneurial activity which disrupted the status quo. In the resulting disorganization, the mayor and the City Council fought for control over economic development. . . . The old guard were obstacles to entrepreneurial activity but were unable to prevent it. . . . As the conflict intensified, the control exercised by the power elites over economic development was reduced, and the level of entrepreneurial activity increased.

Positive value of chaos. Others argue that the very instability of the small business sector aggregates to assure the security and stability of the larger economy.

> Let me put in a metaphor for you—it might help to resolve the paradox. When they first built those huge space-rockets down in Florida, they had a problem of how to get them from the assembly site to the launching pad. It was like moving a skyscraper. So they thought first of building a road—a good, thick, solid, stable road. But they realized that the motion of the truck, combined with the enormous height of the rocket, would set the whole vast superstructure weaving around like a tall tree in a gale. So what did they do? They made the road out of a deep bed of pebbles. Of course the pebbles moved under the weight of the thing—it was hell down there, all that grinding—but the movement, the grinding, compensated for the motion of the rocket, and the overall system was stable and secure.

Birch, 1985, p. 42

Figure 6.2 diagrams the chaotic environment of the entrepreneurial act. It shows how (1) environmental uncertainties (e.g., interest rates, sources of supply, changing consumer tastes, deregulation) and (2) new venture uncertainties, which are more immediate specific aspects of the context (e.g., capitalization, staffing, and location) result in (3) opportunities for the entrepreneur. Acting on some opportunity, entrepreneurial behavior (4) produces a new or transformed organization, adding new values to the social system or marketplace. In the process, entrepreneurial organizations "pulsate," change directions and speeds, and either succeed or discontinue operations. These (5) outcomes of entrepreneurial behavior themselves add to the chaos of the entrepreneurial environment, both generally and specifically.

For example, George and Sarah McCune saw an opportunity in a market niche that their employer (a large publishing house) did not value. They began Sage Publications, a publisher of social science books aimed at researchers and scholars, under conditions of uncertainty (they did not know this market niche and had no formal financing). Since its founding Sage has demonstrated value added to this market segment and subsequent profitability, and this has spawned similar competitive efforts in larger publishing firms.

Implications

We might expect fewer or smaller sprints and pauses and less impact on the context from firms that stay small or start and grow slowly. There is likely to be a bigger splash with a bigger, faster start-up. There could be little or considerable turbulence around an acquisition, depending on whether it is "friendly" and if continuity is strategically called for. We would also expect more turbulence in high-technology niches than in low-technology niches. Survival and advantage may be found and fostered by entrepreneurs who sustain temporal tension (notwithstanding the uncertainty of the future), maintain flexibility and vigilance, and work to maintain alignment of resources to the venture idea.

SOCIAL AND CULTURAL CONDITIONS

The social system, the culture, and "the spirit of the times" within which the entrepreneur begins a venture operate to either encourage or discourage that venture. Entrepreneurial conditions vary across national and other geopolitical boundaries, with differences in history, government, and culture.

FIGURE 6.2   Turbulence and Entrepreneurship

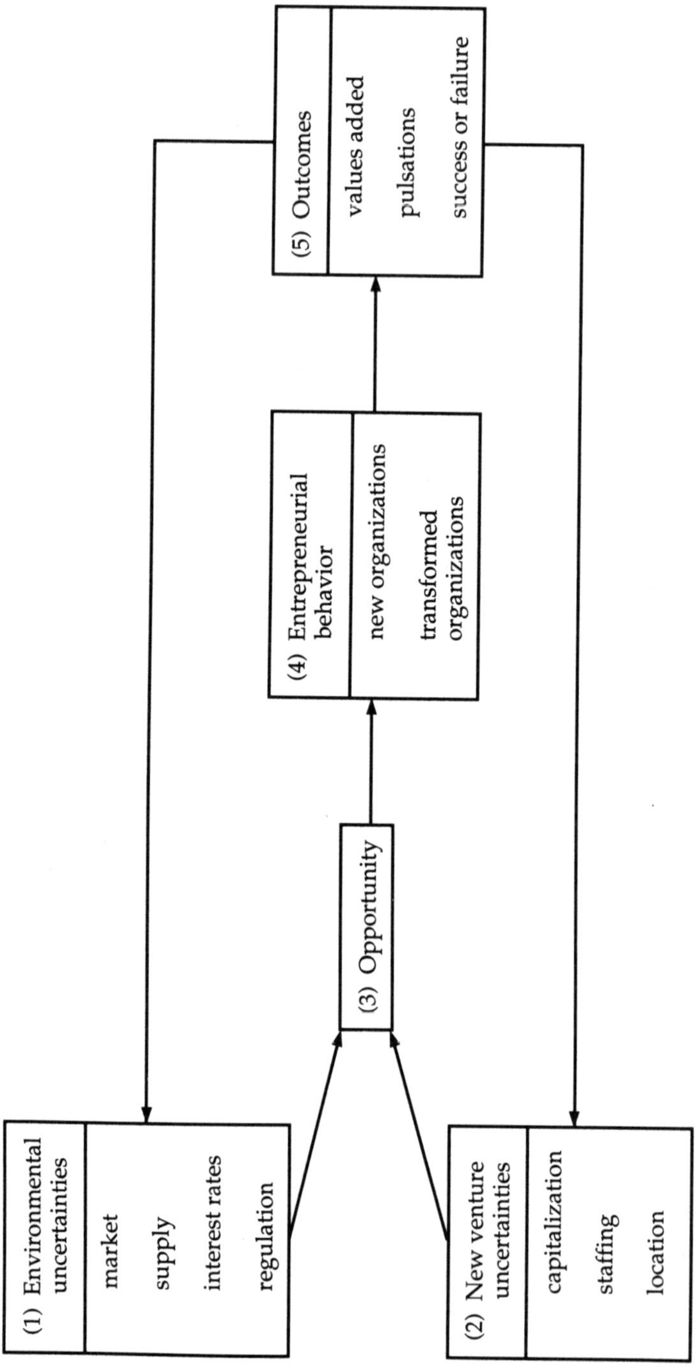

(1) Environmental uncertainties

market

supply

interest rates

regulation

(2) New venture uncertainties

capitalization

staffing

location

(3) Opportunity

(4) Entrepreneurial behavior

new organizations

transformed organizations

(5) Outcomes

values added

pulsations

success or failure

These differences have been used to explain the difficulty policy makers face in fostering new businesses in certain European countries ("The word spreads," 1983).

As cultures change, so do the opportunities for entrepreneurship. For example, recent changes in cultural conditions in Vietnam and the People's Republic of China have apparently given rise to new entrepreneurial activity. Even the United States, facing economic competition in the 1980s, called forth a revival of its ancestral entrepreneurial spirit.

Recent social changes. In the United States, a recently surfaced social need for heroes and the recent publicity surrounding entrepreneurs such as Steven Jobs (Apple Computer and more recently NeXT, Inc.), Mitch Kapor (Lotus Development Corporation), or Fred Smith (Federal Express) make entrepreneurial activities seem both more desirable and more feasible to more people. In addition, "baby boomers" have arrived in the prime age bracket for beginning entrepreneurial careers (30–45 years old), making entrepreneurial activity more probable.

Social forces have also produced record numbers of two-income households and working women. The economic impact of these trends includes "record amounts of personal savings," which make new ventures more feasible because of available start-up capital and the opportunity for one spouse to quit work to start a new venture (Farrell, 1985). In addition, these social changes create demands for new products and services such as restaurant chains, continuing education, and daycare, making these and other new ventures more likely (Drucker, 1984).

Implications

The arrival of entrepreneurial activity in socialist regions may auger other changes (entrepreneurship works best within systems that allow people to make and keep money and that have a public stock market, a pool of talent, and market access). Demographic changes, along with changes in regional policies and social values, will have an impact both here and abroad.

POLITICAL CONDITIONS

Political conditions, as suggested in the earlier description of the need for free markets and private capital, are also necessary to create the context for entrepreneurship. Regions with high taxation, corrupt governments, and government-run industries work against the development of new ventures with growth potential.

Recent political changes. The "entrepreneurial decade" of the 1980s has also been marked by important political changes. Ronald Reagan carried much of the "rugged-individual" and "free-market" ideology with him into the office of president. According to Michael Piore, an MIT economist, "the thrust of the country's economic policy under President Reagan has been the removal of restraints on individual creativity and initiative" (1986). Whether Reagan has always acted consistently with this ideology is not the point. The point is that through deregulation (which opened markets to new competitors) and reductions in capital gains taxes in 1978 and 1981 (which made venture capital economically rational and more widely available), government action has fostered entrepreneurship (Farrell, 1985).

More generally, since political change or turmoil of any kind creates economic disorganization, entrepreneurs may find unique opportunities during or following times of unrest. Specifically, entrepreneurs may find ways to organize currently disorganized resources—thereby adding value and making a profit. Alternatively, political turmoil may actually release resources to be used to build new organizations (Wholey & Brittain, 1986). However, severe and extended political unrest, such as that occurring in many developing countries, may militate against the long term survival and growth of new ventures.

SPECIFIC CONTEXT: DISPLACEMENTS

While organizations are born out of environmental chaos, the individuals who create new organizations are affected by their own personal uncertainties. As discussed in Chapter 5, individuals often carry with them turbulent childhood experiences and a motivation to escape from insecurity and/or poverty.

However, the personal turbulence may be more immediate, occurring in adulthood and "pushing" or "pulling" the individual off his or her current career path and into an entrepreneurial career. Research suggests that many new businesses (both Mom-and-Pop and growth-motivated concerns) are started by people who are socially "displaced." Shapero

(1982b) describes displacement as a "detracking" force that pushes (or pulls) one from a state of inertia into starting a new business. While displacements can be positive pulls (e.g., encouragement and persuasion from a potential partner), most entrepreneurs report a negative push. Negative displacements include being a refugee or voluntary immigrant, having been fired from one's job, job dissatisfaction, being "between things" (as a recent graduate, recently discharged from the armed services, or retired), and being psychologically displaced by a change of health or a "traumatic" birthday (e.g., turning 40).

Shapero theorizes that displacements contribute to individual perceptions of the desirability and feasibility of starting a new business. Figure 6.3 shows the relationship between displacing experiences and perceptions of venture possibilities. When faced with changes in our life paths, we give fresh consideration to the future. As we always have some choice in the direction of our new paths, we consider our alternatives. We *can* choose to become self-employed—to start or acquire an organization. Recall that there are no involuntary entrepreneurs.

At the choice point we review our perceptions of venture desirability. Is the venture concept worthwhile? Do I like the idea? How do others feel about it? Often, entrepreneurship is more desirable than alternatives (e.g., collecting unemployment, working for someone else). Perceptions of desirability are a function of personal and social values developed through family, friends, and prior experiences.

At the choice point we also review our perceptions of venture feasibility. Can I do it? Do I have control over the necessary resources? How long before I generate a positive cash flow? Sometimes, venture feasibility is thoroughly analyzed in the form of a business plan, and this plan is shared with others and refined. At other times it is a quick, personal calculation. Perceptions of feasibility are a function of the support available—one's network and team. Feasibility perceptions are also enhanced by having seen other, similar ventures launched and succeed.

Among middle managers laid off during the streamlining and merger mania of the 1980s, Don Bigda offers an example of how displacement frees up the entrepreneurial spirit. In 1986 his employer, Needham Harper Worldwide, merged with Doyle Dane Bernbach Group, Inc. and BBDO International, and at the age of 40 Bigda was laid off. He took $60,000 of his $250,000 severance pay and bought an equity stake in a small

FIGURE 6.3   Entrepreneurial Event Formation Process

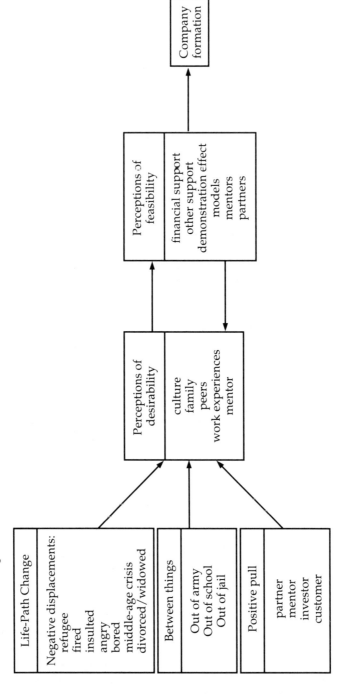

Source: "Entrepreneurial Event Formation Process" from *Some Social Dimensions of Entrepreneurship*, by G. Shapero, p. 15 (1982).

advertising agency started by former colleagues (Cole, 1987). The combination of capital and the time/talent to invest made venturing both feasible and desirable.

In other cases, displaced workers rely on unemployment insurance, considerably less severance pay, and savings, and these shrink with each month a person is out of work. In these situations there might be considerable urgency in getting a stream of income started. Unless the now-unemployed person had been planning a venture before the displacement, a new venture is not likely to be his or her first consideration. Alternative work situations will be explored first, and only if suitable employment cannot be found will a new venture be likely. Once it is considered, though, we would expect those who choose to venture to do so quickly, with minimal planning. They have no "slack resources" for part-time involvement or moonlighting. When based on financial insecurity, these ventures would probably begin with the monetary goal of income substitution. When combined with poor planning, this makes such ventures poor candidates for rapid growth and long-term survival.

SPECIFIC CONTEXT: INCUBATORS OF ENTREPRENEURSHIP

Some organizations have unintentionally fostered entrepreneurship by creating situations in which employees leave to start their own businesses. Other organizations have been consciously created to house and nurture early-stage start-ups. There is considerable confusion among researchers because both types of contexts have been called incubators. Here, we shall use the term *spinoff* to refer to organizations that develop, often unintentionally, from parent organizations. These spinoff organizations can be new start-ups or managerial buy-outs of going concerns, including the purchase by managers of a business unit of the parent organization. The term *incubator* will refer to organizations created to nurture (shelter, support, energize) several fledgling organizations. These will be discussed at length later.

SPINOFF BUSINESSES

Large organizations often create the context for entrepreneurial careers in two ways. First, they can do so by creating autonomous businesses that provide input to the parent firm or extend a technology/service developed by the parent firm.

Such spinoffs are planned and form part of the parent's investment portfolio (i.e., the parent may have the controlling interest). Planned spinoffs constitute about 30 percent of all spinoffs (Allen, 1986).

Second, organizations can foster entrepreneurship by being unable or unwilling to support employee-initiated innovations or otherwise frustrating employee needs, or by laying off, firing, or retiring employees (Cooper, 1972; Martin, 1984). Employees who leave under such conditions may take the entrepreneurial career path, sometimes in order to compete with the parent firm. This form of spinoff is unplanned and constitutes a majority of corporate spinoffs.

EXAMPLE: MEMOREX

In 1969 Alan Shugart left IBM, along with key engineers, to build and lead a Memorex team that designed a successful new hard disk storage system. Shugart, a charismatic leader who was dubbed the "Pied Piper" by his associates, oversaw the projects as vice president of research and development for Memorex. However, in 1973, when the team had completed the project, Memorex "had no real follow-up projects for the charged-up engineers" and was in a precarious financial position. Shugart left, and subsequently started Shugart Associates in 1973 and Seagate in 1979. Another twenty-eight Memorex engineers followed to start their own separate but related ventures, or joined Shugart in one or more of his ventures, which define most of today's disk drive industry (Russell, 1984). Some of these are:

Engineer	Venture
Tony LaPine	LaPine Technology Corp.
James Morehouse	Amcodyne, Inc.
Mike Monett	Memory Technologies, Inc.
Geofrey Lee	International Memories, Britton-Lee
Finis Conner	Shugart Associates, Seagate
Johan Willems	Drivetec, Inc., Storage Technology
Robert Franchini	Drivetec, Inc., Shugart Associates
Herbert Thompson	Shugart Associates, Drivetec, Inc.
Syed Iftikar	Seagate, Syquest Technology
Don Massaro	Shugart Associates, Metaphor Computer Systems

Engineer	Venture
Duane Meulners	Dymek Corp.
Larry Pyle	Shugart Associates, Data Management Labs
Terry Johnson	Miniscribe Corp.
David Brown	Quantum Corp.
David Osborne	Entrepo Inc.
Jugi Tandon	Tandon Corp.

In several studies of spinoff organizations, Cooper (1971, 1972, 1985) and his associates (Cooper, Dunkelberg, & Furuta, 1985) have found the following patterns:

1. Spinoff organizations tend to be located in the same geographical area as the parent organization.
2. Spinoff enterprises tend to use technologies and markets closely related to the parent.
3. Business organizations spawn new businesses more frequently than nonprofit organizations, such as universities and research institutes, spawn ventures.
4. Smaller organizations (i.e., fewer than 500 employees) have higher spinoff rates than large organizations.
5. Parent organizations are frequently the source of entrepreneurial teams, with two or more employees leaving together to start a new venture.
6. When people leave large organizations, the motivation is frequently a "negative displacement," whereas those who leave smaller organizations (including their own previous ventures) do so for more "positive attractions."
7. Those who leave larger organizations are able to start larger-scale businesses with higher first-year sales.

There is another type of spinoff venture, one that involves the purchase of a part of a larger business by a management and investor team. The trend toward divestiture is growing. "If the 1960s was the age of corporate growth through acquisition, the 1980s may well go down as the age of deconglomeration," (Mahar, 1985, p. 78). As large organizations shed their less profitable, less mainstream units in an attempt to streamline, corporate managers frequently become owners. The purchase by managers through highly leveraged buy-outs or venture capital usually benefits all parties—the larger organization frequently gets a premium price for the business; the managers get a chance to fly with their own ideas; investors have a relatively secure investment; and customers can remain satisfied (Mitton, 1982). Organizations that have divested businesses to managers include General Electric, Litton, ITT, and others (Mahar, 1985). Finally, we note that the purchase by an entrepreneur of a corporate business unit protects the venture from the initial liabilities of newness and smallness, since it has been protected by a corporate parent during its early development.

PLANNED INCUBATION

As part of a social movement to foster economic development, technology transfer, entrepreneurship, and innovation, non-profit (and more recently for-profit) centers have developed for the incubation of new start-ups. An incubator is "a building, a section of a building, or proximate buildings where for-profit enterprises rent space. Additionally, the facility must arrange for management consulting services for tenants" (Allen, 1985, pp. iii–iv). Such buildings can be new or renovated industrial, commercial, or educational buildings (e.g., former schools).

The number of business incubators is growing rapidly. In 1985 there were 70 incubators identified in the United States, most of which had started in 1983. As of 1987 there were approximately 200 existing business incubators and many more in some stage of planning (based on the over 400 attendees at the National Business Incubation Association meeting in March, 1987). There are many such centers in the United Kingdom (which used business incubators for business development much earlier than the U.S.), Europe, and Japan; Japan has one in operation and 10 being planned. The growth of the incubator industry can be attributed to recognition by local and regional governments and business communities that planned economic and social conditions (and assistance) can foster business development, job creation, and economic health.

All incubators exist to nurture new and small businesses by providing individuals (entrepreneurs and their teams) with "skills and knowledge about business operations and opportunities and [motivating] individuals to start a business" (Allen, 1985, p. i). However, each incubator is unique, expressing local needs, resources, and opportunities. David Allen (1985) found three additional dimensions to differentiate among incubators—specifically the degree and way in which they provide (1) multitenant, flexible rental space at lower than market rates, (2) business or management consulting services (e.g., legal, accounting, marketing, business planning), and (3) shared "overhead" in the form of physical services (e.g., building maintenance, heat, conference rooms, and so forth) and office support services such as reception, typing, and photocopying. In addition, incubators also provide business contacts and linkage to "networks" that provide access to re-sources—formal and informal investors, customers, suppliers, and so forth. In essence, incubators provide new ventures some protection against the liabilities of newness and smallness.

Types of incubators. Based on his research on 46 incubators in the United States, Allen (1985) suggests that there are three types of incubators: public/nonprofit, private/for-profit, and university-affiliated. Nonprofit incubators are primarily inter-ested in the generation of jobs and secondarily interested in economic diversification, expansion of the tax base, building renovation, and becoming financially self-sustaining (through rents and charges for services). Tenant firms are selected to reflect local labor and political realities and ventures tend to be younger, locally owned start-ups. Length of tenancy is usu-ally limited; the average is about three years. Rents tend to be the lowest among all types of incubators (an average of $2.50 per square foot in 1985).

Profit-oriented incubators tend to fall into two categories: (a) those seeking return on financial investments in tenant firms (a form of venture capital) and (b) those seeking added values through the development of commercial and industrial real estate (i.e., being a landlord). Tenants are admitted on either their potential as an investment or their ability to pay rent, and are least likely to have limits on occupancy time (i.e., they can stay as long as they can pay the rent and they need no additional space). Rents tend to be the highest among all types of incubators (an average of $9.10 per square foot) (Allen, 1985).

University-affiliated incubators serve some of the non-profit and profit objectives above. They differ in that a research university provides important technical consultation as well as a vehicle for the commercialization of faculty research. Tenants are chosen for their relationship to the university's missions/research, for their use of advanced technology, and for being environmentally "clean." Occupancy duration is limited as in nonprofit incubators. Rents are moderate (an average of $6.13 per square foot) (Allen, 1985).

Incubator as a new venture. Like the small businesses they serve and house, incubators are ventures that require the leadership of an "incubateur" or incubator manager who has some of the qualities of the entrepreneur (and, possibly, a prior career as an entrepreneur) and some qualities of the manager. The responsibilities of the incubator manager include fundraising and grant administration, building renovation and maintenance, acting as landlord, providing advice, network liaison, public relations, and so forth. Finally, the incubator manager may or may not participate in the profits from incubator activities (rents or equity in tenant firms).

Like other organizations, incubators go through stages of development and face their own developmental problems. "The start-up stage begins with concept initiation and ends about the time the facility reaches full occupancy [or break even]. Activities during this time are primarily real estate driven" (Allen & Hendrickson-Smith, 1986, p. ii). Concerns begin with site selection and building renovation and culminate with leasing concerns and the desire to fill the building.

The second stage, business development, occurs after about two or three years and is characterized by managers spending more time with tenants, acting as advisors and advocates for them. During this stage, tenant businesses may enter into synergistic trade relations (providing products and services to each other, often at a discount). With facilitation by the incubator manager, seminars may be offered and tenants encouraged to provide mutual support and advice. Incubator managers may become concerned with "graduation" policies and rent structures.

The third stage, maturity, is reached after about four or five years and is characterized by "high demand for space, and comprehensive, sophisticated business services available to tenants" (Allen & Hendrickson-Smith, 1986, p. ii). Because the U.S. incubator industry is rather young, less is known about the problems and opportunities facing mature incubator organizations.

As the incubator industry grows and develops, there is a tendency to move from "general-purpose" incubators that house businesses of all kinds to niche-oriented incubators. Recently, new incubators have focused on specific types of tenants. The Biomedical Research and Innovation Center in Miami and the Kitchen Center (focusing on small food-processing companies) in Spokane, Washington, are two examples (Galante, 1987).

Implications

Both forms of incubation involve a reconfiguration of opportunities and resources. Spinoffs involve individuals capitalizing on experience, contacts, and inventions derived from corporate life. This raises questions of corporate ownership and, if the parent firm does not intentionally create free-standing firms, litigation over proprietary information and trade secrets may ensue. More large businesses are attempting to protect themselves from employees-turned-competitors through contractual employment relationships. For the entrepreneur who leaves, the new venture he or she creates or acquires offers opportunities to lead through vision, alignment, and attunement, linking resources to create values not recognized by the parent firm.

Planned incubation offers financial help in the form of lowered costs and easier access to resources. Incubators are likely to encourage faster entry into venturing as well as independent venturing over other types of entrepreneurship. There is some indication that many incubators are technology- or industry-specific (e.g., light industries only, high-technology industries only, health-care industries only) and therefore help to direct resources and opportunities in narrow contexts.

ECONOMIC, SOCIAL, AND POLITICAL OUTCOMES OF ENTREPRENEURSHIP

New business start-ups and entrepreneurial activity affect the economy, as well as social and political systems. As suggested earlier, entrepreneurship provides the "creative destruction" of the economic and political status quo that is necessary for "self-renewing economies" (Shapero, 1981a). Specifically, new ventures are more likely than older established firms to innovate (Klein, 1977) and in doing so, they are more likely to change the market, the competition, and industry dynamics. New ventures also influence the local context through the creation of new jobs, new taxes, and other transfers of money (Shapero, 1981a). For example, David Birch (economist, professor, and entrepreneur) reports that "66% of all new jobs created between 1969 and 1976 were created by companies with 20 or fewer employees" (1985, p. 36).

As suggested earlier in this chapter, this self-renewing capacity so necessary for growth comes with a social price tag: turbulence, change, and uncertainty. The businesses that exist today may not exist tomorrow (we'll have more on "failure" in

Chapter 11). While products, services, jobs, taxes, and cash flows are created by new business, the continuity or stability of any particular product, service, job, etc. is uncertain.

CONTRIBUTIONS

Politicians, business leaders, economists, and scholars are keenly interested in fostering new ventures, particularly those new ventures that make significant contributions to local, regional, and federal economies. These contributions include the creation of jobs, sales, and exports.

Perhaps the most important of these contributions is the creation of jobs. In 1979 David Birch noted that small and new businesses created more new jobs than the largest firms in the United States. Sales are also important because they result in social, political, and economic benefits through taxes, flow of capital, and vitality instead of stagnation. Exports, especially to other countries, are important contributors to the balance of payments; exports from one state to another contribute to the relative well being of that state.

Paul Reynolds (1987) has longitudinal data for the contributions (jobs, sales, exports to other states) made by new ventures in Minnesota. Most contributions are made by a small proportion of new ventures, specifically by those with high initial sales and rapid growth of sales (16 percent of the firms in his study). Says Reynolds, "The results are unequivocal—high-start up, high-growth [in terms of sales] new firms provide contributions that are 6–20 times greater than low-starting, low-growth new firms" (1987, p. 239).

A more detailed look at the data reveals that for construction, manufacturing, and distribution services, initial personnel problems are positively related to subsequent sales. For producer services, retailing, and consumer services, a management focus on financial problems is positively related to sales. Job creation was positively influenced by initial personnel problems in manufacturing, distribution services, and producer services (except in retailing). Job creation was positively influenced by a management focus on financial problems in consumer services (Reynolds, 1987). Finally, from another study of firms in Pennsylvania, Reynolds and Freeman (1987) find that export-oriented firms (20 percent of the sample) account for 45 percent of total sample sales and 31 percent of total sample jobs. These results suggest that firms in different industries and markets have different growth dynamics and therefore differ considerably in their economic impact. Based on the findings we predict that ventures formed for income substitution and those that are slow in the start-up phase (e.g., part-time ventures) will make fewer contributions. If stakeholders are interested in locating high-potential contributors, they must look at the initial size and early growth patterns of the venture.

ORGANIZATIONAL OUTCOMES

Yet another fruitful approach to entrepreneurial contexts looks at the organization created by the entrepreneur. This approach involves a model of *enactment* in which the entrepreneur organizes reality by labeling, attending to some information while ignoring other input, and interpreting events, resources, and experiences (Ford, 1985; Ford & Baucus, 1987; Weick, 1979). These interpretations and labels are shared with others inside and outside the organization, and become expectations of the future. In this way, the entrepreneur calls forth an organization that becomes "real" or "socially constructed" and later constrains opportunities and resources. Stated another way, the entrepreneur creates an organization with a particular set of beliefs, assumptions, values, and expectations—or, more generally, a culture. This culture develops its own momentum and becomes the context for subsequent venture process and for individual work, including the entrepreneur's work. This aspect of context is elaborated in later chapters dealing with the leadership role of the entrepreneur.

SUMMARY OF CONTEXTUAL FACTORS

Figure 6.4 depicts many of the contextual elements that foster (or impede) technology-driven entrepreneurship. Although the diagram deals specifically with technology-based new ventures, it offers a contextual map for other types of entrepreneurship. The diagram shows how the social and economic climate (includes cultural norms and government policies) interacts with technical resources available in the context (e.g., a university, a supply of engineers from existing firms, a research hospital, etc.) to produce incubator organizations (for spinoff or planned incubation). Incubator organizations give rise to potential start-up teams. The business infrastructure and climate of the context (e.g., potential suppliers and customers; the prosperity of these, etc.) combine with other factors in the quality of life of the region and the presence of start-up teams to produce new technology-

FIGURE 6.4   Dynamic Model of the System for Creating
New Technology-Based Organizations

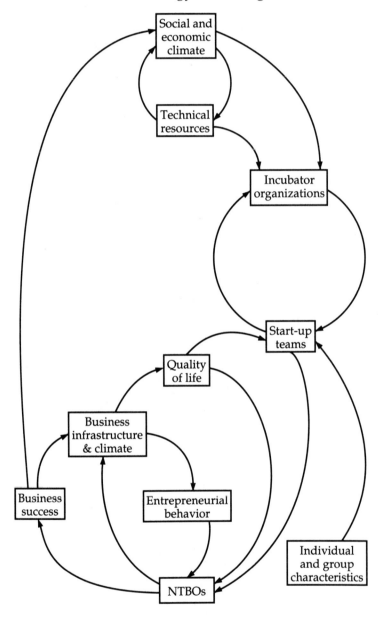

Source: S. Hart and D. Denison, "Creating New Technology-Based Organizations: A System Dynamics Model," *Policy Studies Review*, 6:512-528
(Tempe, AZ: Sage, Policy Studies Organization, Arizona State University,
1987).

based organizations (NTBOs). Hart and Denison (1986) propose that these relationships result in (or fail to result in) a *critical mass* of knowledge, people, experience, and motivation.

> As more firms are successfully created within a given Technology Development Cluster [local context], a perception of entrepreneurial business success begins to emerge. This helps to augment the network of entrepreneurial individuals and groups, technical linkages, capital sources, and business services that can be drawn upon by start-up teams with a technology-based new business idea. Once this system of networks reaches a "critical mass" *it begins to feed off itself, multiplying the experience base.* . . . As this agglomeration process proceeds, *it creates a "culture of experimentation."* . . . [and] has the effect of slowly altering the investment portfolios and risk preferences of an increasingly wide set of more traditional investors and consultants. (Emphasis added)

> Hart & Denison, 1986, pp. 13–14

IMPORTANCE OF CONFLICT

This chapter has described the general and specific contexts of entrepreneurship. These contexts help determine whether or not a given individual will start a venture and how successful that venture or type of venture is likely to be. Contextual variables also determine how many ventures in various industries and niches are likely to begin and/or cease operations in a given region.

The context interacts with individual characteristics described in earlier chapters. That is, entrepreneurial behavior cannot be predicted only by having the "right stuff" as an individual. The situation must foster, demand, or catalyze entrepreneurial tendencies. Nor can entrepreneurial behavior be predicted by merely having a context that supports new ventures. Individuals must be motivated and competent to assume the risks and responsibilities of initiating and sustaining a new venture.

Policy makers interested in increases in entrepreneurship in a given region have two "levers" to press. First, they can attempt to create contexts that allow and nurture entrepreneurial behavior. That is, they can change economic, political, and social infrastructures and create incubators for fledgling organizations. Second, they can attempt to motivate individuals and provide them with experience so that more men and women will take the call to adventure. Incubators can create policies that allow entrepreneurs to reap financial and social rewards for their risk and provide counseling, education, and information to assist the entrepreneurial process.

CHAPTER 7

THE PATH: CAREERS AND LIFESTYLES OF ENTREPRENEURS

INTRODUCTION

This chapter addresses the way that entrepreneurs operate by looking at the paths they take into, through, and away from their ventures. These paths are entrepreneurial careers. The concept of a career involves important individual characteristics (e.g., motivation, personality, styles of behaving) and important characteristics of the situations in which one works. First, we will describe the concept of a career and point to some behavioral theories and models of career processes. We will then extend those theories to look specifically at entrepreneurs. Next we will look at different "types" of entrepreneurial careers, and last, at the stages of entrepreneurial careers.

Most organizational observers agree that the concept of a career "suffers from surplus meaning" (Hall, 1976, p. 1). For most of us the term conjures up notions of the jobs we hold, have held, and hope to hold. Some extend the notion to nonwork activities that help define our lives—our hobbies, avocations, and family life. Hall (1976) lists four assumptions about careers: (1) A career is not an evaluative concept; it does not imply success or failure, fast or slow progress. (2) Career outcomes such as success or failure are best assessed by the focal individual. (3) A career is a behavioral concept with subjective and objective facets. (4) A career is dynamic, not static; it is an experimental process carried out over time, which links us to whatever we call "work." Hall's working definition of *career* is the individually perceived sequence of attitudes and behaviors associated with work-related experiences and activities over the span of the person's life.

Hall, 1976, p. 4

A related definition by Schein (1977) highlights the importance of the person-situation interaction in careers.

The career can be thought of as a set of stages or a path through time which reflects two things: (a) the individual's needs, motives, and aspirations in relation to work, and (b) society's expectations of what kinds of activities will result in monetary and status rewards for the career occupant (p. 52).

Most approaches to careers have looked at the process from three perspectives: (1) the aspirant making an initial career or job choice, (2) the organization selecting and training individuals, and (3) the concerns of career advancement and career change among adults. We will briefly discuss each of these approaches and their application to entrepreneurs. Although the entrepreneur's career is the focus here, this discussion will also have relevance to those *choosing to work for entrepreneurs* and for those *assuming entrepreneurial roles in large organizations* (e.g., intrapreneurs).

CAREER CHOICE

A model of individual career choice is shown in Figure 7.1. The figure shows how individual personalities, abilities, and social situations influence occupational choice. The important variables in career choice are: (1) the individual's awareness of his or her skills, attributes, and abilities; (2) the individual's awareness of his or her career alternatives; (3) the perceived requirements for beginning the career; and (4) the time a career decision is made (early in life, later, or never). These factors influence the entrepreneur's perceptions of venture desirability and feasibility.

As shown in Figure 7.1, aspects of the individual's personality, experience, and background result in "immediate determinants" of occupational choice. For the entrepreneur these determinants include prior industrial or management experiences, the need for independence and control, and other variables mentioned in Chapters 2–5. The figure also shows situational or contextual variables that result in "immediate determinants" of career choice (covered in Chapter 6). For the

FIGURE 7.1   Model of Entrepreneurial Career Choice

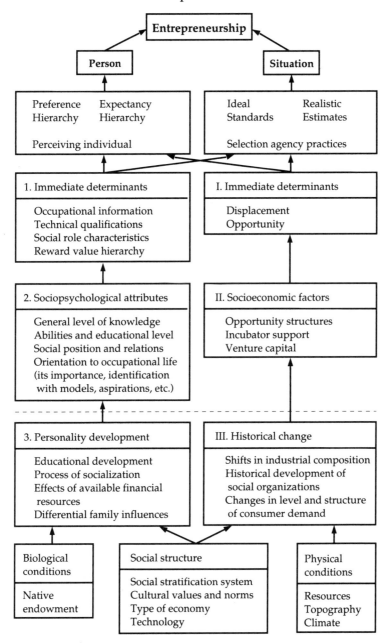

entrepreneur these are displacements and opportunities; for the intrapreneur they may include aspects of the employing organization such as availability of slack resources and reward systems. Discussion of how and why employees of entrepreneurs choose the new, small, and rapid-growth venture as a context for their careers is found in Chapter 8. For now, readers are encouraged to extend the model and speculate.

ORGANIZATIONAL MATCHING OF PEOPLE AND JOBS

Organizations recruit, select, train, counsel, promote, fire, and retire members (employees). It is important to note that individual careers are not constrained to one organization. This applies to the career of the entrepreneur as much as to any other. The entrepreneurial pattern of simultaneous and sequential new ventures will be discussed later in the chapter.

To maximize the value of individual contributions and organizational outcomes, people and jobs must be "matched." Matching is partially accomplished through screening and selection processes carried out by both the individual and the organization. Another important aspect of matching individuals to their jobs (and to the organizational culture) is through socialization, whereby individuals learn the rules and procedures (practiced and "official"). Through informal exchanges and formal training programs, individuals learn the relationships and behaviors expected of them. A third way to facilitate the matching is through job redesign whereby jobs are restructured to suit jobholders.

Recall that entrepreneurs are frequently organizational "misfits," unable or unwilling to be supervised, managed, or controlled by others or by systems. Instead of working for someone else, entrepreneurs choose to work for themselves. Instead of joining already existing organizations as employees, entrepreneurs (particularly founders) build organizations around themselves.

Although entrepreneurs build an organization to suit their needs and desires, once underway the organization can take on a life and direction of its own. One of the biggest challenges facing an entrepreneur with a successful and growing venture is how to adapt to the changing demands placed on the CEO. These role transitions are addressed in more detail in Chapter 10. For now we merely mention that organizational growth can often result in a lack of fit for the entrepreneur and another displacement (through acquisition, investor rebellion, going public, and so forth).

ENTREPRENEURIAL CAREERS

There has been some recent interest in entrepreneurial careers, the sequence of job and work experience that precedes and sometimes follows venture initiation, as well as the job of being an entrepreneur. For the purposes of this book, *the entrepreneurial career is the process of deciding to begin and to continue operating as an entrepreneur.*

Entrepreneurial careers are characterized by unique entry points and processes (e.g., most entrepreneurs did not plan to be entrepreneurs; Ronstadt, 1985a) and unique stages of development. The relationships among career, personal life, organizational development, and organizational strategy are also unique in the entrepreneurial career (we continue the thesis that the person and the organization are holistically related, with personal and career crises tightly coupled to organizational issues, causing special problems and opportunities).

TYPES OF ENTREPRENEURIAL CAREERS

Individuals enter into entrepreneurial careers by choice and by displacement. But even when displaced, entrepreneurs *choose* to start a business rather than seek other employment, training, unemployment insurance, or welfare. Furthermore, entrepreneurs enter with different goals, different entry wedges (start-ups, buy-outs, franchising, etc.), and different strategies (which are also consciously chosen) and these influence the type of career experiences encountered by the entrepreneur. There are many ways to organize the different careers of entrepreneurs; one way is in terms of the entrepreneur's goals. The personal and organizational goals of the entrepreneur (or team) at inception will influence and direct (although not precisely determine) the career outcomes of the individual as well as the outcomes of the venture.

Income-substitution career. Entrepreneurs with the goal of working for themselves and earning a comfortable living enter into entrepreneurship as an alternative to salaried or hourly employment. This category includes the growing number of self-employed craftspeople and professionals as well as many small partnerships, often with no employees other than the owners. It also includes many franchisees, some of those who buy small going concerns, and many family and "marginal" or small, stable, income-substitution businesses (Liles, 1974). The organizations generated by this career tend to be very small (with fewer than ten employees). David Birch (1985) suggests that 80–90 percent of small businesses are created to be stable sources of family income.

Small business career.   Entrepreneurs with a community-oriented goal such as prestige, visibility, and membership in the country club must grow their venture beyond middle-class income-substitution levels. They employ more people (the Small Business Administration considers businesses with fewer than 200 employees to be "small"). Many manufacturers, retailers, construction companies, and local businesses tend to be headed by someone with career goals such as these. These "attractive small companies"

> provide salaries of $40,000 to $80,000 [1974 dollars], perquisites (company car, country club membership, travel, and so forth) to its owner/managers and often flexibility in life-style such as working hours, kinds of projects and tasks pursued, or geographical location.
>
> Liles, 1974, p. 7

In addition, there is considerable ego involvement in the organization, and its success and profitability are frequently taken as personal accomplishments.

Growing concerns.   Entrepreneurs who want to see how far they can go, who like the adventure of testing their limits, and who want to amass wealth and influence enter into entrepreneurship as a path to growth. These are the entrepreneurs found in the *Inc.* 500 fastest-growing firms in the United States. The career intention is to do well, score well (in terms of money), and perhaps start all over again.

> The high potential venture is the company which is started with the intention that the venture grow rapidly in sales and profits and become a large corporation. . . . In the high potential venture we find the genesis of the major corporations of the future and therefore, the source of a growing number of jobs and other contributions to the economy.
>
> Liles, 1974, pp. 6–7

Other types of entrepreneurial careers.   From extensive interviews with entrepreneurs, Brooklyn Derr (1984) developed five career "portraits" that incorporate personal history, career history, and stories of the venture development process. First, *small business entrepreneurs*, mentioned above, "spend their early career years working to build a strong capital base and a reputation for trustworthiness, good service, and excellent business character" (Derr, 1984, pp. 8–9).

> Once successful, their creative energies and organizational talents were recognized by community leaders and they were asked to lead fund-raising projects and other activities. These contacts produced, in turn, new venture opportunities which led to more community service (pp. 10–11).

An example of this type of career is that of Jack Bares (of Milbar, Chagrin Falls, Ohio) whose specialty hand-tool assembly business has enabled other family businesses to develop and has provided Bares with funds to advance some social agendas such as family values and education. Bares was recently recognized by the Cleveland Council on Smaller Enterprises (a community-based small-business development organization) for his ten years of leadership in that organization.

Second, the *technical entrepreneur* has "a powerful love for the content of . . . [his] work" (p. 11) but chooses to move beyond technical craftsmanship to build products and organization.

> Unlike the conventional small business entrepreneur, the technical entrepreneur is personally invested in the product itself and sees it as a great service to humanity. Profits and other concrete measures of success gauge the realization of organizational goals rather than symbols of personal success (p. 12).

Roger Frantz of Westsail Industries (Mentor, Ohio) offers a good example of this type of career. Frantz founded and is sole owner of this product-development company, which specializes in medical products, with sales to major medical supply houses and laboratories. The firm (made up of Frantz and eight employees) manufactures and assembles prototypes and initial production runs of products, but is generally not interested in larger-scale production. The reputation of the firm for high quality and performance allows Frantz to choose only those projects that interest him and challenge the company. More specifically, Frantz looks for opportunities to expand his knowledge of new manufacturing processes and work with new materials and machinery. He prefers "hands-on" work and leaves one or two days a week free of scheduled meetings so he can work on the shop floor with internal improvement projects.

Third, *adventurer entrepreneurs* are "driven by a strong need for excitement, competition, and risky self-tests" (p. 15). These are usually loners, unwilling to trust important details to anyone but themselves and perceived by others as intense and compulsive. They may be intrapreneurs or independent entrepreneurs. They get restless when the organization stabilizes and will move on to new adventures.

Although he doesn't quite fit the description offered above, Doug Tompkins of Esprit is possibly an example of this type. Tompkins is shown rock climbing in the introduction to his business on the videotape program "Entrepreneurs" (1986). The narrator begins:

> Doug Tompkins is a world-class mountain climber and adventure sportsman. Four to six months of every year he is incommunicado in the Alps, Antarctica, or the Himalayas. Between trips he runs Esprit.

Unlike the description offered by Derr, Tompkins has let go of operations and only involves himself in creative aspects of the business that affect the Esprit image and direction. Instead of making business an adventure, Tompkins finds his adventure in his leisure activities.

Fourth, the *artist entrepreneur* is an artist first and a businessperson second. These artists let their work be influenced by the realities of the artistic market. Their goals include profits, reputation, and influence in the art world. Examples include the formation of Apple Recording by singers John Lennon, Paul McCartney, Ringo Starr, and George Harrison and the formation of Sundance Productions by actor/producer Robert Redford. Less-visible examples can also be found in some architectural organizations, media production organizations, and so forth.

The fifth career is that of the *administrative entrepreneur.* This is essentially the corporate entrepreneur or intrapreneur who is not motivated by accruing personal wealth (even as a way of keeping score). "They measure their performance by the number of new programs they generate, the viability of an innovation, and the contribution they were able to make to the organization's well being" (Derr, 1984, p. 14). While considered an entrepreneurial career here, there are important differences between intrapreneurs and entrepreneurs and between the corporate and free-market contexts in which they operate.[1]

Across all types of entrepreneurs Derr (1984) found considerable creativity, value placed on organizational growth, value placed on autonomy, and tenacity. Seen as a career line, entrepreneurs appear to travel spirals rather than the relatively straight, upwardly sloping lines that characterize most managers (and which most students in MBA programs expect). That is, entrepreneurs consider, initiate, and develop many business concepts. Some of these become new ventures and many entrepreneurs are involved in multiple ventures, either sequentially or simultaneously. See the discussion of venture-to-venture entry points below.

PHASES OF THE ENTREPRENEURIAL CAREER

Researchers and observers of entrepreneurs find that the entrepreneur's career *as an entrepreneur* has four phases, marked by entrepreneurial decisions (individual or team). The four decisions are: to start the career, to continue, to expand, and to exit. Each decision point involves distinctly different activity requirements, role demands, and emotional strains.

PHASE 1: ENTRY INTO ENTREPRENEURSHIP

The decision to begin a career as an entrepreneur is either premeditated or serendipitous. A premeditated beginning involves planning one's earlier work and education so as to be positioned and prepared for a later entrepreneurial career, (e.g., getting different jobs in the focal industry). A serendipitous entry involves no planning but may involve "bad luck" (a displacement) or "good luck" (an opportunity comes from unexpected sources) that changes one's career options.

The decision to begin a career as an entrepreneur is also partially determined by the individual's perceptions of his or her readiness and restraints (Liles, 1974). Readiness involves the individual's self-confidence in general—his or her willingness to try something new and expectations of success. It also involves a specific self-confidence in the ability to master the

---

[1] See Kanter (1983), Miller (1983), Pinchot (1985), and Schollhammer (1982) for further information on intrapreneurs.

tasks and problems of the new venture start-up, chief of which is gaining control of resources. Such self-confidence increases with age and experience.

> In terms of his decision to initiate a company and to try to run it successfully, a person's own assessment of how ready he is probably is a good approximation of how ready he really is.

> Liles, 1974, p. 8

Restraints are forces operating against the desirability or feasibility of starting the entrepreneurial career. Restraints include success and satisfaction in one's current career or job, family-security concerns, desire for increased non-work time for recreation and leisure, and limited physical or emotional energy for starting something new. Restraints seem to increase with age after one is about 30 years old. Figure 7.2 shows how

FIGURE 7.2 The Free Choice Period for the Would-be Entrepreneur (Liles, 1974)

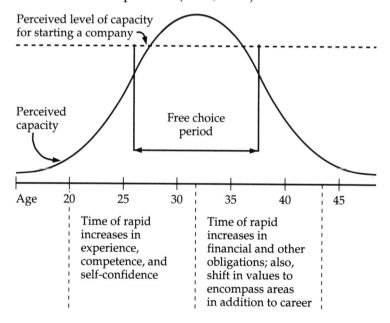

Source: Patrick Liles, "Who Are the Entrepreneurs?" from *MSU Business Topics,* Winter 1974 (East Lansing, MI: Michigan State University).

perceptions of one's own capacity (the curved line) change over time relative to perceptions of the minimum capacity needed to venture (the dotted line).

Career departure points. People enter into entrepreneurial careers from some prior position such as a job, an avocation, or school. Vesper (1980) notes the following five typical departure points.

School to venture. Vesper identifies and details seven types of collegiate entrepreneurial paths. In (1) on-campus and (2) off-campus sidelines, the business is started while in school but is not part of any coursework. On-campus ventures cater to students; for example, UK Student Agencies (an employment agency) was started by Raycon Reynolds while a student at the University of Kentucky. Off-campus ventures market to the larger community; College Pro Painters, Ltd. is a house-painting business begun in 1971 by Greig Clark as a way to support himself while attending the University of Western Ontario. The company now employs 2000 students, and has over 175 franchises, and had gross sales of about $17 million in 1983.

In (3) curricular start-ups and (4) curricular follow-ons, ventures are either started or planned (and later implemented) as a part of a for-credit course. A good example of a curricular follow-on is Softball World, a $2 million private softball facility in Dallas. The venture was conceived by Marty Salfen as a result of combining his personal interest in softball (he pitched for Southern Methodist University) and the feasibility study he did as part of an entrepreneurship course. (5) Extracurricular follow-ons are planned while one is a student (but not for course credit) and implemented after graduation.

In (6) dropout ventures, a student venture succeeds and grows, demanding the full-time involvement of the entrepreneur and precipitating withdrawal from school. In other cases coursework is experienced as unchallenging and unproductive, and dropping out creates a displacement and a context for entrepreneurship. Finally, in (7) direct post-graduate start-ups, entrepreneurship is the first career, there is no planning while in school, and the business is begun directly after graduation. This path is found infrequently. "It appears that unless a student has already worked out an idea for venturing during school, either as part of course work or on the side, the temptation to take a job with a company, rather than drift in search of a start-up, . . . will be too great. If a venture then ensues, it will be after work in another company first" (Vesper, 1980, pp. 66–67).

Job to venture. Vesper suggests that there are four common transitions from prior jobs into entrepreneurship. The first is a direct job outgrowth, where one's prior job created the context for venturing by presenting acquisition opportunities or opportunities to spin off. Perhaps the best example of this is when a former employee buys the business, as happened with Ken Ricci of Corporate Wings (Cleveland, Ohio). He bought the corporate aircraft company in the late 1970s and grew the firm to annual sales of $6 million by 1985. For other examples of employee spinoffs, see Chapter 6.

Second, tangential opportunities may arise from social activities, hobbies, and activities outside the job sphere. For example, a real-estate investment firm may begin with a search for a vacation home, or a day-care center might begin with having trouble finding adequate day care. The third common transition is the sideline start-up, which is started on a "moonlighting," part-time basis and may grow into full-time work. One man began his engineering and architectural firm by moonlighting as a contract engineer while employed. After two years, he left to start the firm, which grew over the next 33 years to employ 120 and attained sales of $7.5 million in 1984.

Finally, planned direct post-job start-ups are planned while still employed but not started until after quitting. Having met his partner while employed at a southern California aerospace manufacturer, John conceptualized and planned four businesses before actually purchasing a firm with undervalued assets, no management, and poor marketing in which the partners could exploit their experience and contacts within the industry.

A recent survey of the readers of *Venture* magazine ("Leaving the Company to Start One," 1985) found the following reasons for leaving previous jobs: (1) independence had been thwarted (55 percent), (2) desire for a new challenge (50 percent), (3) inadequate compensation (39 percent), and (4) lack of employer appreciation (38 percent). Respondents also reported wanting to be able to do things the way they felt they should be done, a need to leave a political situation, and a desire to "write my own destiny." An earlier, more scholarly study suggests that the dissatisfaction with promotion opportunities distinguishes entrepreneurs from managers who have been relocated or promoted (Brockhaus & Nord, 1979).

The job-to-venture path is increasingly popular among black and female managers who see a ceiling to their career aspirations in traditional, white male-dominated organizations (Hymowitz, 1984; Hymowitz & Schellhardt, 1986). A black entrepreneur, whose technology-based firm was twice listed among the *Inc.* 500 fastest-growing private firms, left a *Fortune* 500 firm where he could see no future.

> I could see what my boss's boss had and what he had to do to have it. There was really nothing there to motivate me to continue that track. Rightly or wrongly I felt that I could run more business than they'd ever give me an opportunity to run, for a number of reasons.

One of those reasons was race. After proving himself by running a new business for his multinational employer, the president finally told him the corporation wasn't ready for a black person to be a vice-president.

Unemployment to venture. Shapero (1982b) considers termination, discharge from military service, or the end of formal schooling to be major "displacements" that jar us from our inertia. Such displacements and unemployment contribute to our perceptions of the desirability of starting a new business (see Chapter 4). Vesper (1980) describes four unemployment contexts:

1. Intentional resignation occurs when a person quits a job, usually because of job dissatisfaction, although political disfavor and health problems are also found. After two heart surgeries, HB was forced to take early retirement at age 52. With his wife, who knew that the workaholic HB had to be kept occupied, he investigated and later bought a frame-it-yourself franchise. They now have eight stores and employ 32 people.

2. Layoffs are due to changing economic and technological factors. One report suggests that increasing numbers of laid-off middle managers (15 to 20 percent of the 500,000 laid off between January 1979 and 1984) consider the entrepreneurial career (Freseman, 1985). Laid off from Merrill Lynch Realty Associates in 1984, William Austin (60 years old) and his former boss, Jay N. Torok (48) joined with two other friends to start Lone Pine Industries Inc., an investment firm specializing in leveraged buy-outs (Freseman, 1985).

3. In a discharge a person is fired, usually because the employer is dissatisfied. Thus we might expect increases in faculty entrepreneurship around the time tenure is determined and, in other industrial contexts, after poor performance reviews.

4. The final unemployment context is retirement. Like managers fired from previous employment, retired managers find new ventures a way to fulfill dreams and salvage self-esteem. Those who take action frequently purchase a going concern rather than starting a new one. This was the case for William J. Smith, who retired from American Can in 1982 at age 54 after a 33-year career with the firm. Using the reputation he had built at American Can, Smith acquired a business in the industry in 1983. Asked about retirement in 1986, he says it is "a long time in the future" (Aspaklaria, 1986b).

The transition from employment to entrepreneurship has its own risks—the loss of a retirement nest egg, health insurance, and other benefits—and its own rewards—enhanced self-esteem, challenge, and so forth.

> Of great help in bridging the distance between the two careers [middle management and entrepreneurship] is the discovery that technical expertise, management skills, and business contacts acquired over the years at the corporation are valuable entrepreneurial assets.
>
> Freseman, 1985, p. 60

Home to venture. While we don't know how many new businesses begin out of the home, both low- and high-technology firms have started in apartments, basements, and garages, as seen in the case of Techmar. Techmar produces "add-ons" for IBM, Apple, and other computers. It was started by Carolyn and Marty Alpert to develop and market a technology-based health-care product. The business started in their Cleveland Heights apartment; they later moved into a house where Techmar was initially housed in the basement. The business expanded into all available rooms in the house before the Alperts moved into a formal business setting. Until that move, employees were predominantly "moonlighters."

Although neither fits the Techmar case, two categories of the home-based venture start-up are most common (Vesper, 1980). Homemaker-started ventures are typically begun by women who wish to combine home- and child-care activities with business. These "have tended to be of the stably small venture variety, as opposed to ambitiously growth-oriented" (Vesper, 1980, p. 79) and include handicrafts manufacturing, catering, small retail boutiques, antique shops, small local publications, repair services, day-care centers, and hairdressers.

Family ventures are started by a husband and wife team, sometimes with help from children. These tend to be Mom 'n Pop businesses that provide income (often modest) to the family. Says Vesper (1980) "it is hard to find dramatic success stories initiated by family teams. . . . Few growth companies appear to start this way, and the reasons have yet to be unraveled" (pp. 79–80).

Venture to venture. Some entrepreneurs enter into a new venture during or following an earlier venture—because it is easy and opportunity knocks. "Entrepreneurs tell us it is generally easier to start a second, third, or fourth venture than it is to start the first venture" (Ronstadt, 1984a, p. 106). Ronstadt also points out that, like all learning experiences, the experience of venturing contributes to a learning curve, whereby subsequent venture activities are in fact easier. However, not everyone learns from experiences. Another study reports that the existence of prior entrepreneurial ventures did not differentiate successful from unsuccessful entrepreneurs (Sexton & Van Auken, 1982).

Ronstadt (1984a) reports that over half of the entrepreneurs he studied were involved in multiple ventures. His study suggests that there are two major types of venture-to-venture career movement: (a) sequential (when the entrepreneur ends his involvement with one venture before the other begins) and (b) overlapping (involvement with more than one venture simultaneously). Ronstadt's report shows that 21 percent of Babson College entrepreneurs were sequentially involved and 36 percent had overlapping ventures. These proportions increase when people with longer careers as entrepreneurs are studied (of those practicing for more than six-and-a-half years, 65 percent have had multiple ventures, 21 percent sequential, and 44 percent overlapping).

Other studies support the importance of venture-to-venture career movement (Hornaday & Aboud, 1971; Sexton & Van Auken, 1982). These studies suggest that the exact number of entrepreneurs involved in multiple ventures varies between 20 and 50 percent.

Another way of differentiating multiple ventures is in terms of the similarity between ventures. Vesper (1980) suggests two types of sequential career entry: similar ventures (staying within one technology, market, or industry) and varied ventures (where ventures are significantly different). Multiple ventures probably arise from opportunities perceived because one is already on a venture pathway—what Ronstadt calls the corridor principle (new doorways and paths are invisible until one begins down the corridor). However, more research is needed to reveal just how previous entrepreneurial experience influences current venture development.

PHASE 2: WORKING HARD—THE ENTREPRENEURIAL LIFESTYLE

Once started, the entrepreneur must decide to continue to work as an entrepreneur; ending one's involvement with the venture is always an option. Ronstadt (1984a) considers three factors that influence the decision to continue the entrepreneurial career. The first set of influences are personal qualities such as "persistence, tenacity, creativity and willpower in the face of uncertainty" (p. 52). These qualities reflect the courage and control aspects of personality discussed earlier in the book, as well as a commitment to a way of life (master of one's destiny, self-employed, etc.). The second set of influences are environmental and include continued "displacements," the scarcity of alternatives (depressed labor market), an attitude that "it is somehow wrong for someone who has been, in effect, a lead dancer to 'step back' into the chorus line" (p. 54), and positive anchors such as community prestige. The third set of influences derive from the venture itself and include satisfaction, a sense of accomplishment, excitement, challenge, and the momentum success brings as well as the opportunities that emerge from the entrepreneurial "corridor."

Whatever contributes to the decision to continue, the career and lifestyle of the entrepreneur have unique costs and benefits. Table 7.1 lists some of these as suggested by Boyd and Gumpert (1983) in their study of chief executives of established small companies.

Benefits of entrepreneurship.   The benefits include the ability to control one's own worklife, the financial rewards that accrue to ownership of wealth-producing assets (including the organization itself), the chance to achieve unfettered by a hierarchy, the prestige that follows success, and so forth. The benefits to the person reflect the motivations to choose the

TABLE 7.1 Benefits and Costs of the Entrepreneurial Career

Frequently mentioned benefits*	Frequently mentioned costs*
1. Freedom to make decisions about business	1. Personal sacrifices
2. Accountability only to yourself	2. Burden of responsibility
3. Financial rewards and perquisites	3. Dominance of professional life
4. Feeling of achievement	4. Loss of psychological well-being
5. Involvement in all aspects of the business	5. Lack of human resources
6. Opportunity to respond quickly to change	6. Uncontrollable forces
7. The challenge of taking risks in new areas	7. Isolation in problems
8. Personal contact with employees and customers	8. Friction with partners and employees
9. Having direct impact on company's direction	9. Commitment of personal finances for start-up
10. Absence of bureaucratic and organizational policies	10. Difficulty of finding creative time

*listed in order of frequency

Source: Boyd and Gumpert, "Coping With Entrepreneurial Stress," *Harvard Business Review,* March–April 1983 (Cambridge, MA: Harvard Business School Press, Harvard University).

career. Thus someone with a goal of income substitution will find satisfaction when the venture's cash flow meets his or her income goals. Someone else whose goal is to play the game of business will find satisfaction with the new challenges business development presents. Finally, the benefits to society are aggregate well-being—employment, cash flow, taxation, and so forth.

Costs of entrepreneurship. The costs of the career are less obvious from what has already been said about entrepreneurs and the context of entrepreneurship. Students who begin to study the lives of entrepreneurs are impressed by the following qualities of many entrepreneurial careers.

Entrepreneurs *work long hours for relatively little financial reward, at least in the early stages.* Work weeks of 60–70 hours are common (Hornaday & Aboud, 1971), with one study reporting that nearly one third of the entrepreneurs studied work 70 or more hours a week (Sexton, 1980). Thus entrepreneurs invest considerable "sweat equity" in terms of continuous attention to the business and many sleepless nights. However, the sheer number of hours does not necessarily ensure success and may in fact signal imminent failure. One study found longer work weeks among unsuccessful than successful entrepreneurs (Sexton & Van Auken, 1982), suggesting that the enterprise, having certain "sunk costs," escalates commitment beyond what is rational or that troubled ventures take more time.

Entrepreneurs, especially growth-motivated ones, *rarely take vacations* and when they do, they are frequently achievement-motivated or discovery-oriented, highly intentional activities (Aldrich, 1986). Many entrepreneurs seem to avoid what most Americans call "leisure" and "relaxation." Says Irv Robbins, who started Baskin-Robbins Ice Cream,

> I hated Thanksgiving, Christmas and any holiday when the office was closed, because my list [of things to do] is so long and I gotta go home and play with the kids when I could be at the office cracking away at my list.

Commitment to the venture is expected by others, creating additional psychological investment. Timmons (1978) lists several role demands placed on entrepreneurs by venture capitalists and "generalized expectations." These include the expectation that the venture

> receives top priority for the entrepreneur's time, emotions, and loyalty. . . . Entrepreneurs must be prepared to 'give all' to the building of the business, particularly in the early start-up years. . . . [There is also the expectation that] building a high-potential business requires a total immersion and commitment to that end. [This commitment involves the] . . . investment of life savings, reduction of income, second mortgage, long hours, and neglected family life (p. 12).

As a result of these lifestyle factors, entrepreneurs *need to manage the interface between work and nonwork*—between work and play and between work and family. Some completely separate these spheres of life by not discussing work with their spouses, families, or close friends and having a "no family" policy in terms of hiring. Others merge these spheres and are "unable to easily separate work and play, work and nonwork life, and give almost full attention, energy, and time to starting up a new venture" (Derr, 1984, p. 7). For some of these work is play. It is fun, satisfying, and a source of personal renewal. Many entrepreneurs involve their spouses officially or unofficially as sounding boards, employ their children, and find friends through their ventures.

Despite or because of the work priorities and the boundary problems between work and nonwork, entrepreneurial careers *often jeopardize family life*. The role of the entrepreneur's spouse will be discussed again in later chapters. For now it is sufficient to say that marital tension and divorce are common among entrepreneurs (Wojahn, 1986a), although ventures that are not growth-oriented allow for a greater accommodation of family and community priorities without damaging the business (p. 12). One study reports that 90 percent of the entrepreneurs surveyed felt family time was sacrificed to achieve success (Sexton, 1980), which is not unlike findings among nonentrepreneurial (e.g., managerial, technical) high performers. When entrepreneurship is an unanticipated second career, occurring as a result of termination in middle age, extra stress is often placed on spouses (who may have to return to the workforce for the first time since their marriages) and children (who are college-aged) (Freseman, 1985).

Entrepreneurial work is very stressful. Entrepreneurs tend to behave in a "Type A" or heart-attack prone way. They tend to be "perpetually hurried and impatient. . . . [and] show extreme commitment to the work place" compared to other groups, but are no more hard-driving and competitive than managers (Begley & Boyd, 1985, p. 457). Boyd and Gumpert (1983) list four factors contributing to entrepreneurial stress: (1) loneliness, or having no "peer" to talk to; (2) immersion in business; (3) people problems—lacking interpersonal and human-relations skills, failure to delegate, etc.; and (4) the need to achieve, which drives people to fatigue.

Felt stress is associated with certain key aspects of the entrepreneurial role, namely role overload (obligations that exceed available time), responsibility for people, and situational stressors such as equipment malfunction, defective materials, mistakes of employees, understaffing, conflict among employees, and so forth. In addition, challenges from the environment such as competition for product quality and competition for qualified personnel relate to entrepreneurial stress, where competition for price and for product novelty do not contribute to stress (Boyd & Begley, 1986). Additionally, new ventures involve *intense emotional experiences* ranging from euphoria to terror.

ENTREPRENEURIAL TERROR
WILSON HARRELL, 1987

I would like to address a few words to a particular group of readers, to those of you, young and not so young, who are starting your first company. By that act, you have joined a very special organization. Admission is automatic; permission is neither needed nor sought; tenure is indefinite. Welcome to the Club of Terror.

I myself have been a member of this club, and have known this terror, for close to 35 years. I can assure you that it is unlike anything you have ever experienced before. No longer do you have to be bothered with such ordinary feelings as concern, or frustration, or even fear. Those gentle things are the least of your troubles now. You can put them away as a child puts away toys. From now on, you will be in the grip of a human emotion that the good Lord, or more likely his nemesis, created just for entrepreneurs.

Now, I realize that you didn't bargain on this when you started your company. Terror is something that entrepreneurs don't expect, can't escape, and have no way of preparing for. You won't find any college courses on the subject—Handling Terror 101 and 102, or whatever. Nor are there any on-the-job training programs. To my knowledge, nothing has ever been written about it, either, and few people even talk about it. The truth is that those of us who have experienced entrepreneurial terror seldom admit to it. As a result, it remains a deep, dark secret.

The terror is so secret, in fact, that each of us thinks he or she is the only one who's ever felt it. That's understandable. After all, an entrepreneur is, by definition, a risk-taker who "ain't afraid of nothin'," right? Phooey. Terror is our constant companion, and it scares the hell out of every one of us. If you don't believe me, try something. The next time you meet a fellow entrepreneur—young or old, big or small, male or female—just ask, "So, how are you coping with terror?" You'll probably get a look of surprise or even shock. But if you gaze deep into the other person's eyes, you'll also see a warm expression of recognition. He may smile, or grin, or laugh out loud, if he's got the monster corralled for the time being. Then again, he may cry, depending on the status of his current venture. One thing is for sure, though: he'll know from whence you came.

Let me be clear that by terror I do not mean simply an intense kind of fear. The two are quite different. Fear is the sudden rush of adrenaline let loose when her boyfriend walks in, or when you almost get hit by a drunk driver. It's usually accidental, unexpected, and short-lived. Entrepreneurial terror, on the other hand, is self-inflicted. It occurs

when an otherwise normal person makes a conscious decision that carries him over the threshold of fear into a private
world filled with monsters sucking at every morsel of his
being. There can be no sleep in this world, just wide-awake
nightmares. The terror you feel has its own taste (bile), its
own smell (putrid), and its own gut-wrenching pain. And it
doesn't go away as long as you remain an entrepreneur.

I have often tried to figure out what causes this terror,
what breathes life into these monsters in the first place. It's
not the money. As any successful entrepreneur will tell you,
money is just a by-product of accomplishment, and its loss
is, well, one of the risks you take, usually with your eyes
open. "Fear of failure" is a better explanation, although the
phrase seems awfully inadequate to anyone who ever
felt entrepreneurial terror. The more I think about it, the
more convinced I am that the terror comes from the same
thing that leads us to start companies in the first place—
some basic, semiconscious need to make our mark in the
world, to leave our footprints in the sands of time. What we
really fear, I suspect, is that we might become another member of the herd and pass into oblivion.

Wherever the terror comes from, it is awfully hard to
imagine unless you have been through it. I certainly had no
idea what lay ahead when I started my first company in 1953,
although I had had some experience with fear. That experience came as a fighter pilot during World War II, when I was
shot down behind enemy lines. There, badly burned, I was
picked up by members of the French Underground, who
devised a unique and cynical way to hide me from the Germans: they buried me in a cornfield with a hose stuck in my
mouth so I could breathe. The first time they buried me, I
lay there for four hours—time enough to consider all the
bleak possibilities. I figured the Germans would (1) stick a
bayonet through the dirt and into me; (2) riddle the hole
with bullets; (3) accidentally kick the hose; or, worst of all,
(4) turn on the faucet. For eight days in succession, I was
buried; for eight days, I lived with a new and unwanted
friend—stark, raving fear.

But I also discovered something else during that period,
a kind of exhilaration I had never experienced before. Each
time the French partisans dug me up, I was amazed at how
high I felt. I was elated. I had conquered fear, and I knew it.
Of course, it helped quite a bit that I was still alive.

When I was repatriated, I believed that I had experienced
the ultimate in fear—which was probably true. What I
didn't realize, and couldn't possibly imagine, was that I was
headed for a career filled with experiences every bit as
grueling. In the future, moreover, I would put myself
through this torture of my own free will.

The truth began to sink in shortly after I started my first company, a food brokerage representing companies that wanted to sell their products on military bases in Europe and the Near East. Kraft Foods Co. appointed me its representative, and almost immediately sales went out of sight. Everything I did turned into more and more sales for Kraft. I was flying high and making money hand over fist.

Then one day, when I was visiting the company's executive offices in Chicago, Kraft's president, J. Clyde Loftis, invited me in for a chat. The meeting was great for about 10 minutes, as he heaped praise on me for my selling efforts. The next 2 minutes weren't so great, as he calmly announced that Kraft was letting its own salespeople take over the military market in Germany—which happened to represent about half of my total commission from sales. He assured me that, naturally, I could continue representing Kraft in the other areas, countries like Saudi Arabia, Turkey, and Libya.

I sat there stunned. I felt like a fly on an elephant's ass. My income was about to be cut by 50%, and my profit by 100%. Without Kraft, I was pretty near out of business. My mind was going 90 miles an hour. I could see exactly what happened: I had sold myself out of a job. I had made it look so easy that some smart aleck had been able to convince Kraft's management its own salespeople could do the work better and cheaper. But maybe Loftis himself had doubts. Taking a deep breath, I said, "Mr. Loftis, if you take over in Germany, I'm going to let you take over everywhere."

He looked at me. I looked at him. Absolute silence. I had, of course, stopped breathing and was in desperate need of a pacemaker. Terror had just joined the meeting.

After what seemed an eternity, he said, "Are you sure?" Since I couldn't speak, I just nodded. "We'll let you know," he said.

It took him a month to make up his mind. During every moment of those 30 days and 30 nights, I lived with a terror as vivid and as horrifying as anything I had experienced in the French cornfield. When the letter arrived from Kraft, my hands were shaking so badly I couldn't open it. My secretary read it—and let out a shout: "You did it! You did it!" Kraft had backed down. At that moment, my exhilaration was so overwhelming, the high so intense, that I almost passed out.

Was it worth it? You're damn right it was—a hundred-thousandfold. Thirty years later, my old food-broker company still represents Kraft Inc., not only in Europe, but in the Far East and many other places. What's more, that account became the cornerstone of what eventually grew into the largest military-representative organization in the business. Two years ago, I sold it for more than $4 million.

I suppose it was this episode that confirmed me as an entrepreneur and kept me coming back for more. Aside from the terror, the experience also taught me the second secret of entrepreneurship—its reward. I realized then that the elation you feel more than makes up for the pain you have suffered.

Some people might call this an addiction. I prefer to think of it as a roller coaster ride. In the beginning, you pull yourself slowly up the first incline, making the tough decisions with a growing sense of excitement and foreboding. When you hit the top, there is a brief, frightening moment of anticipation before all hell breaks loose. Terror takes over as you go screaming into the unknown. For a while, you feel nothing but incredible fear, interrupted only by a few bumps along the way. Then, suddenly, the ride is over, and the terror is gone, and the exhilaration is all that remains. It's time to buy another ticket. Somehow, though, you know that your first encounter was the worst. You have, to a degree, learned how to handle terror. Thereafter, the intensity diminishes a bit—unless you find a bigger roller coaster or take up, say, skydiving.

The important thing, obviously, is to get through that first encounter, as some of you are trying to do right now. Don't be alarmed if it seems to be more than you can stand. Recognize the terror for what it is, and get used to it, because it could be yours for life. Learn to look it squarely in the eye and spit on it. If you don't, you probably won't make the club, at least not this time. Of course, there's no limit to the number of times you can join.

Now, I realize that I haven't said a damn thing to help you deal with the terror or make it go away. Unfortunately, I don't have any practical tips to give you. The only technique that I've found useful is to get in my car, all alone, and ride around cursing with every four-letter word in my vocabulary. If, by chance, you don't know many bad words, write me, and I'll send you my list. Then set aside a day or so, because it will take you that long to say all of them.

But cursing aside, let me offer a couple of pieces of advice. First, never try to share your feelings of terror with a friend. You will only be passing along the stuff of which ulcers are made. The other person, after all, may never have been on the roller coaster and may not be a member of the club. The chances are that he or she won't be able to deal with the feelings you describe. By sharing the terror, moreover, you are—in effect—asking the other person to share the blame in case something goes wrong. That's against the rules of the club. It is conduct unbecoming an entrepreneur. Leave that to the big companies, which have a built-in structure for sharing terror (or whatever its *Fortune* 500 counterpart might be). They call it a "committee," or sometimes "the office of the president."

Above all, don't take terror home with you. No matter how sorely tempted you are, do not under any circumstances share terror with people you love, unless they happen to be partners in your company. It will only make them despondent and maybe even sick. They put up with enough just living around an entrepreneur. Besides, you need the experience.

There is, however, something you can, and should, share with the people you love. I'm talking about the entrepreneurial high. By all means, take that home with you.

Back to my Kraft story for a moment. My wife will always remember that episode, not so much because I was such a miserable son of a bitch during the 30 days I was waiting for the reply, but because of what happened afterward. We were living in Frankfurt, Germany, at the time. As soon as I got my love letter from Kraft, I called her with the news and asked her for a date. She accepted. The day of our celebration, I took her to the Frankfurt airport and we boarded a plane to Paris, where I'd made reservations at the most exclusive and outrageously expensive restaurant in Europe. I started the dinner by ordering a 60-year-old bottle of wine, which cost about $500. The maître d' dimmed all the lights and served the wine with great ceremony. I've forgotten how the wine tasted, but I will never forget the way my wife looked at me. The dinner lasted three days. We shared the high.

You will have your own highs to share once you have conquered your terror. In the meantime, you should at least be aware that you are not alone—far from it. There is a whole gang of us out here living with the same monster. And you can take some comfort in knowing that terror is an integral and necessary part of every new business started by anyone, anywhere, at any time. Which means that, for every company in existence, there is, or was, some poor soul who bore the cross of terror for all of the people who have benefited. Whether the name was Mr. Kraft, Mr. Pillsbury, Mr. Ford, or Joe Blow, they all shook hands with the devil and joined the club.

My own belief is that the ability to handle terror, to live with it, is the single most important—and, yes, necessary—ingredient of entrepreneurial success. I also believe that it is the lonely entrepreneur living with his or her personal terror who breathes life and excitement into an otherwise dull and mundane world. From that perspective, the Club of Terror is a very exclusive one. Welcome.

Source: Wilson Harrell, "Entrepreneurial Terror," *Inc.* February 1987. Reprinted with permission, *Inc.* magazine. Copyright © 1987 by INC. Publishing Company (Boston, MA: 38 Commercial Wharf, 02110).

PHASE 3: TO GROW OR NOT TO GROW

In most models of small-business development, there is a stage of business growth. Economist David Birch estimates that 12 to 14 percent of small businesses are growth-oriented (1985). Other researchers find, as expected, that high growth rates are most common among newly established rather than older firms, and that lower growth rates are found in purchased and inherited rather than start-up ventures (Dunkelberg & Cooper, 1982). See Chapter 10 for more on the relationship between entrepreneurs and stages of business development.

As the organization grows and changes, so do the role expectations and career of the entrepreneur. Figure 7.3 shows some of these shifts across five stages of development.

The transition through these changes involves changes from founder to manager, leader, or ex-entrepreneur. Growth requires a leader who is willing to delegate, create structure, formally manage information and resources, and represent the organization to the public. It involves changing relationships among organizational members and, importantly, a changing relationship between the founder and his or her firm. These role transitions, and the toll placed on the individual, will be discussed again in Chapter 10.

Career issues at the stage of growth. To grow an organization seems to require a desire to expand, the perception of growth opportunities, and strategic use of one's expertise at the business (Welsh & White, 1983). In addition, the moderate human-relations skills that are acceptable at start-up need to be expanded and honed as delegation, training, and motivation of others become more important.

> The critical factor in growth is not the enlargement of productive capacity, labour force and sales, but the way in which the management handle the organisational changes

FIGURE 7.3 Management Factors and Small Business Development from Churchill & Lewis, 1983

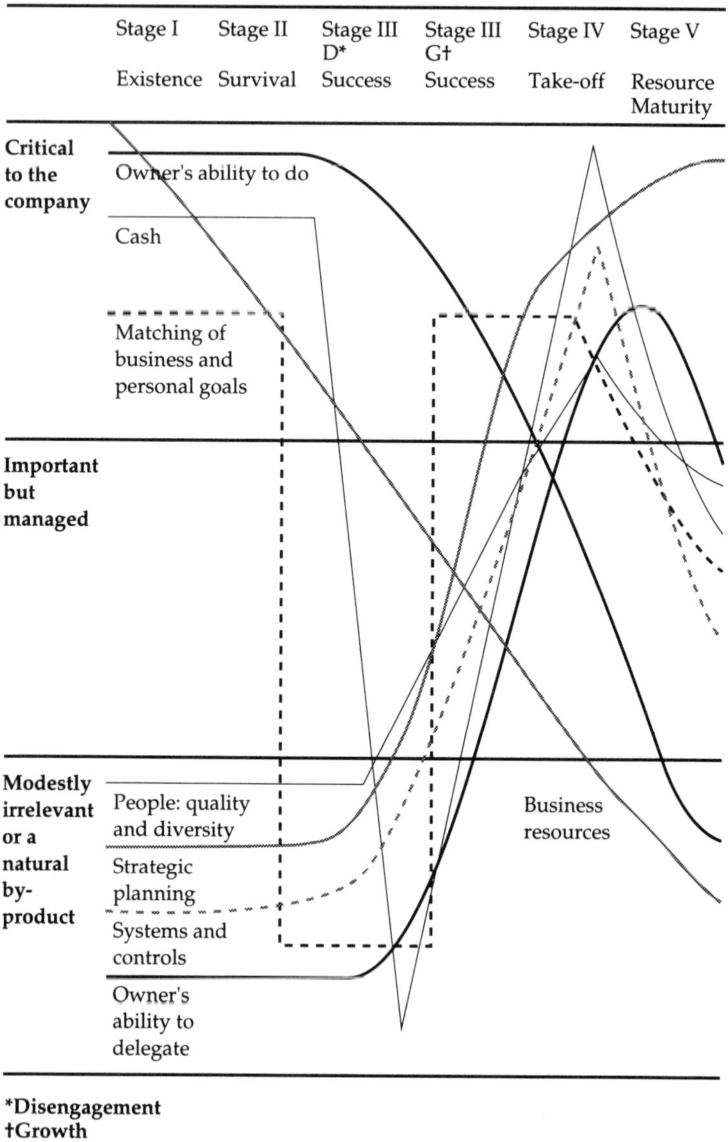

	Stage I	Stage II	Stage III D*	Stage III G†	Stage IV	Stage V
	Existence	Survival	Success	Success	Take-off	Resource Maturity

Critical to the company

Owner's ability to do

Cash

Matching of business and personal goals

Important but managed

Modestly irrelevant or a natural by-product

People: quality and diversity

Strategic planning

Systems and controls

Owner's ability to delegate

Business resources

*Disengagement
†Growth

Source: N. Churchill and V. Lewis, "The Five Stages of Small Business Growth," *Harvard Business Review*, May–June 1983 (Cambridge, MA: Harvard Business School Press, Harvard University).

entailed. An enterprise emerges from its adolescence when it ceases to be a one-man business and becomes a hierarchy by delegation.

Miller, 1963, p. 184

Thus the significant career challenges during the period of growth include: (1) the diffusion of control whereby the organization takes on a direction of its own, no longer dominated by the intentions and will of the founding entrepreneur or team; (2) choosing to manage or to lead rather than implement (research suggests that only 5 percent of entrepreneurs successfully become managerial entrepreneurs; Pinchot, 1985); and (3) stamina to sustain rapid growth or persistence to pursue slower growth. Lacking ability to meet these challenges or lacking the desire to live with the changes that come with growth can result in the entrepreneur's exit from the venture.

PHASE 4: GETTING OUT

All entrepreneurs eventually leave their organizations. For some, the exit is death. For others, there is planned succession and retirement. Some exit when the organization is liquidated or acquired, some when investors demand it.

Leaving the venture is not to be confused with venture failure, because the organization may continue long after the entrepreneur's departure. Nor is leaving to be confused with ending the career of the entrepreneur. We have already pointed out that many entrepreneurs move from venture to venture.

Venture endings fall into three categories. (1) Dissolution for voluntary reasons, possibly with considerable cash upon liquidation, accounts for approximately 90 percent of ventures that cease operations. (2) Bankruptcy and (3) business failure (leaving outstanding debt) account for 10 percent. Another recent study reports 5 percent bankruptcy, 43 percent liquidation, 46 percent sold out to others, and 5 percent unclear in terms of how entrepreneurs left their ventures (Ronstadt, 1985a). This same study reports that nearly half of the exiting entrepreneurs saw their ventures survive them.

Business failure. Many organizations and entrepreneurs vanish from telephone listings, tax records, and other records, making research on the causes of failure and subsequent livelihoods difficult. A recent study of 93 entrepreneurs who had started business in 1975 found that 60 (65 percent) had disappeared while another 11 were no longer in business but available for interviews in 1984 (Brockhaus, 1985). According to David Birch,

> within the first year 20% [of new ventures] are gone, vanished. Then in the second year another 15% are gone, in the third year another 10%, and so on—the curve flattening out. In other words, the chance of your failing in the first seven years in a new business in this country is [approximately] 50%.

The entrepreneur's experience with failure will be discussed again in Chapter 11.

EXAMPLE: JC

JC recently sold his three coffee houses, after more than ten years of struggling to manage debt from a failed attempt to expand. He sold the business to avoid bankruptcy, narrowly avoiding "failure." For JC, having a business that survived his involvement was "success." When asked about his exit, JC indicated that "exit opportunities" had to be found and one had to be acted on. Exiting, like entering, is a matter of timing and he felt he waited too long. He also indicated that the various exits from the venture had different "energies." For him, negative energies, which cast out the entrepreneur, offer more opportunities for growth because the "learning is greater" than when the entrepreneur leaves voluntarily.

Planned and voluntary departures. Entrepreneurs can consciously plan their exit from their venture, passing organizational control to an acquirer, public stockholders, employees, and/or family members. Each of these exits requires a financial analysis of the value of the firm as well as legal, accounting, and organizational expertise. Each requires leadership succession and management development (Gordon & Rosen, 1984). Yet each exit has different organizational dynamics and behavioral requirements of the entrepreneur, his or her team, and the organization.

Other than retirement and selling out for a profit (through acquisition or a public offering), exits are motivated by long hours, disappointing growth potential, low sales volume, and inadequate financing (Brockhaus, 1985). Another study cites "a variety of pressures which . . . produce financial disappointment, personal hardships, and family strain" as the reasons for ending the entrepreneurial career (Ronstadt, 1985, p. 431).

Liquidity—turning organizational assets into cash—is an important incentive in planned and voluntary departures, and is especially important to entrepreneurs with significant venture capital partners whose goal is investment liquidity after five to seven years. So important is this to venture capitalists that they often "screen" entrepreneurs as to their willingness to sell organizational assets in the future. Liquidity is achieved most frequently through being acquired or going public.

Selling the firm means finding a buyer (or being found by a buyer). While growth firms (those "elephants" of the venture capital community) tend to be acquired by larger firms (or the public), small businesses are frequently acquired by other entrepreneurs or entrepreneurial teams. We might suspect (although no studies have been done) that acquisition by another entrepreneur provokes different dynamics than acquisition by a larger organization. For example, when a larger organization acquires a smaller one, there is frequently an attempt to keep the entrepreneur and the entrepreneurial team. Sometimes the entrepreneur becomes a vice-president or CEO; sometimes the transition is managed by retaining the founder as a consultant; and there is often a "non-compete" agreement. These devices may be less common when the acquirer is another entrepreneur. However, the entrepreneurial acquirer can be expected to more significantly transform the firm, adding to the value of the firm (if successful).

"Going public" involves another consciously chosen strategy to achieve liquidity and cash for expansion. By providing continuity of ownership and management, the initial public offering (IPO) creates the context for the entrepreneur's exit from the organization. Of course, people who make the transitions from start-up entrepreneur to manager or leader may stay in executive positions in public companies and "retire" later. Others leave more immediately and involuntarily, as newly formed boards of directors (which usually include the entrepreneur, who retains some of the stock) assume ownership authority and may ask him or her to leave. The role transitions and the relationship with the underwriting "stakeholder" will be discussed again in Chapter 9. For now, suffice it to say that the underwriter's actions influence the future of the company, "not only the valuation of a business, but also the visibility and ownership of its shares" (Sutton & Post, 1986, p. 32).

Employee ownership of the organization, through Employee Stock Ownership Plans or Employee Stock Ownership Trusts, is an alternative some entrepreneurs prefer, based on personal and organizational values. An example of this comes from the entrepreneur of an *Inc.* 500 company.

BP: AN EXAMPLE OF EMPLOYEE OWNERSHIP PLANS

"Right now I'm the only stockholder in the organization and I'm now planning a way in which senior managers and employees can take ownership. If this country is ever really going to compete internationally. . . . What we need to do is transfer the ownership of what people are investing in, to the people, not through a socialism method but simply through ownership. When you do that, you'll unleash a dynamism that will really show what this country can do.

"Ownership is important to me now for control and the ability to give direction and set the dictum and the things in motion. You don't have to negotiate with everybody. But at the point where you have reached an institution that essentially belongs, operationally, to the people who make it up, then you have to transfer that ownership to them so that those same decisions have that level of depth and credibility."

Further discussion of sharing equity with key insiders can be found in Chapter 8.

Another way for entrepreneurs to exit from their ventures is by turning over the business to second-generation family members, retaining private control. Apparently this is fairly common, since 95 percent of American companies are either family-owned or family-controlled and 42 percent of the workforce is employed in these businesses ("Conversation with Richard Bekhard," 1983). Compared to public firms, private firms tend to be found in less capital-intensive industries, respond to more fragmented markets using niche strategies, offer higher salaries, put more money into R & D, develop smaller-ticket items, expand horizontally (rather than vertically), and have less debt and higher cash flow (Ward, 1986). Some of these factors may help explain why family-owned businesses often fare better than public firms. In general, personal control, the ability to re-invest in the venture, and a sense of personal pride in ownership give private firms a competitive edge in the marketplace, as illustrated by the example of Quality Commodity Company.

EXAMPLE: QUALITY COMMODITY COMPANY

The major employer in a midwestern town, Quality was expected to be handed off to the founder's son. Unexpectedly, the son suffered serious health problems that precluded his continued involvement in the firm. The company was sold to a large multinational firm. Later the multinational divested Quality and it again became a family-run business, albeit with a family other than that of the founder.

While held by the multinational, Quality's sales decreased, scrap rate went up (from less than 10 percent to 50 percent), absenteeism increased (from 3–4 percent to 15 percent, with employee turnover of 11 percent), and employment dropped from over 500 to under 200. When acquired by another family system, Quality's sales soared (from approximately $2 million to nearly $11 million), scrap rate returned to less than 10 percent, absenteeism and turnover returned to original low levels, and employment rose to previous levels (Astrachan, 1985).

It is fairly well-understood that giving up control of one's venture is difficult. It may be even more difficult to turn it over to one's son or daughter. With sons, issues of masculinity (rivalry, tests of manhood, struggle for authority) interfere and the age of both father and son as well as the age difference between them affect whether the transition is one of conflict or harmony. Daughters, who are often overlooked as CEOs and considered last-resort leaders, face additional struggles for authority and legitimacy. However, since women/daughters experience different personal-development issues than men/sons, the transition to daughters may involve less conflict (Rogolsky, 1985). Finally, when more than one offspring is involved there is a heightened probability of "sibling" rivalry.

Of course there are many examples of family handoffs that work smoothly, as happened with Color Art, Inc. where founders Bob Rein and Gil Lorenz turned over company control to their respective sons, a group of other family employees, and nonfamily managers (Kahn, 1985). However, evidence suggests that the handoff is usually difficult. The average firm exists for 24 years—the average tenure of most founders (Lansberg, 1983)—and "only three out of ten family-owned firms survive beyond the founder's tenure" ("Conversation," 1983, p. 30). Finally, many cases of second-generation "flops" can also be found, such as the failure of Itkins office-furniture stores (in New York) after being turned over to the sons of two partners/brothers (Posner, 1987).

Involuntary separation. Entrepreneurs, more than other organizational members, have egos bound to the organization. The personal investment of money, time, and sweat equity along with the creative impulse to build a business make the organization and entrepreneur symbiotically related. When the organization outgrows the entrepreneur—when other stakeholders push the founder aside—the parting can be painful.

EXAMPLE: JON BIRCK

When Jon Birck founded Northwest Instrument Systems in 1981, the plan was to build instruments that add onto personal computers. The first product was an oscilloscope device. When revenues did not meet costs and negative cash flow developed, a second infusion of money brought in venture capitalists Kleiner Perkins Caufield & Byers who insisted that Birck hire a general manager. The GM brought in a strong team to design, build, and sell a second product, this time a logic analyzer. The product sold well.

When the time came to decide whether to build digital instruments (the team was in place) or analog instruments (the founder's expertise), a conflict developed. Birck continued to push analog business plans, "not seeing that Northwest now had a momentum of its own" (p. 86).

In 1984, the venture partners and directors of Northwest told Birck that the firm needed a "strong leader who had managed a rapidly growing business already; Birck had not. To attract someone who had, they would have to offer the

CEO's job and they thought it would be best if Birck resigned," keeping his stock and a position on the board (p. 86).

The displacement was painful. "The first week at home he cleaned out the closets, reorganized the kitchen, and went hiking in the mountains for a few days by himself. He didn't know what the founding ex-president of a company was supposed to do. Get another job? Wait for his stock to make him rich? He couldn't imagine spending the rest of his life out of the action" (p. 80). He called upon his network of contacts from Northwest to help him assess his options.

He is beginning again, with a related product and a complete team. This time he intends to build an organization he can work with for many years, as a career (Benner, 1985).

Other entrepreneurs leave reluctantly but without being pushed. They recognize that the skills and talents needed to start a venture and grow it rapidly are not appropriate to sustain and refine the organization. If the entrepreneur lacks management experience or dislikes management processes, he or she faces a difficult decision—to exit the creation. Experienced as "agitation of the spirit" and a "spasm of discontent," the moment of reckoning occurs:

In the fullness of your accomplishment, you find it strangely hollow. The company is too big, too complex. What is that person's name? Where did that family feeling go, and where's the magic? You find yourself stranded in the breach where impulse and improvisation must give way to systems and planning, and the fires of creation are cooling on the routines of disciplined technique. You sense . . . that your own talents, so productive at the start, are no longer of the kind and quality to carry the enterprise further. Others around you see that as well. But it's your enterprise, isn't it? You birthed it. You are its loving parent. How can you let it go? What can you do?

Rhodes, 1986, p. 74

What happens to ex-entrepreneurs? As suggested earlier, when one venture ends or the entrepreneur exits the venture, starting over again is a common pattern. Ronstadt (1985a) reports that 57 percent of former entrepreneurs in his study planned to restart their entrepreneurial careers with another venture.

Some suggest that ex-entrepreneurs (especially those who left with considerable cash) become venture capitalists. However, Mancuso (1974) suggests that "they are seldom effective as venture capitalists. . . . The skills of a successful venture capitalist are at a much higher level of abstraction than those of the entrepreneur" (p. 21).

In an empirical study of eleven former entrepreneurs, Brockhaus (1985) found that six were employed as salespeople, two had started another business, two had found jobs working for someone else, and one was unemployed.

CAREER CRISES AND ROLE TRANSITIONS

All individuals are thought to go through "crises" of mid-life as the biological clock ticks off the years and capacities and interests change. Life changes affect careers, relationships, and self-concepts. Entrepreneurs are no different, although no one has looked at entrepreneurial careers this way. Of particular interest is how the career relationship between entrepreneur and venture changes with life changes.

Because the entrepreneur has a special, deep relationship with his or her creation, he or she has more occasions for career crisis. As one passes through various stages of the entrepreneurial career and as the enterprise passes through the various stages of organizational development, demands from the organization and the abilities of entrepreneurs change. Old roles and old behaviors have to be examined in light of current and future demands. Role transition and learning are always possible. Entrepreneurs can learn to let go of old patterns and acquire new skills. These topics are addressed in Chapters 10 and 11.

Implications

The career pattern of the entrepreneur is a function of his or her values and the goals involved in making this choice. Observers may be able to predict career initiation as well as career outcomes and problems based on an understanding of the goals, personality, age, and developmental stage of the entrepreneur. Conversely, by observing the career of an entrepreneur we are able to deduce something about his or her underlying goals and values.

Although there has been no research to date, we expect that the fast-versus-slow entry into entrepreneurship may be an important career consideration. How do some entrepreneurs manage to "moonlight" while others feel the need to take a plunge? We would also expect that entry into entrepreneurship via independent start-up, acquisition, or franchise and within a corporation would attract individuals with different concepts of their careers and would result in different career options and problems. Similar hypotheses may be advanced for ventures started in different industries (high compared to low technology, service compared to manufacturing) and with different initial structures (solo, partnership, team, etc.).

Would-be entrepreneurs and potential investors can use the career stages to assess venture desirability and feasibility. Forewarned about stress, the critical decisions regarding growth, and the need to exit, would-be entrepreneurs can be forearmed with self-assessments, support from family and friends, and time to prepare for the opportunities that surface.

Families and friends of entrepreneurs can use the career stages as a "reality check" on the interpersonal dynamics that can occur in venturing. Knowing what is "normal" for entrepreneurs helps make sense of experiences outside the venture.

CHAPTER 8

INTERNAL TEAMS: PARTNERS

INTRODUCTION

No one knows exactly how many new ventures are started by teams of individuals, but estimates seem significant. The Bureau of the Census reports that 8 percent of the existing businesses in 1977 (approximately 1,153,000 businesses) were partnerships. We can reasonably assume that many more began as partnerships and have changed to sole proprietorships or corporations. Another report showed that over 57 percent of technology-based new start-ups were begun by groups and 27 percent of the nontechnical companies had a founding team (Shapero, 1972). Finally, an *Inc.* magazine report on the 100 fastest-growing American firms in 1983 showed that two-thirds involved partnerships (Rich & Gumpert, 1985). The authors go on to say: "As this research and our own experience suggest . . . assembling a winning management team is at once one of the most important and most difficult tasks facing a young venture" (Rich & Gumpert, 1985, p. 129).

Estimates of the number of partnerships vary considerably because of differences in when a team forms—before financing/start-up or after. Further ambiguity enters when we include team members who are not partners or "owners" but have key responsibilities, as well as insiders and outsiders who have an equity stake or future stock options. While the focus of this chapter is on partnerships, a few more words on the general importance of venture teams seems worthwhile at this point. Employees are discussed later in this chapter and key outsiders are discussed in Chapter 9.

VENTURE TEAMS

Investors clearly recognize the importance of the venture team. "Most experienced private investors and entrepreneurs know that probably the most critical factor in determining whether a new venture ever realizes sales beyond $5 million a year, and joins the elite 3700 companies with sales over $20 million, is largely attributed to highly effective venture management teams" (Timmons, 1975, p. 1). Even glamorous and exciting proposals that lack a "balanced" venture team will not be considered by 50 percent of venture capitalists (MacMillan, Siegel, & Narasimha, 1985). Finally, venture capitalists in three regions agreed that the ability to build a team, and to attract qualified people with proven skills to create the new enterprise, was more important than entrepreneurial personality and background (Goslin & Barge, 1986).

When we start to consider entrepreneurial teams, *those groups of individuals who come together to start a new venture or who come together during the early stages of the enterprise,* we may be dealing with a special type of entrepreneur. The person who builds a team may have abilities, motivations, and personality characteristics considerably different from the "rugged individualist" who prefers to maintain hands-on involvement and personal control of key decisions. Recall that entrepreneurs tend to have only moderate social skills, have low needs for affiliation and strong needs for autonomy and control, are less conforming, and need less social acceptance than the general population. Entrepreneurs in general do not sound like team players or team builders.

In addition, entrepreneurial teams require a complex level of behavioral analysis. No longer can we localize the entrepreneurial spirit and action in a single person and look to his or her abilities, motivations, and experiences. One person is no longer solely responsible for outcomes, and control is shared. Furthermore, the complexity of entrepreneurial teams increases with size.

TEAM SIZE

The simplest team is composed of two individuals and involves two personalities, two sets of abilities and motivations, and two careers. The relationship rests upon important interpersonal dynamics such as attraction, liking, conflict, leadership, power/dominance, communication, trust, and so forth.

Things get even more complicated when we consider teams of three. With three players, in addition to compounded issues of individual differences in personality, abilities, etc., there are possibilities of "politics," of coalitions, and "two-against-one." In addition, communications become more complex, as do all aspects of interpersonal relationships.

Of course, as the group gets bigger, with four, five, six, and more key players, the relationships become even more complex. Relationships, in terms of the number of possible two-person linkages, grow geometrically. The team becomes a small group, with all the attendant dynamics such as "group-think" or conformity, cohesion, and so forth.

RESEARCH ON VENTURE TEAMS

While there is some research on entrepreneurial teams, it is sparse, mostly anecdotal, and lacks a theoretical base. However, there is considerable theory and systematic research on dyads (e.g., marriage partners, therapist-client relationships) and small groups (e.g., therapy groups, leaderless training groups, T-groups, and work groups in larger organizations). We will posit that because many entrepreneurial teams are composed of individuals "new" to each other (this assumes no previous venture start-ups together) and because these individuals have a common goal, entrepreneurial teams can be compared with other dyads and small groups. Of course, we cannot possibly review all existing theories and research on dyad and small-group dynamics. We will introduce some of the important factors to set the stage for further discussions of entrepreneurial teams—partners and employees.

INSTRUMENTAL RELATIONSHIPS

Entrepreneurial teams are task-oriented groups (rather than relationship-oriented groups such as families, groups formed for therapy, and "leaderless" training groups). Task orientation requires "instrumental relationships" rather than "personal relationships." In an instrumental relationship, *the relationship itself is a tool for the accomplishment of a task or goal.* That is, individuals are presumably more concerned with the accomplishment of work than with developing intimacy, more concerned with a task than with the well-being of group members. (See the section on teamwork tasks below.) Instrumental relationships serve several purposes (Steele, 1979):

- They allow complex tasks to be broken down among individuals with diverse skills.
- They form the core technology in service-oriented organiza-

tions, (i.e., when a service is provided, the server and recipient necessarily form an instrumental relationship).

- For some people with strong needs for affiliation, doing work in a relationship is intrinsically more satisfying than working alone.
- Forming interdependent goal-oriented relationships can help to reduce competition between parties, as when market competitors merge their organizations.
- Forming interdependent goal-oriented relationships can increase competition between parties (e.g., sales contests).
- They seem to be a natural outcome of situations in which one person has sufficient power over others to control their behavior to accomplish his or her chosen goal, as is the case in many privately held firms.

A similar set of reasons can be drawn specifically for the team approach to new ventures (Vesper, 1980, p. 41).

- Teams make available a larger human-resource effort.
- Teams can provide a more complete balance of skills and other resources with which to start.
- With a team, the departure of any given member is less likely to be disastrous for the venture than with a lone entrepreneur.
- With a team, the venture should be able to grow farther before having to expend valuable management effort in seeking out and recruiting additional key talent.
- A willingness and ability on the part of the initial entrepreneur to assemble and work with a team can be symptomatic of his or her ability to attract and manage people.
- The attempt to recruit team members can be a preliminary stage to test the venture idea.

Types of instrumental relationships. There are many different ways to characterize the instrumental relationship and the entrepreneurial team. Steele (1979) describes four types of task-oriented relationships based on the degree of trust among individuals (i.e., friendly or antagonistic) and on whether the goals of the relationship are individual or collective (i.e., competitive or cooperative). Figure 8.1 reflects these four possible types of instrumental relationships: (1) friendly cooperation, where individuals attend to both their common goals and their positive feelings toward each other; (2) friendly competition, where individuals like one another but are competing for some

FIGURE 8.1 Types of Instrumental Relationships

Orientation to other party	Orientation to contributions	
	Cooperative	Competitive
Friendly	(1) Friendly cooperation	(2) Friendly competition
Antagonistic	(4) Antagonistic cooperation	(3) Antagonistic competition

Source: W. Bennis, J. Van Maanen, E. H. Schein, and F. I. Steele, *Essays in Interpersonal Dynamics.* Copyright © 1979 by The Dorsey Press. Reprinted by permission of Brooks/Cole Publishing Company (Pacific Grove, CA).

advantage such as R & D money or budgets; (3) antagonistic competition, where individuals neither like one another nor share a common purpose and a climate of mistrust and hostility exists; and (4) antagonistic cooperation, where individuals do not care for each other but cooperate because of a common goal.

Most likely, start-up teams require cooperation (friendly or antagonistic) where the goals of breaking even, making profits, and growing the enterprise are shared. However, it is possible for a group to shift over time in terms of affection and cooperation, with a friendly group becoming antagonistic or a cooperative group becoming competitive. It is therefore possible that an entrepreneurial team might become friendly and competitive. However, it is hard to imagine a successful team with antagonistic competition. If this arises, the team disbands and sometimes the organization ceases operations. (Conflict between partners is discussed later in this chapter.)

TEAMWORK TASKS

While all instrumental relationships are task oriented, it is commonly accepted that for long- and short-term survival and effective task performance, groups must attend to both task and "maintenance" issues. *Task issues involve what is needed to get the job done,* including work flow, cooperation, and interdependence among contributors (e.g., marketing and production), the technology used (e.g., computer-assisted design or draftsperson design), and so forth. *Maintenance issues involve "team spirit" and group cohesion,* and include the need to deal with the tensions and feelings that normally arise from frequent interaction, the distribution of power, decision making, and responsibility, and the evaluation and compensation of members.

Teamwork requires that members form a psychological contract in which their expectations of each other and the organization are open to discussion and negotiation (Harrison, 1973). Ideally, this contract is under continuous renegotiation as the team and the organization change. In turn, discussion and negotiation require communication skills (both talking and listening), interpersonal risk taking, skills at influence, etc. Effective teams attend to these factors, honing skills and clarifying relationships as they work together.

In fact, most activities designed to enhance team spirit (such as a retreat with a consultant for team building or drinks with the team after hours) affect task performance (i.e., satisfied workers are more productive). Likewise, ongoing task performance affects interpersonal feelings. For example, productive workers tend to be more satisfied, whereas less productive workers recognize their shortfall and tend to be more stressed and less satisfied. In other cases working together results in residual sentiments and feelings, which are not discussed due to time constraints and which may build misperceptions among team members. In turn, both task performance and team spirit contribute to organizational outcomes such as profitability, structure, formality, ethical conduct, and culture.

Figure 8.2 shows how these factors interact to produce individual, group, and organizational outcomes. For an example of how some of these factors operate, see the box on the Fishing Buddies Partnership.

FRIENDSHIP- AND MARRIAGE-BASED PARTNERSHIPS

While we claim that many business partners are "new" to each other, we do not mean that partners have had no prior relationship. Many, if not most, partners choose each other from existing relationships—as family members, as friends from other contexts, or as co-workers.

In these cases, partnership is a new relationship layered over a previously established, noninstrumental, often affectionate, personal connection. A good example of this is a partnership involving a husband and wife.

FIGURE 8.2   Group Task, Maintenance, and Performance

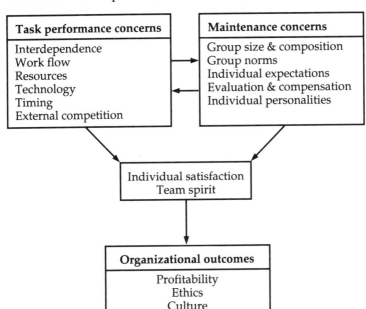

EXAMPLE: TECHNISERVE

Nancy Abbott began Techniserve, a Hinckley, Ohio firm providing data-processing services, as a sole proprietor. A year later, her husband Bob left his electrical engineering job with a *Fortune* 500 firm to become an active partner in the firm, which until recently was run out of the couple's home. A third, silent partner has minority ownership interests in the six-person firm.

Because they have a personal relationship that predates their business relationship by 13 years, the Abbotts claim a level of trust, acceptance of personality differences, and commitment to a common business goal that would be difficult to find in other, nonfamily partnerships. As in most effective partnerships, they avoid conflict by making all important business decisions jointly, and they openly and frequently share their expectations of one another.

One of the perils of combining marriage and business partnerships is the erosion of boundaries between personal and business roles. This was of particular concern to the Abbotts, who housed their business in their home. They recently relocated the business to help separate their business relationship from their personal life as much as possible.

That does not change the 24-hour-a-day nature of their relationship. Other married partners resolve this potential immersion in each other's lives by structuring the business so that each has a special domain. When asked if it is bothersome to spend 24 hours a day with his business partner, Bob responded, "Sometimes I don't like the long hours, and that's a problem being married to your business partner. But it is a two-edged sword. It makes it easier to see each other, and at least your spouse understands when you are tired, worn, and strained after a long day."

FISHING BUDDIES PARTNERSHIP

Having fun together as friends seems to be the underlying purpose of the partnership formed by Andy, Bob, Chuck, and Dave, who make almost all major decisions in recreational settings, mostly fishing and backyard parties (the latter including their spouses and families). Says Andy, "The business is not the whole thing. It's just one of those things we have fun doing together." The others agree; if the business were no longer fun, they would end it.

The four friends, all first-generation immigrants and three with engineering degrees, began PFC, a northern Ohio machine-fabrication business, in 1979. Together they invested a total of $20,000 and own the business equally. Equality of ownership is so important that one of the partners coined the term "all-ership" for their relationship. "Together we own every single thing here. Each helped in creating it, the friendship, the good times, the business. So it's not ownership of parts but all owning all." Chuck explained further:

"You have your fishing rod, I put in my reel, Andy's line and Dave's lure. When you catch a fish, whose fish is it? It belongs to all of us, right? But if we worry about whose fish it is or which part belongs to whom, fishing together is no longer fun. Then what's the use of fishing together?"

The partners' friendship and partnership lives are closely intertwined and the boundary between them is fuzzy. In interviews on their friendship and business partnership, they had a hard time knowing when one aspect (business) was the focus of attention.

As might be expected, the business has developed in ways that reflect the friendships that underlie it. Only Bob works full time in the business, along with three full-time machinists. The others are involved part-time.

To protect Bob should the business fail, the group decided to create a "superfund." This fund was built through regular contributions from the part-time partners out of their regular share of distributed profits. Later, Bob insisted that the scope of the fund be expanded to include unemployment insurance for everyone, and began to make regular contributions from his share of profits.

The interpersonal support and caring that pervades the partnership can be seen in other activities. "We have a set of phone numbers so we can call when we go away. We look out for each other's homes," says Bob.

> "We call each other when we get home late, just to be sure everyone got home ok. Andy's wife leaves work at midnight. She's got our numbers and we know her route home. So if she gets stuck, she can call us, and we know how to look for her" (Chuck).

The friendship has permitted the development of a climate involving hard work, psychological safety, and openness.

> "You never doubt about these guys. They put everything into their work. Their best. They're hard working, and they enjoy doing that" (Dave).
> "Anybody fails we all fail. So we stay alert. . . . We have to so everybody can help before it happens" (Andy).
> "Then it's safe. No one is saying you're stupid or thick headed. . . . It's like an objective exercise, never personal. No egos involved" (Dave).
> "Every night we have a chance to talk. . . . If we can't be here together, we call each other. Share the day's news" (Chuck).

The friendship, caring, and fun shared by the partners seems to have affected their decision-making and conflict-management practices. While decisions are made by consensus, individuals are encouraged to dissent. "It's our duty to one another to say so if we do not agree" (Bob). Disagreements, when they occur, are perceived as opportunities to search for the best combination of ideas and choices, without involving judgments of personal competence. "The best decision? That's what everybody agrees on. If one does not agree, we have to continue talking, searching" (Andy).

To achieve consensus, which is always a time-consuming process, the partners have developed a set of "discussion rules" through which each member is encouraged to detach himself personally from his idea and present both the positive and negative aspects.

> "Even if it takes a long time, what's important is that we're all into it. Then we will have fun implementing it. But what's the hurry? When we fish we don't hurry. When we hurry we don't usually catch anything and it's no fun. Like fishing, we catch some fast, some take patience and a long wait" (Bob).

Finally, when conflict seems imminent,

> "Sometimes it also gets hot. But we try to stop that as soon as possible. Time out right away. . . . Then there's our prayer thing. Part of the time out . . . it works wonders. I mean it brings us back to a safe level . . . no formula prayers. I don't think it's important who we pray to. More important is what it makes us think about—our friendship and good intentions. That's the key. If we start fighting, it's often because we lost sight of our friendship" (Andy).

Leadership of group meetings rotates every six months and is seen as a way for each to learn to be "a leader among equals." The leader is responsible for facilitating group efforts, "to keep our discussion going smoothly and keep us aware of what's happening." No one is boss, no one is chief.

"No one can be boss around here. We're all friends" (Bob).

"We're simple people who see each other as equals, even in power and influence" (Dave).

"We all are at the top. Nobody's higher" (Andy).

From Dumdum (1987)

PARTNERSHIP STRUCTURES

As suggested earlier, there are many opinions and very little data on the importance of venture teams. Some suggest that the more successful entrepreneurs operate alone (Collins &

Moore, 1964). Others suggest that team efforts are more likely to succeed (Baty, 1974) and report that the number of partners is positively related to the venture's sales (e.g., success) (Teach, Tarpley, & Schwartz, 1986). Teams seem to be most important when resources are scattered. When the expertise to start a high-technology firm depends on several different engineering disciplines and on financial and marketing experience, a team may be the only way to begin. Likewise, in disadvantaged regions and Third World countries, resources are both scarce and scattered and team approaches to new ventures might be more prevalent and more enduring than in more organized and advantaged areas.

DEFINITION

Partnerships can be distinguished from other relationships and business forms. *A partnership involves a business context where two or more peers share ownership and responsibility.* An entrepreneurial partnership is one where partners are involved in creating new value through a start-up venture or in the transformation of a going concern.

The peer nature of the partner relationship is essentially one of equality in status, despite differences in capital commitment, expertise, function, personality, motivation, and control. For example, general partners have equal voice in corporate decisions, represent the enterprise to its customers, suppliers, and employees, and can commit organizational resources. This distinguishes partnerships from relationships that are hierarchical (e.g., relationships between superiors and subordinates, leaders and followers, and elders and youth).

Partners bring resources of different value to the venture and may contract for unequal ownership and responsibility (e.g., general versus limited partnerships, although limited partners may better be considered *external* to the organization and the entrepreneurial process). Even among general partners, there may be one or more individuals more highly invested in the venture (in terms of initial capital investment or psychological urgency and ownership) and who take on more leadership responsibilities and control than the others. (For a further discussion of leadership, see Chapter 11.) Partners may also specialize in areas of responsibility (e.g., finance, technology, innovation, and marketing).

Partners may formally or informally contract with each other on issues such as the duration of the partnership, the extension of equity to others, dilution of investments, and so forth. Thus the way that ownership and responsibility are shared among partners may change over time.

EXAMPLE: EXPECTED SEPARATION OF PARTNERS

George had been a manager in large aerospace manufacturing firms for 16 years before he and his partner bought a small contracting firm and began entrepreneurial careers. During his previous career as a manager, he became friends with David. Two years later, because their opportunities were limited in big business, they began looking for a small manufacturing firm to acquire. The only criteria were that the organization have a presence in the industry and be lacking sales.

Such a firm, ROSpace, was found and acquired, with George and David as equal partners. However, they had an informal agreement that stemmed from vital differences in the personal values they placed on their enterprise. David's personal goals for becoming an entrepreneur were financial; George's were to run a growing high-technology firm. Their informal agreement was to make the business as profitable as possible, and to invest profits in real estate with minimal reinvestment in the firm. They agreed to a buy-out after five years, with the liquid assets (such as the real estate) for David and the business for George.

Six years later, the firm has twice been listed in the *Inc.* 100 fastest-growing private firms. Says George:

> "It took us seven years instead of five, because after five years we couldn't fund it. We couldn't fund the divorce. It took us two more years to develop a means of funding the separation of the partnership. David went on to continue his main interest which was real estate. My interest was the further development of the business.
>
> "It was a concession on my part, during those seven years, to stay at that initial low operating level . . . our sales rarely exceeded one million dollars . . . because at a low operating level you have the chance to generate income revenue and assets that can be put into things like real estate. My preference was to take whatever cash flow and return possible and pump it back into developing the operation.
>
> "When I said to him, 'Make me a proposition,' he came back with a position to negotiate. I just looked at some elements that I needed from an operational standpoint and discussed those and to the rest of it I said, 'Fine.'
>
> "We did it. He took the assets that were liquid, I took what was left, which was the operation. It was like starting over again, from a balance sheet standpoint. But from what I had in mind and what I needed to do, I was in very good shape.

"A few people who were close enough to the situation to know what the deal was thought I had made a terrible deal. . . . I have a personal requirement that when I'm involved in a business situation with someone else, like a partnership or a joint venture, the ideal situation is when we both prosper. For my business partner to be more prosperous than I was at the time we separated the business was preferable to me. It was an advantage to have that particular reputation rather than the opposite reputation . . . very prosperous but his partner is off by the wayside, bankrupt."

STRUCTURAL ELEMENTS

A partnership structure refers to relatively fixed and enduring qualities of the individual partners, the relationship itself, and the organization they build. It is upon these "givens" that the dynamics of a partnership rests.

Individual differences. The similarities or differences between individuals in terms of age, sex, race, and personal history are "fixed" in that any change would require changing partners. As mentioned earlier, these differences have an established importance in interpersonal relations (Friedlander, 1973; Hall, 1973) and organizational effectiveness (Kanter, 1977) and thus in entrepreneurial partnerships.

A potentially more malleable category of individual differences are those of personality and expertise, and these have been found to distinguish entrepreneurs from others. Individuals do have means for modifying and changing these aspects of themselves (e.g., through counseling, education, and so forth). However, psychologists and educators have considered certain elements of the person to be difficult to change (e.g., character and deeply embedded habits) while other aspects are more easily changed but still require considerable time—for example, learning style, emotional responsiveness, and expertise. The rate of change is slow enough that these can usually be considered "given" for short-run analysis. That is, a person's future time perspective, risk aversion, need for control, autonomy, confidence, and experience with the industry (as well as other characteristics) take time to change and can be considered stable and fixed when a new venture begins.

Relationship structures. Those who have theorized about interpersonal relationships consider relationship variables such as shared language and meaning structures (Van Maanen, 1979), the "negotiated order" or assumptions that emerge from interaction (Day & Day, 1977), the task and maintenance requirements of groups (Likert, 1961), and role systems of actors and interaction (Katz & Kahn, 1978) as structural elements. These concepts reflect patterns established fairly early in a partnership—routines of interaction that form a foundation for current and future activities. These patterns of interaction change very slowly most of the time. For example, sharing the language and meanings of microchip development, application, and marketing structures the relationship between partners—they can communicate effectively and quickly, relying on jargon and shared assumptions.

In addition to these, the partnership has a structural requirement based on the definition of partners as peers with equal importance to the venture. Of special importance are the *boundaries and distance between partners* (e.g., how much information, decision making, and planning is shared, how much is kept private, and how quickly and effectively the partners can reach each other to share information and make decisions). The peer quality of the relationship assumes that it allows for quick, reciprocal access among partners.

Organizational structure. In addition to those relatively enduring aspects of organizations that are traditionally considered structural (e.g., size, differentiation, integration, centralization, hierarchy, and "shape"), partnerships have unique structures that stem from the interpersonal relationships upon which they are founded. *Shared leadership* has considerable impact on the organization's task specialization or differentiation when partners bring different expertise and create separate domains of decision making (e.g., one partner works "inside," the other works "outside" the firm). Shared leadership also affects conflict management or integration when differences are resolved and synergy is achieved (e.g., no one has authority over the other although one partner is often the "lead" and final decision maker). We might also expect partnerships to evolve with unique structures, shapes, and strategies, retaining the expertise and interest domains created by the originating partners.

In his study of a large partnership group (ten partners), Brown (1986) found four organizing qualities that helped the partners sustain a nonhierarchical structure. These are (1) skill sharing, where an effort is made to teach and share all jobs, (2) legitimizing work, where partners' values of tasks and work processes are shared, (3) consensus decision making, and (4) collective responsibility, in which each takes responsibility for the mistakes of others and tasks are assigned on the basis of skill sharing rather than efficiency.

Although we suggest that partnerships are by definition nonhierarchical, this does not mean equal ownership, investment, or control. Nor does it imply a lack of role differentiation. Many advisors to partnerships recommend early clarification of who is in charge (the ultimate decision maker). Anticipating conflict, they advise partners to write and sign a legal agreement covering the rights and responsibilities of all partners as well as plans for future dissolution of the partnership (e.g., a buy-out agreement). It is interesting to note here that most of the practical advice given to partners is pessimistic, focused on "how to avoid conflict" or "how to get rid of unwanted partners." Little advice can be found on how to structure synergy and build the trust necessary to have an enduring partnership.

We argue that in effective, enduring partnerships, all partners are heard and have influence on venture decisions. However, Philip Thurston, Harvard University professor and consultant to small businesses, argues just the opposite.

> If partnerships do exist, the very structure should undermine any possibility that partners could face one another on equal terms. Indeed, inequality can be the key to satisfactory relationships.
>
> Thurston, 1986, p. 25

In addition to these aspects of organizational structure, a partnership has unique elements stemming from its *legal form*, with accounting, taxation, and liability outcomes. Of particular importance is the partnership agreement that becomes an organizational charter.

DYNAMIC PROCESSES OF PARTNERSHIPS

Dynamic processes are events and activities that result in change and/or growth of individuals, relationships, and organizations. In the partnership relationship, a specific set of interpersonal processes is thought to operate. Figure 8.3 diagrams these dynamics.

FIGURE 8.3   Partnership Dynamics: The Two–Person Example

Attraction

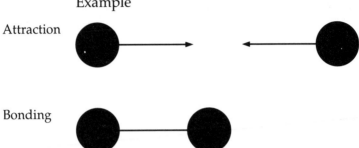

Bonding

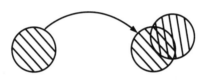

Projection

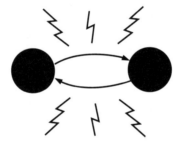

Conflict

Development

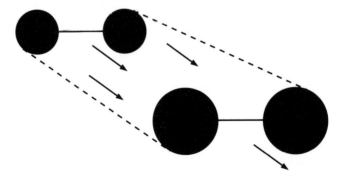

ATTRACTION (COMING TOGETHER)

The partnership begins with two or more individuals coming together to discuss the possibilities of venturing together. According to interpersonal theory, some combination of five qualities predicts who we will choose as a partner:

1. objective likeability (i.e., physical attractiveness, competence, resources)
2. proximity (i.e., closeness in geographical distance and traveling or communicating time)
3. finding the other person rewarding or pleasant to be with
4. similarity of attitudes, interests, and personalities
5. some complementarity of characteristics (e.g., I like working on finance and management, you like sales promotion) (Campbell, 1980; Middlebrook, 1980)

"The method by which entrepreneurs select their partners is, alas, all too frequently random, uncertain, and subject to chance" (Silver, 1983, p. 127). The process of finding partners has also been described as "idiosyncratic" (Timmons, 1975) and "very difficult" (Silver, 1983).

Many partnerships are formed around the individuals' ability to invest capital. Here the primary attraction is to the other person's money. One study of microcomputer software ventures found that 76 percent of the firms raised all initial capital from the partners' personal funds, and that the number of principals was positively and significantly related to the amount of initial capital raised (Teach et al., 1986). However, people with money do not necessarily have the attitudes of an entrepreneur or the skills of a manager.

Another basis for many partnerships is the repertoire of experience and expertise needed to succeed. For example, a woman interested in a retail clothing store for "feminine" professional/office attire lacked critical experience and contacts with clothing manufacturers. She asked an old friend currently employed as a manager by a national chain of department stores to join her as a partner.

Choosing partners based on their ability to contribute financial and human resources (expertise and long hours) is clearly important to the attraction of partners. This focus on resources contributes to the commonly held perception that entrepreneurs are "exploitive" and exchange-oriented in their relationships.

As mentioned earlier, another basis for the attraction of partners is less instrumental and more emotional—when partnerships come from pre-existing friendships (Ladd, Kanter, & Wigan, 1980; "Do Business and Friendship Mix?" 1985) and family relationships (Fooner, 1983; Helm, 1986). The advantage of such partnerships includes the deeper understanding between partners of personalities and personal histories, and presumably better communication. However, what makes for a good friendship or marriage does not necessarily make for an effective business relationship. The woman retailer mentioned earlier found her friend's (potential partner's) personal background and personality (e.g., having been pampered by her parents and former husband, with no need to achieve) and goals (i.e., to make a lot of money right away, without working more than 40 hours a week) were inappropriate for a business partnership. The women ended their business plans and remained friends.

A further disadvantage of friendship-based partnerships is that they may fall into ineffective "leaderless democracies" (Timmons, 1975). In addition, the interaction among partners has two sets of meanings—as contributions to a business and as contributions to a friendship. Events have "double" value, and boundaries between what sustains friends/family and what contributes to business may be hard to draw.

Team composition.   While most "lead" entrepreneurs look for individuals with talents that complement theirs, there is also a tendency to select team members who are similar to the leader. For the most part, we prefer to work with people we can trust, and it is easier to trust others who are more like us than different from us, especially if we do not have a long association with them. People of our same age, sex, race, ethnicity, education, and personal backgrounds are individuals whose values, attitudes, and responses are fairly easy to predict. We find similar others easier to understand, easier to trust, and more attractive. The greater the differences, the more difficult it is to communicate and the harder it is to find common values and agree on problems and their solutions. As a result, we have a tendency to build "look-alike" teams.

However, research suggests that the inclusion of individuals with different experiences, backgrounds, and approaches to problem solving makes for more creative and more efficient groups (Carlsson, Keane, & Martin, 1984/1976; Maier, 1984/ 1970) that are able to avoid "groupthink," or the tendency of group members to conform to one set of assumptions. Thus we would expect the most effective entrepreneurial teams to include complementary skills, as well as differences in experience, style, resource networks, and so forth. Less effective teams would be composed of individuals with overlapping skills and few differences—for example, a team with members from the same hometown who all attended the same schools together, majoring in the same discipline, and who share the same friendship network.

There is some evidence to support this. In their study of microcomputer software firms, Teach and his associates (1986) found that the number of unique educational backgrounds found in the partnership group was positively and significantly associated with venture sales. In addition, chances of success seem to be enhanced by at least one partner having a business degree and one having an engineering degree. "As the number of principals increases, the ability to access a greater variety of educational backgrounds increases and this fact relates to the success of the firm" (Teach et al., 1986, p. 556). Timmons (1982) also reports that homogeneous teams tend to fail in new ventures or have only marginal success.

BONDING (STAYING TOGETHER)

Once individuals interact in a frequent and patterned way, a relationship exists and continues to exist as long as the individuals choose to interact. A partnership begins when individuals start to think of their relationship as having a business or commercial purpose. The continuity of any relationship depends on the strength of the bond between the individuals, their desire to work together, their loyalty, and, for partners, their commitment to the venture.

This bond is built by managing ambivalent feelings of attraction-repulsion (e.g., enjoying the other versus finding him or her irritating and frustrating) and resulting tendencies to seek interaction with the other (e.g., including him or her at meetings and socializing after work versus avoiding such interaction). In addition, partners' commitment to each other requires resolution of conflicting desires for autonomy and independence and the need for interdependence (e.g., giving and receiving help, mutual respect, trust, and status). The conflict implicit in this tension is discussed below.

The bond is also built by managing two sets of relationship "boundaries": (1) those between partners (that is, what responsibilities are mine and which are yours?) and (2) those between the partnership and others (that is, external factors such as spouses' opinions or changes in the marketplace that could influence the partnership). Outside influences such as financial incentives to do other things (e.g., take a better-paying job) and the availability of alternative relationships and/or business opportunities will affect the degree of commitment to the partnership.

Friends, spouses, and family members who are also partners can rely on bonds of affection and loyalty that are developed in other contexts. However, as Henry Scanlon, President of Comstock, Inc., a stock photography agency, commented, "When you go into business with a friend, you have to deal with everything on two levels, which can sometimes produce negative results. . . . More often than not, doing business with friends doesn't work out. But when it works, it works much better" ("Do Business and Friendship Mix?", 1985, p. 27). The same may be said of marriage-based business partnerships.

EXAMPLE: ALAN LADD PRODUCTIONS

In a documented case of friends as partners, Alan Ladd, founder of an independent film production group, comments on his friends and partners, Jay Kanter and Gareth Wigan:

> We're in and out of each others' offices all the time and of course we're required to do certain social things in the evenings—take a writer, director, or producer to dinner, for example . . . our weekends are filled with business. . . . Working this way could be a nightmare if we didn't have good, strong relationships.
>
> Ladd et al., 1980, p. 89

Ladd and his partners work to create a "family" environment in which individuals care for the people they work with, differences are respected, the limits of each person are understood and accepted, and emotions can be expressed without reprisal or evaluation. All three report the importance of being able to trust one another, being able to rely on the others in bad times as well as good, and the freedom to be honest and give criticism without egos being bruised. In this environment conflict is accepted and disagreements are worked out openly.

PROJECTION

When we form ongoing relationships in which there is an emotional dimension, there is often an unconscious process of projection. This involves the individual "seeing" some aspect of himself or herself in the other person (Horwitz, 1983). Projection is thought to initiate and maintain relationships of many sorts, from enemies to lovers. Thus I find "enemies" by seeing my own unconscious dark side or "shadow" (what I like least about myself) in someone else. Likewise, romantic attraction can be considered the result of unconscious projection by women of their inner masculine aspects onto the real man they love and the equally unconscious projection by men of their inner feminine qualities onto the real women they love (Sanford, 1980).

The process of projection is not confined to personal life. If we assume that we all have unconscious parts of ourselves such as forgotten wishes, repressed drives, and habits of which we are unaware and that these parts are active (e.g., they influence our thoughts, feelings, and behaviors), then projection probably occurs wherever and whenever people interact. Thus we assume that projection occurs in organizations, at work, and between partners. A study by analysts Hodgson, Levinson, and Zaleznik (1965) found that projection occurs within the executive role set—those top two or three executives who hold power (i.e., the "dominant coalition"). It also occurs between rank-and-file employees and the CEO/entrepreneur, where employees may heroize (or villainize) the entrepreneur and the executive role set. Seen from the leadership team:

> The executives were sometimes at a loss to understand what was happening as they gave way to subordinates' unnoticed enticements to fulfill the subordinates' hypotheses about them.
>
> Hodgson et al., 1965, p. 470

We assume that the same dynamic operates in entrepreneurial organizations—perhaps more so because of the vitality and visibility of the entrepreneurs.

MANAGING CHANGE AND CONFLICT

An important team dynamic involves group response to changes in the team. Staff turnover is covered in Chapter 9.

Here we address changes in partners, changes in the composition of the partnership group, and sources of conflict among partners.

Partners as individuals change as they grow older, acquiring new tastes and developing new expectations, hobbies, and relationships. Like marriage partners, business partners can "drift apart" and wish to follow separate careers. Just how partners adjust or fail to adjust to the changes each goes through determines the endurance and vitality of the partnership. For more discussion see the next section on interpersonal development.

Just as changes in original partners' predispositions can change partnership dynamics (and create conflict), so can changes in the structure or composition of the partnership. New partners may be added to bring in valuable human and/ or financial resources, and a "piece of the pie" is important to secure their commitment. (Further discussion on sharing equity with employees can be found in Chapter 9.) Each new partner complicates the organization by adding to information, communication, and decision-making processes, requiring office space and support, and so forth. Sometimes these partners are distant and silent; other times they are more active. New partners "dilute" the influence of original partners, and new interpersonal relationships must be negotiated.

Partnership conflict is exacerbated by individual tendencies to avoid or ignore differences in contribution and expertise within the group. Rarely are all partners' contributions equal. Effective teams recognize the importance of the lead entrepreneur and the various talents and do not treat everyone equally. "Nor do they avoid the very difficult, often painful, and time-consuming effort required to come to agreement" (Timmons, 1982).

Besides changes in partners' preferences, differences in goals and different ethical boundaries can cause partners to fall apart. Timmons (1982) reports a case in which two young MBAs formed two ventures, one of which was unprofitable and drained resources from the successful venture. Partner A, while stretching trade payables to the breaking point (some dependable creditors were not paid even though they had been promised payment) also used scarce company funds to pay for his life-insurance policy. Compounding the ethical concerns was the fact that the insurance salesman who received these payments was also a relative. When Partner B found out about these payments, A denied making payments and then denied any wrongdoing. "An unresolvable dispute developed between the partners, and within days their lawyers were their only mode of communication. A few months later the partners had to sell the business at a loss" (p. 71).

There is some evidence that the partnership form of business is inherently unstable, at least in the United States. Collins and Moore (1964) found enough ended partnerships to label a phase of business "getting rid of partners" and Philip Thurston, a consultant to business partnerships, reports (1986):

> When I stress the risks of disagreement to a group of business owners, someone usually speaks up to describe a satisfactory partnership. I know there are such, and more power to the individuals who sustain them. But after one or two success stories, more owners speak of painful [partnership dissolutions] experienced or observed (p. 25).

Thurston suggests that partners anticipate and manage conflict by including in their partnership agreement clauses that cover the "what ifs" of the business and "an escape route" while they are still "within the window of venture enthusiasm and working friendship." That agreement should include what partners will do if they cannot resolve differences themselves. Solutions may range from a buy-sell agreement to an agreement to seek and abide by third-party mediation.

Behind much of the conflict experienced in partnerships (decision-making domains, use of resources, pay and effort equity, involvement of spouses and children, and goals for the firm) are four psychological processes. First, the projection processes described earlier contribute to conflict by distorting perceptions and emotions. A second source of conflict is the polarity of approach-avoidance mentioned above, where sometimes we want to be with the other, including him or her in our projects and decisions, and at other times when we want to proceed alone. A third source of conflict is our tendency toward rivalry versus collaboration, which is probably learned early in life from sibling relationships.

The process of influence is a fourth source of conflict. Partners, as founders and/or key executives, expect to exert control over the organization. However, because they share control, it is often necessary for them to influence and be influenced by each other. Since entrepreneurs (and presumably even those who form partnerships and teams) generally move toward greater autonomy and away from previous experiences of being controlled or interdependent, the partnership can pro-

duce tension. The tension may result in "getting rid of partners," especially if the relationship is based primarily on
resource need (Collins & Moore, 1964).

INTERPERSONAL DEVELOPMENT

As individuals change, so do relationships between them.
Partnerships evolve and grow as a function of the changes the
individuals experience in their own lives. For example, personal events such as the coming of age of children or divorce
are likely to stimulate changes in partnerships. Personal
changes that occur with age, such as "mid-life crises" and
shifts in needs and values (Eriksen, 1950; Rokeach, 1973; Wolfe
& Kolb, 1984) are also likely to change partner relations.

In addition, relationships have their own "ages and
stages" and appear to develop in a patterned way, independent
of the individuals involved. The Neely–Chapman partnership
cases (Harvard, 1970a, b) demonstrate this and many other
aspects of the partnership relationship, and are recommended
reading for those interested in partnerships. The Neely and
Chapman Company is an electrical contracting firm founded
by Richard Neely, who subsequently asked his friend Dale
Chapman to join him as partner in 1956. Their partnership
lasted 13 years and involved both families. The cases center on
interviews with Neely and Chapman and their wives after the
partnership was dissolved, with Neely buying the business
from Chapman and Chapman going to work for someone else.

Neilsen (1982) proposes a developmental model of the two-
person relationship that draws heavily from theories of friendships and marriage and from the Neely–Chapman case. Table
8.1 shows the developmental issues Neilsen identified in the
case.

SUCCESSFUL PARTNERSHIPS

While we have common-sense and operational definitions of
partnerships, we are less quick with our definitions of success.
Is a successful partnership one that lasts for a long time, or one
that changes, or one that ends "cleanly" with everyone "winning" and no ill feelings? Is a successful partnership one that
sustains a growing organization or one that focuses on the
satisfaction of the individual partners' needs? Is a successful
partnership one that is changing or one that remains familiar to the partners? Is a successful partnership one that is
acknowledged by outsiders as being "sound" or is it one

TABLE 8.1 The Developmental Sequence of a Two-Person Partnership

Stage 1	*Mutual Usage versus Mutual Concern*
	Complementary skills of partners make each an important resource to the other (i.e., mutual usage). The sharing of dreams, lifestyles, and social experiences develops into mutual concern. Mutual usage relationships remain fixed at this stage. When partners become friends with mutual concern, they enter stage 2.
Stage 2	*Fusion versus Differentiation*
	Mutual concern results in the possibility of forgetting where, psychologically, one partner leaves off and the other begins. Such fusion results in unconscious coordination and division of labor. Differentiation involves explicit roles and is necessary if the relationship is to continue for a longer period.
Stage 3	*Living Off the Relationship versus Living Through the Relationship*
	Having created role specialization, partners become more efficient with their time and energy. A new dilemma involves whether to use the extra time to pursue personal interests and growing away from each other (i.e., living off the relationship) or to invest these resources in the partnership itself (living through the relationship), which may require "heavy confrontation and mutual adaptation far beyond one's original preferences" (p. 18).
Stage 4	Resisting the Limits of the Other's Willingness to Change versus Tolerating Them
	Continuing to deepen the relationship results in a limit in each person's willingness to change to meet the needs of the other. Continued pushing for change can result in breakthrough understandings of personal values, or in pathological behavior such as irrational fighting, rigidity, and separation. Tolerance of these limits is a sign of mature respect but can also create boundaries that may be limiting in the future.

TABLE 8.1   The Developmental Sequence of a Two-Person
Partnership (*continued*)

Stage 5	**Detente versus Appreciation**
	Having forged an enduring relationship based on acceptance of differences, the last stage is a matter of the attitude toward the relationship— is it satisfactory but not great, or still full of potential?

Source: Adapted from Neilsen (1982)

that "feels good" to the partners? Most likely, a successful partnership is one that fulfills some combination of these criteria.

Although a more clarified understanding of success awaits research, we can reasonably expect certain factors to be important. First, we expect that when partners *share beliefs* about the structure of the partnership, chances of success are enhanced. If the structure is misunderstood, the individuals do not have a common ground for relating; we expect miscommunication and a loss of synergy. Second, we expect that *mutual acceptance* of the existing partnership structure will contribute to success. If structural elements are not accepted, and these cannot be changed quickly (the definition of structure), the partnership may develop interpersonal tensions and destructive conflict. Third, we expect that *individual skills in psychological and interpersonal* work will contribute to success. These skills include active listening (Rogers & Farson, 1984), reflective observation (Kolb, Rubin, & McIntyre, 1984), and use of positive-influence skills (Berlew, 1984). Such psychological and interpersonal skills are expected to contribute to the analysis and acceptance of structure as well as to the ongoing processes of attraction, bonding, projection, and conflict management.

VALUE ADDED

The most obvious way in which partnerships can succeed is through adding value or synergy. *Synergy* is defined as "the working together of unlike elements to create desirable results unobtainable from any combination of independent efforts" (Craig & Craig, 1974, p. 62). By extension, partnership synergy is the transformation of individual contributions into a product that is greater than the sum of the separate contributions. The degree or quality of partnership synergy is a function of the expertise, background, resources, and character of the individuals, the complementarity of their differences, and how these differences are organized and orchestrated.

Concepts of *alignment and attunement* get at fundamental "hows" of synergy (and thus at partnership value). Harrison (1982) suggests that the alignment of people and resources toward a common goal (i.e., establishing internal order) and the attunement of these organizations to a purpose or mission (i.e., finding a healthy relationship with the environment) are important. Looking at leaders, Berlew (1984) highlights the importance of the ability "(1) to maximize energy alignment, and (2) to implement structures and systems which facilitate work and coordinate activities, without wasting human energy or stifling initiative and creativity" (p. 2). Accordingly, we expect partnership synergy to be a function of the individuals' alignment in a team and the team's attunement processes.

BUSINESS SUCCESS

Clearly related to partnership synergy are notions of organizational success. As with partnership success, we are faced with a muddle of concepts to define business success—organizational survival, break even, "excellence," profit, effectiveness, and value.

Whatever criteria used, we expect a partnership to have its greatest impact when the organization is new and/or small. At this stage there are few stakeholders and partners fill many roles: financier, leader, strategist, manager, and often line worker. As new stakeholders are added to internal teams (i.e., employees are hired) and to external teams (e.g., venture capital "partners," bankers, lawyers, stockholders), the partnership relationship becomes less critical to organizational success.

During these critical months or years we expect the partnership's structure, dynamics, and developmental "health" to affect business development and success. Like individual entrepreneurs, partnerships affect the development of organizational culture (Martin, Sitkin, & Boehm, 1984; Schein, 1983), strategy (Guth & Tagiuri, 1965; Hambrick & Mason, 1984), and structure (Bobbit & Ford, 1980). Finally, when partners "fall out of favor" with each other, when feuding starts, the business suffers (Mamis, 1984).

CHAPTER 9

INTERNAL TEAMS: EMPLOYEES

INTRODUCTION

There is evidence that a significant number of new jobs are created by small businesses and entrepreneurial ventures, while jobs are being lost in *Fortune* 500 firms (Birch, 1979). There is also evidence that a large proportion of American workers work in small-business and entrepreneurial contexts; in 1977, nearly 82 percent of retail employees, 80 percent of wholesale employees, 68 percent of service employees, and 25 percent of manufacturing employees worked in firms of fewer than 100 employees (Granovetter, 1984).

However, there is little systematic information on the employment context of entrepreneurial organizations. Most research on human-resource management and organizational behavior derives from studies of large organizations; significantly less is based on stable small organizations. While these studies have general value, the entrepreneurial organization at start-up and during growth may constitute a unique situation for employees—one worthy of research attention. This chapter presents some critical factors to consider when looking at entrepreneurial organizations as employers.

EMPLOYEE MOTIVATIONS

Why do people choose to work for entrepreneurs? There are certain *disadvantages*. At the earliest stages, the job is not secure, the perquisites are minimal, and for many years the pay may be below that offered by larger and more stable firms. Let's look at what motivates people to choose an entrepreneurial environment for their career.

CREATIVE, ADULT ENVIRONMENTS

One theory of entrepreneurial staffing is that employees of entrepreneurs are attracted to new, growth-oriented, risk-taking organizations because their motivations are very similar to those of the entrepreneur (growth, responsibility, and achievement), and some of their motivations are stronger than the entrepreneur's and can be filled especially well in the entrepreneurial context (e.g., advancement, the work itself, and recognition) (Swayne & Tucker, 1973). According to the authors of this essay, salary is not a major motivator for either entrepreneurs or employees. An empirical study supports this, finding that people who work for entrepreneurs tend to be risk takers who are either young and single or part of a two-income household (Hambrick & Crozier, 1985).

Many entrepreneurs recognize that their firms can offer employees creative, adult working environments. In a study of 52 firms led by the founder, Neiswander, Bird, and Young (1987) found that 77 percent claim to provide a "creative atmosphere," "few rules," "freedom to create a challenging job," and "fostering involvement in your job." Nearly one fourth claim to motivate employees by treating them fairly and as adults—the way they would have liked to have been treated when/if they were working for someone else. Other motivational techniques mentioned by entrepreneurs include goal setting and offering employees a "ground-floor" opportunity.

In addition, small firms simply *are* where the jobs are. There is evidence that movement between firms may be more important to the social and economic mobility of American workers than promotions and transfers within large firms. Several reasons can be offered for this. First, large and small organizations tend to have slow or no growth (growth is an exception rather than a rule among firms), and opportunities for advancement or creativity are limited within large pyramidal or small, closely held firms. Second, instead of growing, many large organizations are trimming staff and selling off unintegrated units, frustrating managers' careers and dampening the perception of opportunity within large firms. This results in a perception of expanding opportunity (and displacement incentives) in small-business employment. Third, small-business employers are unlikely to find the right person for each opening within their organizations so they hire from outside (e.g., from other small or large firms).

VISIBILITY AND LEARNING OPPORTUNITIES

Another motivation for working with or for an entrepreneur is the visibility of the entrepreneur and employee to each other. Not only are employee contributions easily seen and employee innovations highly valued (publicly in 20 percent of the cases) (Neiswander et al., 1987), but employees see the entrepreneur/CEO/boss in action on a daily basis. Proximity to an entrepreneur has two social payoffs. Those with a high need for power value closeness to power and decision making, which translates into contact with the boss. Also, seeing an entrepreneur in action and working closely with an entrepreneur offers the employee a chance to learn vicariously. As noted in earlier chapters, entrepreneurs serve as role models for those considering entrepreneurial careers themselves.

"People are often drawn to small firms because they like informality, broad job responsibilities, and being part of a cohesive, intimate team" (Hambrick & Crozier, 1985, p. 35). They enjoy job variety, novelty, and freedom from bureaucracy. They tend to work long and hard hours (80-hour weeks), especially during periods of growth (Mintzberg & Waters, 1982). The rewards for this intense pace include moderate salaries, deferred compensation, and stock options (Hambrick & Crozier, 1985).

PARTICIPATION

One noneconomic motivation is the opportunity for widespread participation in organizational policies and practices, with every employee contributing to and benefitting from the entrepreneurial spirit (Kennedy, 1984). Employees who participate in decision making—especially decisions about their own work and environment—tend to be more satisfied (and therefore less likely to leave) and more motivated (and presumably more productive). In addition, models of innovation suggest that widespread participation is important to the creative development and implementation of new concepts that is necessary to stay competitive (Kanter, 1983; Miles & Snow, 1978; Peters & Waterman, 1982).

Participation can be high in entrepreneurial organizations. Frequently, jobs are not defined (job descriptions are saved for stages of greater bureaucratization and formalization). People who join entrepreneurial organizations, especially in the earliest stages, tend to have broad and evolving responsibilities (with resulting role ambiguity), complex jobs (performing multiple functions, filling in for others, etc.), and high participation in key decisions through frequent informal meetings (Bowen & Jones, 1985; Benner, 1985). Employees will be energized and motivated by participation if they are allowed to share the creative aspects of the work as well as sharing control. This requires the entrepreneur(s) to encourage innovation, to delegate authority and control, and to allow others to influence decisions. Considering the profile of entrepreneurial characteristics and motivation, full participation by employees might be difficult to achieve.

PROFIT SHARING AND EQUITY

Another incentive that delays cash outlays (and is therefore an important consideration during start-up and growth) is sharing future organizational profits and ownership. The sharing of profits is increasingly widespread among large and small organizations, and is perceived as a way to link performance to organizational results, thereby creating a payroll that contains fewer fixed and more variable costs.[1] Thus some organizational consultants recommend that entrepreneurs share profits and/or equity as a way to attract, retain, and motivate key employees ("Do Entrepreneurs Fail to 'Inspire' Employees?", 1986), while others try to help the entrepreneur hold tightly to his or her investment (Baty, 1974).

Because the values of ownership, wealth, and control intermix and vary considerably across consultants and across entrepreneurs, sharing equity is far more controversial than extending participation in decision making. For entrepreneurs, the choice is difficult because good financial and behavioral reasons can be found for sharing equity and equally good reasons can be found for not distributing equity. These reasons are listed in Table 9.1.

Reflecting on his experience as an entrepreneur, Alan Kennedy (coauthor of *Corporate Cultures* and founder of Selkirk Associates, Inc.) says,

> When I call our 22-year-old secretary and say, "Boy, we've got a hot prospect, and we have to get this piece of literature out to him," there's no mystery in her mind that if she works a little bit harder, gets that letter out, gets it in the mail, that that could produce an order. And an order could mean a rise in the value of her company stock, so there is a close identification toward the goals in the company.

Kennedy, 1984, p. 115

[1] This would be an advantage in cyclic economies and industries such as aerospace.

TABLE 9.1 Reasons for Sharing and for Not Sharing Equity Ownership

Reasons For Employee Ownership	Reasons Against Employee Ownership
Financial and/or legal rationale	
To provide additional investment capital	To conserve a relatively undervalued resource, namely equity
To defer the expense of labor	To avoid future litigation
To support the price of shares	To avoid complications in any future sale of the business
To take advantage of tax provisions	
Behavioral rationale	
To acquire and hold key personnel	To increase the long-run likelihood of maintaining control
To be fair or to avoid the guilt associated with being unfair	To conserve privacy
To enhance employee commitment and performance	To avoid the envy caused by knowledge of differences in earnings and accumulated wealth
To reward past service	To avoid future regret
To forestall future requests for stock and control allotments	To avoid the complexity of issues associated with the what, when, how, and who of formulating policy for distributing equity
Ownership results in attitudes of pride and commitment	Ownership results in "feet on the desk" and other entitlement attitudes
Strategic rationale	
An important symbol of control and compensation	Having many stakeholders distracts management with internal politics
A way of sharing risk	Because of complexities in valuation, can be a "form of enslavement" (Posner, 1985, p. 57)
Motivates people to constant innovation	Difficulties in separating the compensation and control aspects of ownership

Source: Adapted from "In the Interest of Equity: Distributing Equity Among New Venture Employees" by W. E. McMullan, in *Frontiers of Entrepreneurship Research 1982*, K. Vesper ed. (Wellesley, MA: Babson College).

Other important questions about the sharing of equity include: (1) Who should receive equity (key employees or everyone)? (2) Should equity be given or purchased? (3) How much equity should be available to employees? (4) What kind of equity should be held by employees (preferred shares or common shares)? (5) How should distribution occur (e.g., by policy or negotiation)? (6) By whose initiative should distribution occur (entrepreneur or employee)? (7) When should distribution occur (as soon as an employee joins or over time)? (McMullan, 1982).

The value of employee ownership will undoubtedly continue to be debated. However, one study suggests that employee buy-outs of entrepreneurs tend to fare well. These are in the form of Employee Stock Ownership Plans (ESOPs). Summarizing recent research on employee-owned organizations, Cohen and Quarry (1986) report that these are "more profitable, more productive, stay in business longer, have higher sales growth rates, and hire more new employees than comparable conventional firms" (p. 59). In their study of firms with ESOPs they found the founder still active in management in 50 percent of the cases, suggesting that shared control and ownership is both possible and profitable. In 50 percent of the cases, the founder was no longer involved and had, in effect, sold the venture to workers. Cohen and Quarry found that the average employment growth rate in the ESOP companies was 3.3 times greater than the industry average (5.6 percent compared to 1.7 percent). Sales in the ESOP firms grew at an average rate of 12.7 percent per year, compared with an industry average of 9.7 percent.

Implications

Employees with different motivations may be attracted to and motivated by ventures started by different types of entrepreneurs. Income-substitution goals of the founder result in slow, if any, growth. The venture *may* provide creativity, visibility, and participation but limited challenge and restricted opportunities for equity participation and getting rich along with the entrepreneur.

Firms started to fill some noneconomic goal may attract and motivate employees who share key values. Thus a firm designed to market humanitarian technology, such as tests of infant intelligence potential (a measure of the learning potential and learning disabilities of premature infants and others at risk), will best be staffed with employees who share the value of caring for infants at risk and alleviating anxiety in parents of these children.

The structure of ownership has clear implications for motivating employees with profit sharing and equity. The more closely held the firm, the less likely equity sharing will be. If closely held ownership is paired with central control by the founder (and/or his or her family), the organization is less likely to feel creative, participative, or full of challenging learning. Employee motivation may become a problem.

ENTREPRENEURS AS BOSSES

ENTREPRENEURS' MOTIVATIONS

Entrepreneurs hire others to work for them for obvious reasons—extra help is needed to meet current demands or to prepare for the future. Entrepreneurs seem to approach hiring from two different perspectives: (1) to have the new hire do what the entrepreneur does, to free the entrepreneur to handle more pressing concerns; and (2) to hire someone with skills the entrepreneur does not have that are needed in the company.

There is evidence that entrepreneurs are often ambivalent about hiring others. Money (usually their own personal savings) is scarce, but so is time. Because time is short, there is often pressure to hire quickly for urgent and current needs. As a result, the entrepreneur may ignore future-oriented concerns such as the employee's fit with his or her style and whether the employee can grow with the firm. Quick hiring also results in employees being put on the job without much orientation and with no training, although they are expected to produce results right away.

The earliest employees often become the top managers of the firm as it grows and form an "inner circle." They often become friends with the entrepreneur as a result of the early "family" atmosphere, and form the early culture of the organization that determines how well the firm competes, innovates, and progresses.

Asked what employee issues they thought were most important (and therefore what they were motivated to do with employees) entrepreneurs mention, in order of importance (Neiswander et al., 1987):

1. hiring an employee
2. morale
3. motivation
4. productivity

5. turnover
6. training
7. compensation

PERSONNEL PRACTICES

The personnel practices in entrepreneurial firms have not been examined empirically with much detail. However, we do know that human-resource problems are the most frequent problems of small businesses (Lewis, Sewell, & Dickson, 1961). The top ten problems cited by the 757 firms studied by Lewis and his colleagues are listed below, beginning with the most serious (Lewis et al., 1961, pp. 68–69).

1. Recruitment of nonmanagement personnel
2. Training of nonmanagement personnel
3. Training of management personnel
4. Sales promotion
5. Recruitment of management personnel
6. Development of distribution channels
7. Cost controls
8. Employee job interest
9. Product diversification
10. Quality control

The hiring of a personnel or human-resource manager is often low on the entrepreneur's list, so entrepreneurs usually end up performing the personnel function themselves. A survey of small businesses found that about half had no personnel manager and that the owner/CEO was most frequently responsible for the following personnel functions (Little, 1986): establishment of wage and salary levels; union/labor relations; recruiting; screening of applicants; equal opportunity compliance; Occupational Safety and Health Act compliance; counseling, complaints, and discipline; evaluation of employees; and training and development. Another survey of the presidents, CEOs, or owners of small businesses partially confirms this, finding that 74 percent were responsible for training and development decisions (Banks, Bures, & Champion, 1987).

There is some recent information on early-stage hiring, but very little on how employees are "brought on board," socialized, and trained or on how long they stay with an entrepreneurial organization. We have virtually no information on any of these concerns for firms in periods of rapid growth.

RECRUITMENT AND HIRING

A recent survey of northeast Ohio ventures in wholesale/retail, service, and manufacturing industries yielded 52 responses (an 18 percent response rate) to questions on early-stage hiring practices (Neiswander et al., 1987). This study found that most entrepreneurs use a "hit or miss" approach to hiring. Especially in the early stages, money is scarce and none is available to hire executive-search consultants. So most early employees are found through family, friends, and business associates, a finding verified by other research that shows that most employees enter small firms through personal contacts (Granovetter, 1984).

Entrepreneurs will probably review an average of 12.6 résumés and interview over four candidates for any one position. Interviews with potential employees tend to focus on the candidate's goals and objectives over the next five years, and on his or her experience and ability to solve particular problems and learn quickly. In addition, entrepreneurs tend to look for "entrepreneurial attitude, drive, self-motivation, initiative, and action orientation" (Neiswander et al., 1987, p. 5).

In addition, entrepreneurs are particularly interested in "chemistry"; it's what entrepreneurs look for in terms of style, personality, and synergy. Does the employee "fit" with the entrepreneur (his or her boss) and with the existing team members? There are no pat answers to questions of chemistry and entrepreneurs seem to look for it through lengthy and multiple interviews. Others use psychologists to assess their own personality and the personality of management candidates to find those who will "click" with the entrepreneur.

EXAMPLE: BP

BP spends a considerable amount of time with each managerial candidate to assess which of three basic types of person each is: marines, infantry soldiers, or garrison soldiers. Marines prefer to be "on the firing line" where things are hot and changes are coming fast and furious. They enjoy risk and being first on the "island" (e.g., innovation). Infantry soldiers prefer to use technology and expertise to advance existing products or services or "clear the island" (e.g., capture market share, set up operations). Garrison soldiers prefer to maintain order once the island is secured (i.e., control, systematize, and formalize operations). Whether hiring for accounting, sales, or operations, BP attempts to identify which type of environment the person will flourish in and whether that function is in need of innovation, advancement, or stability.

By looking at the person's character (after qualifications have been met), BP attempts to match the person's "chemistry" with the department's "culture." By doing so he expects to have more highly motivated and satisfied managers.

The first employee. On the average, the first employee is hired when the company has $25,000 of capitalization (in 75 percent of the cases, the company was self-financed, so the entrepreneur was spending his or her own money). In more recently founded firms, the first employee was hired in the same month as the first sale; older firms were more conservative, hiring within six months of the first sale. The most important functions warranting hired help were operations (production), secretarial/administrative, and sales, and the first employee had an average of 2.3 functional job responsibilities (e.g., sales, accounting, and engineering). Technically oriented entrepreneurs were more likely to hire additional technical help earlier than those without technical backgrounds (Neiswander et al., 1987).

Operations managers, office managers, and sales managers are the most important early hires. Later, entrepreneurs consider hiring a marketing manager, a purchasing manager, and a controller. Much later (and of far less perceived importance) are R & D, information systems, and human-resource managers (Neiswander et al., 1987). As suggested earlier, entrepreneurs probably fill these functions themselves.

The problems with "old-timers." Old-time employees are not necessarily old in age. Consider entrepreneur Steven Jobs, who at age 20 joined with Steven Wozniak, then age 25, to begin a venture that later became Apple Computer. The key employees who joined early on are their peers, and several remained with the organization during its rapid growth and transformation. These young men and women are the old-timers at Apple.

Old-time employees may be those with five, ten, or thirty years with the firm. All present a similar dilemma for the growth-oriented organization—the changing requirements of management versus loyalty to those who endured early uncertainties and became friends along the way.

> The managerial skills needed in a 1000-person company are different from a 100-person company, and are usually in short supply when the company has reached that size rapidly. . . . Managers now need to direct departments instead of doing the tasks themselves. A vice-president of operations who was a first-rate plant manager, for example, may not be a good manager of three other plant managers. . . . In addition, there is the problem of shifts of substantive expertise required. In this case, the vice-president of operations who made his mark by being able to get new facilities going quickly may not have the expertise to squeeze costs out of a product line that is under price attack from new competitors.
>
> Hambrick & Crozier, 1985, p. 36

The problem is compounded by the entrepreneur's sense of fairness, derived from a family of feelings (e.g., if one early team member is made vice-president of sales, the engineer on the team may expect to be made vice-president of operations). "Few situations so starkly pit a CEO's sense of himself as a company leader against his sense of himself as a decent and humane person, a good employer" (MacRury, 1986, p. 101).

Two solutions to the problem of old-timer obsolescence seem possible. Management training may be able to upgrade the skills and expertise of old, loyal, and valued employees. Indeed, successful growth organizations do invest in hiring top-notch human resource managers and in developing professional training programs (Hambrick & Crozier, 1985).

The second solution involves hiring new managers, with appropriate expertise, and giving them authority and resources. This option often involves replacing a member of the original team. Baty (1974) proposes three equally imperfect ways to do this: (1) fire the employee (but by now he or she is a friend and well-liked by the team, and his or her termination may affect organizational morale); (2) bring someone in above the employee (perceived as a demotion and may demotivate); and (3) create a token job, with little responsibility (this can be expensive and fools no one). There tends to be agreement among consultants that ineffective employees should be let go, despite the emotional difficulties.

From the perspective of organizational effectiveness, old-timers may be perceived as problems. But from the perspective of long-term employees *and* from the perspective of the entrepreneurs themselves, the organization may be the problem. For those who started or joined the new venture for the excitement of hands-on work with a small group of key people, or for the control that is possible during early development, growth means organization, systems, meetings, reports, and bureaucratization. Growth brings both the rewards of a job well done and the loss of team spirit and the old sense of family. Further discussion can be found in Chapter 11.

The problems with newcomers. New employees present the organization with another set of problems. In order for them to participate effectively with the entrepreneur and his or her initial team, they must be brought up to speed on current work in progress. This is difficult because, in a growing business, current team members are already working long hours with 150 percent effort and there is no one to properly train new managers and workers. There are no job descriptions or procedures manuals. In addition, newcomers have to learn the core values and norms of the firm. Beside lacking time to attend to this important socialization process, many entrepreneurs (and their teams) are unaware or inarticulate about these values and norms or find them unimportant.

Timing of hiring. There is controversy about when hiring should occur—should vision (e.g., future needs) or demand (e.g., current sales and volume) drive the decision to invest in human resources? Presumably based on his consulting practice, Baty (1974) argues that hiring for the future means hiring overqualified people today with the following costs: (1) overpaying relative to what is needed to get the job done today, (2) the possible loss of equity, (3) the expense of perquisites, and (4) a loss of effectiveness as the overqualified employee leaves big business luxuries and moves into the more Spartan entrepreneurial context. However, as large corporations are trimming middle management ranks, many managers are finding that jobs with small and entrepreneurial organizations are both available and attractive, even without the perquisites and equity (Bennett, 1986). In an empirical look at this question, Neiswander et al. (1987) found that "early hires were usually brought on board to be responsive to a set need at the time" (p. 5) and the future fit with and ability to grow with the firm were not taken into consideration.

The other side of the argument comes from an empirical study of 74 firms in the "*Inc.* 100" and the "*Inc.* Second 100" fastest-growing firms in 1981. This study found that successful growing firms hired managers and external directors with experience in larger firms who had the skills needed to move the organization from its entrepreneurial origins to maturity. These managers and directors were recruited *before* the firm reached the size where the skills and perspectives were critical. Those who "stumbled" on the growth curve "tended to appoint such people only after they had encountered trouble. In a rapid growth environment, this is often too late" (Hambrick & Crozier, 1985, p. 37). Of course, not all entrepreneurial organizations are growing concerns and the hiring practices are expected to differ based on growth objectives, environmental conditions, and the strengths of current management.

Nepotism. Another controversy must be mentioned. Recall the introduction to Chapter 8 and how entrepreneurs, like all of us, want team members they can trust. As mentioned then, this results in "look-alike" groups subject to groupthink, the tendency to ignore individuals and data that do not support consensus and to avoid conflict. Another serious problem is nepotism, the hiring of family members, and cronyism, the hiring of friends and the family of friends. While these individuals may be more trustworthy, they may not bring the skills and divergent perspectives needed to maintain innovation and sustain profits. Other concerns with such favoritism are the fairness of promotion and compensation as well as leadership succession.

Nepotism and cronyism occur in closely held and family businesses. Of course, not all family-controlled or closely held businesses practice such favoritism. However, if we assume that it occurs in 10 percent of these organizations, the numbers can be startling. Recent estimates suggest that 90 percent of "all corporations (including 35 percent of the *Fortune* 500) are either owned or controlled by a family" (Lansberg, 1983, p. 39) and that 42 percent of the American workforce is employed by family-controlled organizations (Beckhard, 1983).

Family firms are caught in the dilemma of having two sets of values, norms, habits, and relationships that intersect (Kepner, 1983). The family accepts all blood relatives and most relatives by marriage without condition. Healthy family systems are based on unconditional love and support, and permit and encourage the expression of emotion. In families, the norms of fairness are based on need or equality among siblings. In contrast, most organizations are based on instrumental relations mentioned in Chapter 8, namely, hiring and retaining members based on their competence and skills. Organizational well-being requires the efficient production of goods and services and profitability, as well as norms of fairness based on merit (e.g., pay for performance or pay for longevity/seniority).

Renn Zaphiropoulos, founder of Versatec, the largest producer of electrostatic printers and plotters (acquired by Xerox after it demonstrated a growth rate of 25 percent a year) has this to say to his employees (whom he personally greets):

> Remember that your supervisor is not your father or mother. Your father and mother accept you unconditionally. That is not the responsibility of your supervisor. There are conditions under which you're accepted in business or in industry. You have to perform according to the agreement you make. And therefore although one can let off steam in tantrums and scream all this at home, it doesn't work here. I wish it did. Here you have to be accurate.
>
> Xerox Creative Services, 1980

Issues of fairness in hiring, rewards (e.g., salary, bonus, stock options, and promotions), appraisal, and training are frequently raised when nepotism and/or cronyism are practiced. In fact, bureaucratic human-resource practices were developed to circumvent both nepotism and cronyism.

Hiring, training, and firing family members puts additional strains on the lead entrepreneur.

> Typically, relatives feel entitled to "claim their share" of the family business; they flock to the firm demanding jobs and opportunities regardless of their competence. The rationale rests on the family principle that unconditional help should always be granted to relatives who are in need. From a business standpoint . . . the founder knows that the firm cannot be allowed to become a welfare agency.
>
> Lansberg, 1983, p. 41

Although less severe, the same pressures can come from friendship groups.

The approach to hiring is a function of the goals the entrepreneur has for the organization (see Chapter 1) and his or her family culture. Some entrepreneurs anticipate these pressures and develop policies of "no relatives." Others appreciate the commitment and convenience of hiring relatives, especially in the formative years (Lansberg, 1983).

As the organization grows, nonfamily members join family members. Recall that family norms of fairness differ from currently accepted norms of business practice. However, family business norms of "fair pay" may be different from what we expect.

> Contrary to commonly held beliefs about nepotism, studies have shown that founders tend to under-reward their relatives who work in the firm. While this practice is relatively harmless during the formative stages of the firm, it creates considerable problems in the mature family business. Under-rewarding relatives, regardless of their competence, may lead to a situation in which incompetent family employees are retained while competent family employees are driven to seek employment elsewhere.
>
> Lansberg, 1983, p. 42

TRAINING AND DEVELOPMENT

Entrepreneurial organizations, especially those in phases of growth, are changing the composition and organizational position of the entrepreneur and members of his or her team (partners or early hires). New members join as new talents and resources are required. Original members leave voluntarily or by request. Arrivals and departures change the size and composition of the team and, as a result, affect interpersonal relationships. As we know from studies of organizational change in other contexts, there is often considerable discomfort and resistance to planned and unplanned change (Zander, 1950/1982). Entrepreneurial team members may experience change as do other executives when the team changes "as . . . a loss of the clear, satisfying, emotionally and motivationally economic conceptions they held" (Hodgson et al., 1965, p. 471).

As a result of these changes, the entrepreneurial organization faces three important personnel problems: the need to bring new people "up to speed" quickly while retaining the core values of the small intimate team; the need to develop old-timers in the context of changing demands that result from growth; and the need to manage the conflict between old-timers and newcomers.

Orientation of new employees. As the team expands or changes, new members must be brought up to date and informed of the work in progress, group norms, values, standards, and so forth. This process is known as adult socialization (Van Maanen & Schein, 1977) and occurs whenever individuals enter into new organizational contexts. Time costs for this process can be considerable.

The orientation of new employees is something entrepreneurs tend to ignore, thinking that training is something done only in big organizations or is a low priority during periods of "sprinting" and crisis management brought on by start-up and rapid growth. However, experts tend to agree that employee training is crucial for entrepreneurial companies "where everything is still evolving, from the purpose of the business to its methods and procedures" (Posner, 1986, p. 74). Indeed, successful growth-oriented firms "spend a great deal of time and money in training and development of all employees but especially managers" (Hambrick & Crozier, 1985, p. 37). Without training, employees are thrown into their work and expected to learn by trial and error and by asking questions of peers. When peers are themselves new and/or poor communicators, the lack of training can result in poor quality, loss of customers, and dissatisfied workers who feel an urgent need to act but lack clarity about what to do.

Skyway Freight Systems, Inc. recently instituted an extensive employee orientation program. Founder Jim Watson finds the benefits of the program exceed its costs.

> It's helped the company upgrade its service and create a loyal—and growing—clientele. At the same time, it has had a demonstrable impact on employee morale and turnover. This, in turn, has allowed the company to concentrate on finding new people for expansion, instead of having to hunt down replacements.
>
> Posner, 1986, p. 75

Development. Recall that the entrepreneur, CEO, or president tends to be *the* decision maker with regard to training and development in 50 to 75 percent of small businesses (Banks et al., 1987). This group also identified their priorities with regard to training topics, which are ranked below beginning with the highest priority.

1. management skills for new managers
2. communication skills
3. leadership
4. problem solving
5. motivation

6. decision making
7. delegation
8. time management
9. negotiation
10. goals and objectives

In most cases, small business owners tend to use a limited range of training resources with most using only trade associations, college seminars of less than five days, and in-house personnel staff when such exist (Banks et al., 1987).

Conflict. Although we expect that growing firms would have considerable cónflict from the inadequate integration of newcomers, the "old-timer" problems, and stress and burnout, there is little evidence—systematic or anecdotal—on conflict in the entrepreneurial environment. We do know that old-timers tend to self-focus (but so do functional areas) when recalling organizational history. Old-timers (more than newcomers) tend to identify with the perspective of the entrepreneur but otherwise are not very different in their perception of the enterprise (Martin, Sitkin, & Boehm, 1984). This suggests that the old-timer-versus-newcomer conflict may be less important than anticipated.

Another clue about entrepreneurial conflict management comes from data on labor relations and unions, where less than half have employee bargaining units. In most cases company officials (probably the entrepreneur or an early team member) negotiate with the unions (Lawyer, 1963).

Implications

The recruitment, hiring, and training and development of employees is a key component of the new venture's internal alignment of resources. As discussed in Chapter 1, if the entrepreneur wants to move the venture in an intended direction—toward growth or toward stability—the human resources must align with his or her vision and values. This alignment occurs as people join the firm. Do they share core values? Are they interested in the challenges of venture growth or in the rhythm of stability? Do their monetary goals line up with those of the entrepreneur? The competency of the entrepreneur in recruiting and selecting employees is important to this process.

Alignment also occurs as people develop their jobs, overcome the problems of tenure (old-timers and newcomers), and progress within a family or nonfamily firm. Training and re-training become important as ventures grow and/or undergo changes in markets, products, technology, and regulation. Be-cause entrepreneurs hold onto the human-resources/personnel function for a long time, his or her competency in developing and motivating employees is critical.

THE ENDING OF THE TEAM

A final dynamic in entrepreneurial teams involves how mem-bers deal with the issue of their continuity as they build an organization that later absorbs and controls them. For a grow-ing organization, the "team spirit" often disappears.

> You take an idea and a little money, find a handful of be-lievers, and together set out to build a new enterprise against all odds. The quarters are cramped, the hours are long, the pay is thin, but it doesn't matter. There is a magic in the work, a special shine. You are a family, bonded to-gether in common purpose and commitment. Exuberant, enthusiastic, and dedicated, you accomplish prodigies of endurance and self-sacrifice. The idea takes hold, and the company grows. . . .
> . . . In the fullness of your accomplishment, you find it strangely hollow. The company is too big, too complex. What is that person's name? Where did that family feeling go, and where the magic?
>
> Rhodes, 1986, p. 74

In such growth contexts, teams and individuals need to deal with their transformation from entrepreneurs to top man-agers. The role transitions of lead entrepreneurs are discussed in Chapter 11, and are obviously more complex when several people are involved. Builders of a growing firm can expect changes in the nature of one's responsibilities, changes in group norms and values, and changes in organizational culture.

Not all entrepreneurial ventures grow into hierarchical, formalized, and self-perpetuating organizations. Some remain stable and small, often because the team members like it that way (either consciously or unconsciously); others stay small because the market cannot support larger firms. With a stable, small firm, the team faces the challenge of remaining innova-tive and vital and avoiding pressures toward "groupthink" (e.g., "that's how we do it here," avoiding conflict and confron-tation, etc.). Even successful long-term relationships seem to benefit from occasional renewal experiences where individuals bring in new ideas or people (such as consultants), recontract with each other, and find new ways to express appreciation and commitment.

SUMMARY AND CONCLUSIONS ABOUT INTERNAL TEAMS: PARTNERS AND EMPLOYEES

> The age of the lone wolf entrepreneur has passed. Launching and managing successful growth companies are both much too complex.
>
> Silver, 1983, p. 130

Chapters 8 and 9 have outlined the key team members who operate inside the entrepreneurial organization. These key players—partners and employees—with leadership from the entrepreneur(s), make entrepreneurial events happen, adding value and organization as the process unfolds.

These chapters have drawn considerably from the insights of consultants. There are two comments to be made on this. First, there is a need for more empirically based research on partners and employees of entrepreneurs. Second, consultants are frequently called for by entrepreneurs to help them with their human resource/interpersonal problems. This makes sense when we consider that many entrepreneurs lack sophisticated human relations skills (although many also have excellent skills). Entrepreneurs use consultants in lieu of hiring personnel managers and consider the behavioral side of their enterprise to be a place to save money rather than a place to invest money. Finally, consultants tend to see systems that do not work well. We must assume that there are many entrepreneurial organizations where employment processes work and evolve adequately.

We do know that the entrepreneur's relationships with key team members will be instrumental in the accomplishment of his or her goals (unless the goal is to remain solo self-employed). Therefore, the entrepreneur, potential entrepreneurs, employees and partners of entrepreneurs, as well as outside team members (to be considered next) might do well to attend to the internal team composition, size, dynamics, and relationships as well as the relationship of inside teamwork to organizational performance.

CHAPTER 10

EXTERNAL
RELATIONSHIPS

INTRODUCTION

Just as entrepreneurs form key relationships within their organizations, they also
form relationships with outsiders—ven-
ture capitalists, boards of directors, "strategic alliances,"
professional advisors, family and friends, and networks. These
relationships involve different types of "psychological contracts" and are formed with different intentions than those
formed with insiders. Before we go on to explore each of these
relationships in some detail, we ought to ponder why external
relationships are considered so important to entrepreneurial
success and why they are named "external teams" by Vesper
(1980).

ENTREPRENEURIAL ENVIRONMENT

One of the ways to look at the entrepreneurial organization is
as an organism in a competitive niche or environment. As with
large, established organizations, entrepreneurs face environments with many dimensions (see Figure 10.1). Each dimension can be more or less complex, with greater or lesser
differentiation and integration (e.g., well segmented markets
versus mass markets; low versus high technology, etc.). In addition, each dimension can be changing more or less rapidly.

   Organizational survival, growth, and profitability (and
thus increase in net worth and insider job security and promotion opportunities) are thought to be dependent on how
well the organization adapts to the complexity and change in
its environment. Organizational analysis reveals that effective
organizations *scan* the environment for important changes and

FIGURE 10.1   Domains in an Organization's Environment

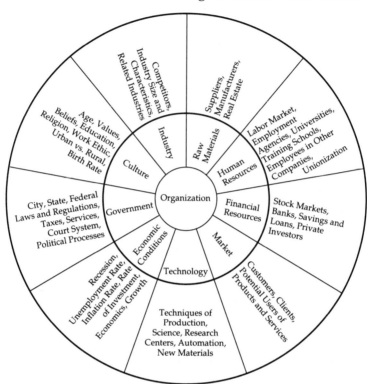

Source: Reprinted by permission from *Organization Theory and Design,*
Richard L. Daft. Copyright © by West Publishing Company. All rights
reserved.

trends, *proact* on the environment to create change beneficial
to the organization, and *strategize* to achieve niche/market su-
periority. Entrepreneurial organizations are no exception.

Indeed, we may hypothesize that entrepreneurs with organizations that have the most growth potential achieve this
by intentionally entering chaotic, turbulent, and volatile environments where opportunities and competitive advantage are
hard to determine (Valentine, 1985). In these environments
vision and vigilance—along with a good measure of intuition,
common sense, and luck—seem to be of value.

Entrepreneurial organizations can adapt to such environments in ways that larger or more rigid organizations cannot.
Entrepreneurial firms are small, with shorter chains of command and less staff than their larger cousins, and are more
aggressive and innovative than the traditional small business.

As a result, entrepreneurial organizations are capable of making faster and more finely tuned adjustments in products or services and are more responsive to selected segments of markets (these are both aspects of attunement, which is part of entrepreneurial intention as described in Chapter 1). In contrast, large organizations survive because they have momentum, market share, and access to more resources than smaller firms.

In order to capitalize on the unique characteristics of the entrepreneurial organization, Michael Piore, coauthor of *The Second Industrial Divide,* suggests that entrepreneurs engage with their environments.

> [G]et outside your company. You get dynamism, you find market niches, and you get ideas by traveling—that is, looking at other companies, moving around, going to trade fairs, looking at new equipment. You can almost judge the difference between a dynamic and a nondynamic company by how much the management in these small companies gets outside their own company.
>
> Piore & Sabel, 1985, p. 41

Yet another way to conceive of entrepreneurial organizations is as bridging or brokering opportunities and resources, which may in fact be held by other people. In this model, the entrepreneur, seeing an opportunity in one place and time, connects this opportunity with resources in another place (or time). As with the model of organism survival and growth, environmental awareness is of great importance to the entrepreneur, as are the intentional competencies suggested in sustaining temporal tension, maintaining strategic focus, and choosing strategic posture.

ENVIRONMENTAL SCANNING

Empirical studies show that small-business owner-managers spend more time than large-business managers in scanning the environment for information (two hours a day compared to one and one-half hours), and have greater concern about the marketplace and growth potential than managers in larger organizations (Kuehn & Johnson, 1986). This same study showed that small-business managers (like those in larger firms) gather most of their information by talking and listening (especially with customers). However, small-business managers connect with suppliers and distributors more often than managers in larger firms, who tend to use group meetings and informal networks more often than the small-business manager. Although the subjects in this study were not founders or entrepreneurs, the results are suggestive of what external relationships might be valuable to the entrepreneurial organization.

Resources other than information are also critical to entrepreneurs: capital, customers, suppliers, employees, physical plant and equipment, and so forth. In scanning for resources and information, entrepreneurs rely on interpersonal relationships. These relationships can vary in importance on two dimensions: (1) the *quality and quantity of resources* and (2) the amount of *active involvement and commitment* of the outsiders who provide them. Individuals with significant information and resources who are actively involved with the business are often called "external team" members (Vesper, 1980).

Important relationships outside the organization are with those who have a stake or interest in the organization's success, growth, and profitability (e.g., venture capitalists and private investors, boards of directors or advisors, corporate partners and strategic alliances, professional advisors, family and friends, and networks). Let's look at each of these stakeholders in turn.

VENTURE CAPITAL

Of all the external relationships formed by entrepreneurs, that with venture capital is probably best understood. There has been increasing interest in the functioning of venture capital decisions because of the vast amount of money involved (approximately $16.3 billion dollars in the venture capital pool, with $3.25 billion committed to portfolio companies in 1984) (Gorman & Sahlman, 1986). As a result, we have considerable information on the relationship between capitalist and entrepreneur.

DEFINITION

"Venture capitalism is the business of developing business. The venture capitalist typically makes long term investments in high risk businesses with long term potential for significant capital gains" (Robinson & Pearce, 1984, p. 69). Expected gains are 25 to 50 percent compounded over an investment duration of five to seven years, a 300 to 1000 percent gain. Actual gains average 155 percent (Brophy, 1986) with newsworthy financings receiving twenty-to-one returns (Mahar, 1986).

Although we frequently refer to the venture capitalist as an individual, most venture capital is found in funds with individual and institutional investors. The funds are run by an organization headed by several partners, who make substantial personal investments, raise funds, scout and make "deals," and monitor investments. In our look at this external relationship, we will focus on the behavior and interpersonal interaction of the venture capital partner(s) and the entrepreneur and his or her team. Solo venture capitalists are often called "angels" or "private placements" (Logan, 1986; Neiswander, 1985) and are a source of funds and nonmonetary support that is less well-understood than venture capital firms.

NATURE OF THE RELATIONSHIP

The *ideal* relationship between venture capitalists and entrepreneurs goes through the following stages:

1. An entrepreneurial team, looking for first-round financing,[1] writes a "winning" business plan, and personally impresses a venture capitalist.

2. The internal team is "balanced," experienced, and committed, involves a strong lead entrepreneur, and is not extravagant in its plans.

3. The team wants "intelligence capital" (e.g., expertise) as well as money.

4. The venture capitalist puts together a set of venture partners from other firms (thus distributing risk). One takes the role of "lead" investor, and is responsible for monitoring the new enterprise, organizing the other investors, and intervening as deemed appropriate.

5. The venture capital group provides money, while the lead investor, in addition, provides advice—all for a share in the equity of the firm (often a controlling interest).

6. A "deal is cut," involving term sheets that "lay out the equity interest acquired, the price paid by investors, voting rights, board seats, and who will pay for the registration of future issues" and a legal document, the purchase and sales agreement, which puts these agreements into legal language and "adds any other conditions that have to be met

---

[1] In 1985, 18.9 percent of venture money went to seed and start-up ventures (compared with 33 percent in 1986), in 1985 18.7 percent went into later-stage ventures (8.8 percent in 1986); while follow-on and leveraged buy-out financing remained about the same in 1985 and 1986 ("The venture index," 1986).

before the sale." The document serves as a financial disclosure statement of the company receiving the funding (Jubak, 1986, p. 134).

7. Later, if more money is required, the lead investor and the original investment group make a rational assessment of the future prospects of the enterprise. They drop the "losers" and make additional investments in the "winners."

8. After four to seven years of steady growth the company (investment) is sold—through a public offering, in a corporate acquisition, or back to the founders who buy out investors.

9. Investors make money, entrepreneurs make money, and the company flourishes.

The reality of venture capital-entrepreneur relationships differs widely from the ideal. There are long hours of *courtship and sizing up* where opportunities, risks, and individuals are assessed *by both parties* by a process called "due diligence." Venture capitalists screen business ideas, seeing hundreds of proposals a year. They fund less than 6 percent of those seeking "seed" financing (for business development, prototype development, etc.) and only 16 percent of start-ups (Brophy, 1986). These figures will decrease substantially, following economic upheaval such as that of October 19, 1987. The screening process *attempts to pick winners* both at early stages and in later rounds.

Research suggests that venture capitalists make their initial funding decisions based on a two-tier system. First, the business proposal or business plan must pass financial, market, and technology criteria and second, the entrepreneur and his team must be seen as adequate to the task (MacMillan, Siegel, & Narasimha, 1985). In the latter category of evaluation personality, "chemistry," integrity, and interpersonal styles and skills begin to take on unique value. Logic and rationality hand decision making off to feeling and intuition.

Specifically, venture capitalists assess *four critical factors of the entrepreneur and his or her team*: (1) personal motivation of the entrepreneur (does he or she have the "right stuff," charisma, staying power, and the ability to handle risk?); (2) organizational skills such as leadership and team building; (3) executive experience, especially with the target market; and (4) technical skills (MacMillan et al., 1985; Robinson & Pearce, 1984).

The entrepreneur is also making an *assessment of the venture capitalist and the psychological "price" of capital* (e.g., handing over considerable ownership and often control). Sometimes this assessment is cursory, where a financially strapped entrepreneur is so focused on operating income that he or she enters a relationship in which values such as wealth creation versus organization building may clash (Kotkin, 1984). At other times a thorough assessment results in entrepreneurs having difficulty finding venture partners with "intelligence equity" as well as money (Kotkin, 1984b).

There follow days, weeks, or months of *negotiating* between entrepreneurs who have "good deals" and need cash and venture capitalists who have cash and need good investments. However, the issues negotiated have little to do with money and a lot to do with *control.*

> There's only one issue [between entrepreneurs and venture capitalists] and that's ownership. . . . Any other terms can be bought off by giving up a bigger percentage of ownership.
>
> Andrew Egendorf of Symbolics Inc.,
> in Jubak, 1986, p. 134

There are also long hours of negotiating among the investor group on issues of control (e.g., dilution of original holdings with subsequent rounds of financing), participation in subsequent rounds of financing, and composition of the venture partnership group. After the initial investment, the decision to stay with the investment or "bail out"—a decision that is often a mix of logic and emotion—can divide investment partners and require additional negotiation. The investor group structure and dynamics have implications for the group's relationship with the focal entrepreneur. For example, a group divided on the issue of subsequent financing or "firing" the entrepreneur can put considerable pressure on the relationship with the entrepreneur.

The importance of shared values. As in finding and developing a partnership relationship, the synergy of the venture capitalist with the entrepreneur depends on shared values and mature negotiation. Ideally, both parties value organizational growth and want to "cash out" within a certain period of time. They keep communication channels open and candid, disclosing both bad news and good. There are few surprises interpersonally.

Relationships fall short of the ideal because of value divergence and/or poor communication. Values change. Venture capitalists seem to fear that entrepreneurs, tasting success with some benchmark in personal wealth (like $1 million) will stop being attentive to the venture. A venture capitalist with a well-known Cleveland bank says:

> If the guy who never had anything in his life has all of a sudden built something and says, "Jesus, what if I lose it" and all of a sudden becomes very conservative in his business strategy, the opportunity cost to my money all of a sudden went right through the roof. I don't have that asset growing in the same way I did the day before he made that philosophical change.

Just as much of a concern is the possibility that the entrepreneur will come to enjoy the responsibilities of leadership of his or her enterprise and resist efforts to sell the company later, since with the transfer of ownership often goes control and autonomy.

Of course, entrepreneurs have their own concerns. Among these are: Will the venture partner exert stifling control? Will the venture partner stick with me if more money is needed later? Will the company be sold too soon? Can the pace of growth be chosen for the long-term benefit of the organization?

Communications can be impaired if trust is not present, if degree of involvement/distance is not understood (articulated during the phase of "psychological contracting"), and if norms of asking for help/being helpful are not understood. Equally important is the ability of both parties to "speak the same language," which reflects the "intelligence equity" of the venture capitalist and the managerial orientations of the entrepreneurial team.

Qualities of the relationship. Relationships between investors and entrepreneurs vary considerably. One of the most frequently used words is *partner.* Says Don Valentine, founder of Sequoia Capital,

> On a tactical level we are at best a partner, but mostly a cheerleader. For example, during the wooing process—when the decisions are made whether to invest or not—we try to avoid having any of our ideas taken up as part of the concept of the company, lest we distort the entrepreneur's or management's view of what's supposed to happen. . . . We want to make sure that the company is one where the entrepreneurs are having *their* ideas financed, and that they are passionately committed to those ideas.

Valentine, 1985, p. 46

Another word that is often used is *marriage.* Another Cleveland-based venture capital partner said:

> It's the worst kind of marriage because once we're married, there is no divorce. We can't sell our stock. We can't get out if we change our mind a year later. Now we have to make the marriage work. We have fights just like other married people do but we have to make this marriage successful.

Venture partnerships vary in terms of *active involvement* in the firm. Some venture capitalists keep "hands off," while others spend more time involved with entrepreneurial management. Proponents of the hands-off approach are entrepreneurs who do not wish to lose control and investors who believe that entrepreneurs do best when left alone. Hands-on investors believe that they bring more to the investment than money and wish to secure or control their investment. A partner with Morgenthaler & Associates says:

> We believe that young companies, no matter how experienced the management, benefit from an active, involved member of the board of directors who takes the position of ownership, counsels with management, interfaces with management, doesn't play a day-to-day management role but plays an active counseling and looking out for the interests of shareholders kind of role.

Entrepreneurs who recognize that their firm has grown beyond their competencies might also welcome hands-on venture partners (although such recognition is apparently rare).

A measure of hands-on involvement is the time spent by investors in direct contact with the entrepreneur and his or her firm, such as in telephone conversations and on site visits. Indirect contact also occurs, and involves networking, research, etc., on behalf of the entrepreneurial firm. A recent study of venture capital firms showed that investors are spending from zero to 450 man-days a year (a man-day is the equivalent of one person working for one day), with an average of 34 man-days, in direct contact with the entrepreneurial organization (Robinson & Pearce, 1984). Another study found considerably less time—only two hours per week from the lead investor and an additional 45 minutes a week from non-lead investors (Gorman & Sahlman, 1986). This same study reports that first-round investors spend ten times more direct hours than those who join later. "Typically, a lead-investing venture capitalist shows up frequently, one-and-a-half times a month, but stays only five hours each time" (Gorman & Sahlman, 1986, p. 424).

Venture capitalists tend to *like* the entrepreneurs they finance. They seek open, trusting give-and-take during their relationship. This means having immediate access to each other, sharing off-hours activities, and developing a personal relationship. A venture capitalist at a large Cleveland bank says:

> I honestly can't think of another business where you get to pick your friends going in. I'm on seven boards of portfolio companies and in every single case, whenever I'm there or anywhere nearby, and I have some time, I'll stop and have dinner with the CEO and his wife. It doesn't have a damn thing to do with my investment. They're friends of mine.

However developmental, friendly, and helpful the relationship, there are some peculiar twists to it. For one, "venture capitalists assume that few entrepreneurs will actually accomplish what they say they will," with one venture capitalist saying 90 percent of his investments fail to meet their written targets (Andrews, 1986, January, p. 33). Such an expectation is clearly not optimistic nor that of a "cheerleader." Likewise, an entrepreneur with few other sources of financing can be vulnerable and dependent on investors who keep "their favorite entrepreneurs hungry for cash" and with little room for error or learning (Andrews, 1986, January).

VENTURE CAPITAL CONTRIBUTIONS TO THE ENTERPRISE

We see that venture capitalists often contribute considerable time and "intelligence equity" in addition to money. The list below shows the kinds of assistance that venture capitalists provide, in order of decreasing frequency (Gorman & Sahlman, 1986, p. 426).

1. Help obtaining additional financing
2. Strategic planning
3. Management recruiting
4. Operational planning
5. Resolving compensation issues
6. Introducing potential customers and suppliers
7. Recruiting board members
8. Managing the investor group
9. Helping entrepreneurs find professional services such as accounting, law, consultation
10. Being the entrepreneur's sounding board

In addition, it often falls on the venture capitalist, along with the board of advisors, to *replace the entrepreneur and other top managers when this is deemed beneficial*. Apparently this is done frequently (Gorman & Sahlman, 1986).[2] Although always a tense and difficult transition, the firing of the entrepreneur can be handled in different ways, resulting in good continuing relationships (e.g., when severance is based on shared values for the growth of the company) (Gupta, 1986) or in ill will (e.g., when severance involves ego needs or is based on the exercise of power).

EXAMPLE OF "DEAR JON"

Dear Jon,

Duniway Park, Portland, Ore., August 6, 1984—At 6:35 a.m. the sun is breaking over the tops of the trees, and the air is cool and clear, although a bit hazy over Mt. Hood. Yesterday Vice-President Bush and his Secret Service men ran here, and the regular runners at this downtown track couldn't figure out why three men in suits were sitting in a car blocking the entrance to the parking lot. But today the lot is open, and Jon Birck has parked his Honda and is stretching. He wears red shorts and a black T-shirt with "The Seventh Annual Cascade Run-Off" in purple letters across the front.

"I'll be back in about 42½ minutes," he says. He pushes in the stopwatch button of his watch and takes off, half a lap around the track and then up a path through the trees, in a slow, springy stride.

A few months earlier, as chief executive officer of a small but fast-growing company, Birck had trouble finding the time to run. Northwest Instrument Systems Inc. was then three years old and poised to scale up development, production, and sales of a radically new kind of electronic instrument for electrical engineers. The fledgling enterprise had obtained the backing of world-respected venture capitalists, recruited top people from two of the area's most prestigious high-technology companies, developed an instrument it expected to become the core of its first product line, and moved to a new building. And, as Northwest's founder and president, Birck had become part of a new Portland-area elite—people who had risked all to start their own companies.

---

[2] This contrasts with the "building-men" attitude of capitalists such as George Doriot and raises questions about entrepreneurial role transitions, which will be discussed in Chapter 11.

To an ambitious electrical engineer from the Midwest who had no formal training or experience running anything like the company his dream had become, it was both scary and exciting. At dawn, Birck would slip out of bed while his wife slept, grab a bowl of Cheerios, and race off to the plant—13,000 square feet of glass and cement in an up-and-coming industrial park west of Portland. He kept a shirt and shorts and a pair of Nikes at the office, but often as not he skipped running, settling right down at his desk or walking around to talk with the 60 or so people who were building and selling Northwest's instruments. Although by this time he was no longer working until 11 or 12 at night, as he had during the company's earliest days, he still practically lived at the plant, and most nights he took work home. Not that he minded for a minute. Starting Northwest was one of the most exhilarating things he had ever done.

Then, suddenly, Birck was out. In May of 1984, after three years of working harder than he ever had in his life, he was asked to leave by his venture capitalists, who told him they needed a more experienced CEO to protect their investment. Now, cocooned in a swank, borrowed office on the 23d floor of a Portland bank building, he was driving ahead on plans for a new company—and sorting through the pieces of the old.

If he had been born a generation earlier, Jon Birck might have spent his career managing a research group for a large company. But he came of age in an era when people with bright ideas started companies in garages and sometimes made millions and appeared on the cover of *Time* magazine. Maybe his company had outgrown him, as his financial backers claimed, although Birck didn't think the problem was that simple. But the real question he had to answer was: How could he make sure, when he started his *next* company, that he wouldn't get divorced from it so soon?

At first, Birck couldn't even think about Northwest without his stomach acting up. The first week at home he cleaned out the closets, reorganized the kitchen, and went hiking in the mountains for a few days by himself. He didn't know what the founding ex-president of a company was supposed to do. Get another job? Wait for his stock to make him rich? He couldn't imagine spending the rest of his life out of the action.

Like a lot of young electrical engineers in the late 1960s, Birck moved to California to be "where things were happening." In June of 1970, he got married and moved to Santa Clara to work for an aggressive young company called National Semiconductor Corp. He found a lot to like—and not to like— in Silicon Valley.

At first, he found it tremendously exciting to work for a company on the cutting edge of an important new technology. Charlie Sporck, National's president, would get up at quarterly meetings and talk about doubling the company's size in the next year and putting up three more buildings. "We all thought it was a big joke," Birck says, "but the company grew from $20 million to $200 million a few years later."

There was another side to the semiconductor industry, however, that made Birck uncomfortable. He saw engineers hired away from competitors, then "sucked dry and given nothing jobs" until they went to work for someone else. It wasn't unheard of for an engineer who wanted a promotion to purposely obstruct the projects of other people in line for it.

"I grew up on team sports," Birck says. "I thought we were supposed to be working for the common good. I kept wondering: Is this necessary? Is this reasonable? Is this all there is?" Eventually he went to work at a small company called Precision Monolithics Inc., to learn about linear circuitry. Then, after a couple of years, he headed off to graduate school at Stanford University.

Tektronix Inc., the Oregon company Birck joined after Stanford, showed him that it was possible to build a business with the kind of values he had grown up with. Tek managers talked about treating employees and customers well, nurturing relationships for the long haul, and giving people enough rope to make their own decisions and mistakes.

The years at Tek tested his one-problem, one-answer model of the world. He went to seminars on such topics as conceptual blockbusting, heard associates in the research group talk about creative analogies, and took some classes in business at Portland State University. There, the chairs were arranged in a circle and the case studies had more than one right answer. That may not sound like much to a liberal arts major, he says, "but to an engineer from Purdue, it was a Big Aha."

All of this might have added up to nothing more than personal fulfillment had Birck not been disturbed by a sense that Tektronix had a narrow view of its future. Decisions were made not to enter the computer market and not to pursue business applications of the technology that the company had developed for engineers—decisions that some of the young managers found hard to understand.

Birck never talked much about wanting to start a company, but the idea had been in the back of his mind since his days at Purdue. Being an engineer, he figured the opportunity would present itself as a technology window, so he just waited patiently for one to open up.

In 1979, the window appeared, in the form of the Apple II personal computer.

To many engineers, the first personal computers looked like sophisticated toys. Birck saw them as a "probe into the model"—a new factor that could change the way people viewed electronic instruments. Traditional intelligent instruments relied on dedicated control computers usually built into each instrument. The intelligent instruments could then be hooked up to small computers to analyze the data. Birck speculated that if someone figured out how to work an instrument off the computing power of a personal computer, the user could avoid the duplication of intelligence that occurs when each instrument has its own, and could use the personal computer to document and manage products. He bought an Apple II and took it home to see what it could do.

His first experiments were fairly basic. He made an electronic controller for a kiln he used for stained glass work; tested a solar collector he had built; and hooked up the family security system, the lights, and the heat to a control system that would turn everything on and off. It was hobbyist stuff, but it indicated that larger things were possible.

Karen Birck was not particularly thrilled when her husband told her in June of 1981 that he wanted to quit his job to work fulltime on a business plan. As a CPA, she was capable of supporting the two of them indefinitely—except that she was pregnant with their first child. She was concerned that Birck hadn't done anything like running a company before.

The lack of operating experience didn't bother her husband, however. Other founders he admired—Bill Hewlett, David Packard, and Tek's Howard Vollum and Jack Murdock came to mind—had learned on the job. He told Karen they would be better off if he got some momentum going while she was still working. Perhaps by the time the baby arrived, he would be back on a payroll.

After convincing his wife, telling his boss didn't seem particularly momentous. Two weeks later the people in his research group gave him a cake and wished him well.

Birck doesn't remember celebrating the big day at home, although he does recall signing for a second mortgage on his house. Mostly, however, he remembers developing a business plan and starting to show it around. One of the people he showed it to was a guy he played softball with at Tek, Rick Cordray, a program manager who was also experimenting with instrumentation and Apple computers.

The idea, Birck explained to Cordray, was to design and build a new and more efficient kind of instrument. Birck said he was going to literally match the capabilities of instruments that sold for anywhere from $500 to $30,000 with computer modules that would plug into a personal computer, perform the same functions, and sell for $1,000 to $10,000. The first product would be two cards in a metal case that would perform the functions of a basic oscilloscope. He wanted Cordray to design and build it.

Birck was blunt about money. He planned to bootstrap the company on his savings and the cash he had gotten from remortgaging his house until he had a prototype to show potential investors. Not only was there not enough for salaries, but Cordray would have to keep his job at Tek for a while so he would have some cash to contribute. If they were successful, Cordray would share the wealth and be the young company's vice-president for engineering.

For Cordray, a dark and unassuming PhD from Rice University who had spent most of his life in school and in research labs, the appeal lay mainly in the chance to learn something about business. He had no long-standing ambition to start a company, though. "Northwest happened to be an opportunity that came up when I was ready," he says. "It was not the dream of my life."

Working nights and weekends, Cordray took charge of the engineering side of things, and Birck did "everything else," which included figuring out where to buy the stuff Cordray needed, figuring out how to pay for it, and continuing to work on the business plan. Birck knew they were going to need more help eventually—in marketing, for example, about which they knew little or nothing—but he and Cordray couldn't afford more bodies as yet.

Sometimes the two men talked like revolutionaries, speculating that they might completely change the way people made and used instruments. A big part of the thrill lay in how they were doing it—not in years with squadrons of people on the campus of one of the industry leaders, but in a few months with a couple of guys in a 200-square-foot space where the desks and the bench were in the same room. It was a back-room engineer's dream—no meetings, no conflicting priorities, no bureaucracy telling them that what they were building wasn't what the market or the company needed. They were going to build something, put it out there, and see what the world said.

The business press is full of stories about entrepreneurs being outgrown by their companies. But "outgrown," as it is often used by the press and by venture capitalists, is a catchword. The outcome can be as much a question of direction as speed. And a company's direction can change imperceptibly, one step at a time.

In the months after Northwest's birth, Birck found that he had underestimated the costs of just about everything—

people, equipment, materials, space. By November, the money was nearly gone. He arranged a small financing with a local investment company and received promises of more. Birck and Cordray added a secretary-administrator, a second engineer, and more space.

That month they also got their first response to an ad they had placed in *Byte* magazine—an order from the University of South Florida, which said it wanted to use Northwest's oscilloscope to measure the impact of boats running into piers. In December, they boxed one up, then shared some wine. "It was exciting," Cordray says. "We were only four employees, and we shipped a product. It was the first selling I'd ever done."

Pretty soon they were shipping 5 to 10 oscilloscopes a month. The sales were encouraging, but by spring, Birck was beginning to wonder about the company's rate of growth. His heroes at Hewlett-Packard Co. and Tektronix had built their companies slowly on savings and revenues from early products. Yet, while revenues were coming in as Birck had planned, costs continued to be much higher than expected.

By February, when the local company still hadn't produced the promised second infusion of cash, it was clear that Northwest would have to look elsewhere for money. Cordray had gone to school with the wife of a partner in one of the more well-respected venture capital firms in northern California—Kleiner Perkins Caufield & Byers—and Birck decided to give them a call. Jim Lally, the Kleiner Perkins general partner who eventually urged the firm to invest, told him to stop by next time he was in the Bay Area.

Lally, like most venture capitalists, prefers to invest in an entrepreneur who has started a company before—or at least one who previously led a fast-growing division. But his second choice is an entrepreneur who recognizes what he doesn't know, and Birck seemed to fall into this category. Lally said he thought Northwest needed a general manager, and suggested someone he had worked with at Intel Corp., Mike Maerz. Birck agreed to call Maerz, and Lally promised to start lining up some money.

Mike Maerz had the kind of bottomline business experience that Birck and Cordray both lacked. He had earned degrees in electrical engineering, worked for IBM Corp. as a design engineer, done a stint in the Navy, worked at Intel for six years in marketing and as a product manager, and gone on to run the microcomputer division at Tektronix.

Maerz also had Intel-type hard edges. He talked fast, tended to quantify things, and had integrated Intel's results-orientation and constructive-confrontation techniques into his management style. He was not a guy Birck could imagine putting his feet up with and "blue-skying" about some Utopian vision. Maerz was the kind of guy, Birck thought, who would want to know what Utopia *looked* like—what kind of trees were there and how high the hills were.

But Birck wanted a manager, and he figured managers needed to think that way. Besides, he wanted the backing of Kleiner, Perkins, and he wasn't sure he would get it without Maerz. So he hired him. And by May, Kleiner Perkins— along with Sevin Rosen Management Co., another venture capital firm—had committed $800,000.

The second product called for in Birck's plan was the logic analyzer, the basic test tool of the digital designer, and Mike Maerz had some strong ideas about how it should be executed. Birck and Cordray had been willing to compromise some performance standards to meet price objectives, but Maerz was not. He was convinced that the people who used a logic analyzer were much more concerned about what it could do than how much it cost.

Achieving the kind of performance Maerz had in mind would require two changes in Birck's specifications: a separate instrument chassis and a slightly higher price tag. But even so, Maerz pointed out, Birck's basic goals—that the box hook up to a personal computer and sell for significantly less than competing instruments—would still be met.

Birck said fine. His job was to set goals. Maerz's was to execute. Neither man saw this shift as a major strategic change.

The money from the venture capitalists—combined with the sexiness of a world-class project—allowed Maerz to attract a strong team to design, build, and sell the logic analyzer. And it was this team, according to Cordray, that made the biggest contribution to Northwest's evolution. "A lot of the engineers came from Tek," he says, "and at Tek, the attention was on high performance, not low cost. It was a case of letting people follow their noses into what made sense."

What made sense to the engineers was an instrument as good as the industry's best. Apparently, the venture capitalists agreed: Early in 1983, Sevin Rosen and Kleiner Perkins put in another $1.3 million.

The week that the logic analyzer was introduced, Northwest made the covers of two electronics magazines. People at the company were euphoric. They had set high standards and met them, and customer reaction was even better than they had hoped. Soon the logic analyzer was selling better than the oscilloscope ever had.

Birck was pleased—and ready to move on to the third step in his plan.

There are two major segments of the instrument industry: analog instruments (the traditional test and measurement tools, such as oscilloscopes, used by everyone from television repairpeople to physicists in order to measure continuous electrical currents) and digital instruments (which are used primarily by engineers designing hardware and software to measure electronic pulses in computer circuits). Birck's expertise lies in the analog area, but he had planned all along to develop both kinds of tools. Northwest's first product, the oscilloscope card, was an analog instrument; its second, the logic analyzer, was digital.

The next part of Northwest's plan called for bringing in analog people. Although Maerz and many others who had worked on the logic analyzer were eager to stay focused on digital design, Birck was not. He hired a 19-year veteran of Tektronix to develop a proposal for further analog development. But when the proposal came in a month later, it was clear that the project was larger than Birck had predicted, and would demand more resources by a factor of two to three.

"We couldn't afford to do both," Birck says—at least not on the scale originally planned. Northwest got a third infusion of cash that September ($3.3 million, from a group led by Hambrecht & Quist and J. H. Whitney), but the young company's engineering budget was already the appropriate size for its stage of development. So Birck argued for scaling down the digital project and going ahead with a revised version of the analog program. There were strategic advantages, he was sure, to playing in both leagues.

To Maerz, vice-president for sales Jim Fischer, and Northwest's board of directors, Birck's proposal didn't make sense. The logic analyzer was a solid revenue producer. Northwest's marketing people and designers had digital backgrounds. Although the analog market was bigger, the digital market was growing faster. And analog competitors, such as Tek and HP, were more entrenched.

Birck didn't seem to be facing the reality of what his company had become: a team of people who had built a successful, high-performance digital product. He kept talking about his plan, not seeing that Northwest now had a momentum of its own.

No one had foreseen the exclusion of analog instruments from Northwest's future, but on a wave of logic-analyzer momentum, Maerz, Fischer, and the board pushed for it. And after a three-month debate, in December of 1983, Birck gave in.

"There was an opportunity in each hand," he says. "And we were set up to take advantage of the digital one."

"Companies exist not because some guru started with some great vision," says Rick Cordray, looking back on the decision, "but because some people had some ideas about what they could do, and got started, and worked hard. Sometimes there are big course corrections."

Five months after the decision to go digital, Birck flew to San Francisco with Maerz and Fischer for what he thought was going to be a routine board meeting. It was unusual for the directors to call a meeting in the Bay Area, and on the way down Birck wondered about the effect of his battle for the analog option. His position was less clear in the new, more narrowly defined Northwest. Everyone agreed that one of his strengths was as a long-term product strategist, looking into the future to see where new markets and technologies intersected. With the company focused on a technology that wasn't part of his background, what role was he now to play?

The night before the board meeting, Birck had a meeting scheduled with two of the lead investors, Jim Lally and Dave Best (of Hambrecht & Quist), in a conference room at the airport hotel. Lally and Best gave the news to him straight: Northwest needed a strong leader who had managed a rapidly growing business already; Birck had not. To attract someone who had, they would have to offer the CEO's job, and they thought it would be best if Birck resigned. He would keep his stock and a seat on the board.

Birck says he was stunned. "Life after Northwest wasn't part of my mental set." He had dedicated three years to the company. He had left a secure job, put his marriage on the line, taken out a second mortgage on his house, given himself a below-market salary (and then, for a while, not even cashed his paychecks), exposed his dreams and naïveté to bankers, lawyers, and investors, fought to keep his company committed to its original strategic direction, and given in when he couldn't convince his team that he was right. And now that the company was poised for what all of them hoped would be a period of steady growth, Lally and Best—the investors he had recruited and trusted—were asking him to bow out gracefully.

But he said OK. Just like that. "You know when you're beat," he says. "They had all the cards. They didn't come to that room to negotiate.

"Sure I was upset. Wouldn't you be? I could have screamed and stamped my feet, but where would that have gotten me? I had an interest in seeing Northwest continue as a prosperous company. I didn't want attention focused on the conflict."

A couple of days later, he had cleared out his desk.

"People ask me what I do all day," says Birck from his new office, loaned courtesy of Wayne Kingsley, a Portland venture capitalist who didn't invest in Northwest. "They seem to think I sit here and look out my pretty window." The view is nice—Portland bisected by the Willamette River, from 23 stories up—but Birck has more on his mind than scenery.

After he got over the shock of his dismissal, he made the rounds of people he had worked with at Northwest—venture capitalists, accountants, lawyers, suppliers—and asked for help in assessing his strengths. Two pieces of advice Jim Lally had for anyone starting a new venture made a particularly strong impression: Surround yourself with the best people you can find, and make sure everyone has the same goals.

As Birck set out to define his new company—its products, he says, will be "cousins" of Northwest's—his top priority was recruiting. So far, he has signed up four people, all of whom are "gainfully employed" and expected to remain so until the rest of the key players are in place. The five meet one evening a week to work on a business plan. Although Birck has talked to enough potential customers to feel sure his idea is a good one—and enough venture capitalists to think he can get the backing he needs—he will take the idea no further until the team is complete.

In fact, if he doesn't get the kind of team he wants, he intends to drop the idea. He doesn't want to be what Jim Lally calls a "decathlon champion entrepreneur"—a Nolan Bushnell–type who starts a company and then goes on to the next event. This time, Birck wants to build something he can stay with for the long haul.

Source: Susan Benner, "Dear Jon," *Inc.* February 1985. Reprinted with permission, *Inc.* magazine. Copyright © 1985 by INC. Publishing Company (Boston, MA: 38 Commercial Wharf, 02110).

A CHANGING RELATIONSHIP

Traditional venture capitalists, those who have led the current venture capital explosion, were more actively involved in taking care of the companies they financed than newer capital fund managers. Georges Doriot, one of the first highly successful venture capitalists, claims to have been more than a source of funds, that he has "built men and companies."

> To do that required, above all, patience and loyalty. Doriot often worked with a company for a decade or more, through good times and bad, before realizing any return at all. Small wonder he came to refer to his companies as his "children."

Kotkin, 1984b, p. 68

More recently, the relationship has changed, reflecting the rapid growth of the venture capital industry (from $2.5 billion committed to business in 1976 to over $10 billion in 1983). This growth has led less experienced (and some would argue less competent) managers with MBA backgrounds to make venture capital decisions. The lack of "intelligence capital," combined with perceived arrogance on the part of some unproven venture managers, has worked to turn some entrepreneurs away from this source and toward alternatives such as investment banks, insurance companies, the venture capital arms of large banks and accounting firms, and strategic alliances with big businesses (Kotkin, 1984b).

In addition, the pressure for financial performance of new ventures has increased and timeframes have been shortened. "We have the symptoms of the heightening of greed among venture capitalists and entrepreneurs," says Burgess Jamieson, a venture capitalist (Kotkin, 1984b, p. 72). This translates into increasing demand for return on investments and pressure to "short-cut the whole process. Instead of giving companies five or six years to grow, they try to do it in two years. Some companies have been rushed and grossly overfinanced as a result" (Kotkin, 1984b, p. 67).

Obtaining venture capital changes the entrepreneurial organization, and venture capitalists have begun to pay attention to how their money is spent. Overfinanced firms tend to spend the money they have, rather than pinch pennies and seek the greatest value for the money spent (Buskirk, 1982). Says George Tate, cofounder of Ashton-Tate:

> The key thing is you have to go through the pain. If you sense pain in the beginning, the chances are you won't have to deal with it later. . . . If some [venture capitalist] just handed us $5 million, it would have sucked the blood out of us. The only way to stay focused is pain—and not being able to make the rent if you screw up.
>
> Kotkin, 1984b, p. 75

Another important change is in the offing. With a change in the capital gains tax, which became law in 1987, the size of the venture capital pool may change. With that change, the venture capital community may lose its prominence as a source of funds for venturing. The tax law revision is also likely to influence the structuring of "deals" (equity, capitalization, control, sell-out aspects) and the relationship between entrepreneurs and venture capitalists. Likewise, the crash of October 19, 1987 temporarily halted the popularity of initial public offerings—a favored way to achieve liquidity for venture capital. Following that crash, venture capital firms were reporting fewer new investments, and were reserving their capital for second and third rounds of financing for their existing portfolio of ventures.

BOARDS OF DIRECTORS AND ADVISORS

One of the tasks of the venture capitalist is to assemble a board to advise the entrepreneur. Usually, the venture capitalist, along with one or more co-investors, represents the investor group; other outsiders are recruited to form a board, which also includes key members of the inside top-management team. The board can direct or advise the entrepreneur. A *board of directors* is financially responsible to investors and owners and controls the top-management group. Although they frequently are expected to do more (Mace, 1986), at a minimum directors should:

- hire, fire, and set the compensation for the chief executive/entrepreneur
- monitor the environment to challenge boardroom assumptions
- endorse corporate strategy (Norburn, 1984).

A *board of advisors* has no such control. Instead, it serves as a group of consultants to executive decision making.

Entrepreneurs without outside investors often elect to form such a board. A recent study of privately held companies found that 20 percent had an independent board of advisors and that the CEOs who have such boards find them useful ("Challenges," 1985). We will look at the pros and cons of having a board, the structure of the board, and finally, recent changes to board dynamics.

PROS AND CONS

Most entrepreneurs realize that outside advice is helpful, but resist setting up a board of outsiders to give such advice. Says Kenneth Hendricks, CEO and founder of ABC Supply Co. (#2 on the 1985 *Inc.* 500 list of the fastest growing privately held firms),

> The energy that goes into setting up a board, and then periodically sitting down with them, is a reduction in productivity. . . . A board is a convenient way for an entre-

preneur to shift responsibility to other people. I like being responsible for this company. I'm a hands-on kind of guy, and the buck stops here. I love the independent environment at my company, and I don't want to change it.

Persinos, 1986, p. 80

Fear of loss of control, fear of not being able to move quickly, lack of trust in others and a desire to keep certain information secret, and a desire to appear competent and strong create such resistance to outside advisors. Clearly there are enough "war stories" told by entrepreneurs about boards that usurp their power (e.g., Adamsak, 1984; Hartman, 1986) to warrant these concerns.

The advantages of having a board involve the development of leadership, management of leadership transitions, better decision making, and better corporate image. Having a board of outsiders who question the decisions and behavior of the entrepreneur and his or her team can result in the entrepreneur taking on more of a *leadership role* (e.g., doing more strategic thinking) and being less of a hands-on activist (Persinos, 1986). Thus the board may help the entrepreneur learn new attitudes and behaviors and ease the transitions that accompany growth (see Chapter 11 for more discussion of role transitions). Boards of directors/advisors can also help with concerns about leadership continuity should the founder leave.

Boards contribute to *decision making* by questioning the assumptions and information underlying entrepreneurial decisions. Bringing assumptions to the surface has been shown to help strategic decision making (Mason & Mitroff, 1981). Richard Parker, founder of a $15 million direct-mail fundraising company, says:

Just the process of meeting, and having to prepare ahead of time, helps me think more clearly. . . . From having a board I've discovered that if you can't logically explain what you want to do, it's probably not worth doing. . . . A board helps you face things a CEO would be tempted to deny or sweep under the rug.

Persinos, 1986, p. 82

Furthermore, boards contribute a diversity of backgrounds (with members chosen for their different expertise), which in general contributes to better decision making (as discussed in the formulation of partnerships).

The *image* of the entrepreneurial firm can be measured, in part, by those who serve as directors/advisors. Russell Cox, president of Resort Management Inc., serves on boards of large and small organizations and advises entrepreneurs to take special care in selecting the first director. "The caliber of people you get depends on who you start with. . . . If you start with a good individual, you can get other good people who want to be associated with him" (Jacobs, 1985). The image of the board and the enterprise can affect the recruitment of managers as well as the respect of bankers, lawyers, and other professionals.

STRUCTURE OF THE BOARD

The usual structure for a board tends to favor insiders to outsiders. However, some companies have decided that outside views and expertise are important enough to tilt the board in favor of outsiders. Consultants advise entrepreneurs to form a board with five members, three from outside the company (Jacobs, 1985). The other voice in board composition is that of the lead venture capitalist, who may insist on a majority of seats for investors, and otherwise recruits and manages board members.

Boards composed of representatives of strategically important organizations clearly aid in environmental scanning. Strategically important organizations will differ for each venture, depending on technology, markets, size, regulations, and so forth. Boards will usually meet regularly—once a year, quarterly, or monthly—as needed by the venture or as board member availability may dictate.

CHANGING DYNAMICS

In the late 1980s organizations of all sizes and stages of development were faced with a Directors and Officers (D&O) liability insurance crisis. For new and small businesses, the problem results from litigation based on soured initial public offerings of high-technology start-ups. This has forced D&O premiums up (three to ten times higher in 1986 than in 1985) and coverage down, making coverage expensive and difficult to secure. As a result, entrepreneurial businesses have faced tough questions about boards of directors. Some "go bare," but lose directors who do not want their personal assets exposed to this risk. Other organizations find incentives— agreements not to sue from within the firm, warrants that become stock upon exercise—to recruit and maintain board members (Andrews, 1986). Many have opted for a board of advisors, who provide the outside views but who have no control over management. However, advisors have less influence on management decisions and on the image of the firm, and ultimately, they may not be exempt from suits (Andrews, 1986).

The liability crisis has brought new concerns to the board-room and into the relationship between the entrepreneur and his or her advisors. It may mean fewer advisors for new ventures, with less shared information and resources and less control by outsiders.

CORPORATE PARTNERS AND STRATEGIC ALLIANCES

Another set of important external relationships exists for entrepreneurs who form alliances, joint ventures, and other cooperative relationships with larger corporations. The core of this relationship is the exchange of "entrepreneurial spirit" for organizational resources. There is no data on whether entrepreneurs or large organizations more frequently initiate strategic alliances of various types. Most of the research in this area is on joint ventures, and these are usually initiated by large companies as a way to expand research and development, quickly develop new products, tap into new technologies, and have existing technologies tailored to their existing manufacturing processes. When entrepreneurs initiate alliances they do so to acquire capital, loan guarantees, equipment, marketing channels, access to technology, and so forth. Frequently, the large corporation receives minority interest in the new venture.

The number of corporate alliances has increased over the past few years. One count found 200 such investments in 1984, three times the number made in 1981 (Posner, 1985). *The Wall Street Journal* reports that $475 million in corporate venture capital was invested in 1984, with most of this channeled through venture partnerships and less than $200 million through the corporation's own programs (Asinof, 1985). This increase reflects a change in the strategy of big business toward smaller enterprises, from one of acquiring innovative firms (which often results in the founder leaving and, as a result, the new acquisition having considerably less value) to that of investing in them ("The age of alliances," 1984; Posner, 1985).

NATURE OF THE ALLIANCE

As with partners of any kind, this relationship is one where early agreements on values and expectations, as well as developing good communications, works to keep the parties collaborative and the relationship productive. Most research on this relationship deals with the parties to joint ventures Harrigan (1985) characterizes as "parents" who spawn a third entity, the "child" venture. Apparently, joint venture partners need well-honed interpersonal and political skills.

> The [joint] venture's management team must possess both diplomatic skills and entrepreneurial aggressiveness in order to balance the need to represent each . . . [party's] viewpoint fairly to its partners against the need to make the venture an economic success.
>
> Harrigan, 1986, p. 1

As with venture capital, corporate partnerships require extensive negotiating and trust building (both parties must believe that the venture will work and that each party is committed to the venture's success). When trust is missing or when either party is uncertain about the importance of the alliance (e.g., how such alliance fits in with overall corporate strategy), continuity and collaboration are difficult. Says venture capitalist John Mumford:

> You've got to be sure that the product line in the [corporate investor's] company is on solid ground, and that the guy who's running it is a champion in the company, and you've got to have a good relationship with the guy who controls the P&L [statement].
>
> Jubak, 1986, September, p. 49

During the course of the relationship, skills at overcoming differences in organizational cultures and managerial styles are important, since entrepreneurial organizations are less bureaucratic, more informal, and often staffed with younger personnel than the larger partner. In addition, the relationship requires ongoing negotiation about issues of control, autonomy, and changing needs of the two organizations (e.g., succession planning, shifting markets, etc.) (Harrigan, 1985).

FINDING AN ALLY

For some entrepreneurs, finding a corporate partner may be as simple as returning to a former employer with the opportunity to invest. Others use a formal and logical process to find partners and structure agreements. If there has been a previous round of venture capital, the lead venture capitalist is also involved. There is a preference for finding partners with previous experience in joint ventures since, as with all roles, experience makes people better (and more formidable) negotiators and communicators (Harrigan, 1985). Apparently, experienced corporate partners know how to make the relationship enduring and of mutual benefit.

UNANSWERED QUESTIONS

Considering the paucity of research on this relationship, it remains to be seen what structures emerge within the larger partner to accommodate the new venture. Of more interest to the subject of entrepreneurial behavior are questions about the career of the entrepreneur and the fate of his or her firm. Does this relationship evolve into an acquisition by the larger firm? What can be done to help or prevent that process? What role transitions does the entrepreneur-partner face? Will there be a transfer of technology (one-way or reciprocal)? Will there be a transfer of culture (i.e., will the entrepreneurial firm become more rational, systematic, and administrative? Will the larger firm become more entrepreneurial?)?

THE CASE OF RICHARD SEBASTIAN AND ACME-CLEVELAND

All across the heartland of American industry, such antique companies as Acme-Cleveland, a machine-tool manufacturer, are scouring the countryside for business innovators that can help them bring technological changes to their markets and retool their factories for the future. Their motive—survival—is as basic as their industries. The pulse of the heartland, pressed by low-cost foreign competition, is slowing down. Plants are out of date; products are being rejected as irrelevant or inferior; layers of management, once thought indispensable, now stand revealed as so much cotton batting. Competition has turned the gaze of these giants outward and downward—to the world of small companies, sometimes to copy their procedures, sometimes to harness their genius, always to find the spark that will enable the large companies to live and grow.

The effort takes many forms. One of the most talked-about is intrapreneurship, as when such industrial behemoths as IBM Corp. and 3M Co. discover that product innovation thrives best when employees are turned loose to function like independent entrepreneurs. Another is the corporate start-up, as when such companies as Control Data Corp. and Tektronix Inc. offer capital and support to restless employees eager to go out on their own. The trend can be seen as well in the changing relationships between large manufacturing companies and their small suppliers. And even General Motors Corp. is rejiggering its legendary bureaucracy in hopes of fashioning a more nimble, decentralized operating system. Indeed, GM chairman Roger B. Smith himself has appeared on "The Phil Donahue Show," explaining to the nation's housewives why executives of the new Saturn subsidiary will have total freedom to invent new ways of manufacturing automobiles.

All these maneuvers reflect an apparent change in big-company attitudes toward small enterprise. The giants, to be sure, have long recognized that smaller companies offered things they wanted. Historically, however, their approach has resembled that of a sultan in search of a new favorite for his harem. Acquisition was the goal, whether in the short run or the long, and as often as not the acquired company didn't protest. But funny things happened on the way to the seraglio. For one thing, the small company founders tended to take their money and run, leaving little more than the shell of a business behind. Then there were the cultural conflicts—notably the attempts by large companies to impose highly developed management systems on entrepreneurial ventures. A case in point was Exxon Corp., which bought or spawned several new businesses in the late 1960s and early '70s, smothered them with management, then watched them expire one by one. Other big companies learned similar hard lessons, which put a temporary halt to their search for small company "windows on technology."

But along about 1980, a new kind of relationship began to appear, primarily in the computer, telecommunications, and pharmaceutical industries. In these relationships, the large company would buy a minority stake in a small company without seeking to acquire or even control it. Thus, for example, Memorex Corp., a leader in computer-memory storage, bought 4% of a young disk-drive company called

DMA Systems Inc. General Instrument Corp., a big force in the cable TV equipment industry, settled for less than half of Sytek Inc., a computer networking company. Such companies as Abbott Laboratories took minority interests in young, avant-garde medical research companies.

These deals had two things in common. In each, both parties were intimately involved in research and technology, and the focal point was new products. What the large company wanted was a leg up on products and markets it felt would be important to its future. The alliance was a way of extending its internal research and development effort at relatively low cost, while protecting its approaches to potential new markets. What the small company wanted was money, without giving away its freedom and incentive to create a viable business.

And the newfangled arrangements worked, or at least some of them did. They certainly became very popular. During 1984, the number of minority investments by big companies in small companies financed by venture capitalists soared to 200, almost three times the level in 1981, according to Venture Economics Inc., in Wellesley Hills, Mass. There was also a wave of deals between young technology companies in the United States and more established European and Japanese companies, and this was paralleled by another wave that linked big American companies and smaller ones abroad. Meanwhile, some growing companies began to explore alliances with each other. Cullinet Software Inc. and Lotus Development Corp., for example, worked out an agreement to develop software links that will provide users of 1-2-3 and Symphony with access to mainframe-computer databases. Then there was the deal last December between Jack Eckerd Corp., the $2.6-billion Florida drug retailer, and a California start-up called HomeClub Inc., which is developing a chain of home-improvement centers. In addition to acquiring about 20% of HomeClub's stock, Eckerd agreed to have its chairman, Stewart Turley, serve on the smaller company's board.

But perhaps the most startling development has been the appearance of such alliances in the industrial heartland, where some of the woolly mammoths of American enterprise have begun teaming up with hot, young technology companies in an effort to rejuvenate their operations and adapt to changing environments. The incongruity of such partnerships aside, these new industrial alliances represent a significant broadening of the trend, for their goals are quite different from those of the earlier technology alliances. Unlike Memorex, General Instrument, and Abbott, the large companies involved in these heartland deals are generally not looking for new products. Rather, they are seeking ways to streamline and upgrade their manufacturing processes, in hopes of competing better in international markets.

General Motors is perhaps the foremost example of the heartland's new outreach policy. For generations, the auto giant chugged along on a proud tradition of internal R&D. Almost overnight, it has struck up operating alliances with six small companies, all but one of them in the fast-emerging area of machine vision, which uses computer-controlled cameras during manufacturing for such activities as quality- and process-control. Besides providing the companies with equity capital (it owns about 10% of each of them), GM has signed multimillion-dollar R&D contracts.

Another example is Caterpillar Tractor Co., which is looking to alliances to restore its overseas competitiveness. Last February, its venture capital arm put $2 million in a three-year-old Arlington, Tex., company that develops systems for factory robots. Caterpillar is now considering other, similar deals.

So, too, is Rockwell International Corp., the $9.3-billion defense and aerospace giant. Last November, it paid $1.2 million for a 5% interest in Micro Linear Inc., a young San Jose, Calif., company with expertise in the design and manufacture of semicustom linear integrated circuits. Rockwell expects to be one of Micro Linear's major customers during its first year of operation.

It remains to be seen, of course, how these relationships will work out, but already new questions are arising and new issues emerging:

How, for example, should a deal be structured to maximize the chances of success? How much ownership is too much, or too little? Companies are experimenting with different equity percentages, development contracts, and licensing deals. A few big-company partners have discovered, to their dismay, that the wrong deal can present entrepreneurs with the same irresistible temptations to maximize short-term over long-term objectives that the big company executives are so often accused of falling into.

How do you cope with the inevitable cultural differences between industrial giants and small, entrepreneurial companies? Robert J. Eaton, a vice-president at General Motors, remarked recently that he had been meeting with guys in jeans and sneakers who rode to work on 10-speed bicycles. "They don't wear suits," he said. "I'm not sure some of them even *own* suits." On a more serious level, skeptical observers wonder whether big companies will be able to restrain themselves from imposing their own decision-making structures, their compensation policies, their very language, on smaller, more fragile partners.

What about the independence that lies at the heart of the relationship? To what extent should the small company be allowed to set its own agenda? How much latitude should it have? As a minority owner, the big company can try to persuade; it can't order. On the other hand, its persuasion can be mighty persuasive, and this has already made for some interesting discussions between large and small partners. The chief executive officer of a GM-allied machine-vision company, for example, recalls a dispute over the responsibilities of the man whom GM wanted to sit on his board. He insisted that the director's duty, first and foremost, was to foster the small company's interests, not GM's. "We went round and round on that issue, before they saw our point of view," he says.

What sort of commitment is needed from the big-company partner? Will deals initiated by high-level corporate managers be accepted in the operating divisions? Maybe not, or so some companies have discovered. Their experience suggests that the most successful alliances are those that speak to the particular needs of line managers.

Questions like these drive home the point that alliances are no magic bullet, no instant cure for the ills of basic industry. Rather, they constitute an experiment to try to tap the very different resources and cultures of large and small companies. Like most experiments, they proceed by trial and error, on a case-by-case basis, through the gradual accumulation of knowledge and experience. And therein lies the advantage of companies that have begun acquiring such knowledge and experience—companies like Acme-Cleveland.

Source: Bruce G. Posner, "Strategic Alliances," *Inc.* June 1985. Reprinted with permission, *Inc.* magazine. Copyright © 1985 by INC. Publishing Company (Boston, MA: 38 Commercial Wharf, 02110).

PROFESSIONAL ADVISORS

Anyone who has been to an entrepreneurship forum, a venture club, or a meeting of a small business booster organization will recognize that many in attendance are those whose business is to provide professional services to entrepreneurs—accountants, lawyers, and consultants. (See the section on networks for discussion about these meetings.) Since many new and entrepreneurial organizations choose not to hire such professionals as employees, and since their services are necessary in early stages of organizing, professional advisors cannot be ignored. CEOs of privately held firms were asked with whom they would consult on important business decisions. They reported most likely to consult with their accountant (63 percent), lawyer (50 percent), a business associate (45 percent), and banker (32 percent) ("Challenges," 1985).

Unfortunately, we know very little about what kinds of professional-entrepreneur relationships work well. We do know that the norms, values, and goals of professionals tend to be very different from those of managers and entrepreneurs (Kerr, Von Glinow, & Schriesheim, 1977).

LAWYERS

Legal advice may be the first and most critical outside help used in the earliest stages of venture creation. Lawyers are involved with drafting articles of incorporation and partnership agreements, checking contracts, insurance, etc. (Vesper, 1980; Baumback & Mancuso, 1975; Rich & Gumpert, 1985; Ronstadt, 1984a; Swayne & Tucker, 1973).

More important than the presence of legal counsel, however, is how that counsel is chosen and how the relationship develops. A recent survey of readers of *Venture* magazine showed that most entrepreneurs have had considerable difficulty in finding acceptable legal counsel, with 96 percent changing lawyers at least once. The biggest problems are lack of competence, poor business advice, and high fees ("Entrepreneurs and their attorneys," 1986), suggesting that basic trust may be most critical and most difficult to achieve.

Selecting a legal counsel often involves a personal recommendation. However, most writers advise a more thorough search (see Ronstadt, 1984a for guidelines). Once chosen, lawyers can become a source of business advice and networking (though often not as useful in this regard as accountants). The quality of that advice and the quality of the relationship may depend on "due diligence" by the employing entrepreneur. An early study found "both typical and more successful engineers [turned entrepreneurs] utilized outside advisors, but that more successful entrepreneurs exhibited more specific knowledge of what advice was needed and why" (Woodworth et al., 1969, in Vesper, 1980, p. 43).

Finally, and with some recent increase in frequency, lawyers are investing in the companies they serve. Sometimes the investment is *quid pro quo,* sometimes because the lawyer (and his or her firm) recognize the capital appreciation potential of their client's enterprise. Because of strong professional values among lawyers, issues of conflict of interest remain problematic (Bekey, 1984).

ACCOUNTANTS

Even less is known about the relationship between the accounting professional and the entrepreneur. Accountants are the key resources in assembling the financial information for a business plan that may be used to solicit funds (Rich & Gumpert, 1985) and for regular financial reports required by investors and bankers. At a recent conference, "Banking on the Entrepreneur," sponsored by Enterprise Development in Cleveland, Ron Cohen, CPA, pointed out that accountants can provide straight (although often not encouraging) advice about the entrepreneur's and the venture's credit worthiness. The accountant can also help determine the type and amount of loan needed and help in the search for a bank. Besides this function, accountants may provide inventory and management advice and actively network client businesses for sources of funds, personnel, and other resources. One study revealed that about half of the entrepreneurs surveyed rely more on their accountants than on their lawyers for business advice, and 43 percent found accountants a better source of business contacts than their lawyers ("Entrepreneurs and their attorneys," 1986).

BANKERS

It is generally accepted that bankers, whose business is to loan money at a profit, have a different set of values and expectations than entrepreneurs seeking cash. Where the entrepreneur will "bet it all" on an idea or early-stage business, bankers are conservative, risk-averse, and more bureaucratic.

"After six months of sky-rocketing sales and unimpeachable credit [entrepreneurs Robert Tracht and Bruce Gilman of Comteck Import/Export Ltd.] were suddenly 'invited' by their bank . . . to take their business elsewhere" because new loan officers were uncomfortable with the start-up firm (Kotkin, 1984, May, p. 112). Says Tracht:

> We called 35 banks, and they all gave us the same answer. Everyone said you have to have been in business for at least two years and have $100,000 in working capital. It was like they were all reading the same cue card.

Kotkin, 1984a, May, p. 112

However, not all banks follow these rules of thumb. Some, like those featured by *Inc.* magazine (Kotkin, 1984a) are specifically interested in new and smaller businesses and focus on tailoring loans to the needs of the individual firm. These small and medium-sized banks, with a majority of loans to smaller businesses, can outperform larger banks because they focus on the all-important relationship. "They regard themselves more as service companies than as 'financial institutions . . .' they consider the customer the heart and soul of their business" (Kotkin, 1984a, p. 112). The customer (entrepreneur) is happy because the banker takes a personal interest in the business, remains accessible, and is able to respond quickly to the venture's needs. Finally, there is some evidence that banks in regions where entrepreneurship is most active tend to be more open to providing credit to new ventures. It is important to note that banks frequently see small-business loans as high risk, and, indeed, research suggests that, overall, banks lose money on these loans (Churchill, 1988). However, the same research suggests that these banks *make money by holding the deposits of these same small businesses.* Thus the total banking relationship—loans, deposits, and other services—turns out to be profitable for the banks who serve small businesses.

The previously mentioned conference, "Banking on the Entrepreneur," held in January, 1988, also addressed the theme of the interpersonal relationship, especially trust, developed between a particular loan officer, the entrepreneur, and his or her partners and key employees. Because the loan process often takes considerable time (a minimum of three months for a loan extension and more than six months for a first loan) and involves a bureaucratic movement of loan approvals through committees and up the hierarchy, a good relationship between individuals is necessary to maintain momentum and ensure that good loans are made to worthwhile ventures. Other than the usual interpersonal concerns such as "chemistry" (bankers and entrepreneurs advise finding a loan officer the entrepreneur can trust), problems emerge with banking policies of assigning junior account executives to small-business sectors and frequently moving junior officers, requiring the entrepreneur to educate and re-educate bank personnel about his or her firm.

An entrepreneur (Seth Harris, President, Harris Wholesale Company) and an attorney (James Aussem, Principal, Seeley, Savidge & Aussem) combined to give advice to entrepreneurs seeking a business loan. First, understand who is borrowing—the entrepreneur, other investors, spouses, and/

or key employees. Second, determine what you, the entrepreneur, have to offer, including collateral (which often extends to personal assets) and key employees who can live with restrictive covenants placed on dividends, salaries, etc. Banks make loans to people; organizations are collateral. Third, be able to describe the business. Here a business plan is valuable, but the use of common language in oral presentations is vital. Fourth, explain why a loan is needed. Fifth, find the right bank, through networks, and meet with the right person at the highest level possible. In meeting the banker, Harris and Auseem (1988) offer the Do's and Don'ts in Table 10.1.

TABLE 10.1   Do's and Don'ts in Meeting with a Banker

DO

1. dress for a banker.
2. clean up the office, factory, plant, and personnel the day the banker visits.
3. prepare for your presentation (up to ten hours rehearsal for each hour of presentation).
4. prepare your own analysis and projections.
5. prepare your staff and key individuals for discussion with the banker.
6. personally write the story of your business, its history, its strong points and its weak points. Use your own language.
7. sell your firm as you would to a customer. Present brochures.
8. rely on professional advisors to open doors and help you avoid pitfalls.
9. give the bank a few of your customers to contact.
10. take the banker on a call with you.
11. avoid surprises—the one thing the bank *dreads*.

DON'T

1. mail anything. Do hand deliver, face to face if possible.
2. give the bank an opportunity to say "no" to cold facts and figures. Make them say it to *you*, face to face.
3. assume they know your business. Take time to educate them.
4. negotiate alone. Use your professional advisors as a buffer.
5. lose your temper.
6. assume the first deal offered by the bank is the best deal.
7. rush it.
8. mislead your banker.
9. be afraid to ask questions.

Source: Seth Harris, Chairman and Chief Executive Officer at Harris Wholesale Company (the largest privately owned wholesale drug company in the U.S., with sales of $1 billion).

Bankers are also a key resource for locating businesses to acquire. Loan officers are a good source of information about companies in trouble, where a "turnaround" entrepreneur could buy low and later sell high. Trust officers, who work with entrepreneurs in planning their personal estates, are good sources of information for possibly less troubled acquisitions (Vesper, 1980).

In choosing a banking relationship, consultants recommend using the same careful consideration that goes into the choice of a lawyer or accountant. Specifically, they recommend using one's network, referrals from other professionals, one's own intuition, and the bank's reputation in the small-business sector to make the choice (Baty, 1974). More than relationships with lawyers and accountants, the relationship with a bank tends to be long-term (since debt is long-term). However, rapidly growing firms can outgrow a specific (e.g., branch) banking relationship and may need to restructure the debt and the relationship.

For their part, entrepreneurs can help make the banking relationship one that is mutually productive by: (1) keeping the banker informed about the business, (2) making personal contact, (3) borrowing, and (4) meeting one's targets on time and on budget (Baty, 1974).

OTHER ADVISORS

Public-sector advice, such as that provided by Small Business Development Centers, has been found to contribute to the creation of viable new businesses that more than return taxpayer dollars in new employment and taxation (Chrisman & Hoy, 1985). Others argue (but do not present evidence) that *business consultants,* especially those with start-up or small-business practice, add to venture success (Osgood & Wetzel, 1977). We do not know the number or importance of consultants to smaller businesses and entrepreneurs, what they do for the new venture, nor what value is added by their services. Clearly more research on these relationships is warranted.

PERSONAL SUPPORT SYSTEMS: FAMILY AND FRIENDS

The influence of a personal support system cannot be overestimated, given two perspectives that have already been mentioned. First, the family of origin or natal family contributes to the likelihood of becoming an entrepreneur through three factors: (1) the presence of a role model; (2) early (childhood) independence training, which contributes to achievement motivation; and (3) a desire to escape childhood poverty and family tensions. Second, the life of an entrepreneur is one of considerable stress and tension; having an emotional support system is crucial for healthy management of these tensions.

To these reasons we will add the following: Families can be an important source of financial support, especially in the earliest stages. However, concerns about family integrity and well-being can inhibit entrepreneurial momentum. Finally, the inclusion of friends and family members in a new venture creates a new and important level of complexity in the business.

FINANCIAL SUPPORT

In most new business start-ups, family and friends are the most important source of early financial help (Birley, 1985), although the extent of family financing is not known. One possible source of financing is an existing family business, which may fund unrelated businesses of second and subsequent generations. Poza (1984) proposes the establishment of *family venture capital firms*, which would support new ventures beyond the founding generation as an alternative to traditional succession plans and estate planning.

An often unrecognized source of funds is the *savings and sacrifices of the entrepreneur's family*, where the spouse and children forego a regular monthly income of one provider, often living on accrued savings or the second income. As a result, "their families may experience a shortterm [sic] drop in their material standards of living" (Martin, 1984, p. 278).

Friends are also a source of seed and early-stage financing. However, some entrepreneurs like to keep friendships separate from business, especially where money is concerned. Of those who responded to a *Venture* magazine survey only 14 percent preferred to work with friends; 47 percent were reluctant and 6 percent opposed the idea entirely. When entrepreneurs do borrow from friends, they are "hard-nosed . . . just as likely to borrow money from friends but only 39% [of the *Venture* survey entrepreneurs] paid or offered to pay interest" ("Do Business and Friendship Mix?", 1985).

NONFINANCIAL BUSINESS ASSISTANCE

Besides start-up capital, often in the form of a loan or partnership, family and friends may provide access to important business resources. Recall that most entrepreneurs tend to be long-term residents of the place where their business starts, and by inference so are their friends and family. People with roots and connections in a community may turn these to the entrepreneur's benefit.

> Family and friends are the most useful where local issues are concerned, as with the seeking of location and employees. This applies to sales also and may explain in part the concentration upon local sales in most of the companies studied.

> Birley, 1985a, p. 113

VALUE CONFLICTS

Entrepreneurs often face a role conflict and/or a conflict of values between family/leisure-time priorities and work. As with all values issues, the decision is personal, but the most common opinion is expressed below.

> [Entrepreneurs] should be totally committed to the success of the venture, which should take priority over all other commitments, including (in a sense) their responsibilities to their families.

> Martin, 1984, p. 278

Thus we expect that most entrepreneurs will make some *presumably short-term sacrifices of family security and financial well-being* for the good of the new venture. In addition to giving financial priority to the business, *time and intimacy are prioritized in favor of the venture,* especially since the entrepreneurial career demands a seven-day, 60- to 90-hour work week. The lifestyle makes it difficult to develop and sustain close personal ties—family and friends must tolerate relatively infrequent contact.

The focus on business and distance from intimacy with family may become a preferred way of living, making ultimate disengagement from the venture (selling out or retiring) very difficult. At the same time, developing such a lifestyle preference makes disengagement from family and friends easier. We would expect more sacrifices of intimacy and family from those with growth-oriented firms than from those whose firms were created as a substitute for income.

While the business limits family life, family may limit the new venture. The various commitments and expectations arising from *family roles may act as a hindrance or distraction* in the decision to undertake an entrepreneurial career (Liles, 1974). Based on the timing of men's lives, family security issues that arise in the early 30s and 40s (i.e., marriage and the birth of children) make men less able (or willing) to undertake a new venture career. Likewise, these obligations, stemming from the "good provider role" (Bernard, 1981) make continual risk taking (the entrepreneurial spirit) difficult to maintain.

Spousal relationship.   One center of the family-versus-business conflict is in the relationship between the entrepreneur and his or her spouse. Most studies have looked at male entrepreneurs and their wives; there are a few anecdotal stories but no studies to date on female entrepreneurs and their husbands, and few studies on children. Wives have played an important role in the career decisions of men for a number of years, if not throughout recorded history (Jolson & Gannon, 1972). For half of the entrepreneurs in a recent study, the spouse was an active support and/or sounding board (two of these spouses were also partners). Of these, an older entrepreneur spoke most appreciatively about his wife:

> She sacrificed an enormous amount to let me do all these crazy things. It's been tough on her because I've been so totally involved that very often I'm not very good company. Eight kids later, how she's sane at all, I don't know. She always ran the home and never complained. Whenever I got home there was always something to eat. She never pulled relative rank, something I could never thank her for.

> Bird, 1986, p. 12

While exaggerated on the side of appreciation, this comment reflects the role and importance of a "significant other" on the home front.

The mutuality of the marriage relationship is so important to American couples that Martin (1984) advises that the decision to begin a new venture should be made by both spouses.

> Apart from the fact that both husband and wife must make such a commitment jointly, if they have a viable marriage, it is unlikely that an individual would be able to withstand the psychic strain of new venture creation without familial support.

> Martin, 1984, p. 278

Of course, marriages end, and when entrepreneurs enter divorce proceedings, the business enters as well—suffering from lack of attention, at risk in a property settlement, and the focus of much debate (Wojahn, 1986a).

Family and friendship in business. Family businesses have special strengths, weaknesses, and problems. Most fundamentally, the business and family/friendship systems overlap, creating value conflicts and considerable confusion with regard to authority, leadership, compensation, promotion, discipline, and so forth.

> The *family* must satisfy deep social and emotional needs for belonging, affection, and intimacy, and it must provide a sense of identity that includes experiencing one's self as a source of influence and power.
>
> Kepner, 1983, p. 60, emphasis added

> The family's primary social function . . . is to assure the care and nurturance of its members. Thus social relations in the family are structured to satisfy family members' various developmental needs.
>
> Lansberg, 1983, p. 40

Friendship offers a similar potential for clashes of values since friendship is a relatively permanent, emotionally salient relationship, involving "a strong love between two persons not based on sex or the social arrangements of marriage." Friendship operates on norms of reciprocity, trust, sharing, and emotional vulnerability (Brain, 1977, p. 123).

In contrast, the norms and values of *business* are those of economic rationality.

> The fundamental *raison d'etre* of business . . . is the generation of goods and services through organized task behavior. As a result, social relations in the firm are, on the whole, guided by norms and principles that facilitate the productive process.
>
> Lansberg, 1983, p. 40

The overlap produces early hiring and training advantages. For example, family members and friends are readily available and presumed trustworthy, loyal, honest, and hard working, so psychological contracts take less time to be formed. However, the overlap results in later role conflict for the entrepreneur, specifically in decisions to reward, promote, fire, or discipline an employee. Other fuzzy areas include the training of family members (especially second generation)—should children move up the ranks or take their apprenticeships and early jobs in other, nonfamily businesses (Zaslow, 1986)? Of particular concern to organizational survival are issues of leadership succession (Lansberg, 1983).

Succession. Leadership succession and business continuity often generate important value-laden questions. Should control of the firm be passed on to family members? If friends are partners, whose family takes control? Should control be passed to professional (and nonfamily) managers? How should this decision be made and implemented? What alternatives exist? What is the impact of this decision on family relations? What is the impact of this decision on employee satisfaction and motivation?

Since only 30 percent of family-owned firms survive beyond the tenure of the founder ("Conversation," 1983), the continued existence of family businesses depends on how these and other questions are answered and how the process of transition is managed. However, family control relates to more than survival. In one well-documented case, continued family control was found to be more effective in producing sales and employment and in reducing scrap and turnover than control by a larger acquiring firm (Astrachan, 1985).

Behind the questions of succession may lie considerable unacknowledged rivalry between father/entrepreneur and son/successor (Levinson, 1971) and intergenerational conflict that stems from the different needs of older and younger men (Davis, 1986). In addition, there is possible sibling rivalry as sons and daughters line up for positions of control in the firm's second generation.

Some entrepreneurs foresee these problems and have strict "no kids" and/or "no friends" rules and conscientiously avoid nepotism and cronyism. Some bring family members into the business at an early age to combine family time and work time. A special linkage between family and business occurs in the home-based business, which seems to be increasing in popularity, especially among women (Lublin, 1984).

NETWORKS

A network is composed of people with whom the entrepreneur discusses business, and includes all of the external relations previously mentioned. In addition, a network includes formal organizations designed for "the dynamic use of contacts" and informal associations.

FORMAL VERSUS INFORMAL NETWORKS

Formal networks are organizations designed to facilitate the exchange between entrepreneurs, capitalists, and service providers. These include business booster clubs (Chambers of Commerce, Rotary Clubs, Young Presidents Organizations), venture capital clubs, small business/start-up seminars, and exclusive CEO groups such as SoCal TEN.

Clubs and seminars for entrepreneurs are increasingly popular; most attention is being focused on *venture capital clubs*, which are being formed in many places and at a rapid rate (Ioannou, 1984). In addition, club membership has grown dramatically. For example, the San Diego Venture Group expected 91 people for its first meeting in February 1985 and 201 showed up; two months later, club membership was 340 (Asinof, 1985, April 10). There is even a newsletter, *Venture* magazine's *Capital Club Monthly*, to link these formal groups together into an even more encompassing network.

Informal networking takes place in men's clubs, health clubs, and golf clubs, which tend to be sex-segregated. Women rely more on formal networking organizations, especially those designed for women (Black, 1986). Interestingly, more men than women attend venture capital club meetings (Asinof, 1985, April 10).

FUNCTIONS OF THE NETWORK

The network provides the entrepreneur with access to resources, training, and a psychological release, which are thought to be particularly important during start-up and other periods of rapid change (Aldrich, Rosen, & Woodward, 1986). Networks may also operate in the larger social system to boost awareness and prestige of the entrepreneurial role, to organize for political impact, and to promote social change.

For example, venture capital clubs, often started by venture capitalists to get an inside line on new companies, provide entrepreneurs with the opportunity to promote their companies. Some (but not many) entrepreneurs get funding from direct presentation to venture capital clubs. For example, the

Boston group of the Private Equity Fund "generated $3 million to $4 million in deals in its first nine months in 1983, . . . having grown substantially since then" (Asinof, 1985, April 10). Other networks provide investment funds, have special relationships with local banks (such as the Women's Economic Development Corp. of St. Paul), or add clout to negotiations with investors (Black, 1986).

The training function of networks is not so much "information sharing" as problem solving and learning from other people's experience (Black, 1986; Kahn, 1985). Sharing experiences with "peers" (who are difficult to find inside an organization one is building) serves the function of social release and escape from entrepreneurial loneliness.

Finally, networking groups have a potential beyond serving the economic, social, and psychological self-interests of members. Specifically, these forums become "metafirms" or "transorganizations," where learning crosses company lines. The umbrella identity takes on unique value (i.e., another new organization is created), and collective action can result in larger social change (Kahn, 1985).

QUALITIES OF NETWORKS

Besides being formal or informal, the networks of entrepreneurs can be described in terms of their content, interpersonal ties, age, activity level, and "multiplexity."

Content. Networks *composed of mostly business contacts* (compared with family and friends) are thought to have more of the resources needed by an entrepreneur. Research has shown that people starting a business tend to have networks with more business relationships than people who have no plans to be entrepreneurs, are thinking about being entrepreneurs, or are currently running a going concern (Aldrich et al., 1986).

Interpersonal ties. Relationships between individuals in a network can be described as "strong" (close friends with long histories together) or "weak" (strangers). Granovetter (1973) argues that the *resources of a "weak" tie network are greater than those with "strong" ties.* Aldrich et al. (1986) found that "networks of entrepreneurs in the beginning stages of business had higher proportion of strangers than networks of respondents at other stages of business" (p. 12). Comparing the number of years the entrepreneur has been in business with the number of years he or she has known his or her network contacts,

Aldrich et al. (1986) found that 50 percent of the CEOs in their study had networks younger than their business, suggesting that *entrepreneurs may change their network relationships to serve a business rationale.* These results suggest that while the network, like the business, is new, it may be richer in resources than older and closer networks.

Activity level. Activity level refers to the number of contacts and the amount of time spent with network members. Aldrich et al. (1986) found that *starting entrepreneurs have more contacts and spend more time developing contacts than established business owners and non-owners.*

Multiplexity. Network multiplexity refers to the overlap in the roles played by members of the network, or

> . . . the number of multiple relationships that exist between [starting entrepreneurs] and their network members. . . . For example, in a high density network, one network member may be a friend, a banker, and a former college roommate. . . . In a low density network, members would tend to have fewer multiplex relationships.
>
> Aldrich et al., 1986, p. 15

Research shows that entrepreneurs do not differ from established business managers or non-businesspeople in the complexity and overlap of their network (Aldrich et al., 1986). Entrepreneurs spend more time developing contacts, have more contact with key advisors, and have networks in which members have more ties than those who consider but do not begin a new venture. Finally, entrepreneurs with younger profitable ventures (less than three years old) spend more time maintaining network relationships and have more multiplex networks than entrepreneurs with older ventures. Older ventures that are profitable are more closely associated with the size of the entrepreneur's network (Aldrich et al., 1987).

WEAKNESSES IN NETWORKING

Although networks are apparently necessary to get started and to stay informed about changes in the environment, there are some potential disadvantages of relying on network relationships. First, they require personal compatibility, and therefore exclude some individuals whose styles, temperament, or habits differ from those at the core of the network. Second, they take time to establish and maintain. Third, they require reciprocity—giving resources as well as receiving.

Finally, there is some suggestion that networks with strong ties, long duration, and high "multiplexity" might in fact be detrimental to the entrepreneurial spirit by inhibiting risk and change (Aldrich et al., 1986). That is, as the members of the network accumulate experience with each other, relationships tend to become relatively stable and overlapping, and "entrepreneurs [come to experience] . . . decreasing ability to replace members even when resource needs change" (Aldrich et al., 1986, p. 14).

Implications

Clearly entrepreneurs of different types form relationships with different external parties. Entrepreneurs with growth goals are likely to seek or be courted by venture capital firms, whereas those with income-substitution or predominantly noneconomic "missions" are avoided by venture capital. Likewise, venture capitalists expect full-time commitment from the entrepreneur. Furthermore, some venture firms specialize their portfolio of investments by technological-industrial niches.

Entrepreneurs with technology-based ventures are likely candidates for strategic alliances with larger firms. We would expect service-oriented firms, such as those that "lease" employees by taking over administrative overhead, to form customer or client relationships with larger firms and not strategic alliances.

External advisors are important to all types of entrepreneurial ventures. However, banks are not likely to enter into loan relationships with firms in the early stages, and they are likely to be critical to entrepreneurs who acquire going concerns. External advisors may be specialized to deal with ventures in certain industries or of certain sizes and growth potential. Shopping for advisors through networks appears to have some value.

All external relationships reflect intentional competencies of the entrepreneur. These relationships are usually future-focused and require the sustaining of temporal tension. As founders move between operations (present focus) or tactics (short-term future focus) to planning and strategizing with venture capitalists, bankers, boards of directors, networks, and others, the time horizon shifts to longer-term futures (five to seven or more years). Temporal agility, along with patience, seems very important. Even relationships with family and friends contain temporal tension, as short-term sacrifices are made for uncertain future affluence and leisure time.

Likewise, all external relationships reflect the ability of the entrepreneur to tune in to (attune to) the environment. The ability of the entrepreneur and his or her team to form strategic relationships that are information and resource channels seems critical, especially in environments that are changing, such as those using or producing high technology, those with changing government regulations, and those that must be internationally competitive. Central to this competency is the ability of all parties to discuss and agree on values in the early stages and to keep communication open. Recognizing integrity and developing and maintaining trust are important. Again, this truth applies as well to family and friendship relationships.

CHAPTER 11

THE ENTREPRENEURIAL ROLE: THE EVOLUTION OF A LEADER

INTRODUCTION

One way to consider entrepreneurial behavior with regard to internal and external teams is by looking at the entrepreneurial role, or how entrepreneurs interact with others in the pursuit of their goals. Of specific interest is the entrepreneur as leader. Changes in the entrepreneur's role and changes in the organization are discussed later in this chapter.

ROLE THEORY

The concept of *role* derives from social psychology and refers to the characteristic ways in which an individual (here an entrepreneur) interacts with one or more other individuals in the pursuit of individual or shared goals. Roles result from the common human desire for predictability in interactions. Roles develop—or, more accurately, we learn and modify our roles through shared expectations of behavior.

Roles are reciprocal. To have a leader, there must be a follower; teachers require students; there cannot be a husband without a wife, a mother without a child, and so forth. Reciprocity implies give-and-take between individuals in mutual role definition. Thus entrepreneurs learn what is expected of them from venture capitalists, partners, and others, while venture capitalists and partners learn what is expected of them from entrepreneurs and others.

Many of the roles we take on are context-specific, developed and used in specific situations or in interaction with specific other individuals such as "at the office" or "with my husband." Entrepreneurs, because they are generalists, interacting with a wide variety of insiders and outsiders, "wear many different hats." Those with "many hats" are involved in many roles, and the ability to appropriately shift roles requires considerable flexibility and cognitive complexity.

A MODEL OF ROLE-DEVELOPMENT

Because roles emerge, change, and stabilize over time through interaction, we can diagram the process in terms of role sending and receiving (see Figure 11.1). This figure shows individuals and team members, in role sets, developing expectations about the role behavior of the entrepreneur. Their expectations are communicated verbally (directly and indirectly) and nonverbally to the entrepreneur (i.e., "You need a business plan with two years of cash flow analysis," or "As an entrepreneur you are expected to take personal responsibility for all facets of your firm").

These expectations, as understood by the entrepreneur, are a framework that narrows the range of acceptable behavior for the entrepreneur. While entrepreneurs carry the halo of the "rugged individualist," they cannot create value alone. Meeting the expectations of customers, bankers, partners, and employees is critical to success. However, individuals differ in how they perceive and value the expectations of others and in how they proceed. For example, a person can use a spreadsheet program to write a business plan or can take a course on writing business plans; he or she can be personally involved in all operational decisions or delegate to others. Finally, the behavior of the entrepreneur, whether conforming to expectations or not, influences what others come to expect of him or her in the future (e.g., "she pays attention to details," "he can't delegate") and how these others behave in their own roles as watchdogs, friends, or devil's advocates.

Role sets are individuals or groups of individuals who have an important relationship with the entrepreneur and have a stake in his or her behavior. Some role sets have only one

FIGURE 11.1   A Model of the Role Development Process

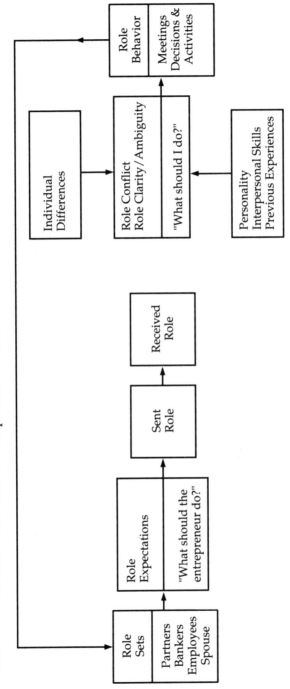

Source: Data from D. Katz and R. L. Kahn, *Social Psychology of Organizations*, 2nd ed. (New York, NY: John Wiley & Sons, 1978).

person in them (e.g., a spouse) while others include several individuals who share a common relationship with the entrepreneur such as employees, customers, or investors.

The *sent role* is made up of the expectations of the relevant role sets. For example, bankers and investors have certain expectations about the way an entrepreneur should prepare for funding, how he or she should interact with the financial community, and what priorities should dominate the entrepreneur's venture. Very different expectations might be expected from early-stage employees or customers. Expectations are communicated through face-to-face interaction and through written and secondary sources such as gossip or hearsay. Some expectations come from one's personal history (such as those from deceased parents or distant mentors) and are brought into play through memory.

The entrepreneur perceives or misperceives these expectations. This is the *received role*. Here the entrepreneur's "veridical perception" (Schrage, 1965) is important to successful, conflict-free, and rewarding interactions. Having accurate perceptions of the expectations of lenders helps one prepare for the loan application. Likewise, attunement to employee expectations can help build a cohesive management team or forestall collective bargaining.

The entrepreneur's own expectations, beliefs, needs, drives, and motivations interact with the expectations of others to "flavor" the *role behavior*. Here personality, previous experience, and personal goals and values influence the individual's behavior. Thus the entrepreneur whose need for autonomy is great will tend not to delegate, even though managers and venture partners expect it. Likewise, the creative entrepreneur will tend to focus on new projects rather than control systems while building a stable organization for employees and partners. Finally, the entrepreneur whose goal is adequate income to support his or her family will be less receptive to the expectations of growth held by others such as venture capitalists or ambitious brothers-in-law.

This general model of role taking applies to all organizational roles. However, entrepreneurs differ from managers, employees, and the general population by having unique leadership and executive responsibilities in the organizations they create and transform. Thus, in addition to role taking (through sending and receiving expectations), entrepreneurs *make or create their roles to suit themselves*. Let's look more closely at the roles created and taken by entrepreneurs.

ENTREPRENEURIAL ROLE TASKS

Entrepreneurs have responsibilities such as hiring, strategic planning, and setting policy that are common to all executives. Other responsibilities, such as the creation of organization, the initiation of new organizational systems, the birth of a new culture, and the creation of new products or services are more or less unique to entrepreneurs. In addition, the entrepreneur, who is invested in and identified with his or her enterprise, takes these responsibilities more personally than most managers.

The entrepreneur's chief role task is to effectively link himself or herself (his or her ideas, resources, and skills) with the new venture and with external resources (bankers, customers, etc.). In establishing his or her role the entrepreneur needs to consider five variables (Hodgson, Levinson, & Zaleznik, 1965).

1. *The organization,* as it exists and where it is going, its size, profits, market, etc.: Is it growth-oriented or intended to produce income? Will the entrepreneur maintain private control or bring in partners, investors, and shareholders?

2. *His/her concept of his role and other organizational roles*: What does he expect to do? not do? What role model does he hold? What are employees and managers to do, and how? What roles are outside investors expected to play?

3. *His/her self-concept* including beliefs about his or her abilities: Is he or she a generalist or a specialist such as "an idea person" or "a salesperson"? Does he or she know how to perform certain key functions or how to learn these functions? Is he or she a doer, a dreamer, a manager, or a leader?

4. *His/her commitment to the organization and its commitment to him/her*: How long does he or she plan to stay with the organization? With how many new ventures is he or she involved concurrently? Do other organizational stakeholders value his or her contributions? Has the firm outgrown him or her?

5. *The work itself*: Does he or she enjoy fire-fighting, daily decision making, long hours, negotiating, promoting, planning, etc? Does the work energize or deplete him/her?

ROLE DILEMMAS

There are two role-related dilemmas identified by social psychologists—*role ambiguity* and *role conflict*. As we begin new roles, when we lack information about what to do, when contexts are ambiguous, or if we are uncertain about how others will respond, we experience role ambiguity—What should I do now? Because entrepreneurs create their own positions and write the rules of the game for their organizations, we don't expect them to experience much role ambiguity, although conceivably first-time entrepreneurs and entrepreneurs without a role model might experience some.

If we wear different hats (e.g., employee, part-time entrepreneur, wife, mother, and athlete), we may experience role conflict. This happens when the expectations of others are incompatible with each other or incompatible with our own expectations—Should I spend time with my family or work on accounts receivable? Four types of role conflict have been identified (Rizzo, House, & Lirtzman, 1970):

1. Inter-sender conflict occurs when different role sets make inconsistent demands of the entrepreneur. For example, the entrepreneur's banker and employees have different expectations about how profits should be spent. Likewise, the entrepreneur's partner and spouse (assuming they are different individuals) have different expectations about how time should be spent.

2. Inter-role conflict occurs when the person occupies two different positions in one organization, as when the entrepreneur is both chairman of the board and vice-president of marketing, reporting to a president hired to manage the firm. (See Richman, 1985c for the case of Billy Ladin of ComputerCraft.)

3. Intra-sender conflict occurs when the individual's abilities and resources are not adequate to the situation. This results in role overload, when one is "faced with obligations, which taken as a set, require him to do more than he is able in the time available" (Froggatt & Cotton, 1984, p. 207). If an entrepreneur lacks personal commitment, time, energy, or the ability to learn, or resources such as a network and capital, failure would be expected.

4. Person-role conflict occurs when the entrepreneur's values and standards are perceived to be incompatible with those of the role set. For example, many struggling entrepreneurs face ethical dilemmas not unlike those of John DeLorean, who apparently turned to illegal activities to keep his business dream alive.

High levels of role ambiguity and role conflict are expected to result in lower satisfaction and productivity and in higher levels of stress (Miles & Perreault, 1982), although some individuals thrive on and seek out ambiguous and/or conflictful situations (Froggatt & Cotton, 1984). To date, only one study has looked at the entrepreneurial role and that study did not address role ambiguity or role conflict. It did find that role overload (e.g., time limitations) and responsibility for other people were strong predictors of entrepreneurial stress (Boyd & Begley, 1986). Clearly, more research is needed on the role tensions of entrepreneurs.

TYPES OF ENTREPRENEURIAL ROLES

In his study of managers, Mintzberg (1973) found that they filled ten roles: figurehead, leader, liaison, monitor, disseminator, spokesman, disturbance handler, resource allocator, negotiator, and entrepreneur (i.e., "intrapreneur," innovator, risk taker). Entrepreneurs may take on any or all of these roles as their organizations grow (see the section on leadership for discussion of how entrepreneurs differ from managers). In addition, entrepreneurs take on the roles of partner, employer, and client as discussed in earlier chapters on internal and external teams. Let's now look at some unique roles of the entrepreneur.

CREATOR OF ORGANIZATION

The most obvious role of an entrepreneur involves his or her function as the instigator, the "prime mover," "parent," and author of the organization he or she begins. In this role, personal values are implemented. Entrepreneurial values and attitudes directly influence the product or service provided by the organization, and entrepreneurs often craft the prototype or provide the original service themselves. As others join the venture, entrepreneurs teach them their methods, values, and interpersonal "rules of the game."

Entrepreneurial values also underlie the philosophy and purpose of the firm and directly influence early strategic, structural, and policy decisions. Through these early actions and decisions, the entrepreneur's values and attitudes become core aspects of the emerging corporate culture (Bennis & Nanus, 1985).

> . . . [Entrepreneurs] have strong assumptions about the nature of the world, the role their organization will play in that world, the nature of human nature, truth, relationships, time, and space.
>
> Schein, 1983, p. 17

In turn, early products and initial corporate culture influence a stream of future decisions, traditions, thought forms, and ways of doing things, which contribute to (or diminish) the firm's ability to survive or grow (Barney, 1986). A good example of how personal values influence organizations is found in the case of Robert Swiggett.

THE CASE OF ROBERT SWIGGETT

Skip Griggs, 50, the president of one of Kollmorgen Corp.'s 16 divisions, once worked for a well-known manufacturer of household appliances. He supervised two assembly lines that produced electric toothbrushes and knives. Each day, the people who worked on this assembly line were given half an hour for lunch and two eight-minute breaks, during which they could eat a candy bar or a sandwich and also go to the bathroom before the assembly-line belts started up again. The company would not allow the workers to use the nearby cafeteria for their breaks, so they took them in the bathroom instead.

"Management figured," Griggs says, "that if you let them use the café, they'd eat and hang around and when the belts started up again, *then* they might remember to go to the bathroom. They couldn't even be trusted to do that by themselves. Management just didn't seem to be able to see that this was a little attention that could produce great results. You know, little things mean a lot to people, and you can't do anything without people. I just couldn't stomach that. I mean, eating in a bathroom, come on. So I opened the café on my own and everybody cheered, but I got chewed out like you couldn't believe.

"It was very frustrating. I never met the president of the company, not even once. I had a boss in Chicago. If things were going well, he'd come and visit me. If things were going poorly, I had to visit him. And all the while you're worrying, 'Lord, what did I do now?' You didn't know for sure, you just had to sit there and worry what it might be. It was an atmosphere of suspicion."

In time, Griggs was fired. He came away from the experience not so much embittered as confirmed in the belief that management mistrust of employees was the natural state of the corporate world. He would be a hard man to convince otherwise.

In 1974, Griggs interviewed for a job as manufacturing manager at the Inland Motor Division of Kollmorgen in Radford, Va. Corwin Matthews, the personnel manager, explained to Griggs that Kollmorgen—a $79-million-a-year electronics company—was not like other corporations. There was a new philosophy at work there, Matthews said, which disagreed strongly with the precepts of traditional authoritarian management. People came first at Kollmorgen, he said, and they were seen as basically good, well-intentioned, willing to work, responsible, and creative. Everyone was treated as an equal in an environment grounded on mutual trust and respect. Here people felt secure and could talk openly about their opinions and problems.

Griggs listened politely to this description of what seemed like a mythical kingdom, and took the job, reasoning: "I looked at it as one of two things—a gold mine or a disaster. Either way, I felt I'd know soon enough."

A year passed, and even after Griggs listened to Robert L. Swiggett, Kollmorgen's chairman of the board, chief executive officer, and leading evangelist, describe the company's new corporate vision at a meeting in Hartford, he was still uncertain. Maybe the vision was only that, he thought, fun for a sunny day but quick to evaporate when business got tough. "Maybe then they'd say, 'Let's go back to the old way and tell those dumb bunnies what to do,' " he recalls thinking. "I thought it was working in our division, but what about the others? You know you go so far, but you sometimes tread lightly. I still had some vague reservations. Let's face it, freedom and respect for the individual are just different."

Four more years passed. Storm clouds came and went and, if anything, the "bunnies" were given more freedom. Meanwhile, Griggs' division also witnessed extraordinary growth. From 1974 to 1979, the company's sales nearly doubled, from $79.1 million to $154.5 million, while earnings almost tripled, from $3.3 million to $9.8 million. Yet Griggs still had some doubts.

Then, in 1980, Swiggett published the company's philosophy in a seven-page brochure that was widely distributed. Griggs was ecstatic. "I knew he had to mean it because he put it in black and white for the world," he says. "He was putting his reputation and all his experience on the line. I said to myself: 'I'm in this for the rest of my life.' "

The Kollmorgen Corporation Philosophy is philosophy of a very practical sort, as well it should be. After all, Bob Swiggett the philosopher-author is also Bob Swiggett the chairman of the board of a company with 5,000 employees, 16 divisions, and 25 manufacturing locations, not to mention approximately 4,500 shareholders—a generally skittish crowd favoring results more than contemplation. Thus, Swiggett declared his intentions as early as the front cover of the brochure.

"Freedom and respect for the individual," he wrote, "are the best motivators of man, especially when innovation and growth are the objectives." To avoid misunderstanding, "innovation" was quickly defined as "technological leadership" and "first to market with the best" in the company's three business segments: printed circuitry and associated technology, special direct current motors and controls, and electro-optical instruments. And "growth" was identified as doubling sales and earnings every four years while exceeding a 20% return on shareholders' average equity.

Traditional forms of management cannot sustain these goals, Swiggett went on, particularly in larger companies. In order to achieve innovation and growth, a company must maintain "a free-market environment for every individual in the company," wherein "each employee is exposed to the risk and rewards of the market . . . [and is] primarily responsible for using his abilities and for his own success or failure." The best way to encourage such entrepreneurial commitment is to break a company into small, autonomous "profit center" teams.

"Within each small, close-to-its-market business unit," Swiggett wrote, "each person can accurately assess the contributions of the other team members. Each can feel like a partner. Each can feel he contributes, and feel confident that his contribution will be recognized. . . . Each feels responsible. Each individual is every other's judge."

There is a compelling personal conviction throughout this statement that carries with it the incontrovertible certainty of revelation. It is hard to believe, based on the fluid exposition of his cosmology, that Swiggett, like Griggs, came to his faith slowly, awkwardly, and once, even reluctantly. Like any good laboratory scientist, he placed a premium on activity for its own sake, always trying this or that until he or a colleague stumbled across a breakthrough. Then he kept going, content to figure out the theory later.

Swiggett traces the origins of his faith back to a day in 1967 when he stood on the edge of the production floor and watched some of his company's 500 employees moving through the complex patterns of their individual enterprise. The company's name was Photocircuits Corp.—it later merged with Kollmorgen—and it was a model of traditional, rational management. Indeed, there were more than 1,000 open orders out there on the floor, each one with a different set of manufacturing requirements, often 50 process steps long, and each one passing through 10 or 15 different departments. "It was a classic case of confusion," Swiggett recalls. "Later, when we began to analyze what it took to get an order through the shop, [we realized] we were lucky ever to ship anything."

That landscape, which for so long had seemed to Swiggett the natural and fruitful condition of a traditional, centrally controlled, functionally structured organization, had turned hostile and threatening. Something was missing out there, some unifying first principle, some elemental sense of design, and its absence was confounding the company's future.

Photocircuits's primary business was the manufacture of printed circuit boards. The company had, in fact, pioneered the field, which in turn had revolutionized electronics-assembly technology. Before the advent of printed circuits, each of the myriad capacitor and resistor joints on a terminal board had to be soldered by hand. The printed circuit board allowed mass soldering and automatic assembly of electronic components, and later fertilized numerous other technologies.

The company's first big breakthrough came in the mid-1950s, when it obtained an agreement to make half of the printed circuit boards for computers being used in a new continental air defense system. According to Jim Swiggett, Bob's brother, who joined the company in 1953, the deal "contributed about $1 million a year until [the program] petered out in 1967." These were significantly larger revenues and responsibilities for a company that had, until then, been operating out of a garage, a cellar, and a basement beneath a bar.

"We had a minimum of management skills," Jim recalls. "It was definitely the dark ages all the way. I mean, you had to take your used pencil to the accounting department to get a new one. It was just a bunch of guys trying to get something done." Deciding that it was time to acquire the accoutrements of a real business, Jim Swiggett hired a consultant, who helped him rough-in the framework of a traditional, centrally controlled, functionally managed corporation.

As the business grew, so did the new management structure, but in time the company found itself resorting more and more frequently to distinctly nontraditional operating tactics. The impetus came from new, smaller printed circuit companies, which frequently won business at Photocircuits's expense because they could respond more quickly to the customer's needs. In order to meet this challenge, Photocircuits would often organize a small, dedicated task force to solve particularly urgent problems. Invariably, this task force, which operated without cost systems or formal scheduling and with utter disregard for the precepts of modern management theory, bulled its way to a solution. The idea proved so successful that it was institutionalized in 1960 when the company established a so-called Proto department.

Although the Proto department was originally set up to make prototypes of new production business, it soon became a small-quantity, quick-turnaround business in its own right, with its own list of customers. There were only 35 people in the department, but they could turn around an order for a new type of printed circuit board in 1 to 3 weeks, as opposed to the 6 to 10 weeks normally required. What's more, the Proto department was the most profitable part of the company. "The Proto guys had one game," Bob Swiggett says, "and that was to satisfy the customer. The other people in production were playing departmental games, like who has the best score for efficiency in their department. To them the customer was only a job number."

It is one of those ironies of history that Swiggett, even with the evidence right in front of him, couldn't see in the Proto department the very substance of what Skip Griggs would later read in the Kollmorgen Philosophy. It was all there: the importance of small groups of individuals acting autonomously, the profitability, the customer satisfaction, the innovation and growth. But to Swiggett, the Proto department was somehow tangential to the company's main operations, a renegade of sorts meant to have little impact on the status quo. Besides, he was totally preoccupied with building the business in a more traditional manner.

From 1957 to 1967, Photocircuits nourished an intense effort to diversify the business and overwhelm the competition. "We couldn't deal with competition," Swiggett says. "We wanted to have something the other guys didn't have." Routinely spending 10% of sales on research and development, the company accelerated its chemical-engineering research and established a product-development operation. By 1967, it had come up with a number of new technologies that promised substantial additions to the company's $10-million sales base.

Perhaps it was this flurry of activity that obscured the subterranean rumblings of approaching disaster. In any case, when Swiggett finally heard them on that day in 1967, it was nearly too late. Somehow Photocircuits had trapped itself in a paradox of self-defeating success. "Rarely did we meet promised deliveries," Swiggett recalls. "Quality problems were enormous; profit performance was erratic; morale was poor. Production managers burned out quickly. Functional departments fought with one another. Only the rapid growth of the market and the even more disorganized condition of our large competitors sustained us."

As it happened, Swiggett and some of his colleagues had just returned from a tour of an IBM Corp. plant in Endicott, N.Y., where they had seen what IBM had done with computer-aided manufacturing management. "The complexity of our production routine was so mind-blowing that we thought something like the IBM process control system was what we needed," Swiggett recalls. "We said, 'Boy, what we're going to do is put this whole business on line in real time, and we're going to know where every part is. We're going to be able to have scheduling, we'll have loading algorithms, we'll have all those things.' We were smart guys, at least we thought so, and we wanted to do things right. We weren't willing to trust our gut."

Jim Swiggett, then vice-president of manufacturing and production, was put in charge of developing System 70, a customized method of scheduling and management that was to produce daily departmental scheduling by 1970. The project was successfully completed in late 1969 at a cost of around $500,000. Then it bombed. "Statistically, we got everything we wanted," Bob Swiggett says. "We could spit out printouts that would cover the wall in about 15 minutes. The computer worked beautifully, but company performance, if anything, got worse. Foremen were preoccupied with printouts instead of people. Managers spent time worrying about internal systems instead of our customers. People couldn't relate to those printouts, and they resented the control."

The failure of System 70 triggered Jim Swiggett's survival instinct. Time after time, Jim traced back over his experiences, searching for a solution to the company's dilemma, and time after time, he paused at the idea of small, dedicated teams, an idea he called "team manufacturing." He began to see it as something more than a temporary expediency. Meanwhile, the recession of 1970 had made cost-cutting imperative, and that meant either eliminating crucial R&D projects or junking System 70, the shibboleth of modern management. But if System 70 died violently, what would take its place?

These were weighty matters indeed, so Jim packed his bags and went to Harvard University's Graduate School of Business Administration to consult "the world's leading guy on production control," whose name is now shrouded in the mists of time. "I must have talked for quite a while," Jim says, "but he was very patient. Then he said, 'Here you are in the modern age, with computers, control theory, and you've just spent two hours telling me how you want to abdicate your responsibilities. Forget this team manufacturing you've got lurking in the back of your mind and go with what you're doing. You're doing it absolutely right.' "

While Jim was off to see the guru, Bob was home signing the final papers on the merger of Photocircuits and Kollmorgen. As if the crash of System 70 and a recession weren't enough to worry about, Photocircuits needed outside capital to support its growth. Bob had consulted with investment bankers who told him that Photocircuits would be worth $9 million in a public offering. Shortly thereafter, his old friend Dick Rachals, the president of Kollmorgen, telephoned him with an offer.

At first, Rachals only wanted to buy Photocircuits's printed motor business, but, after subsequent discussions, he ended up proposing a merger. To Swiggett, it looked like a good fit: Photocircuits had sales of roughly $15 million, while Kollmorgen's sales were about $23 million. Moreover, both were involved with high-technology products, and the price was right—440,000 shares of Kollmorgen worth about $14 million, considerably better than the expected proceeds from a public offering. In February 1970, the merger was completed.

"There we were," Bob Swiggett says, "newly merged at a great price, and naturally we wanted to look good. So you can imagine the chaos when Jim came back from Harvard saying, 'The hell with it. We're going to throw out System 70. We're going to throw out the whole thing.' "

To Bob and many of his colleagues, especially those who had worked on System 70, Jim's intuitive leap to team manufacturing was actually a stunning setback. "To give up modern management technology for something simpler," Bob says, "to throw that out meant to all of us at that time that we were giving up on another pioneering effort, and we didn't want to ever give up." But within six months, Photocircuits doubled its output per employee, and its on-time delivery rate rose from 60% to more than 90%. "In the middle of a depression," Bob says, "what could've been a disaster turned into a real good money-maker. So we really had it burned into our souls that small teams can be terribly effective."

As soon as the decision was made, Jim Swiggett went to work on what Bob describes as "a chaos of empire shattering." Using the Proto department as a model, Jim and his wrecking crew first broke up the company into some half dozen teams, each with an average of 75 people, and differentiated them by product line, market segment, or customer group. A manager was chosen to lead each team and was given responsibility for the team's profits, losses, and balance sheet. Then they threw out the standard cost system and eliminated most functional manufacturing and overhead departments, including customer service, order processing, production control, and quality control, all of which were turned over to the teams. Every manager was expected to deal directly with customers or field salespeople, set prices, bargain with other product managers for machine time and overhead allocation, and take monthly physical inventories in person.

"In spite of the yelling, almost magically everything improved," Bob Swiggett once said in a speech. "Customers were happier, pricing was better, profits rose, inventories turned faster, troublesome book-to-physical-inventory variance surprises disappeared. Morale rose with the evidence of success."

Shortly after the Photocircuits merger and resurrection, Kollmorgen itself took sick. In 1971, the company recorded an operating loss, as its eight divisions went about reenacting the confusion Swiggett had observed once before from the edge of the production floor at Photocircuits. These problems were exacerbated by leadership conflicts. By 1973 Bob Swiggett was firmly in control and had a clean slate in upper management.

Swiggett was no longer a neophyte; he was by now a seasoned practitioner, as well as a serious student of a new, essentially self-taught management art. He set about reorganizing Kollmorgen's eight divisions as if each were a small Photocircuits. Henceforth, they would stand free, with no centralized manufacturing and overhead departments to rely on. Every division, he said, must be an "autonomous profit-center," and he meant "autonomous" in the sense of being strong enough to go public. Next, Swiggett pushed the same responsibility as far down into the divisions as he could by creating small profit-center teams arranged by product, process, market, customer, contract, or whatever logical method presented itself.

In a series of meetings, the corporate officers committed themselves to superior performance in three areas: innovation, growth, and profitability. As growth objectives, they chose a doubling of sales and earnings every four years because such a growth rate would ensure recognition in the investment community, a high price-earnings multiple, and easy access to investment funds. Similarly, they wanted a conspicuous rate of return on equity and settled on a goal of roughly 20%, or about one and a half times the existing industrial average.

There was also a commitment to freedom and respect for the individual at work, a commitment that was later given form in the so-called partners statement, built word-by-word by 20 corporate officers and division presidents huddled for three days in a hotel in Stamford, Conn. That statement reads: "The purpose of the partnership is to fulfill its responsibility to Kollmorgen shareholders and employees by creating and supporting an organization of strong and vital business divisions where a spirit of freedom, equality, mutual trust, respect, and even love prevails; and whose members strive together toward an exciting vision of economic, technical, and social greatness."

Together, the technological goals, the financial goals, and the partners' statement constitute the Kollmorgen "vision." Having thus defined the game and set up the teams, Swiggett and his colleagues went on to find a way of keeping score, a ballpark, and some rules of good sportsmanship— or, respectively, a bonus plan, an organizational structure, and a corporate culture.

Swiggett wanted each division to struggle in the free-market arena. He also needed a method for making sure that the financial goals of the divisions conformed to those of Kollmorgen as a whole, without sacrificing divisional autonomy and a vigorous spirit of individual self-interest. What he came up with was "RONA," for "return on net assets," in which "net assets" are defined as the sum of receivables, inventories, and net fixed assets, minus payables.

The RONA plan was extremely versatile. It was easy to understand; it correlated with the company's overall objective for return on equity; and it was universally applicable among the divisions. "We had out the argument whether each division should be judged by the same economic performance," Swiggett says. "We studied all the SIC codes and found that in every SIC code, regardless of the kind of business, the leaders were making it and the others were doing poorly. So no matter what the business, the money market— which is blind to the nature of your business—judges you, and you ought to be able to do the same return on net assets."

As the basis for a new bonus plan, RONA also gave individuals a handy way of keeping score. If a division has a good year, even its least skilled workers can gain an additional 15% to 20% of their gross annual salaries. And indeed, the RONA plan quickly proved to be a powerful motivator. It was introduced throughout the company in the first quarter of 1975; six months later, receivables and inventories had been reduced by $11 million. "When people started thinking about an asset," Swiggett says, "they found they had five years worth of drills, five years worth of sheet metal, five years worth of everything. We practically didn't buy a thing for six months after putting in the bonus plan, and we ran the business beautifully."

Kollmorgen also needed an organizational structure that would ensure divisional autonomy, yet allow for coordination at the corporate level. After some experimentation, Swiggett and his colleagues hit on an ingenious solution: Every division president would communicate quarterly with his own board of directors. Each board of directors would generally be composed of three corporate officers, two other division presidents, and a senior technical person from another division. The boards would offer guidance and suggestions but never commands. "After all, what's the role of a leader?" Swiggett asks rhetorically. "It's to create a vision, not to kick somebody in the ass. The role of a leader is the servant's role. It's supporting his people, running interference for them. It's coming out with an atmosphere of understanding and trust and love. You want people to feel they have complete control over their own destiny at every level. Tyranny is not tolerated here. People who want to manage in the traditional sense are cast off by their peers like dandruff."

Such a relationship between a division and its board can sometimes create painful dilemmas. "You can see a situation deteriorating," Doyle says, "but doing something about it that's effective and not damaging to the long-term health of the division can only be done locally by people who are really part of that organization. It's their business; their business got in trouble, and they take the necessary actions."

In addition to the divisional boards of directors, Swiggett and friends also designed a forum, similar in spirit, to review each division's actual operating results and projections. Now, once a month, every profit-center team gives its division president a financial statement detailing its operating results for the past several quarters and projecting results 12 months out. These are then sent to corporate headquarters for consolidation, along with a statement from the division president reflecting the operating results of the division as a whole.

In this manner, more than 50 statements are submitted each month. When all are in, the corporate officers spend the next day around a conference table reviewing each one of them by telephone with the division presidents and project managers. Says Allan Doyle, "The real strength of our system is that, in times of adversity, there is no pressure within the system not to communicate what the division president or product manager sees in his markets. The only way people get into trouble really is by surprising other people. They don't get into trouble by saying, 'Hey look, we've got a problem here.' And here it comes out very early in the process."

Swiggett adds, "The boards and the statement meetings are both ways of growing the business without enlarging the corporate staff very much." This is a remarkable understatement, given that the entire company is "run" by only 11 corporate officers, 2 of whom are senior scientists.

At some final and irreducible level the Kollmorgen culture appears to rest on an act of faith in which individuals experience the company's vision in very personal terms. They are not "sold" on the vision; they commit themselves to it voluntarily because they perceive it as essential in shaping the meaning and significance of their own lives. Culture, then, is created every day as employees give life to the values of their shared belief. Management cannot control, nor even ensure, the moment of its flowering, but it can prepare the soil.

Swiggett himself goes to extraordinary lengths to foster the Kollmorgen culture. Twelve times a year, he leads so-called Kolture Workshops, designed to "keep the fires burn ing and spread them broadly." These workshops are either one or three days long and include from 35 to 100 people. At the three-day session, Swiggett reviews the history of Kollmorgen and, using a relaxed, Socratic method, examines the philosophical issues that inform the company's culture. "Do you think this philosophy can work in a corporation?" he asks. "Do you think it can work at Kollmorgen? Is it working now? How can we improve it?"

Through the Kolture Workshops, the company articulates its vision, over and over and over. At the least, the process bears witness to the potential of that vision; at best, it becomes part of a self-fulfilling prophecy. "Actually, it's very simple," Swiggett says. "We preach trust and the Golden Rule, and we're very careful that what we do is the same thing as what we say."

Accordingly, there are no time clocks at Kollmorgen, no policy or operations manuals, no information monopolies, no cafeterias closed during breaks. All such things, according to Swiggett, are "signals" that belie lofty rhetoric, and employees read them unerringly.

If you want openness and trust, Swiggett urges, then you have to act openly and with trust, every day. Thus, every division president sees the monthly financial statements prepared by every other division president. And the employees are similarly kept informed at monthly meetings that cover the company's progress, as well as the division's specific performance and its effect on the RONA bonus.

In the words of the Kollmorgen Philosophy: "Trusting people to be creative and constructive when given more freedom does not imply an overoptimistic belief in the perfectibility of human nature. It is rather a belief that the inevitable errors and sins of the human condition are far better overcome by individuals working together in an environment of trust, freedom, and mutual respect than by individuals working under a multitude of rules, regulations, and restraints imposed on them by another group of imperfect people."

Source: Lucien Rhodes, "The Passion of Robert Swiggett," *Inc.* April 1984. Reprinted with permission, *Inc.* magazine. Copyright © 1984 by INC. Publishing Company (Boston, MA: 38 Commercial Wharf, 02110).

FIGURE 11.2   Entrepreneur's Impact on the Organization

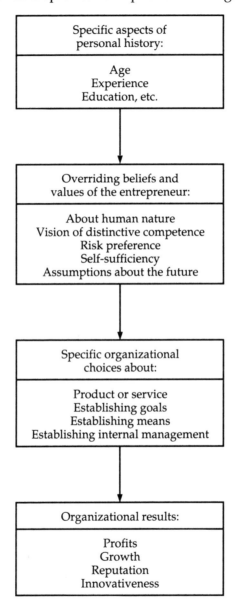

Source: From Donaldson & Lorsch (1983)

Figure 11.2 shows how the entrepreneur's personal experience, beliefs and values, and resultant corporate decisions relate to one another. Further discussion of the role of the entrepreneur as *cultural leader* will be found in the section on leadership.

TRANSFORMER OF ORGANIZATION

Entrepreneurs also buy out or buy into existing organizations. In these cases, entrepreneurs apply their unique perspectives and abilities to going concerns with the goal of adding value (often accompanied by the goal of realizing a subsequent increase in personal wealth). In this role we find individuals and teams who initiate and manage (1) takeovers or acquisitions when there is an outright purchase of a firm, (2) leveraged buy-outs, where existing managers or outsiders make a relatively small personal financial investment and borrow the rest of the purchase price against the firm's assets, and/or (3) "turnarounds," which occur when an entrepreneur takes some ownership of an ailing firm with the intention of fixing it and increasing its value.

Compared to those who initiate new ventures, these entrepreneurs have fewer degrees of freedom (i.e., fewer undetermined variables or unstructured activities). There are existing systems, employees, banking relationships, customers, etc. that must be accepted and used, at least initially. However, what the entrepreneurs lack in freedom, they compensate for with experience; most successful acquirers tend to have had considerable *management experience*, often with a larger business (Richman, 1986a) and often in the same industry. This experience, derived from a constrained bureaucracy, provides important insights into improving a going concern.

The turnaround case is probably most similar to the start-up in that resources are limited and there is a sense of urgency, chaos, and uncertainty. Turnaround entrepreneurs, like those who initiate new ventures, tend to be adaptable, flexible and opportunity driven (rather than resource driven). A major issue, requiring unique leadership expertise, is the absence of enthusiasm and low morale within the troubled acquisition (Mangan, 1986).

THE CASE OF PT

PT has had a career of 18 years as a turnaround executive, first with a Fortune 500 firm and most recently as an independent agent (entrepreneur), brought in with the incentive of stock options by the board of directors of a robotics firm in Northeastern Ohio. Although venture capitalists consider him an entrepreneur, PT thinks he's different on two dimensions—risk and management competence. According to PT, turnaround executives risk only their reputations (and these are more or less protected by a big company with deep pockets), while entrepreneurs "mortgage their house, their wives and go start in the garage." And while turnaround experts need to be excellent general managers, according to PT, entrepreneurs tend to be "lousy managers."

The turnaround process at the robotics firm followed a pattern of change PT has used before. First, and most important to the success of a turnaround, is the timing of the decision to bring in the turnaround executive.

> Typically, what happens when you go into a turnaround situation is that the people who are left are the ones who don't have any confidence in themselves. They didn't have enough balls to go and get another job and you are left with the dregs.
>
> Good people will put up with a given [troubled] situation for only so long. If they don't see change when they think change should take place, they'll leave because they have confidence in themselves, they know it's not getting any better, and they know they have to get another job.
>
> I have gone into companies who were in trouble for five years and boy, there was nothing left. And, I have gone into companies who have had trouble for about two years and it's not so bad because usually you can salvage some of that.

So, because morale and confidence are low, PT demands pride from employees and gives them a "win" as quickly as possible.

> Let them win at something whether it is getting the first shipment out on time or whether it is a reorganization that they participate in. The sooner you can get them to buy into it and demand of them that they live up to what their potential is, then the prize starts coming.

Other actions in the robotics turnaround involved firing both of the cofounders and bringing in a new management team during the critical first 90 days. Overall turnover was 73 percent the first year. This particular situation required a "restart" of the business, which involved raising money (which claimed 50 percent of PT's time), developing a second-generation product, fixing the first-generation product, and significant management change.

As a leader, PT began autocratically and created a "pressure cooker." After about a year he shifted to a more administrative, "support and guidance mode."

> If I'm going to find out where the strengths and weaknesses are in the organization I just beat the living hell out of it—push everybody against the wall. Just drive them and drive them. If you're gonna turn it around, you've got to find out where the cracks are right away so that you know which ones to plug up.

In addition, PT juggled many different engineering, operational, and financial decisions and didn't have time to communicate well with employees.

> You don't have time to pat people on the back. This upsets people because they need a lot of interaction and they don't understand where you're going or how you're going to get there. They get confused and upset and they don't see progress.

Because of the demands from the turnaround executive, his willingness to change direction abruptly, his lack of time for in-depth communication, and his eventual shift from autocrat to administrator, employees get confusing signals. Recognizing this, PT calls the director of human resources the "most important position" in the turnaround. This manager "should always wear the white hat" and be able to get access to the thoughts and feelings of people on a daily basis. His or her responsibility is to keep the turnaround entrepreneur aware of what is really going on in the organization.

PROMOTER

The promoter role of the entrepreneur involves selling ideas to others—to financial backers, employees, customers, suppliers, and so forth. Initially, the task is to convince others that one's business is worth their investment of money, time, or commitment. It involves the skills of persuasion, inspiration, vision, and negotiation. No business can exist without others who believe in the business's value.

Howard Stevenson (1985), professor of business at Harvard University, contrasts promoters with trustees in terms of attitudes and decision making. While the promoter says "I can make this happen," the trustee is concerned about guarding current resources. See Table 11.1 for the dimensions of comparison between the promoter and the trustee.

Another way to think of the promoter is in relation to his or her investors. Others invest in a new venture at considerable risk, so they expect to exert some control and/or reap considerable rewards from the businesses that succeed. The entrepreneur-as-promoter can structure the investment in terms of ownership of equity and payout rates. One way of measuring the promotional ability of entrepreneurs is by looking at the financial contract. At one end is the entrepreneur who keeps controlling interest in the firm and pays out 125 percent of the investment, in essence convincing investors to "trust me." At the other end is the entrepreneur who keeps only a small percentage of interest in the firm and pays out 200 percent of the investment, and in essence says to the investors "control me." The first entrepreneur is more of a promoter than the second.[1]

MENTOR AND ROLE MODEL

Entrepreneurs serve as examples to others, as our discussion of their background shows us. Most entrepreneurs have had a role model who was self-employed, a business owner, or an entrepreneur. Role models are sometimes fathers or family members, sometimes former bosses, and sometimes friends who either succeed, struggle, or fail. The role model may have been someone the entrepreneur admired and sought to emulate, or someone the entrepreneur disliked (e.g., "If that so-and-so can run his own business, so can I"). Just as entrepreneurs are influenced by their role models, they become role models for others—their children, employees, and friends.

Some entrepreneurs are aware of the example they are setting for others and consciously work at being good examples and sharing their experience. Some, like Jack Bares, founder of Milbar in Chagrin Falls, Ohio, become active in small-business support groups such as the Small Business Administration, growth associations, and chambers of commerce.

Some take on teaching responsibilities for associations as well as universities and colleges. Examples include John Van Slyke, founder of American Management Company and fac-

[1] A special thanks to David Wright, President of The Plechaty Companies of Cleveland, OH for insight into the financial aspects of the promoter role.

TABLE 11.1 Promoter Orientation Compared with Trustee Orientation

Pressures Toward This Side	Promoter	Key Business Dimension	Trustee	Pressures Toward This Side
Diminishing opportunity streams Rapidly changing: Technology Consumer economics Social values Political rules	Driven by perception of opportunity	STRATEGIC ORIENTATION Entrepreneurial Domain → ← Managerial Domain	Driven by resources currently controlled	Social contracts Performance measurement criteria Planning systems and cycles
Action orientation Short decision windows Risk management Limited decision constituencies	Revolutionary, with short duration	COMMITMENT TO OPPORTUNITY Entrepreneurial Domain → ← Managerial Domain	Evolutionary, of long duration	Acknowledgment of multiple constituencies Negotiation of strategy Risk reduction Management of fit
Lack of predictable resource needs Lack of long-term control Social needs for more opportunity/resource International pressure for more efficient resource use	Multistaged with minimal exposure at each stage	COMMITMENT OF RESOURCES Entrepreneurial Domain → ← Managerial Domain	Single-staged with complete commitment upon decision	Personal risk reduction Incentive compensation Managerial turnover Capital allocation systems Formal planning systems

CONTROL OF RESOURCES

Pressures toward this side	Entrepreneurial Domain →	← Managerial Domain	Pressures toward this side
Increased resource specialization	Episodic use or rent of required resources	Ownership or employment of required resources	Power, status, and financial rewards
Long resource life compared to need			Coordination
Risk of obsolescence			Efficiency measures
Risk of opportunity			Inertia and cost of change
Inflexibility of permanent commitment to resources			Industry structures

MANAGEMENT STRUCTURE

Pressures toward this side	Entrepreneurial Domain →	← Managerial Domain	Pressures toward this side
Coordination of key non-controlled resources	Flat, with multiple informal networks	Formalized hierarchy	Need for clearly defined authority and responsibility
Challenge to legitimacy of owner's control			Organizational culture
Employees' desire for independence			Reward systems
			Management theory

Source: H. H. Stevenson, "A New Paradigm for Entrepreneurial Management" in *Entrepreneurship: What It Is and How to Teach It* by Kao and Stevenson (Cambridge, MA: Harvard Business School Press, Harvard University 1985).

ulty member at Harvard University, and William Bygrave, founder of High Voltage Engineering Corporation (a NYSE company and pioneer on Route 128 near Boston) and faculty member at Babson College. Despite the bureaucracy involved with governmental agencies and higher education, and often with considerable opportunity costs (e.g., time not spent making businesses successful), many entrepreneurs are interested in sharing their wisdom and experience with others. This is evidenced by the recent positive response to a program designed to help entrepreneurs be better teachers (the Price-Babson Symposium of Entrepreneurship Education). Others actively encourage employees to try starting a venture—sometimes by providing resources to the new venture—as an independent spinoff or as an "intrapreneurial" effort (resulting in a wholly or partially owned subsidiary).

INVESTOR AND SOCIAL FIGURE

Two outcomes of successful new ventures are money and status. Money allows the entrepreneur to change hats and become an investor, philanthropist, teacher, politician, or "beach bum." Status produces larger audiences interested in the entrepreneur's business and personal life, and as a result produces great social and political influence and less privacy.

Entrepreneurs-turned-investors are an important, informal source of venture capital for the next generation of entrepreneurs. Such entrepreneurs are often known as "angels" who make private investments in start-ups, ranging from a few thousand to several hundred thousand dollars. The entrepreneur/angel is doubly loved—beside providing money, he or she respects the entrepreneurial need for control and tends to leave the new venture alone. Another term used for entrepreneurial investors is "adventure capitalist," connoting "a bold, swashbuckling, risk-taking plunge into an amorphous business situation and an undefined market—a gamble for which 'venture' is too tame a term" (Mamis, 1984, p. 94).

Entrepreneurs who become philanthropists, teachers, and politicians are using the freedom (from daily work) that their money can buy them and the influence their status provides in working for social values outside their enterprises. Examples include Harold Willens, cofounder of Factory Equipment in Los Angeles, who after having "done well" went on to "do good" by initiating various organizations aimed at the promotion of peace. Jeno Paulucci, founder of Chun King (later sold to R. J. Reynolds) and Pizza King (sold to Pillsbury), is described as a "public figure with clout and political influence who never worries about protocol or elections" and spends most of his time "using his wealth and business skills, not to mention the force of his personality, in the service of an unorthodox brand of social responsibility" (Wojahn, 1986b, p. 77).

In some cases, previous entrepreneurial experience is an asset to subsequent roles or careers. One's leadership, risk acceptance, exchange-oriented skills, and network of resources are all assets to philanthropy, teaching, and politics. In other cases, previous experience is almost a liability because nonprofit arenas move slower, use consensus or voting in decision making, and are more "theatrical" than profit-oriented businesses (Brownstein, 1985).

Being a social figure, teaching, creating, transforming, and promoting can all be considered aspects of an over-arching concept, that of the entrepreneur as leader. We will next take a brief excursion into current leadership theories and how they apply to entrepreneurs.

ENTREPRENEURIAL LEADERSHIP

The entrepreneur's leadership ability, philosophy, and style are important to the entrepreneurial process, the resulting organization, and the performance of the organization. In the beginning and during the organization's formative years, the entrepreneur calls the shots. He or she makes decisions, hires people, allocates resources, garners commitment, and in general makes things happen. He or she is, by definition, a most powerful leader.

As chief decision maker and the person with the control, responsibility, and authority, the entrepreneur makes choices about goals, people, and methods and communicates verbally and nonverbally about the firm, its mission, and his or her position in it. Through these decisions and actions, the entrepreneur creates organizational policy, structure, strategy, and culture. The organization, in turn, produces goods and services, jobs, profits, taxes, etc. that influence larger social systems (refer to Figure 11.2).

Evidence shows that certain entrepreneurial characteristics that influence behavior and decisions significantly influence organizational performance. In one study of top managers, Grimm and Smith (1986) showed that "younger, less experienced but more educated managers [are] more likely to pursue innovation strategies and that they [are] more likely to alter their strategy with changing environmental conditions" (p. 2). The same holds true for entrepreneurs, we presume. Entrepreneurs tend to be younger than those who consider but do not start a venture (Ronstadt, 1984a), and successful entrepreneurs tend to be younger than unsuccessful entrepreneurs (Sexton & Van Auken, 1982). Furthermore, high-performing firms are significantly more likely to have a founder who is still involved, often as CEO, than less successful firms (Virany & Tushman, 1986).[2]

LEADERSHIP COMPARED TO MANAGEMENT

In looking at entrepreneurs as leaders, we must first distinguish leadership from management. In simple terms, leaders think and act strategically (i.e., do the right things) while managers are concerned with daily operations (i.e., do things right) (Zaleznik, 1977). They also tend to differ in personality, needs, and attitudes.

> Managers enjoy relating with people, attain much of their sense of self from such activities, and work to maintain order. Leaders are loners, risk takers, and visionaries.
>
> Burke, 1984, p. 17

Others have portrayed leaders as charismatic, creating intense emotions in followers, whereas managers take a transactional orientation (trading favors, pay-for-performance) toward employees and others. Table 11.2 describes transformational leaders and transactional managers.

Finally, entrepreneurs tend to be opportunity-driven, whereas managers are resource-driven. Seeing an opportunity, an entrepreneur asks "How can I gain control of the resources to profit from this opportunity?" Managers facing a similar opportunity ask themselves "Is this the best way to spend the resources allocated to me?" Refer to Table 11.1 for more comparisons between those who promote opportunities (i.e., entrepreneurs) and those who take trusteeship of resources (i.e., managers).

ENTREPRENEURS AS MANAGERS

We should briefly note that entrepreneurs tend to make poor managers, with one exception. Research suggests that entrepreneurs often start their own businesses as a way to escape

---

[2] See Bobbitt and Ford (1980), Donaldson and Lorsch (1983), and Hambrick and Mason (1984) for theoretical support for the impact of CEOs and entrepreneurs on their organizations.

TABLE 11.2   Transformational Leaders and Managers

Dimensions for Comparison	Leaders	Managers
Emotional involvement	Emotional involvement is with the institution and with ideals/vision	Involvement is with the task and the people associated with the task
Personal life	Work & personal, private life not that distinguishable	Separates work from personal, private life
Achieves commitment via	Inspiration	Involvement
Holds people accountable via	Implicit guilt induction; wants whole person	Explicit contractual transactions; wants task accomplishment
Value emphasis	Terminal; end-state	Instrumental; means
Problems	Create them	Fix them
Plans	Long-range	Short-range
Appreciates from followers/ subordinates	Contrariness	Conformity
Engenders in followers/ subordinates	Intense feelings— love, sometimes hate; desire to identify with; turbulent	Feelings not intense; relations smoother and steadier

Source: W. W. Burke, p. 67 in "Leadership as Empowering Others" from *Executive Power* by S. Srivastva and Associates (San Francisco, CA: Jossey-Bass, 1986).

bureaucracy, systems, and managerial roles. Furthermore, the motivations of entrepreneurs are different from those of corporate managers (Smith & Miner, 1983). Because they like to control their operations, they are poor at delegating. Because they are here-and-now oriented, they tend to be poor at planning and setting up control systems. Because they like their autonomy, they are not comfortable with teams and ignore developing political systems. In contrast, good managers delegate, plan, control, and use groups and political systems to accomplish their own and organizational goals.

The exception mentioned above involves entrepreneurs with previous management experience. Increasing numbers of former managers are taking up entrepreneurial careers, as middle management ranks are pared back and managers face displacement (Freseman, 1985; Richman, 1986a) or ceilings to advancement. Frequently, managers become entrepreneurs by acquiring and transforming existing businesses rather than by starting up totally new ventures. This path into entrepreneurship makes sense, since managers tend to have the financial resources and connections to leverage their purchases (Kelly, Pitts, & Shin, 1986). In addition, a going concern is one of the best ways to add value by capitalizing on one's management experience.

For entrepreneurs who can't manage, three options seem possible. (1) They can become institutional leaders, hire managers, and delegate certain functions and/or operations. (2) They can keep their ventures small enough that managerial systems are not required (something not permitted by most outside investors). (3) If outsiders gain control, the entrepreneur can be forced to give up management of the firm (see the section on role transitions).

ASPECTS OF LEADERSHIP

Warren Bennis, Professor of management at the University of Southern California, interviewed 90 top leaders in the United States and has developed a four-dimensional model of effective leader behavior (Bennis & Nanus, 1985). In one dimension, effective leaders focus *attention through vision;* their personal convictions and beliefs energize and direct the behaviors of others. "Visioning" directs action by drawing a desired future state into the existing consciousness of oneself and others. The energizing aspects of a vision come from its scope, as big dreams—especially those shared by others—tap the emotional and spiritual resources of the enterprise.

Second, effective leaders provide *meaning through communication.* "Leaders articulate and define what has previously remained implicit or unsaid; then they invent images, metaphors, and models that provide a focus for new attention" (Bennis & Nanus, 1985, p. 39). More specifically, leaders tend to search for answers to "why" questions rather than "how" questions, and focus more on problem finding than problem solving. In both their talk and their behavior, effective leaders communicate core values and create an organizational culture.

In a third dimension, effective leaders achieve and maintain *trust through positioning*, which is conceived as the action side of vision. Positioning involves making oneself known (i.e., being available and candid) and one's positions, values, and methods clear. Others come to trust a leader when his or her position is consistent. Consistency results from a persistence of beliefs and a continual reinforcement of the vision.

Fourth, effective leaders *deploy themselves through positive regard*. Positive self-regard involves recognizing one's strengths and compensating for weaknesses, continuing to hone skills and talents, discerning the fit between one's skills and the job requirements, and being able to see one's mistakes as ways of learning, not failures. In addition to finding positive self-regard in effective leaders, Bennis found emotional maturity and positive regard for others, involving the following specific skills:

- *Empathy,* "the ability to accept people as they are, not as you would like them to be" (p. 66).
- *An avoidance of the past,* "the capacity to approach relationships and problems in terms of the present rather than the past" (p. 66).
- *Appreciation of others,* "the ability to treat those who are close to you with the same courteous attention that you extend to strangers and casual acquaintances" (p. 66).
- *Trust in others,* despite the apparent risk.
- *Self-confidence,* "the ability to do without constant approval and recognition from others" (p. 67).

LEADERSHIP RESPONSIBILITIES

While Bennis did include some founders in his study, the findings did not distinguish entrepreneurs from other leaders. Let's look at how existing research on entrepreneurs demonstrates effective leadership.

Visioning. Most entrepreneurs have a vision, although they might not "see" it in their "mind's eye" (imagining apparently involves visual, auditory, and/or kinesthetic centers of the brain). Visions of a venture will differ according to the goals of the founder. For some, the vision involves an innovation or an idea for a new product or service, as was found among the entrepreneurs featured in Flower's (1984) article, "Those Visionary Entrepreneurs." For others, the vision involves some improvement over existing businesses in areas of technology, marketing, or service. Still others include in their entrepreneurial vision some larger purpose or mission, such as that of Bill Millard of ComputerLand.

> "Bill has a vision that extended way beyond managing stores and profits," says Gordon Star [Millard's chief of staff]. "He wanted to create a worldwide network, with the intention that it would contribute to worldwide peace. Individual franchising would transcend political boundaries. . . ."
>
> Crister, 1986, p. 72

People are curious about where vision comes from (see Chapter 2). In general, it comes from being open to ideas, listening to others, and reading. When asked about the source of his visions for Federal Express, founder Fred Smith replied:

> I think it is the ability to assimilate information from a lot of different disciplines all at once—particularly information about change, because from change comes opportunity. . . . The common trait of people who supposedly have vision is that they spend a lot of time reading and gather information, and then synthesize it until they come up with an idea.
>
> Federal Express's Fred Smith, 1986, p. 46

Vision is used by entrepreneurs to prepare business plans, deal with emotions, find money-saving techniques, and indoctrinate or socialize employees (Rockey, 1986). However, theorizing, researching, and discussing the importance of vision is often easier than enacting it.

> It's really hard to share the vision so that people will get with it. . . . We ought to be able to say "Look, this is a beautiful vision. It's got you at the center of it. Isn't that great? Let's get it done." People ought to pick it up real quick, but unfortunately, they don't.
>
> Donald Burr of People Express;
> "Bitter Victories," 1985, p. 26

Although these anecdotes seem intriguing and there is much talk about vision in leaders and entrepreneurs, no studies report the extent to which entrepreneurs engage in visioning. As a result we are reluctant to draw generalizations or conclusions about entrepreneurial vision.

Communicating and structuring. Entrepreneurs create organizational cultures and social structures through their early decisions and actions. There have been numerous stories about unique organizational cultures, purposefully created by founders to implement certain noneconomic values, including the previously cited Sequent Computer Systems Inc. (Benner, 1985). Another is Marquette Electronics whose cofounder, Mike Cudahy, has created an organization that values fun and disorder and whose managers agree that they are "bad managers." "Maybe we're not managers at all," says one manager. "Provocateurs—that may be closer" (Wojahn, 1986c, p. 78).

Through their words and deeds, founders tend to establish and maintain core corporate values. Sometimes these values are not optimal in the short run, but because they reflect the founder's personal values they are the foundation for many years of subsequent decisions. One entrepreneur in microcomputer training created the "Rules of the Game" shown in Table 11.3 (Bird, 1983). When an employee inadvertently broke one of the rules, the entrepreneur, or someone else well-socialized to her ideology, would confront the employee and clear up the misunderstanding of the rules. According to the entrepreneur, if employees were unwilling or unable to play by her rules, they could choose to work somewhere else.

Values are often communicated less formally, in the telling of stories, in the design of physical spaces, in the criteria used for recruitment, selection, and promotion, and in the symbolic actions of the entrepreneur (what he or she pays attention to, how he or she reacts to crises) (Schein, 1983). These behaviors may be the "best way—perhaps the only way—for a founder to control his [or her] company's destiny" (Linden, 1984, p. 90).

In addition to providing values for the organization, the founder initiates structure through hiring employees, delegating responsibilities, establishing reporting relationships, and determining rewards. The entrepreneur also structures time by setting a timetable.

Timetables. The timetable usually involves expectations, formally stated in a business plan and informally held by the founder, about how long it will take to make a prototype, find financing, achieve a first sale, achieve break even, and so forth. In many instances this timetable is relatively fixed in

TABLE 11.3   One Entrepreneur's Rules of the Game

---

1. Be willing to only make agreements you intend to keep.
2. Be willing to make every attempt to keep agreements you make.
3. Clear up, by communication, any broken agreements at the earliest possible moment.
4. Always tell the truth with compassion.
5. In any communication, be aware and accept that the other individual is telling the truth as he or she sees and feels it at that moment.
6. Be supportive in all your communications.
7. Be responsible for your communications by providing correction without invalidation.
8. Be willing to speak only when it has good purpose.
9. Communicate any problem you encounter immediately to the person who can solve the problem.
10. Suggestions or requests on any matter concerning the organization should be submitted in writing to the person who can decide on the action or reply.
11. All written suggestions or requests should be responded to by phone or in writing within 24 hours of the receipt of the request.
12. Take responsibility by not justifying or laying blame.

Source: Bird (1983)

the founder's mind, either because of external demands from backers or because of certain personality characteristics such as authoritarianism, stubbornness, or compulsiveness (Saranson, 1972).

"Although the reasons for it may vary, the existence of a fairly definite timetable can and usually does have an enormous influence on the beginning context" (Saranson, 1972, p. 62). The timetable, as communicated by the founder's words and deeds, influences how "our experience of the present interferes with or facilitates the achievement of our purposes" (Saranson, 1972, p. 64)—the exhilaration of being ahead of schedule, the pressure of being behind. It also influences how individuals spend their time (on immediate concerns versus planning) and how much time they spend working. Recall that entrepreneurs work in excess of 60 hours during start-up, periods of rapid growth, and crises, and they tend to expect the same from others.

Because entrepreneurs tend to overestimate what can be done in the short run (today, this week) and underestimate the time needed to achieve longer-term outcomes, timetables may be unrealistically ambitious (Bluedorn, 1987). Thus entrepreneurial timetables are more likely to produce "behind-schedule" experiences and create pressure and stress for people engaged in the new venture. The result, after a while, can be "burnout" and turnover.

Positioning and ethics. Entrepreneurs build trust by being relatively consistent in their positions. Those who vacillate fail to gain employee commitment and outsider support. For example, the founding partners (a married couple) of a nursing registry vacillated about delegating and failed to clarify their individual roles. Their office manager, who was responsible for supervising their staff and daily operations, was constantly undermined by the founders' direct involvement with nurses and hospitals. The staff was never sure who was the boss; people got different messages from three individuals, and as a result turnover was well over 100 percent for several years.

Trust also comes from practicing ethical behavior. There is a widely held belief that entrepreneurs are unethical. This negative stereotype comes from the days of "robber barons," when greedy white men seized the means to make wealth and pushed away all others who had values, interests, and needs different from theirs. Selfishness, greed, insensitivity, and narrowness characterize the stereotype. Another negative stereotype (again with a grain of truth) is that of the desperate entrepreneur who chooses unethical and even illegal means to ensure business success.

Those who have interviewed, surveyed, observed, or counseled entrepreneurs and would-be entrepreneurs know that these stereotypes contain limited and distorted perceptions. There are many entrepreneurs who place high value on their "people resources," and who attend to noneconomic and social values. Most recognize that their success requires developing a reputation for honesty and integrity with suppliers, customers, and financiers. However, because entrepreneurs are ends-oriented and opportunistic about means, there is always the chance that their decisions will slide into the gray and unethical areas.

The resolution to the dilemma is not regulation of entrepreneurs or the new venture process. Such regulation would destroy entrepreneurial contexts, adding bureaucracy to a process that works because it circumvents existing expectations, rules, and procedures. Instead, scholars and practitioners argue for courses and programs to promote self-management skills and understanding "that winning at any price is too high a price" (Lipper, 1985). These skills along with Bennis and Nanus's (1985) fourth attribute (learning, style, and self-management) will be discussed in Chapter 12. One entrepreneur says:

> We minimize risk, enhance success guided by enlightened self-interest. We have no duty to do so. We do so because other behavior would be unenlightened, increasing risk, diminishing success.
>
> Dr. J. H. Carbone of NEXUS

Implications

Activities of leadership relate directly to the intentions of the entrepreneur and his or her ability to sustain temporal tension, maintain flexible focus, and determine a strategic posture. Intentionality is thus linked directly to effective entrepreneurial leadership, and we would expect this linkage across different types of entrepreneurial ventures.

ROLE TRANSITIONS

> Once you've earned the title of "entrepreneur" you don't necessarily get to keep it—
>
> Jack Bares, founder and CEO of Milbar

Start-ups, young companies, and growing companies change rapidly. They grow in size and value, adapt to markets, assimilate new members, and structure and restructure. The entrepreneur, as leader, faces an ever-changing organization in a dynamic and usually competitive environment. His or her role changes as the organization grows. The case of Mitch Kapor of Lotus demonstrates some of the pressures to change.

 EXAMPLE: MITCH KAPOR

Kapor, now 36, started Lotus Development Corporation (maker of Lotus 1–2–3 and Symphony software programs) in 1981. In 1986 he left the company he had started. He found that leading a venture that had grown to a $275 million company employing 1350 people was within neither his competence nor his interest.

His skills were designing software and working with small groups of people to combine technical expertise with intuitions about the marketplace. The company's needs were to serve the existing two million customers who were not very interested in new features in their software.

His personal commitment and enthusiasm for his role as leader waned as the organization grew. He enjoyed working closely with one or two others "because it has an intimacy and directness of conversation." He was too impatient, perfectionistic, and assertive to lead through systems and by coordination, and became frustrated with the growing complexity and interdependence in Lotus. He was stressed by the two hats he wore—technical expert and chief executive—because the roles held conflicting values (technical elegance on the one hand and financial performance on the other). Finally, Lotus began to be less important in giving meaning to his life.

To his credit, Kapor recognized that he was ill-suited to the role of chief executive of a large firm. Says Kapor:

> If you're going to be responsible for running a business, you have to be responsive to the requirements of the business situation, not what you want to do as the founder or chief executive officer.
>
> "1–2–3," p. 31

> The honorable and responsible thing for me to do—and the best thing for me and for 1,350 employees and for several million customers and all of that—was to remove myself from the company sooner rather than later.
>
> "1-2-3," p. 36

So he left, voluntarily, over a period of two years as part of a conscious plan to remove himself from his own success. However intentional, leaving was still difficult, involving a very deep and personal questioning and considerable pain.

> I spent several days at one point in pure agony about the issue personally, about the fundamental separation of identity between myself and the company. . . . It was over a long weekend, so I had a lot of time to think about it. And it felt like it feels when you're breaking up with somebody. It's a sense of loss, emptiness, anger, helplessness.

This example illustrates how the organization's size and the founder's role are closely bound together. We'll now examine some of the dynamics of organizational growth, how organizations at different stages require different leadership skills, and, finally, how entrepreneurs respond to organizational growth.

STAGES OF ORGANIZATIONAL GROWTH

The growth we are interested in here is the actual and relative increase in the number of employees, sales, and assets of a new venture. We are most interested in growth that is internally generated (compared with acquisitions), since internal growth is more clearly a product of the entrepreneur's behavior.

Growth curve. Organizations, products, careers, and even lives can be simplistically portrayed by a growth curve, as shown in Figure 11.3. The figure shows two curves, one with slow steady growth at the beginning and another with more rapid growth. Both curves show exponential growth leveling out and perhaps declining.

The growth curve is so familiar to business students that we come to assume its general truth. However, empirical results are conflicting. Economist David Birch estimates that

FIGURE 11.3 Organizational Growth Curves

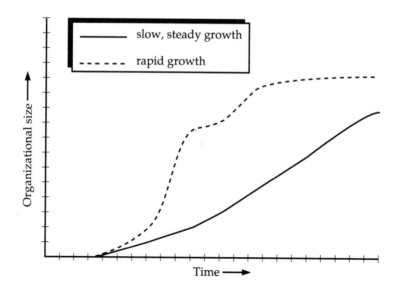

12–14 percent of all small businesses are growth-oriented (1985). Dunkelberg and Cooper (1982) surveyed 1805 small businesses in 1979. They found a median growth rate of 0–4 percent, with 14 percent declining in size, and only 16 percent having growth rates of over 15 percent per year (most of these were newly established). They also found that growth rate depended on whether the entrepreneur had started the firm, with the highest growth rate among owner-managed firms compared to those purchased or inherited.

A conflicting study done by Birley (1986) shows that most organizations do *not* grow significantly. Her survey of 160 firms that were one to six years old in St. Joseph County, Indiana, found that more than 60 percent had had no changes in personnel since the start of the firm, apparently independent of the age of the firm. There were some differences across industries, and nearly 20 percent of the firms were either marginal, part-time, self-employment, or "paper" companies without full-time owners.

Value of growth. For some observers and theorists, if an organization is not growing, it is "mature" and/or declining. Growth, like youth, is attractive.

> The business press . . . bestows plaudits and notoriety on entrepreneurs who create the most from the least in the shortest time. The investment community, from venture capitalists to institutional portfolio managers, looks for growth the way college admissions officers look for high test scores, and places its bets accordingly. Entrepreneurs themselves, goaded by the press, the market, or simply by pride in their own accomplishments, frequently measure their success by sales-and-revenue curves, and forget about everything else.
>
> Richman, 1984, p. 69

Stages of organizational growth. Despite the conflicting evidence about the rate of growth for most new ventures, we find it useful to use the growth curve to locate organizations in terms of the stages of their development. Anytime people talk about stages of development in a continuous process (e.g., stages of life, career stages, growth stages) they run into the problem of creating logical boundaries between segments of development when these boundaries are not part of the phenomenon. That is, we create stages; stages are not found in nature. A second problem with using the concept of stage of growth is determining "how many" stages best explain organizational experience.

Kazanjian (1984) reviewed existing articles on organizational stages and found three-, four-, and five-stage models. He concludes that a four-stage model best describes the dominant problems of organizational growth. Table 11.4 describes the orientation of people, type of structure, nature of the rewards, the planning process, and the role of the chief executive in organizations at each stage. Figure 11.4 shows these stages on the growth curve. Refer back to Chapter 1 for a more detailed list of the milestones of entrepreneurship.

PROBLEMS ASSOCIATED WITH GROWTH

There are many good reasons to resist, slow, or stop growth, which explains why few organizations grow beyond 20 employees and why even fast-growing firms eventually slow down. Growth has personal and organizational costs. From the entrepreneur's point of view the most important problem is *sharing control of the organization* and losing valued independence, although owner-managers of "supergrowth" firms tend to look at growth as a welcomed opportunity rather than a threat to freedom (Ray & Hutchinson, 1983).

Investors are one stakeholder group jockeying for control of the growing venture.

> During the start-up of the new business, investors typically allow the entrepreneur a relatively free hand in operation. When the entrepreneur has created something of value, they find it nearly impossible to avoid staying in contact and being fully informed about their investment. . . . The entrepreneur perceives this new interest as interference and reduced confidence in his or her ability.
>
> Welsch & White, 1983, p. 62

Control may also be shared (in terms of equity and participative management) with team members who are frequently instrumental and necessary to achieve growth objectives (Ray & Hutchinson, 1983; Benner, 1985).

Seen from the outside, the problems of growth include: (1) *instant size*, with resulting disaffection, disorientation, inadequate skills among "old-timers" and top managers, and inadequate systems for decision making and action; (2) *a sense of infallibility* where success breeds arrogance and a tendency to not remain open to criticism or other new information;

(3) *internal turmoil and frenzy* because newcomers lack experience, work demands are great, and conflicts between people emerge; and (4) *extraordinary resource demands* for cash and for talent, often requiring additional infusions—more money, more space, and more employees (Hambrick & Crozier, 1985).

Controlled growth. For these reasons, some entrepreneurs choose to control growth "just as one controls other variables in the calculus of business" (Richman, 1984, p. 71), by refusing sales, limiting the market, and retaining earnings. However, even for slower-growing firms size eventually demands new systems, skills, and resources. Slower-growing firms have the opportunities to develop managers within their ranks and use profits to fund expansion. Of course, slower-growing firms are not as well loved by outside investors (whose expectations often include annual growth of 25 percent or more) and, as suggested earlier, conflict between investors and entrepreneurs over goals and control may ensue. Sometimes, the entrepreneur is ousted.

Even fast-growing organizations seem to need to control growth, to consolidate and take a "breather" (Burr, 1986). Growing organizations seem to "pulsate" (Birch, 1985), alternating between periods of sprinting and pausing.

> . . . Leaders must . . . sense when "enough is enough" of sprinting. They may have a personal sense of overextension, may be personally exhausted, may be unable to keep up with all the changes. Or they may realize the effects on key managers in terms of long working hours, fatigue, frayed tempers, sagging morale. In any event, *the timing of pauses would seem to be critical in order to sustain entrepreneurial success.*
>
> Mintzberg & Waters, 1982, p. 493, emphasis added

LEADERSHIP AT DIFFERENT STAGES

As organizations grow they get more complex, requiring expertise outside the entrepreneur's experience and requiring different reporting relationships as structures develop. Competencies important during start-up may be less important during stages of growth and/or maturity.

> Initially, growth stems largely either from sales or from production—depending on the need—and then from the other, as pressures for distribution follow initial expansion of output, or as expanding sales place more emphasis on

TABLE 11.4 Important Aspects of Organizations at Different Stages of Growth

	Pre-start-up	Start-up	Growth	Maturity
Problems/ Organization design	Invest and develop product technology Build prototype Sell the concept Define business idea Build multiple prototypes	Develop production technology Acquire facilities and plant Produce, sell, distribute in quantities/volume Define prod./tech. design Meet demand Acquire talent	Avoid shakeout Maintain growth momentum/position Attain profitability Balance profits vs. future growth	Dominate prod./mkt. niche Develop 2nd generation Balance bureaucratic vs. innovative tasks
People	Generalists Technologists Non-professionals Consultants, part-timers	— — — — — — — — — — — — — — — — — — — —	— — — — — — — — — — — — — — — — — — — —	Specialists Bureaucrats Professionals Career employees
Structure	Informal Market reliant Group centered	Formalized Centralized Functional	Formalized Decentralized Planning and budget overlays	Formalized Decentralized Profit centered

Rewards	Equity (for few)	———————————————	Compensation/benefits
	Ground-floor opportunity	———————————————	Career development/experience
	Non-bureaucratic setting	———————————————	Stable, secure, growth-oriented setting
Planning processes	Informal	———————————————	Formal
	Centralized	———————————————	Decentralized long range
	Undifferentiated	———————————————	Specialized
	Short range, single time horizon	———————————————	Multiple time horizon
	Integrated	———————————————	Integrated

Source: R. K. Kazanjian, p. 148 in *Frontiers of Entrepreneurship Research 1984*, J. Hornaday, F. Tarpley, J. Timmons, and K. Vesper, eds. (Wellesley, MA: Babson College).

FIGURE 11.4   An Organizational Growth Curve Showing
Stages of Development

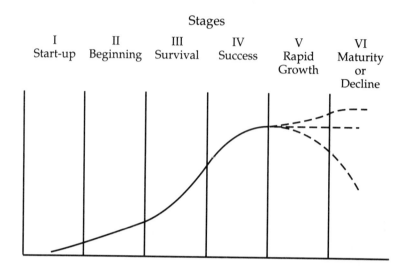

Stages

I	II	III	IV	V	VI
Start-up	Beginning	Survival	Success	Rapid Growth	Maturity or Decline

production. Later in the cycle, financial control is added, followed by a separation of administrative from operative management.

Filley & House, 1969, pp. 447–448

Figure 11.5 shows a five-stage model of organizational change, including the changing shape and structure of the organization as well as the changing relationship between the founder and the business. The figure shows a turning point when success has been achieved (Stage 3), and the entrepreneur decides to continue expansion or stop growth and thereby free his or her time for other interests such as leisure activities, family, and politics (i.e., disengagement). It should be noted that the decision to slow growth and disengage may be an unconscious or irrational one as well as consciously planned. Whether continued growth is pursued or not, the role of the entrepreneur as leader changes as the organization he or she has created changes.

Along with frequent changes in structure and pressures from the environment, growth means the inclusion of more people with different backgrounds and interests. And this destroys the coziness of the small, cohesive start-up team, changes the culture of the organization (Miller, 1963; Rhodes,

FIGURE 11.5 Changes in Structure and Entrepreneur Involvement Across Stages of Small Business Development

	Stage I Existence	Stage II Survival	Stage III-D Success-Disengagement	Stage III-G Success-Growth	Stage IV Take-off	Stage V Resource maturity
Management style	Direct supervision	Supervised supervision	Functional	Functional	Divisional	Line and staff
Organization	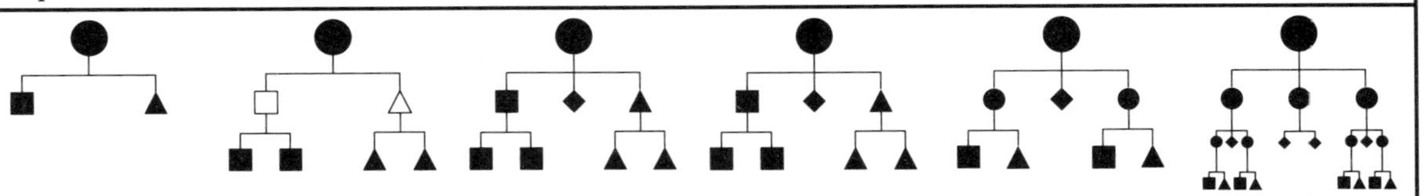					
Extent of formal systems	Minimal to nonexistent	Minimal	Basic	Developing	Maturing	Extensive
Major strategy	Existence	Survival	Maintaining profitable status quo	Get resources for growth	Growth	Return on investment
Business and owner*						

* ○White circle represents owner. ●Shaded circle represent business.

Source: N. Churchill and V. Lewis, "The Five Stages of Small Business Growth," *Harvard Business Review*, May–June 1983 (Cambridge, MA: Harvard Business School Press, Harvard University).

1986), creates communication problems, and requires different interpersonal skills from the entrepreneur, as the cases of Milt Kuolt (below) and Mitch Kapor suggest.

> Fear of the obligations and the impersonality that come with increased size is understandable. . . . A healthy business must grow, and a healthy-minded businessman must accept the strains of growth.

> Miller, 1963, p. 158

 **EXAMPLE: MILT KUOLT**

Kuolt has founded two firms, Thousand Trails, Inc. (a chain of campgrounds) and Horizon Air Industries, Inc. (a regional airline headquartered in Seattle), and he has had the experience of being outgrown by both. He found that his skills of starting a new venture and running a small business—by using sheer energy to overcome obstacles and using family-style interactions—were inadequate for the larger firms that resulted. He says, "The worst mistake an entrepreneur can make is to think that the abilities he had to run a company of 20 employees are good enough to run a company of 850 employees."

In their start-up stages the ventures required only an idea, a little money, a small number of believers, cramped quarters, and long hours with little pay. However, there was magic in the work and self-sacrifice, a sense of family togetherness and commitment to a common goal.

As the ventures grew, Kuolt began to feel uncomfortable and unhappy, the magic disappeared replaced by systematic or "professional" management. Because he had "never cozied up to bureaucracies," he left.

> "I felt that I was much better in the formative stages of a company, in the creative stages, in coming up with new concepts, as opposed to taking a proven product and making it 5 to 10 times its size. I felt that takes a whole new type of discipline, a new type of management thinking."

> Rhodes, 1986

Of the interpersonal skills needed during growth, the *ability to use power effectively* seems most important. In the early days, the entrepreneur holds all or most of the power and makes most decisions directly and personally. Interpersonal influence is face-to-face; conflicts are addressed immediately and directly, and momentum is maintained. As the organization grows, delegation of responsibility and authority is required, and other individuals take on power. The entrepreneurial leader must shift to less-direct involvement in decisions and working interpersonal relations to both empower others and maintain a sense of control. The skills of working with coalitions of subordinates rather than with one small, loyal team, and of using persuasion, common-ground, and "bridging" influence styles (Berlew, 1981) rather than assertion, are required for continued leadership by the entrepreneur.

A study of Canadian small businesses (with mean sales of $31 million and median employment of 100) by Miller and Toulouse (1986) found that small organizations perform better financially when decision making is delegated to trained professional managers and technical experts, and when the organization adopts "a more aggressive and analytic mode of decision making guided by an explicitly codified strategy" (p. 59).

> The hoarding of power and the tendency for some CEOs to try to do everything themselves are common and dangerous aspects of many small organizations. The dangers increase as organizations grow and become too complex for any one person to run single-handedly. This is especially true when the environment is changing and innovation is required (p. 55).

In addition, the study found that smaller firms benefit more from strategies of innovation, which are often difficult for small organizations to sustain since many do not have the resources to pay for continuing education and professional development of engineers, technicians, managers, and salespeople. Larger firms benefit more from cost containment, explicit strategies, and analytic decision making. The same study found that CEOs (and presumably entrepreneurs who were part of the study) with fewer years as CEO tended to have organizations that were more profitable and growing faster.

Together these results suggest that entrepreneurs need to shift their attitudes about control, independence, and planning, and shift to rational instead of intuitive decision making. There is also evidence here that leadership change may be important to organizational success.

THE ENTREPRENEUR'S CHOICE: TO CHANGE OR LEAVE THE GROWING FIRM

Recall that entrepreneurs tend to have experienced a displacement and need autonomy, independence, control, and an opportunity to see the direct results of their own behavior. Because prior jobs, careers, and roles did not suit them, they began their own business. In doing that, their personal identity (answers to "who am I?") got intertwined with the organization they built.

Also recall that entrepreneurs can choose to grow or not to grow with their firm. From this point on we assume the path of growth. If the organization grows beyond the "Mom 'n Pop" size (estimated to be "around 30 employees and $750,000 in assets" by Smith and Miner, 1983), the entrepreneur experiences the paradox of success mentioned in the case of Milt Kuolt. He or she comes to feel like an employee in his or her own firm, dependent on others (rather than independent), with increasing need for systems, procedures, and bureaucracy.

What entrepreneurs do at this juncture depends a great deal on their personalities, goals, and the situations they have constructed. They have three choices. (1) They can leave the organization (by choice, as Mitch Kapor, or forced by others; see Chapter 5). (2) They can change their behaviors, styles, and feelings to fit into managerial roles in the organization. (3) They can create new roles for themselves in the now-changed organizations. To stay with the organization involves significant adjustments, and it is these we now address.

A model of role development. A recent model (Nicholson, 1984) of role transitions suggests that individuals such as entrepreneurs, with strong desires for control and roles with high discretion (e.g., "the capacity to choose goals, the means for achieving these, the timing of means-ends relationships, and the pattern of interpersonal communications, influence, and evaluation surrounding them") (Nicholson, 1984, p. 178) face unique choices about how to manage transitions in their roles. As they leave prior employment roles to become entrepreneurs, they tend to engage in *personal development;* that is, they change their personal frames of reference, values, and identities. As they change with the growing new venture, entrepreneurs tend to engage in *role development;* that is, changing their own and others' expectations of their role to better match their talents, needs, and identity. Examples of the second transition can be found with Mitch Kapor (p. 334) and Billy Ladin (Richman, 1985c). Ladin, founder, majority stockholder, and chairman of ComputerCraft, chose to hire a general manager (President Paul Frison). Ladin himself took the role of marketing vice-president (his area of expertise) and in this capacity reports to the man he hired. Thus Ladin changed his expectations and surprised others into changing their expectations about what an entrepreneur/founder is supposed to do in the organization he created.

Depending on whether the entrepreneur has ever been a manager or leader before, the adjustment to the new role of manager/leader can be one she *determines* (where the entrepreneur knows what is needed of a leader and "actively determines elements in the content or structure of the role," Nicholson, 1984, p. 176) or one she *discovers* (where the entrepreneur is changing aspects of herself and the role she is molding for herself).

Whichever way, entrepreneurs' role transitions are accompanied by changing feelings, stress, and new learning curves. Role sets change in their relative importance, with entrepreneurial leaders trying to meet the expectations of "fellow members of the firm . . . and more especially, . . . outsiders such as other businessmen" (Stanworth & Curran, 1976, p. 104). Values change to include an interest in management training and development and personnel policies, use of management consultants, increasing concern over possible unionization (more likely with larger organizations than smaller ones), participating in mergers, finding acquisitions, and going public.

Finally, as leader of a growing organization, the entrepreneur is faced with a changing lifestyle. It is one of considerably less privacy. For example, Graydon Webb (founder of G. D. Ritzy, Inc., one of *Inc.* magazine's 100 fastest-growing firms in 1985) used to play keyboard and sing with a Columbus, Ohio, rock group. Now he just sits in on occasion because he's concerned about his image as chairman of a public company (Richman, 1985a, May). Other successful entrepreneurs worry about appearing ostentatious or conspicuous in their lifestyles.

Implications

Entrepreneurs face inevitable role changes, especially when the venture changes through growth, retrenchment, and a changing environment. We would expect more role transition concerns and problems among entrepreneurs whose goals are profits and firm growth, among start-ups (compared to acquisitions or franchises), and in high-technology industries, since in these circumstances, the venture and/or environment will change more substantively or more rapidly.

The ease with which an entrepreneur changes his or her role may relate to the qualities of temporal agility and the strategic zoom lens, which also allow/require flexibility. Sensitivity to alignment and attunement requirements may also make role transitions more predictable (by anticipating changing demands within the firm and from outsiders) and therefore potentially easier.

CONCLUSIONS ABOUT ENTREPRENEURIAL LEADERSHIP

We conclude that the role of the entrepreneur in building and leading an organization is indeed complex and multifaceted. We find that entrepreneurs have to be generalists as well as specialists (especially in the early stages when the team is small). The competencies of the effective entrepreneur range from visionary to manager, from insider to statesman. We note that the multidimensional qualities of this role predispose entrepreneurs to role conflict and probably contribute to stress in two ways—from overload (too much to do, too little time) and from being pulled (or pushed) in two or more directions at one time (e.g., work with new employees versus meet with customers versus spend time with family).

The grace and comfort of the entrepreneur's career, his or her change from being alone with an idea to leader of a fast-growth, large-payroll firm, depend on his or her abilities to manage himself or herself and to learn from experiences. These competencies are addressed in the next chapter.

CHAPTER 12

LEARNING, SELF-MANAGEMENT, AND OTHER COMPETENCIES OF SUCCESSFUL ENTREPRENEURS

INTRODUCTION

Many important lessons about business and life in general seem to come from our experiences rather than from books or lectures by teachers, colleagues, and friends. Among our experiences, we seem to learn better from our mistakes than from our continuing progress or success. Mistakes and failures, large or small, get our attention. They are full of information and feedback. We retrospectively "debrief" the events, actions, decisions, and circumstances of the mistakes or errors we and others have made, and in doing this, we learn. We make sense of our experiences (admittedly with considerable psychological bias and rationalization) and we correct our decision making or change our behavior to prevent the same mistake from happening again.

In contrast, "smooth sailing" generally provides less feedback and less information. Often we don't know which of our decisions or actions contributed to the outcome and which were irrelevant or even dampened the outcome. We live by the axiom: "If it isn't broken, don't fix it."

Entrepreneurs live in a very concrete classroom, their enterprise. It is filled, ideally, with many moments of success and good judgment, but more important for this discussion it also includes a supply of mistakes, feedback, failures, and other lessons. *How* entrepreneurs learn from their experiences with their ventures (their process) has a lot to do with their subsequent success or continued difficulty. *What* entrepreneurs learn (the content) will depend on their current competencies (or lack thereof) and the industry, market, and economic conditions surrounding their enterprise. Most, if not all, successful entrepreneurs learn a great deal about self-management— deploying one's strengths, compensating for weaknesses, and developing new competencies. Thus we now turn to look at the learning process of entrepreneurs and their self-management abilities.

THE LEARNING ENVIRONMENT: A LOOK AT FAILURE

The entrepreneurial event is fraught with opportunities to make mistakes, surrounded by competition and larger social systems about which the entrepreneur has limited information (i.e., environmental uncertainty) and which may be changing rapidly (i.e., environmental turbulence). Because every new venture is unique, experience with prior ventures, while helpful, does not ensure accurate perceptions, optimal decisions, resource availability, or success. There is always room for mistakes such as: (1) errors in perceptions of the current situation and people, (2) errors in inferences about the future, (3) errors in inferences about the consequences of our actions, and (4) errors in executing our actions (Knight, 1921).

Because mistakes can result in poor business performance, financial loss, or business failure, many individuals, including would-be entrepreneurs and their backers, would like to know if failures can be anticipated (and presumably avoided). Unfortunately, little is known about new venture failures. In part this is because successes are more exciting to study (and offer a continuing stream of information and possible "deals"). In part, it is because we prefer to ignore failure. Finally, it is hard to locate and obtain the cooperation of businessmen and women who have failed.

FAILURE RATES

Opinions vary widely about the rate of business failure. Consider the following statistics:

- "A business failed every forty-five minutes in 1980, a rate more than 75 percent higher than it had been only two years before" (Platt, 1985, p. 1).

- Out of 250 high-technology firms founded between 1960 and 1969, 39.2 percent had been merged or acquired, 38.4 percent had been discontinued, and 22.4 percent were still surviving and independent in 1984 (Bruno, Leidecker, & Harder, 1986).
- " 'Every year, several hundred thousand firms are started, almost an equal number discontinued, and even more transfer ownership or control,' but only a small number—6,619 in 1978—fail. In fact these statistics have been so misused that Dun and Bradstreet now warns that 'these (failure) statistics do not represent survival rates of new businesses, a frequent and widespread misinterpretation' " (Dun and Bradstreet, *The Business Failure Record*, in Star & Massel, 1981, p. 88).
- The average survival rates for 17,252 retail businesses in Illinois in 1974 was 81.4 percent after the first year and 33.2 percent after the fifth year (Star & Massel, 1981).
- A study of the entries and exits from the Columbus, Ohio, yellow pages found only 34 percent exiting after two years and 50 percent after five years (Shapero & Giglierano, 1982).
- "Out of the 550,000 business closing each year, only 15,000 or so are bankruptcies" (Birch, 1985, p. 32).
- The 1982 recession resulted in a "record number of bankruptcies, running at annual rate of over 2000 companies," representing only 1 percent of the new ventures established in the previous five years (Ronstadt, 1984a, p. 37).
- The *Journal of Accountancy* ("Small business-dominated industries," 1986) reports business failure rate by industry, noting that "the 10 industries with the lowest failure rates were largely industries in which companies with fewer than 500 employees accounted for at least 60 percent of industry employment, sales, or both," whereas the higher failure rates were found in industries dominated by bigger businesses.
- Students expect that 90 percent of all new companies fail in their first year, and academics often cite a failure rate of 65 percent failing by their fifth year. Both of which are myths (Shapero, 1981b).

TYPES OF ENDINGS

Discussions of business failure inevitably need to clarify the type and way in which a business discontinues. Most statistics report discontinuances or dissolutions "when the organization ceases to carry out the routine actions that sustain its structure, maintain flows of resources, and retain the allegiance of its members" (Freeman, Carroll, & Hannan, 1983, p. 694). These statistics do not distinguish among bankruptcy (10 percent of endings), liquidation, or selling the business for a profit

(90 percent of venture endings). While each of these exits involves a transformation of the organization created by the entrepreneur, each has clearly different lessons for him or her. Each may be considered a "failure" by the entrepreneur and/ or venture teams, and the non-bankruptcy endings may be "successes."

Business failure, then, may be a matter of degree and does not necessarily mean bankruptcy. Platt (1985) offers four categories of business failure in increasing severity:

1. Opportunity losses; minimal earnings
2. Negative profits; losing money
3. Technical insolvency; unable to meet current obligations
4. Bankruptcy

Likewise, the process of failing can involve making "one overwhelming disastrous decision that leads to rapid demise" or making a "series of ill-conceived choices that may result from poor management or from the onset of panic following earlier mistakes" (Platt, 1985, pp. 1–2).

SOURCES OF FAILURE

Those who do look at business failures try to diagnose "what went wrong." Two factors stand out in studies of new venture failures: (1) the *liability of newness*—the greater risk of failure among new organizations "because they depend on the cooperation of strangers, have low levels of legitimacy, and are unable to compete effectively against established organizations" (Freeman et al., 1983, p. 692); and (2) the *liability of smallness* because new organizations are smaller and lack human and capital resources. Other researchers have gone into more detail on these factors. For example, one study shows that the lack of external legitimacy is more important to failure than the lack of internal coordination (Singh, Tucker, & House, 1986). Table 12.1 presents three lists of failure factors, the first generated from a study of 250 high-technology firms in Silicon Valley (96 discontinuances; Bruno et al., 1986), the second from a survey of 49 venture capitalists (Gorman & Sahlman, 1986), and the third from a study of 95 manufacturing startups in Michigan in 1959–1960 (Hoad & Rosko, 1964).

RESPONSE TO FAILURE

As suggested in the chapter on entrepreneurial careers, one response to ending one's venture, through business failure,

TABLE 12.1 Source of Entrepreneurial Failure

High-technology founders

Product/market problems

Product timing difficulties
Product design problems
Inappropriate distribution or selling strategy
Unclear business definition
Over-reliance on one customer

Financial difficulties

Initial undercapitalization
Assuming a debt instrument too early
Problems with the venture capital relationship

Managerial/key employee problems

Poor team building
Human failings (e.g., spending money on image, ego, sense of
   infallibility, unethical behavior)

Venture capitalists[1]

Management problems

Ineffective senior management
Ineffective functional management

Market problems

End-user market failed to develop as expected
Company failed to capture share due to: poor channel
   selection/channel resistance
   competition
   poor product/market fit

Product problems

Development delayed/unsuccessful
Manufacturing failure
Poor product performance
Inadequate quality control

Manufacturing entrepreneurs

Market and marketing

Strong competition
Cyclical industry
Nonaggressive selling
Poor pricing policy
Slow collection and accounts receivable
Dependence on personal contacts
Small customer base

TABLE 12.1   Source of Entrepreneurial Failure (continued)

Financing

Initial undercapitalization
Shortage of working capital
High debt level
Chief owner-manager not insured

Management

Dependence on survival of CEO
Little drive or ambition
Management seriously understaffed
Lack of experience

Others

Unwise investment of capital in equipment
Improper application of capital
Financial disagreement with partners
Lack of one strong manager
Family pressures

---

[1] listed in order of importance to venture capitalists

merger/acquisition, or being ousted or fired by a board of directors, is to start again. A recent *Wall Street Journal* article on "fallen entrepreneurs" in Silicon Valley (Bellew, 1985) reads:

> Almost anywhere else, a business failure taints a career, hurting relationships and hampering efforts to start anew. Here, though, perhaps the only dishonor is not to try again. Failed high-tech entrepreneurs write articles for trade magazines, give interviews for books on high-tech history, entertain job offers and establish new ventures of their own. They ski in Aspen, sunbathe in the South Seas, and when time permits, they read their fan mail.

Does failure taint one's career?   There is some suggestion that the relative lack of stigma attached to failure in the United States makes it a better context for new ventures than other countries. Indeed, many start over again and find few obstacles in the minds of other people. However, many more (the exact numbers are not available) disappear and are untraceable by researchers, suggesting a departure to avoid creditors, to save face, or to start with a clean slate somewhere else.

Although the United States tends to be forgiving of entrepreneurial failure (one entrepreneur said that if you hadn't been bankrupt at least once, you hadn't really learned much about business), some important resource managers are not. Investors and bankers who lose money in failed ventures are often unwilling to give those entrepreneurs a second chance. "If the source of failure is blatant negligence and blindness, often the case, our tolerance for that individual is rare" (Peter G. Gerry, president of Citicorp Venture Capital Ltd., in Aspaklaria, 1986). Other unforgivables include entrepreneurial megalomania, greed, and dishonesty.

Emotional responses. Business failure can result in feelings of anger, shame, guilt, and lingering frustration and depression. One way to cope with these negative emotions is through denial and finding blame elsewhere. This is a useful *short-term* tactic.

> . . . the ones that [sic] get back up usually don't take it personally. Instead, many deny that they had much to do with their enterprise's demise. That denial—and the conviction that failure owes much of its origins to uncontrollable forces—helps keep entrepreneurs psychologically afloat.
>
> Aspaklaria, 1986, p. 58

However, as will be shown, recovery of entrepreneurial spirit requires a sense of control, and that requires taking responsibility.

Like the death of a loved one, the loss of one's business (often experienced as a child and/or mistress) results in feelings that take time to heal. Based on his interactions with entrepreneurs, Shapero (1981a) estimates three years are required before starting again—time to think about past mistakes and ways to remedy them next time, time to develop new business ideas and find resources, and time to wait for the right opportunity.

A LARGER SYSTEM PERSPECTIVE

Although painful for the individuals involved, business failures are not all social costs or losses. "The resources, human and material, are still there, though they've been redistributed. What people learn from business failure may even be a gain for society" (Shapero, 1981a). In many cases, firing the entrepreneur results in a greater probability of venture survival (Singh, Tucker, & House, 1986). Finally, because many entrepreneurs try again, new organizations are born and the second or third venture may be one with greater stability and survival/growth potential.

MISTAKES

Of course business failure is in some ways the "ultimate" failure for an entrepreneur, although no one has asked entrepreneurs what failure means to them. Short of venture endings, entrepreneurs can and do experience small failures and mistakes.

A Los Angeles publisher of guidebooks, RW, sees failure as the only way to make progress. It's only when things do not work as expected that he figures out how to improve. He also sees a continuum of failings.

> There is long-term failure, which people think about when you use the term *failure*. Long-term failure has to do with being fired from a job or losing a war. Then there's momentary failure. You're constantly dealing with failure in everything you do. "That doesn't work, let's try this." There's infinitesimally short-term failure and there is very long-term failure. I believe you should live . . . and understand all those moments of failure, of jeopardy, of risk, of terror at the same time you have to have confidence in order to operate.

The opportunity to fail is one of the reasons RW likes to create and organize conferences, which are "more public ways of failing."

> It's immediate and you do it in public. Every conference fails in many ways. That's something that interests me because you can get right at it. It's just so f---ing scary to run a conference.

In daily interaction and decision making the entrepreneur, like any other adult learner, faces potential error in judgment, clumsy execution, and ignorance. Entrepreneurs can learn from these and self-correct their behavior and style, thereby adding even more value to the firm.

LEARNING FROM EXPERIENCE

In order to learn from experience, including mistakes, we need accurate perceptions and honest self-appraisal. If our failings are solely the result of outrageous fortune in the form of economic conditions or governmental interference, we can do nothing to improve our particular situation. However, we know that entrepreneurs tend to have a strong desire to feel in control, and successful ones tend to be more honest with themselves than less-successful ones (Schrage, 1965). So while denial may work to heal the wounds to pride and self-esteem that failure can bring, the successful rebound entrepreneur is likely to have done considerable thinking about his or her mistakes, as suggested by Shapero (1981a) above.

In addition, reflection on one's past experience is important to adult learning (Kolb, 1984) and peak performance (Garfield, 1986). However, entrepreneurs tend to ignore the past, being oriented to the here-and-now, with one foot planted firmly in some future vision. "The [technical or innovative] entrepreneur, unlike the traditional leader, rejects the experience of the past: To him, experience is not always the best teacher after all" (Filley & House, 1969, p. 447). This suggests that entrepreneurial learning might be limited by the entrepreneur's bias for action and preference for trial-and-error learning. Furthermore, this limitation might be overcome through self-management (learning to reflect) or accepting the influence of a team member who has this competency.

ACTION LEARNING

As previously suggested, entrepreneurs are characteristically action-oriented, learning from trial-and-error (Lessem, 1983). In the language of adult learning theory, they make many "active experiments" (i.e., accepting risks, acting under uncertainty) thereby generating many "concrete experiences" (e.g., ventures, changes, new relationships) (Kolb, 1984). Miles and Randolph (1980), who studied organizational creation through a simulation exercise, consider this the "enactive" approach to learning. This approach produces immediate consequences, and these events provide entrepreneurs with critical information about the product, service, market, competition, government regulations, and so forth. Miles and Randolph found that early failures result in greater organizational learning and that action learning is a better strategy in new and different settings, as when entering new markets with new products. Thus successful entrepreneurs court small failures or mistakes, accept "negative" feedback, and change quickly.

What is learned? A study of 24 technology-based ventures (of which 12 were founded by individuals with no previous entrepreneurial experience and 12 by individuals who had had previous involvement in founding and managing a technology-based venture) showed that the following lessons were learned from the experience (Lamont, 1987):

- Contract engineering is highly unstable (either feast or famine). Experienced entrepreneurs develop and market proprietary products, whereas inexperienced entrepreneurs perform contract activities.
- Access to venture capital, the ability to make a convincing presentation to potential investors, and perceptions of less risk in product-oriented (compared with service) ventures make it possible to obtain adequate initial capital. Inexperienced entrepreneurs were undercapitalized, lacking these competencies and positions.
- Weak venture teams contribute to early problems and business failure. Experienced entrepreneurs have teams with production, marketing, and general management skills. Inexperienced entrepreneurs start firms with scientists and engineers who have only casual interest in the business side of venturing.

Thus individuals who "do," who undertake a new venture, learn from the process—from acting, adjusting, changing, trying again, "listening" for feedback, etc. Past action or experience is an important teacher of entrepreneurs (Collins & Moore, 1964; Vesper, 1980).

CONCEPTUAL LEARNING

There is considerable debate among entrepreneurs and educators on whether or not entrepreneurship can be taught to others and, if it can be taught, how. On one side is the argument that formal business education, and particularly the MBA, actually turns individuals away from entrepreneurship by reinforcing risk aversion and skills, attitudes, and assumptions more suited for careers in big business management. On the other side is testimony from MBA students and alumni that education helps, especially with business planning (Robinett, 1985). In addition, observers note that entrepreneurs in the 1980s have critical-thinking competencies derived from formal education along with the bias for action (Ronstadt, 1985b). We will therefore consider the development of critical thinking skills and the content of educational programs in entrepreneurship.

Critical thinking. Miles and Randolph (1980) consider the conceptual processes of planning to be a part of the "proactive" approach to learning in new organizations. They found that proactive approaches result in higher initial performance, and consider them best in new settings where expertise transfers from a prior setting. Knowing how and when to proact and avoid reaction are elements of critical thinking, and critical thinking requires that divergent views be considered and anticipated.

Another study compared high-performing (growing) ventures to low-performing ventures and found that company performance was positively related to the preference for abstract thinking in the entrepreneur (Bailey, 1986). However, "thinking back to past solutions" did not discriminate high from low performance, nor did a preference for active experimentation. Clearly abstract thinking is a critical conceptual competency, but so is reflection (Boyatzis, 1982; Kolb, 1984). More research is necessary to resolve this anomaly.

Based on his experience with the Caruth Institute of Owner-Managed Business at Southern Methodist University, and on his own experience as an entrepreneur, John Welsh (1975) describes the entrepreneur as learner:

> [The entrepreneur] is a generalist. He dabbles in learning a broad spectrum of things, but specializes in none. Trying to fill his head with all the accumulated knowledge on any particular subject bores him and inhibits his natural tendency to conceive of relationships among seemingly unrelated things. He has superior conceptual abilities. He solves problems faster than his peers. He learns more quickly than most of us (p. 279).

Critical thinking is important to effective performance as a CEO or manager and to the performance of the firm. However, critical thinking is not a course taught in most university business management programs, nor is it a seminar topic or the focus of a "how-to" book. Most often, we expect these skills to develop in the process of absorbing content and working through problems assigned by faculty.

Content of entrepreneurship programs. The number of colleges and universities offering entrepreneurship coursework increased from 104 in 1975 to 253 in 1985 (Vesper, 1986). The content of courses includes the following topics, which demonstrate the conceptual frameworks for entrepreneurship (Vesper, 1986).

- venture finance
- venture marketing
- entrepreneurial management
- innovation management
- product design and development
- feasibility analysis
- economics of entrepreneurship
- entrepreneurial behavior
- entrepreneurial history
- internal corporate venturing
- venture accounting and taxation
- venture law

LABELLING AND FRAMING

Psychologists and organizational researchers recognize that a big part of learning and changing behavior has to do with the words or concepts used to label experience and the framework of assumptions used to understand it. For example, CEO use of terms such as *opportunity* or *threat* to label experiences faced by a venture result in very different (and possibly irreversible) actions (Dutton & Jackson, 1987). Likewise, the entrepreneur's use of terms such as *failure* compared to *mistake* will tend to frame the experience with different degrees of perceived control. Indeed, successful entrepreneurs are more likely to label a setback as a learning opportunity, and unsuccessful ones are more likely to label it a "real problem" (Sexton & Van Auken, 1982). Another observer notes that effective leaders "simply don't think about failure, don't even use the word, relying on such synonyms as 'mistake,' 'glitch,' 'bungle,' . . . 'false start,' 'mess,' 'hash,' 'bollix,' 'setback,' and 'error' " (Bennis & Nanus, 1985).

Obstacles and barriers. A variation of the labelling process involves the way that *obstacles or barriers are perceived*, experienced, and eliminated. One observer of the creation of new "settings" or organizations notes:

> . . . it is important that we recognize that aborted efforts to create a setting may not always, or even frequently, be due only to the fact that our external worlds present us with difficulties. Our own ways of thinking about what we wish to create may be as much of an obstacle as external hostility or indifference.

Saranson, 1972, p. 46

This suggests that there are two "frames" for labelling problems—one that sees the problems outside as others and the environment, and one that looks inside at one's own psyche. Objectively, the problem resides in either or both places. (This author has come to believe that many of the problems we experience are outer manifestations of inner conflict or uncertainty. That is, the problem is both inside and outside.) Subjectively, most individuals are biased to externalize problems (i.e., blame problems on circumstances; take personal credit for success).

In a study of child-care program start-ups, Van de Ven (1980) found five specific implementation obstacles, which are shown in Table 12.2. Depending on whether an entrepreneur looks outward or inward when encountering these barriers, obstacles can be projected onto others or events, or introjected as the entrepreneur's responsibility.

One study of the barriers experienced by entrepreneurs (Bird, 1983) reports that obstacles were variously described as a struggle, a fight, a limitation, or a lack of smoothness in the unfolding of events. Of the four entrepreneurs studied, only one internalized business problems by asking "What did I do to create that and why?" This entrepreneur did considerable reflection and "posture adjustment." The others saw limited resources "out there" and other people's attitudes and beliefs as the major source of obstacles to their ventures.

The entrepreneur's experience with obstacles has also been noted by David Silver, a former entrepreneur and now a venture capitalist. For him, entrepreneurs display courage in their inability to accept failure while engaging in valuable "downside reasoning" or developing worst-case contingencies. "Obstacles may have to be jumped, danced around or crawled through—or maybe they'll find new paths. But obstacles will not stop them" (Silver, 1983, p. 50).

Implications

Successful entrepreneurs seem capable of learning from their experience in "real time" and from past experiences. The pace of activity, urgency of action, and long hours on the job may interfere with this competency, which requires time for reflection and analysis. We expect experiential learning to be more difficult and thus more important in determining success in high-technology and rapid-growth ventures (fast-changing situations) and when the entrepreneur operates alone (with less opportunity for feedback). We would expect learning facility

TABLE 12.2 Outward and Inward Perceptions of Start-up Obstacles

Obstacle[1]	Outward view	Inward view
Staff recruitment	"There are no qualified candidates" "Qualified candidates expect too much money"	"I have not tapped the best network to find candidates" "I have not inspired candidates with my vision"
Lack of involvement and support of others	"Other agencies don't care about child care" "Other agencies feel competitive"	"I have not found a way to obtain their support" "I have not shown them a win-win scenario"
Funding	"Foundations have no money for child care" "Banks won't loan to a start-up"	"I have not located the foundations that can support this" "I have not learned from early loan rejections how to apply for a loan and get it"
Lack of clear program goals	"The planning consultants failed to do their job" "The staff is undermining our efforts"	"I have not developed clear program goals" "I have not articulated my goals so staff knows what to do"
Lack of knowledge of specific implementation steps	"The planning consultants failed to do their job"	"I have not consulted with those who know what to do"

[1] from Van de Ven (1980)

Source: Data from Van de Ven in *The Organizational Life Cycle*, Kimberly and Miles eds., (San Francisco, CA: Jossey-Bass, 1980).

to contribute to and/or result from the ability to sustain temporal tension (today's mistakes change future actions), flexibility of focus (determining what details are important), and strategic posture, since feedback is important to both alignment and attunement.

SELF-MANAGEMENT

Successful entrepreneurs and leaders seem to have high self-esteem or *positive self-regard* without becoming excessively narcissistic or megalomaniacal. Recall that the unrealistic extremes of self-confidence are "unforgivable" if they contribute to business failure. Healthy and positive self-regard involves a moral centeredness and knowledge of one's own worth. Warren Bennis (1982), whose recent study of 60 top American leaders was mentioned in Chapter 11, found three attributes: (1) effective leaders know their own talents and strengths, (2) they find ways to develop and nurture these strengths, and (3) they are able to discern the relationship between their strengths and their organizations. Such leaders maintain a sense of personal effectiveness and satisfaction in their work and personal lives (e.g., a sense of mastery, competence, self-direction).

Related to positive self-regard and personal effectiveness is the capacity for self-management. Self-management includes *self-control* (e.g., will power, control over impulses and emotions) and much more. It includes *self-observation*, and especially "awareness of impaired performance in tight or difficult situations," which correlates with the ability to "tune in" to both customers and employees and results in more successful entrepreneurial behavior (Schrage, 1965, p. 59). It includes the *conscious design of work environments* to remind and reinforce desired behavior in oneself and others. It also includes *rewarding and occasionally berating (punishing) oneself* for achieving or failing to achieve goals (Manz & Snyder, 1983).

Another self-management competency is that of *self-directed change of one's own behavior* (Winter, Griffith, & Kolb, 1970). This involves two factors: *a strong personal commitment to change* and *the willingness to receive feedback or criticism* (Kolb, Winter, & Berlew, 1968; Bennis & Nanus, 1985). While willing to change their organization to meet business opportunities and respond to changes in the environment, little is known about entrepreneurs' willingness to change their own behavior, and thus their role in the venture. Some do and some don't, as evidence on role transitions suggests. Clearly more research is required.

There is some anecdotal evidence that effective entrepreneurs attend to criticism. Werner Erhard, founder of est seminars, has been criticized by many people over many issues. Based on his experience, he suggests that "meeting the attack" with defenses interferes with learning. Instead, one must understand and appreciate the criticism.

"The attack must somehow be included . . . accepted—but by accepted I do not mean 'agreed with.' By accepted I mean 'allowed' to be there if one is to be on this path. "Then the question becomes, 'How can I use it? How does this attack move me along on this path?' "

Bennis & Nanus, 1985, p. 74

Because entrepreneurs play a crucial role in the early stages of organizational development and set examples for others to follow both within the firm and in other "spin off" ventures, their ability to be self-managing is important. The abilities of controlling one's own behavior and emotions, motivating oneself, looking objectively at oneself, and intentionally changing one's own behavior (to create an evolving role) are the marks of a competent entrepreneur-leader. However, the only empirical study of entrepreneurial competencies found that the cluster of competencies related to self-management (i.e., self-confidence, expertise, recognizing own limitations) did not discriminate successful from less successful entrepreneurs (McBer and Company, 1986).

OPPORTUNISTIC BEHAVIOR

In addition to self-management and the ability to learn from mistakes, entrepreneurs are characterized by competencies in discerning and acting on opportunities. In general, the new venture opportunity is knowledge that allows the entrepreneur to add value to resources (other goods and services) and thereby make a profit. The processes used by entrepreneurs to identify and act on opportunity are the focus of this section.

OPPORTUNITY IDENTIFICATION

In one of the only studies of entrepreneurial opportunism, Long and McMullan (1984) describe an opportunity identification process with four stages: (1) pre-vision, (2) point of vision, (3) opportunity elaboration, and (4) decision to proceed. Much of what they call pre-vision is discussed in Chapter 2 of this book and essentially suggests that opportunity, like creativity and insight, favors a prepared mind and that *vigilance is an important entrepreneurial competency.* Entrepreneurs collect a lot of information by being open to new experiences and investing time and energy in "looking." Says a man who built a successful investment management organization:

Suppose you and I start walking from here to downtown. You walk very slowly with your eyes in front of you. Meanwhile I walk much faster and stop in every single place and say "Hi." Every single store, every single factory, all the way down the line. And we both arrive downtown at the same time. I will come out with awfully funny experiences and probably have been thrown out of a few places, have met some people, and probably have had more opportunities. You say, "Aren't you lucky." You would have been lucky too if you had kept your eyes open.

Another competency in pre-vision involves the kinds of internal questions posed by entrepreneurs as new information is acquired. The more-competent entrepreneurs (e.g., those with ventures growing in sales, value of the firm, and number of employees) tend to *pose more opportunistic questions* (e.g., "How can I make this happen? How can I gain control over the necessary resources?") while low performers are more concerned with social aspects such as the well-being of participants, status, and power (Bailey, 1986).

Vision. The point of vision involves a more or less sudden coming together of the pieces of the new venture idea into a "gestalt," the "aha" experience, also discussed in Chapter 2. Among the four entrepreneurs interviewed by Long and McMullan, two had a sudden realization that the business idea made sense, while two slowly became aware of the opportunity.

Elaboration. Opportunity elaboration involves a frequently extended process of filling in the details of the business concept and anticipating problems. Long and McMullan (1984) found that time between initial vision and subsequent commitment to go ahead ranged from a few weeks (in the case of a serial entrepreneur in his third venture) to seven years (the same entrepreneur in his first venture). They argue that different individuals may use different strategies for opportunity elaboration.

Whereas some might automatically scale back opportunities to fit their existing resources, others might upscale resource accessibility to fit opportunities (p. 572).

While they did not formally study this particular element of opportunism, they did find different types of elaboration, some more systematic than others. Strategies included making useful contacts, forming a venture team before commitment, rigorously studying industry problems and existing solutions, and actively seeking feedback on the business idea.

Commitment. The commitment stage of the opportunity process involves writing a business plan, signing leases, negotiating with bankers and investors, making sales calls, and the other activities mentioned in Chapter 1.

THE CORRIDOR PRINCIPLE

Another way to look at opportunities is as doors that open off a corridor, or paths that branch from the path one is on. Often these doors or branches in the road are not visible as one begins the journey. Among entrepreneurs, the initial venture begins on a particular pathway, which opens new horizons and new opportunities that were not visible or available before getting into *this* business (Ronstadt, 1984a). Ronstadt's research suggests that the path to a successful enterprise frequently results from a branch off the original path. That is, the final, successful venture is often not the first venture, but rather an opportunity discovered while involved in an earlier activity.

OPPORTUNISTIC PERSONALITY

Not everyone is equally prepared to seize unanticipated opportunities, or branching pathways. In an article on the impact of chance encounters, psychologist Albert Bandura (1982) suggests that those who have "entry skills" (personal developmental histories that provide access to certain sets of people) and who are able to form emotional attachments to people found in chance occasions are more likely to be influenced by unanticipated opportunities. He also suggests that a form of open-mindedness, in which values are less fixed, also predisposes one to follow an opportunity. It is important to note that Bandura's work addressed unwholesome and negative impacts (e.g., how some people get enmeshed in cults) rather than the opportunism of entrepreneurs. His work, however, has implications for opportunism in general.

A model of entrepreneurial behavior based on predispositions compares craftsmen-entrepreneurs with opportunistic entrepreneurs (Smith, 1967). These groups are distinguished mostly in terms of their lifestyle/workstyle goals versus business-development goals (see Chapter 1). In a study of entrepreneurship in stagnating economic environments, Peterson

(1985) found that opportunistic (business- or goal-oriented) entrepreneurs tended to be more successful and craftsman (lifestyle- or means-oriented) entrepreneurs less successful.

David McClelland and his associates (McBer, 1986; McClelland, 1987) found that certain elements of the achievement cluster of competencies discriminated successful from less-successful entrepreneurs in three countries. These are "Sees and acts on opportunities," "Efficiency orientation," "Concern for high quality of work," and "Commitment to work contract." Those that *did not discriminate* were "Initiative," "Persistence," and "Information seeking."

LUCK

A discussion of opportunistic behavior inevitably raises questions about the role of luck in entrepreneurship. Despite their strong internal locus of control, entrepreneurs can usually tell a story about luck, or about being in the right place at the right time. Since it is a pervasive human quality to take personal responsibility for "good" outcomes and to blame "bad" outcomes on others or the environment (Jones & Nisbett, 1972), we would expect entrepreneurs to tell bad-luck stories.

However, in a study of entrepreneurial perceptions of luck, entrepreneurs display a surprising *respect for good luck*. A lucky break or fortunate "fork in the road" are considered major turning points in many organizational histories (Bird, 1983).

EXAMPLE: IRV ROBBINS

Irv Robbins, discharged from the army following World War II, decided to open an ice-cream store in California. He began to search for a store to rent in the San Francisco bay area—a search that had a lucky, unexpected ending.

"I couldn't find a location in the peninsula area. If you recall right after the war there were no empty locations and nobody was building. I was there a month and didn't find a location. I was going nuts. Well, I [decided to] take a weekend off and change my luck, as the saying goes.

"I came down to Los Angeles to visit some friends of mine. After the visit, I left about 5:00 in the morning. I'll never forget this . . . but you talk about the forks in the road of life. I turned right instead of left at a street that should have put me on San Fernando Road in Glendale, and I got lost.

"All of a sudden I bump into some great big gates and it says 'Forest Lawn Memorial Park.' I said 'My god, I don't know what I'm doing here, but I have never seen Forest Lawn' and I'd heard about it. It's where all the movie stars go to get buried. I thought I'd like to look at this place. I drive up to the gate and there's a sign 'Closed. Open 9:00 AM.' I look at my watch, 6:00. I said to myself, 'Well, I'll kill a little time, I'll drive around here and see what's going on and come back at 9:00.'

"So I'm driving around and I don't know where the hell I am. All of a sudden I drive by a building that has an empty store with a sign 'For Rent.' I say, 'Isn't that the craziest thing, I've been looking for a store for a month and couldn't find any. Here's a store for rent, but that's Southern California, a terrible place to live, all the sharpies in town. Well, maybe I'll look at it just to learn something.' "

In fact, Robbins rented the store. To make a long story short, he built his business into Baskin–Robbins Ice Cream, still headquarterd in Los Angeles.

Robbins defines luck as any change from the norm. His response is to turn it into an opportunity. He reports several lucky opportunities in the course of his entrepreneurial career.

"Some comedian on NBC had an ice-cream joke and he wanted to get some ice cream so he sent out a gofer at the studio to get some cones and some scoops and all the stuff needed for a little skit that he wanted to do. Luck. The comedian was named Johnny Carson. Luck. He was on NBC nationally. Luck. I happened to be in the store at the minute the gofer came there and fixed him up. And boy, he got everything in spades."

Other researchers have noted the importance of luck in entrepreneurship. In a study of British entrepreneurs, Miller (1963) notes:

Chance or luck, as the superstitious call it—has a hand in every undertaking, and in none is its role a subject of greater curiosity than in that of the business entrepreneur, whose progress offers a succession of hostages to fortune (p. 153).

Luck also enters into how modern technological advances are brought to market.

Technology tends to advance through a series of random—
often intuitive—insights frequently triggered by gratuitous
interactions between the discoverer and the outside world.

Quinn, 1985, p. 76

 ### EXAMPLE: GEORGE FOSTER

George Foster, a Columbus, Ohio, entrepreneur
deeply involved in his laser-technology firm, had
an idea for new computerized aviation equipment and
formed another organization.

"I knew what I had to do but I personally didn't have
very good skills at that and I didn't have the time. So I
needed a guy to do something for marketing . . . who is a
pilot, who has technical training, and ideally with some
teaching background. Our products are new, innovative and
different; they require explaining to people how to use all
this stuff.

"I went home that night and at 8:00 in the evening, an
associate called me from Cleveland and said 'I don't know
why I'm calling you but I've got a very unusual young man
sitting in my living room here. He's a pilot and a graduate
in physics and he has decided he doesn't want to teach
anymore and he has just resigned from vice president of
marketing for this pulley company.' I said 'Holy cow, I
can't believe this.' "

Foster went on to create an aviation-technology business
with the fortuitous arrival of the precise human resource he
needed.

These stories suggest that to other opportunistic behavioral competencies we might add the willingness to accept random, irrational, and unanticipated resources. The ability to
seize a "lucky break" provided by nature, caprice, serendipity,
or God and the ability to "make your own luck" through ex-
troversion and vigilance seem equally important to the fast-
moving, action-oriented entrepreneur.

OTHER COMPETENCIES

The study by McClelland (1987) and his associates (McBer,
1986) shows that other competencies may discriminate between successful (nominated as such by local leaders) and less

TABLE 12.3   Competencies of Successful Entrepreneurs

From this text:

Sustained temporal tension
Zoom lens for focus on details and overview
Alignment of self and others
Attunement to environments
Learning from experience
Role development

From McClelland (1987):

Initiative
Assertiveness
Sees and acts on opportunities
Efficiency orientation
Concern for high quality of work
Systematic planning
Monitoring
Commitment to work contract
Recognizing the importance of business relationships

successful entrepreneurs. Table 12.3 shows the competencies noted in this text and in the McClelland studies, which differentiate successful entrepreneurs. Other competencies did not distinguish between more and less success (but may differentiate entrepreneurs from managers or surviving ventures from failures). These include: self-confidence, persistence, persuasion, use of influence strategies, expertise, information seeking (McClelland, 1987), credibility, integrity and sincerity, concern for employee welfare, training for employees, building capital, and concern for image of products and services (McBer, 1986).

OTHER SUCCESS FACTORS

This chapter began with a discussion of business failure, and it is appropriate and symbolic to end the chapter and the book with a discussion of factors that contribute to success. We first look at empirical studies of success factors, then conclude with a description of the behavioral competencies that contribute to venture success.

CHARACTERISTICS OF SUCCESSFUL VENTURES

When looking for characteristics of successful ventures, we raise questions about the criteria by which success is measured. Certainly one mark of success is survival and another is growth of sales (cash flow), payroll (jobs), and profits (value added). However, we are likely to get different perspectives when we ask entrepreneurs and those who evaluate their efforts from the outside. The outside perspective was taken in a recent study of venture capitalists whose staffs screen hundreds of business plans for the handful that are considered as possible investments, and who personally interview principals and conduct "due diligence" on the venture and the entrepreneur(s). Some of the firms they follow fail; others show only moderate growth; and a few become "elephants" or big-profit investments. We conclude that venture capitalists will have informed judgment about what makes for a successful venture.

However, we must remain aware of the values of the venture capitalist, whose interest is ultimately return on investment. What characterizes the successful "deals" of venture capitalists has a great deal to do with making lots of money (200–1000 percent of the initial investment) in relatively short periods of time (four to seven years). Entrepreneurs have some of the same values (they like money to support a lifestyle or as a way of keeping score) as well as other values that are perhaps more important to them: controlling one's economic destiny, creating something from nothing, building an organization that implements noneconomic values, and so forth. With this in mind, let's look at what venture capitalists consider success factors.

The study (Timmons, Muzyka, Stevenson, & Bygrave, 1987) surveyed 47 American and international venture capital firms and a few private investors. Respondents were asked what characterized successful ventures, and five factors emerged.

Product-market structure. Successful entrepreneurs identify the true market for the venture's product and clearly define the economic payback to the customer for purchasing the product (that is, the time after which a customer realizes financial benefit from the product, usually less than 18 months). Successful ventures tend to serve mid-sized markets ($10 million to $100 million in sales) with moderate growth potential (30 to 60 percent per year). Finally, successful ventures have a product that can be legally protected and involves unique manufacturing processes and/or higher quality that differentiate it from competitive products. Behavioral competencies needed to achieve this product-market structure involve creativity, market wisdom, and the ability to discover or create niches with appropriate characteristics.

Competitive dynamics. Successful ventures face limited or passive competition, where it is possible to compete based on product differentiation and technological innovation. The ability to attain and maintain significant market share, the opportunity to enter a market without barriers, and the opportunity to erect barriers once under way contribute to success. Finally, entrepreneurs with innovative products that can be expanded or extended to other uses (e.g., clear product-line growth possibilities) have greater chances at success with venture capitalists. Behavioral competencies associated with competitive dynamics involve achievement motivation (love of competition), "veridical" perception of the competition, creativity, and "cleverness" in finding ways to protect the firm from competition.

Business economics. Ventures with a clearly understood position in the value-added stream tend to be more successful than those with low or volatile value added. A way to measure value added is in profit margins, and ventures with larger margins do better than those with smaller margins (smaller margins put greater pressure on managers for efficient organization). Successful ventures frequently have special relationships with suppliers and/or distributors. Venture capitalists look favorably on having a planned stream of venture financing (i.e., several discrete infusions of capital) where performance is assessed as capital is infused. Finally, from the venture capitalists' perspective, a planned way to liquidate their investment makes for greater success. Entrepreneurial competencies associated with business economics include vision, creativity, and "cleverness" as well as time agility and interpersonal skills in negotiating and working with external team members such as suppliers, distributors, and venture capitalists.

Business performance. Venture capitalists look favorably at ventures that can reach break even and positive cash flow in 18 to 36 months, and can be "harvested" in four to seven years through an Initial Public Offering (IPO). Ventures with a chance to attain durable, after-tax profits of 10 to 15 percent are more likely to succeed. Behavioral competencies involved with business performance relate to managerial competencies of the top-management team (see Boyatzis, 1982).

Management. The entrepreneur's (and team's) prior experience with managing start-ups and in the industry of the current venture are important predictors of success of the venture (especially if one of the team members is an industry "superstar"). A management team that agrees on goals and has complementary skills and good rapport is also a sign of success. Leadership with vision, focus, and the ability to provide appropriate incentives to managers is important to success as well. The behavior competencies involved in new venture management include the abilities to learn from experience, work cooperatively with internal team members, and attend to the human side of organization—in a word, leadership.

OTHER CHARACTERISTICS

Another study evaluated success in terms of "significant growth" over four years and computed success with failure (i.e., no longer running one's own business) (Sexton & Van Auken, 1982). The researches found that successful entrepreneurs:

- have more education (college degrees)
- are long-term residents of the community where the business is begun
- are motivated by financial independence and self-satisfaction (not by making money or being one's own boss)
- attribute success to their ability to work with others
- attach higher priority to family and lower priority to the job (note: this finding is discrepant with other studies)
- view setbacks as learning opportunities
- have more stable previous work experiences (fewer number of previous positions)
- have previous experience that relates to current venture
- rely more on family assistance in financing and less on banks
- work 40 to 60 hours a week

Of course, factors that are presumably not controlled by the entrepreneur also have a strong correlation with success. Economic upturns and downturns, changes in governmental policies and supports, the presence, power and resourcefulness of business support groups, and so forth, contribute to success. While simply "there" as part of the context of the start-up, some successful entrepreneurs attempt to influence these factors later in their careers. For example, 1800 small-business leaders met in Washington in August 1986 to recommend changes in federal policies for small businesses.

SUMMARY OF ENTREPRENEURIAL COMPETENCIES

Based on material covered in the text, we can summarize the behavioral competencies of various types of entrepreneurs. At the earliest stages, most entrepreneurs will tend to be more or less creative, visionary, opportunistic, intentional, and controlling. As their enterprises begin to take on lives of their own, intentional action competencies (e.g., sustaining temporal tension, strategic focus, choosing ends and/or means, and alignment of self and others into internal and external teams) will take on increasing importance. As an organization grows, the ability to learn from one's experience, the ability to be self-managing, and the ability to create appropriate roles for oneself become critical. If the organization is to remain small, the entrepreneur's competency as a manager (which is often minimal) will likely come into play. If the organization is to grow, the entrepreneur's competency in creating and learning new roles, especially the role of leader, will be essential if he or she is to remain involved.

Throughout his or her career as entrepreneur, a competency in recognizing and prioritizing work and nonwork roles will be of concern. In addition, the ability to either link work-life with family, play, and leisure life or to maintain very separate and distinct life spheres will likely be developed, especially if home-life success is of value.

Throughout the entrepreneurial career, relationships with others—internal teams and external teams—must be cultivated. Interpersonal competencies in forming mutually satisfying, instrumental relationships are significant throughout the process. This involves communication skills such as listening, inspiring, and finding "common ground" for win-win negotiations. It involves the ability and willingness to share the value added by the venture with key stakeholders through salaries, incentives, equity, authority, and so forth. Greed, egoism and paranoia undermine the success scenario.

Also, throughout the entrepreneurial career, a bias for action, experimentation, and a willingness to accept risk will be found. This bias will be moderated by learning, which requires vigilant and accurate perception, reflection, and analysis.

CONCLUDING NOTE

This book has looked at the behavioral dynamics of entrepreneurs—their personalities, backgrounds, and motivation. The creativity of entrepreneurs has been highlighted, as have the values and family contexts of entrepreneurs. The career paths of entrepreneurs have been described and the key relationships detailed. Relationships with partners, employees, and key outsiders have been examined. The various roles played by entrepreneurs, and the role transitions that accompany organizational growth, have been described. Finally, we have suggested that successful entrepreneurship involves behavioral competencies such as self-management, learning, opportunism, and time agility.

APPENDIX A

NOTES ON RESEARCH RIGOR AND RELEVANCE

The following factors pertain to the rigor and relevance of the studies surveyed in this text. Since the text is not a critique of the research literature, the reader is advised to bear these factors in mind when evaluating results of studies.

Who is studied? In some studies it is the person who starts up a new business. Other studies include those who purchase an existing business, and other studies look at corporate entrepreneurs.

When and where did the study take place? Studies of industrial start-ups in the 1940s or 1950s involve entrepreneurs who differ in life experiences—and possibly in personality—from those who started in 1980. Those who chose manufacturing may differ from those who enter retail sales or services. Those who locate in the Midwest may differ in temperament and character from those who locate in the South or West.

What size is the organization at the time of the study? The entrepreneur who is running a large organization may have different motivations and values than one whose organization never grows beyond a certain size.

With whom are entrepreneurs compared? We want to know what makes entrepreneurs different from other types of workers—from managers, from scientists, from the general population ("the man on the street"). We also want to know the differences in the type of work, the lifestyle, the career, etc. and how entrepreneurial organizations differ from other organizations. We want to know what differs between successful and unsuccessful entrepreneurial endeavors.

How rigorous is the research? Given a field of study that has only recently become popular, very few large-scale studies have been conducted. Most research involves case studies and small sample sizes—generalizations are limited. Those studies that do sample more rigorously (a sample of 100 is considered reasonable for most statistical analyses) can be questioned on how well the various variables (e.g., risk-taking propensity) are measured. Frequently, new scales and items are introduced without reports on the reliability of the measures. (Do individuals tend to give consistent responses to the questionnaire, or do responses vary so much that today's response cannot predict tomorrow's? In this case, there can be no reliable findings.) Reliability is a bare minimum for valid studies of personality, attitudes, values, decision-making styles, perceptions of business success, reputation, beliefs, time orientations, interpersonal or leadership style, etc.

What is the place of the person in the process? Another important consideration is whether we focus on what causes entrepreneurial behavior (e.g., individual action and social forces) or on what results from entrepreneurial behavior (e.g., the creation of organizations, jobs, business failure, environmental change, etc.). In the first case, entrepreneurial behavior is the dependent variable; in the second it is an independent variable.

APPENDIX B

LOCUS OF CONTROL

Below are some statements that pertain to life outcomes. Please indicate how much you agree with each statement by circling the appropriate response, using the following key:

1	2	3	4	5	6
STRONGLY AGREE	AGREE	MILDLY AGREE	MILDLY DISAGREE	DISAGREE	STRONGLY DISAGREE

	SA	A	MA	MD	D	SD
1. Whether or not I get to be a leader depends mostly on my ability.	1	2	3	4	5	6
2. To a great extent my life is controlled by accidental happening.	1	2	3	4	5	6
3. I feel like what happens in my life is mostly determined by powerful people.	1	2	3	4	5	6
4. Whether or not I get into a car accident depends mostly on how good a driver I am.	1	2	3	4	5	6
5. When I make plans, I am almost certain to make them work.	1	2	3	4	5	6
6. Often there is no chance of protecting my personal interest from bad luck happenings.	1	2	3	4	5	6
7. When I get what I want, it's usually because I'm lucky.	1	2	3	4	5	6
8. Although I might have good ability, I will not be given leadership responsibility without appealing to those in positions of power.	1	2	3	4	5	6
9. How many friends I have depends on how nice a person I am.	1	2	3	4	5	6
10. I have often found that what I think is going to happen will happen.	1	2	3	4	5	6

1	2	3	4	5	6
STRONGLY AGREE	AGREE	MILDLY AGREE	MILDLY DISAGREE	DISAGREE	STRONGLY DISAGREE

	SA	A	MA	MD	D	SD
11. My life is chiefly controlled by powerful others.	1	2	3	4	5	6
12. Whether or not I get into a car accident is mostly a matter of luck.	1	2	3	4	5	6
13. People like myself have very little chance of protecting our personal interests when they conflict with those of strong pressure groups.	1	2	3	4	5	6
14. It's not always wise for me to plan too far ahead, because many things turn out to be a matter of bad fortune.	1	2	3	4	5	6
15. Getting what I want requires pleasing people above me.	1	2	3	4	5	6
16. Whether or not I get to be a leader depends on whether I am lucky enough to be in the right place at the right time.	1	2	3	4	5	6
17. If important people were to decide they didn't like me, I probably wouldn't make many friends.	1	2	3	4	5	6
18. I can pretty much determine what will happen in my life.	1	2	3	4	5	6
19. I am usually able to protect my personal interest.	1	2	3	4	5	6
20. Whether or not I get into a car accident depends mostly on the other driver.	1	2	3	4	5	6
21. When I get what I want, it's usually because I worked hard for it.	1	2	3	4	5	6
22. In order to have my plans work, I make sure that they fit in with desires of people who have power over me.	1	2	3	4	5	6
23. My life is determined by my own actions.	1	2	3	4	5	6
24. It's chiefly a matter of fate whether or not I have a few friends or many friends.	1	2	3	4	5	6

Scoring: Add your scores for the following items:

3, 8, 11, 13, 15, 17, 20, 22   P = _____

and for items:

2, 6, 7, 10, 12, 14, 16, 24   C = _____

and for items:

1, 4, 5, 9, 18, 19, 21, 23   I = _____

P = Beliefs about control by *powerful others*. High scores indicate that other people control your outcomes. High scores might be found among those in highly political organizations.

C = Beliefs about *chance control*. High scores indicate that unordered, chance, or random events control your outcomes.

I = Beliefs about *individual control*. High scores indicate you believe that your outcomes are controlled by you—that your current situations and your rewards are direct outcomes of things you control.

Source: H. Levenson, "Locus of Control," *Journal of Personality Assessment* 38:377–83 (Hillsdale, NJ: Society for Personality Assessment, Lawrence Erlbaum Associates, Inc., Publishers, 1974).

REFERENCES

'1-2-3' creator: Mitch Kapor. 1987. *Inc.*, January:31–38.

Adams, J.L. 1980. Emotional blocks. In H. Leavitt, L. Pondy, and D. Boje (eds.). *Readings in managerial psychology* (3rd ed.). Chicago: University of Chicago Press.

Adamsak, P. 1984. How a board scuttled one vision. *Venture*, March:54–58.

Adorno, T., E. Frenkel-Brunswik, D. Levinson, and R. Sanford. 1950. *The authoritarian personality.* New York: Harper and Row.

Aldrich, H., and E. Auster. 1986. Even dwarfs started small: Liabilities of age and size and their strategic implications. *Research in Organizational Behavior* 8:165–98.

Aldrich, H., B. Rosen, and W. Woodward. 1986. A social role perspective of entrepreneurship: Preliminary findings from an empirical study. Paper presented to the Babson Entrepreneurship Research Conference, Wellesley, MA.

Aldrich, H., B. Rosen, and W. Woodward. 1987. The impact of social networks on business founding and profit: A longitudinal study. Paper presented to the Babson Entrepreneurship Research Conference, Malibu, CA.

Aldrich, N.W., Jr. 1986. Power trips. *Inc.*, April:65–68.

Allen, D.A. 1985. *Small business incubators and enterprise development.* U.S. Department of Commerce, Economic Development Administration Research and Evaluation Division.

Allen, D.A., and J. Hendrickson-Smith. 1986. *Planning and implementing small business incubators and enterprise support networks.* U.S. Department of Commerce, Economic Development Administration Research and Evaluation Division.

Allen, D.N. 1986. Personal communication, November.

Andrews, E.L. 1986. Keeping directors aboard. *Venture*, June:36–39, 42.

Andrews, E.L. 1986. Running out of money. *Venture*, January:32–35.

Andrews, L. 1981. *Medicine woman.* San Francisco, CA: Harper and Row.

"Are you a risk taker?" 1986. *Venture*, July:24.

Asinof, L. 1985. Small firms turn to big business for capital, markets, technical aid. *The Wall Street Journal*, 2 November.

Asinof, L. 1985. Venture capital clubs become hot spots for entrepreneurs seeking to make deals. *The Wall Street Journal*, 10 April.

Aspaklaria, S. 1986a. Down but not out. *Venture*, March:58–60.

Aspaklaria, S. 1986b. Startups after sixty. *Venture*, September: 30–34.

Astrachan, J.H. 1985. Family firm and community culture: An optimal fit. Paper presented to the Academy of Management. Working paper, Yale University School of Organization and Management.

Atkinson, J.W. 1957. Motivational determinants of risk taking behavior. *Psychological Review* (64):359–72.

Babbit, H.R., and J.D. Ford. 1980. Decision-maker choice as a determinant of organizational structure. *Academy of Management Review* 5:1–13.

Bailey, J.E. 1986. Learning styles of successful entrepreneurs. In R. Ronstadt, J. Hornaday, R. Peterson, and K. Vesper (eds.). *Frontiers of entrepreneurship research 1986*. Wellesley, MA: Babson College.

Bandura, A. 1982. The psychology of chance encounters and life paths. *American Psychologist* 37(7):747–55.

Banks, M.C., A.L. Bures, and D.L. Champsion. 1987. Decision making factors in small business: Training and development. *Journal of Small Business Management*, January:19–25.

Barlow, D. 1984. The executive as manager of human energy. In S. Srivastva (Chair), *The functioning of executive power*. Symposium conducted through Case Western Reserve University, Cleveland, Ohio.

Barney, J.B. 1986. Organizational culture: Can it be a source of sustained competitive advantage? *Academy of Management Review* 11:656–65.

Baty, G.B. 1974. *Entrepreneurship—Playing to win*. Reston, VA: Reston.

Baumback, C.M., and J.R. Mancuso. 1975. *Entrepreneurship and venture management*. Englewood Cliffs, NJ: Prentice-Hall.

Beckhard, R. 1983. Conversation with Richard Beckhard. *Organizational Dynamics*, Summer:29–38.

Beckhard, R., and W.G. Dyer. 1983. Managing continuity in the family-owned business. *Organizational Dynamics*, Summer:5–12.

Begley, T.M., and D.P. Boyd. 1985. Company and chief executive officer characteristics related to financial performance in smaller business. In J. Hornaday, E. Shils, J. Timmons, and K. Vesper (eds). *Frontiers of entrepreneurship research 1985.* Wellesley, MA: Babson College.

Begley, T.M., and D.P. Boyd. 1986. Psychological characteristics associated with entrepreneurial performance. Paper presented at the Babson Entrepreneurship Research Conference, Wellesley, MA.

Bekey, M. 1984. Lawyers turned investors. *Venture,* September: 98–102.

Bellew, P.A. 1985. Modern phoenixes: Fallen entrepreneurs in Silicon Valley find failure is not disgrace. *Wall Street Journal,* 30 April.

Benner, S. 1985. Dear Jon. *Inc.,* February:79–86.

Bennett, A. 1986. Laid-off managers of big firms increasingly move to small ones. *The Wall Street Journal,* 25 July.

Bennis, W. 1982. Personal communication.

Bennis, W., and B. Nanus. 1985. *Leaders: The strategies for taking charge.* New York: Harper and Row.

Berlew, D. 1981. Positive power and influence program. Plymouth, MA: Situation Management Systems, Inc.

Bernard, J. 1981. The good provider role: Its rise and fall. *American Psychologist* 36:1–12.

Birch, D.L. 1979. *The job generation process.* Cambridge, MA: MIT Program on Neighborhood and Regional Change.

Birch, D.L. 1985. Matters of fact. *Inc.,* April:31–36,39–42.

Bird, B. 1986. Entrepreneurial behavior: What do entrepreneurs do? Paper presented at the Babson Entrepreneurship Research Conference, Wellesley, MA.

Bird, B.J. 1983. *Intentional maps of entrepreneurs.* Ph.D. diss. University of Southern California.

Bird, B.J. 1986. Implementation of entrepreneurial ideas: The case for "intention." Working paper, Case Western Reserve University.

Bird, B.J., and D.N. Allen. 1987. Faculty entrepreneurship in research university environments. Working paper, Case Western Reserve University.

Bird, B.J., and W.B. Gartner. 1985. Academic interest in entrepreneurship: A survey of the Academy of Management entrepreneurship interest group. Paper presented at the Babson Entrepreneurship Research Conference, Philadelphia, PA.

Bird, B.J., and R.S. Jordan. 1987. Measuring managerial time. Working paper, Case Western Reserve University.

Bird, B.J., and D.K. Neiswander. 1987. Entrepreneurial hiring and early stage management. Working paper, Case Western Reserve University.

Birley, S. 1984. Finding the new firm. Working paper, College of Business, University of Notre Dame.

Birley, S. 1985a. The role of networks in the entrepreneurial process. In J. Hornaday, E. Shils, J. Timmons, and K. Vesper (eds.). *Frontiers of entrepreneurship research 1985*. Wellesley, MA: Babson College.

Birley, S. 1985b. The role of networks in the entrepreneurial process. *Journal of Business Venturing* 1:107–17.

Birley, S. 1986. The small firm—set at the start. In R. Ronstadt, J. Hornaday, R. Peterson and K. Vesper (eds.). *Frontiers of entrepreneurship research 1986*. Wellesley, MA: Babson College.

Birley, S., C. Moss, and P. Saunders. 1986. The difference between small firms started by male and female entrepreneurs who attended small business courses. In R. Ronstadt, J. Hornaday, R. Peterson, and K. Vesper (eds.). *Frontiers of entrepreneurship research 1986*. Wellesley, MA: Babson College.

Bitter victories. 1985. *Inc.*, August:25–35.

Black, P. 1986. A little help from her friends. *Venture*, July:52–58.

Blau, P.M., J.W. Gustad, R. Jesson, H.S. Parnes, and R.C. Wilcox. 1956. Occupational choices: A conceptual framework. *Industrial and Labor Relations Review* 9:531,537,543.

Bluedorn, A.C. 1987. Strategic decision making and entrepreneurial time dilation. Paper presented to the Academy of Management, New Orleans.

Bobbitt, H.R., and J.D. Ford. 1980. Decision-maker choice as a determinant of organizations structure. *Academy of Management Review* 5:13–23.

Borland, C.M. 1975. Locus of control, need for achievement and entrepreneurship. Ph.D. diss., University of Texas, Austin. University Microfilms 75–16:644.

Bowen, M.G., and A.S. Jones. 1985. Informal strategic non-planning for survival in start-up ventures. In G. Roberts (ed.). *Proceedings: Discovering entrepreneurship*. Orlando, FL: First Biennial Conference, U.S. Affiliate International Council of Small Business.

Boyatzis, R.E. 1982. *The competent manager: A model for effective performance*. New York: John Wiley.

Boyd, D.P., and T.M. Begley. 1986. The effects of occupational stress on executive strain and financial performance in smaller businesses. Paper presented to the Academy of Management, Chicago.

Boyd, D.P., and D.E. Gumpert. 1983. Coping with entrepreneurial stress. *Harvard Business Review,* March-April:44–64.

Brain, R. 1977. Somebody else should be your own best friend. *Psychology Today,* October:83–84,120,123.

Brockhaus, R.H. 1980a. Risk taking propensity of entrepreneurs. *Academy of Management Journal* 23:509–20.

Brockhaus, R.H. 1980b. Psychological and environmental factors which distinguish the successful from the unsuccessful entrepreneur: A longitudinal study. Paper submitted to the Academy of Management meeting.

Brockhaus, R.H. 1982. The psychology of the entrepreneur. In C. Kent, D. Sexton, and K. Vesper (eds.) *Encyclopedia of entrepreneurship.* Englewood Cliffs, NJ: Prentice-Hall.

Brockhaus, R. H., and W.R. Nord. 1979. An exploration of factors affecting the entrepreneurial decision: Personal characteristics vs. environmental conditions. *Proceedings '79,* Academy of Management.

Brockhause, R.H. 1985. Is there life after death: The impact of unsuccessful entrepreneurial endeavors on the life of the entrepreneurs. In J. Hornaday, E. Shils, J. Timmons, and K. Vesper (eds.). *Frontiers of entrepreneurship research 1985.* Wellesley, MA: Babson College.

Brophy, D.J. 1986. Venture capital research. In D. Sexton and R. Smilor (eds.). *The art and science of entrepreneurship.* Cambridge, MA: Ballinger.

Brown, I.E. 1986. Sustaining the entrepreneurial vision in cooperative firms. Paper presented to the Babson Entrepreneurship Research Conference, Babson College, Wellesley, MA.

Brownstein, R. 1985. So you want to go into politics? *Inc.,* November:98–100,104,107.

Bruno, A.V., J.K. Leidecker, and J.W. Harder. 1986. Patterns of failure among Silicon Valley high technology firms. In R. Ronstadt, J. Hornaday, R. Peterson, and K. Vesper (eds.). *Frontiers of entrepreneurship research 1986.* Wellesley, MA: Babson College.

Buchsbaum, S. 1984. Tea and sympathy. *Inc.,* June:97–100.

Bureau of the Census. 1981. *Statistical Abstract of the United States* (102nd ed.). Washington, D.C.

Burke, W.W. 1984. On empowerment. Paper presented to Case Western Reserve Symposium on The Functioning of Executive Power.

Burns, J.M. 1978. *Leadership.* New York: Harper and Row.

Buskirk, R.H. 1982. The dangers of overcapitalization in the start up stage. In K. Vesper, (ed.). *Frontiers of entrepreneurship research 1982.* Wellesley, MA: Babson College.

Caborne, J.H. 1986. Letter to the editor. *The Entrepreneurship Newsletter* 2(2):10.

Campbell, J. 1980. Complementarity and attraction: A reconceptualization in terms of dyadic behavior. *Representative Research in Social Psychology* 11(2):74–95.

Carland, J.W., F. Hoy, W.R. Boulton, and J.C. Carland. 1984. Differentiating entrepreneurs from small business owners. *Academy of Management Review* 9:354–59.

Carlson, B., P. Keane, and J.B. Martin. 1984. R&D organizations as learning systems. In D. Kolb, I. Rubin, and J. McIntyre (eds.). *Organizational psychology: Readings on human behavior in organizations.* Englewood Cliffs, NJ: Prentice-Hall. (Originally published 1976.)

Carsrud, A.L., K.W. Olm, and R.D. Ahlgreen. 1986. Comparison of female entrepreneurs and M.B.A. students: Groomed for success or doomed to failure? Working paper 85/86–4–19, University of Texas, Austin.

Cartwright, D. 1971. Risk-taking by individuals and groups: An assessment of research employing choice dilemmas. *Journal of Personality and Social Psychology* 20(3):361–78.

Chrisman, J.J., and F. Hoy. 1985. The budding entrepreneur and public sector assistance: Assessing the impact of pre-venture counseling. Paper presented to the Academy of Management, San Diego.

Churchill, N., and V. Lewis. 1985. Bank lending to new and growing enterprises. In J. Hornaday, E. Shils, J. Timmons, and K. Vesper (eds.). *Frontiers of entrepreneurship research 1985,* Wellesley, MA: Babson College.

Churchill, N.C., and V.L. Lewis. 1983. The five stages of small business growth. *Harvard Business Review,* May/June:30–50.

Cohen, A., and M. Quarry. 1986. Performance of employee-owned small companies: A preliminary study. *Journal of Small Business Management,* April:58–63.

Cole, W. 1987. Lemons into lemonade. *Venture,* December:73–77.

Collins, O.F., and D.G. Moore. 1964. *The enterprising man.* East Lansing, MI: MSU Business Studies.

Conversation with Richard Beckhard. 1983. *Organizational Dynamics,* Summer:29–38.

Cooper, A.C. 1971. Spin-offs and technical entrepreneurship. *IEEE Transactions on Engineering Management, EM–18,* February:2–6.

Cooper, A.C. 1972. Incubator organizations and technical entrepreneurship. In A. Cooper and J. Komives (eds.). *Technical entrepreneurship: A symposium.* Milwaukee, WI: Center for Venture Management.

Cooper, A.C. 1985. Incubator organizations and entrepreneurship. Paper presented to the Academy of Management, San Diego.

Cooper, A.C., G.E. Willard, and C.Y. Woo. 1986. Strategies of high-performing new and small firms: A reexamination of the niche concept. *Journal of Business Venturing* 1:247–60.

Cooper, A.C., W.C. Dunkelberg, and R.S. Furuta. 1985. Incubator organization background and founding characteristics. In J. Hornaday, E. Shils, J. Timmons, and K. Vesper (eds.). *Frontiers of entrepreneurship research 1985.* Wellesley, MA: Babson College.

Craig, J.H., and M. Craig. 1974. *Synergic power.* Berkeley: Proactive Press.

Critser, C. 1986. The est factor. *Inc.,* August:69–76.

Daft, R.L. 1983. *Organization theory and design.* St. Paul: West.

Davis, J.A. 1986. Bivalent attributes of the family firm. Paper presented to the Academy of Management, Chicago.

Davis, S.M. 1982. Transforming organizations: The key to strategy is context. *Organizational Dynamics,* (Winter):64–80.

Day, R., and J. Day. 1977. Review of the current state of negotiated order theory: An appreciation and a critique. *Sociological Quarterly* 18(1):126–42.

de Castillejo, I.C. 1973. *Knowing woman: A feminine psychology.* New York: Harper and Row.

Deal, T.E., and A.A. Kennedy. 1982. *Corporate cultures: The rites and rituals of corporate life.* Reading, MA: Addison-Wesley.

Dean, B.V. 1984. The management of innovative start-up firms. Technical Memorandum #548, Case Western Reserve University.

DeCarlo, J.F., and P.R. Lyons. 1979. A comparison of selected personal characteristics of minority and non-minority female entrepreneurs. In R. Huseman (ed.). *Proceedings '79.* Atlanta, GA: Academy of Management.

Derr, C.B. 1984. Entrepreneurs: A careers perspective. Paper presented to the Academy of Management, Boston.

Do business and friendship mix? 1985. *Venture,* March:27.

Do entrepreneurs fail to 'inspire employees? Yes' says survey" 1986. *Journal of Accountancy,* July:26–27,30.

Donaldson, G., and J. Lorsch. 1983. *Decision making at the top.* New York: Basic Books.

Driver, M. 1979. Individual decision making and creativity. In S. Kerr (ed.). *Organizational behavior.* Columbus, OH: Grid.

Driver, M.J. 1979. Career concepts and career management in organizations. In C. Cooper (ed.). *Behavioral problems in organizations* (79–140). Englewood Cliffs, NJ: Prentice-Hall.

Drucker, P. 1984. Our entrepreneurial economy. *Harvard Business Review,* January-February:59–64.

Drucker, P. 1985. The discipline of innovation. *Harvard Business Review,* May-June:67–72.

Drucker, P. 1985. The entrepreneurial mystique. *Inc.,* October: 34–58.

Duffy, P.B., and H.H. Stevenson. 1984. Entrepreneurship and self-employment: Understanding the distinctions. In J. Hornaday, F. Tarpley, J. Timmons, and K. Vesper (eds.). *Frontiers of entrepreneurship research 1984.* Wellesley, MA: Babson College.

Dumdum, L.Y. 1987. Inquiry into partnerships. Candidacy paper presented to the Department of Organizational Behavior, Case Western Reserve University, Cleveland, OH.

Dunkelberg, W.C., and A.C. Cooper. 1982. Patterns of small business growth. In K. Chung (ed.). *Academy of Management Proceedings '82.* New York: Academy of Management.

Durand, D., and D. Shea. 1974. Entrepreneurial activity as a function of achievement motivation and reinforcement control. *The Journal of Psychology* (88):57–63.

Dutton, J.E., and S.E. Jackson. 1987. Categorizing strategic issues: Links to organizational action. *Academy of Management Review* 12:76–90.

Emery, F.E., and E.L. Trist. 1969. The causal texture of organizational environments. In E. Trist (ed.). *Systems thinking,* pp. 241–57. New York: Penguin Books.

"Entrepreneurs." 1986. Nathan/Tyler Productions, P.O. Box 1102, Waltham, MA 02254.

Entrepreneurs and their attorneys. 1986. *Venture,* June:24.

Eriksen, E.H. 1950. *Childhood and society.* New York: Norton.

Fagenson, E.A. 1986. The values of entrepreneurs/business owners. Paper presented to the Academy of Management, Chicago.

Fallows, J. 1986. The case against credentialism. *The Atlantic Monthly,* December:49–67.

Faraday, A. 1974. *The dream game.* New York: Harper and Row.

Farrell, K. 1985. There's no stopping now. *Venture,* February:41–48.

Feigen, G.L., and L.M. Arrington. 1986. The historic role of SEICs in financing the young and growing company. Paper presented at the Babson Entrepreneurship Research Conference, Wellesley, MA.

Female owners try to make life easier for employees—Sometimes too easy. *The Wall Street Journal,* May 28, 1985.

Fenn, D. 1985a. Mothers of invention. *Inc.,* May:108–13.

Fenn, D. 1985b. The lord of discipline. *Inc.,* November:82–88, 95.

Filley, A.C., and R.J. House. 1969. *Managerial process and organizational behavior.* Glenview, IL: Scott, Foresman.

Flower, J. 1984. Those visionary entrepreneurs. *Venture,* March: 46–52.

Fooner, A. 1983. 24-hour-a-day partnerships. *Enterprise,* October:148–52.

Ford, J.D. 1985. The effects of causal attributions on decision makers' responses to performance downturns. *Academy of Management Review* 10:770–86.

Ford, J.D., and D.A. Baucus. 1987. Organizational adaptation to performance downturns: An interpretation-based perspective. *Academy of Management Review* 12:366–80.

Fred Smith. 1986. *Inc.,* October:35–38,41,42,45,46,49.

Freeman, J., G.R. Carroll, and M.T. Hannan. 1983. The liability of newness: Age dependence in organizational death rates. *American Sociological Review* 48:692–710.

Freseman, J.O. 1985. Starting over. *Venture,* December:58–62.

Friedlander, F. 1973. Emerging blackness in a white research world. In W. Bennis, D. Barlow, E. Schein, and F. Steele (eds.). *Interpersonal dynamics* (3rd ed.). Homewood, IL: Dorsey.

Froggatt, K.L., and J.L. Cotton. 1984. Effects of sex and type A behavior on overload- and underload-induced stress: A laboratory investigation. In J. Pearce (ed.). *Academy of Management Proceedings '84.* Boston: Academy of Management.

Galante, S.P. 1987. Business incubators adopting niche strategies to stand out. *The Wall Street Journal,* 13 April.

Garfield, C.A. 1986. *Peak performers: The new heroes of American business.* New York: Morrow.

Gartner, W.B. 1986. Entrepreneurial work. Working paper, Georgetown University.

Gartner, W.B. 1985. A conceptual framework for describing the phenomenon of new venture creation. *Academy of Management Review* 10:696–706.

Gasse, Y. 1977. *Entrepreneurial characteristics and practices: A study of the dynamics of small business organizations and their effectiveness in different environments.* Sherbrooke, Quebec: Rene Prince Imprimmeur.

Gasse, Y. 1978. Characteristics, functions and performance of small firm owner-managers in two industrial environments. Ph.D. diss., Northwestern University.

Gatewood, E., F. Hoy, and C. Spindler. 1984. Functionalist vs. conflict theories: Entrepreneurship disrupts the power structure in a small southern community. In J. Hornaday, F. Tarpley, J. Timmons, and K. Vesper (eds.). *Frontiers of entrepreneurship research 1984*. Wellesley, MA: Babson College.

Getzels, J.W., and M. Csikszentmihalyi. 1976. *Creative vision: A longitudinal study of problem finding in art*. New York: John Wiley.

Gilder, G. 1984. Fear of capitalism. *Inc.*, September:87–94.

Gordon, G.E., and N. Rosen. 1984. Critical factors in leadership succession. In W. Rosenbach and R. Taylor (eds.). *Contemporary issues in leadership* (162–91). Boulder, CO: Westview Press. (Originally published 1981.)

Gorman, M., and W.A. Sahlman. 1986. What do venture capitalists do? In R. Ronstadt, J. Hornaday, R. Peterson, and K. Vesper (eds.). *Frontiers of entrepreneurship research 1986*. Wellesley, MA: Babson College.

Goslin, L.N., and B. Barge. 1986. Entrepreneurial qualities considered in venture capital support. In R. Ronstadt, J. Hornaday, R. Peterson, and K. Vesper (eds.). *Frontiers of entrepreneurship research 1986*. Wellesley, MA: Babson College.

Granovetter, M. 1973. The strength of weak ties. *American Journal of Sociology* 78:1360–80.

Granovetter, M. 1984. Small is bountiful: Labor markets and establishment size. *American Sociological Review* 49:323–34.

Grimm, C.M., and K.G. Smith. 1986. The organization as a reflection of its top management: An empirical test. Paper presented to the Academy of Management, Chicago.

Gupta, U. 1986. Hands-on venture capital. *Venture*, January:43, 46–50.

Gurin, P., G. Gurin, R. Lao, and M. Beattie. 1969. Internal-external control in the motivational dynamics of Negro youth. *Journal of social issues* (25):29–53.

Gush, W.D., and R. Tagiuri. 1965. Personal values and corporate strategy. *Harvard Business Review*, September-October:123–32.

Hall, D.T. 1976. *Careers in organizations*. Pacific Palisades, CA: Goodyear Publishing.

Hall, E.G. 1973. Proxemics in a cross-cultural context: Germans, English, and French. In W. Bennis, D. Barlow, E. Schein, and F. Steele (eds.). *Interpersonal dynamics* (3rd ed.). Homewood, IL: Dorsey.

Hambrick, D.C., and L.M. Crozier. 1985. Stumblers and stars in the management of rapid growth. *Journal of Business Venturing* 1(1):31–45.

Hambrick, D.C., and P.A. Mason. 1984. Upper echelons: The organization as a reflection of its top managers. *Academy of Management Review* 9:193–206.

Hannan, M.T., and J.H. Freeman. 1977. The population ecology of organizations. *American Journal of Sociology* 82:929–64.

Harrell, W. 1987. Entrepreneurial terror. *Inc.*, February:74–76.

Harrigan, K.R. 1985. *Strategies for joint ventures.* Lexington, MA: Lexington Books.

Harrigan, K.R. 1986. Managing for joint venture success. Symposium presentation to the Academy of Management, Chicago.

Harris, S., and J. Aussem. 1988. Fine tuning your presentation to the bank. Presentation to "Banking on the Entrepreneur" conference, Cleveland, OH.

Harrison, R. 1973. Role negotiation: A tough-minded approach to team development. In W. Bennis, D. Berlew, E. Schein, and F. Steele (eds.). *Interpersonal dynamics: Essays and readings on human interaction* (3rd ed.), Homewood, IL: Dorsey.

Harrison, R. 1982. *Leadership and strategy for a new age: Lessons from "conscious evolution."* Unpublished manuscript.

Hart, S.L., and D.R. Denison. 1986. Creating new technology-based organizations: A systems dynamics model. Paper presented to the Academy of Management, San Diego.

Hartman, C. 1986. Requiem for an entrepreneur. *Inc.*, February: 68–75.

Harvard Case Clearing House. 1970a. *Mr. Richard Neely.* 9–470–015.

Harvard Case Clearing House. 1970b. *Mr. Dale Chapman.* 9–470–016.

Hawken, P. 1983. *The next economy.* New York: Holt, Rinehart & Winston.

Hebert, R.F., and A.N. Link. 1982. *The entrepreneur: Mainstream views and radical critiques.* New York: Praeger.

Helm, S. 1986. Perfect partners. *Venture*, July:36–40.

Hennig, M., and A. Jardim. 1977. *The managerial woman.* Garden City, NJ: Doubleday.

Hetherington, E.M. 1973. Girls without fathers. *Psychology Today*, February:47–52.

Hisrich, R.D., and C.G. Brush. 1985. Women and minority entrepreneurs: A comparative analysis. In J.A. Hornaday, E.B. Shils, J.A. Timmons, and K.H. Vesper (eds.). *Frontiers of entrepreneurship research 1985.* Wellesley, MA: Babson College.

Hisrich, R.D., and C.G. Brush. 1986. *The women entrepreneur.* Lexington, MA: Lexington Books.

Hoad, W.M., and P. Rosko. 1964. *Management factors contributing to the success and failure of new small manufacturers.* Ann Arbor, MI: Bureau of Business Research, University of Michigan.

Hodgson, R.C., D.J. Levinson, and A. Zaleznik. 1965. *The executive role constellation.* Boston: Harvard University.

Hornaday, J.A., and J. Aboud. 1971. Characteristics of successful entrepreneurs. *Personnel Psychology* 24:141–53.

Hornaday, J.A., and K.H. Vesper. 1981. Alumni perceptions of entrepreneurship courses after six to ten years. In D. Sexton and P. Van Auken (eds.). *Entrepreneurship education.* Waco, TX: Baylor University.

Horwitz, L. 1983. Projective identification in dyads and groups. *International Journal of Group Psychology* 33(3):259–79.

Hull, D.L., J.J. Bosley, and G.G. Udel. 1980. Renewing the hunt for the heffalump: Identifying potential entrepreneurs by personality characteristics. *Journal of Small Business Management* 18: 11–18.

Hutt, R.W. 1984. Preferred activities of an entrepreneur's organization: Start-up and early stage firms vs. established firms. In J. Hornaday, F. Tarpley, J. Timmons, and K. Vesper (eds.). *Frontiers of entrepreneurship research 1984.* Wellesley, MA: Babson College.

Hymowitz, C. 1984. Taking a chance: Many blacks jump off the corporate ladder to be entrepreneurs. *The Wall Street Journal,* 2 August.

Hymowitz, C. 1986. The glass ceiling. *The Wall Street Journal,* 24 March.

Ioannou, L. 1984. Venture capital clubs. *Venture,* September:64, 68,89.

Jacknis, I.M. 1987. The art of hiring '10s.' *Inc.,* October:145–46.

Jacobs, S.L. 1985. A well-chosen outside board gives owners peace of mind. *The Wall Street Journal,* 21 January.

Jaques, E. 1976. *A general theory of bureaucracy.* Exeter, NH: Heinemann.

Johnson, F.P., Jr. 1985. The entrepreneurial climate. In J. Kao and H. Stevenson (eds.). *Entrepreneurship: What it is and how to teach it.* Cambridge, MA: Harvard Business School.

Johnson, R.A. 1977. *She: Understanding feminine psychology.* New York: Harper and Row.

Jolson, M.A., and M.J. Gannon. 1972. Wives—A critical element in career decisions. *Business Horizons* 15:83–88.

Jubak, J. 1986a. In the land of giants. *Venture*, September:46–49.

Jubak, J. 1986b. Investors tighten the terms. *Venture*, May:134–36.

Just like dear old dad. 1985. *Venture*, November:24.

Kahn, J.P. 1985a. A perfect pass. *Inc.*, June:68–71.

Kahn, J.P. 1985b. Networking: A little help from your friends. *Inc.*, June:55–64.

Kanter, R.M. 1977. *Men and women of the corporation*. New York: Basic Books.

Kanter, R.M. 1983. *The change masters: Innovation and entrepreneurship in the American corporation*. New York: Simon & Schuster.

Kao, J.J. 1985. The corporate new wave: Entrepreneurship in transition. In J. Kao and H. Stevenson (eds.). *Entrepreneurship: What it is and how to teach it*. Cambridge, MA: Harvard Business School.

Katz, D., and R.L. Kahn. 1978. *Social psychology of organizations* (2nd ed.). New York: Wiley.

Katz, J., and W. Gartner. 1986. Properties of emergent organizations. Paper presented to the Academy of Management, Chicago.

Kazanjian, R.K. 1984. Operationalizing stage of growth: An empirical assessment of dominant problems. In J. Hornaday, F. Tarpley, J. Timmons, and K. Vesper (eds.). *Frontiers of entrepreneurship research 1984* (144–58). Wellesley, MA: Babson College.

Kelly, J.M., R.A. Pitts, and B. Shin. 1986. Entrepreneurship by leveraged buy-out: Some preliminary hypotheses. In R. Ronstadt, J. Hornaday, R. Peterson, and K. Vesper (eds.). *Frontiers of entrepreneurship research 1986* (281–92). Wellesley, MA: Babson College.

Kennedy, A. 1984. Every employee an entrepreneur. *Inc.*, April:116–17.

Kent, C.A., D.L. Sexton, and P.M. Van Auken. 1982. Lifetime experiences of managers and entrepreneurs: A comparative analysis. Paper presented to the Academy of Management, New York.

Kepner, E. 1983. The family and the firm: A coevolutionary perspective. *Organizational Dynamics*, Summer:57–70.

Kerr, S., M.A. Von Glinow, and J. Schriesheim. 1977. Issues in the study of "professionals" in organizations: The case of scientists and engineers. *Organizational Behavior and Human Performance* 18:329–45.

Kets de Vries, M.F.R. 1977. The entrepreneurial personality: A person at the cross roads. *Journal of Management Studies* 14:34–57.

Kets de Vries, M.F.R. 1984. Can you survive an entrepreneur? Teaching Note (9G–484–081). Boston: Harvard Business School.

Kets de Vries, M.F.R., and A. Zaleznik. 1975. Myth and reality of entrepreneurship. In M.F.R. Kets de Vries and A. Zaleznik (eds.). *Power and the corporate mind.* Boston: Houghton-Mifflin.

Kets de Vries, M.F.R., and D. Miller. 1984. *The neurotic organization: Diagnosing and changing counterproductive styles of management.* San Francisco: Jossey-Bass.

Keyes, R. 1985. *Chancing it: Why we take risks.* Boston: Little, Brown.

Kimberly, J.R. 1981. Managerial innovation. In P. Mystrom and W. Starbuck (eds.). *Handbook of organizational design, Vol. 1.* Oxford: Oxford University Press.

Klein, B. 1977. *Dynamic economics.* Cambridge, MA: Harvard University Press.

Knight, F. 1921. *Risk, uncertainty, and profit.* New York: Houghton Mifflin.

Kogan, N., and M. Wallach. 1964. *Risk taking: A study in cognition and personality.* New York: Holt.

Kolb, D.A. 1984. *Experiential learning: Experience as the source of learning and development.* Englewood Cliffs, NJ: Prentice-Hall.

Kolb, D.A., I.M. Rubin, and J.M. McIntyre. 1984. *Organizational psychology: An experiential approach* (4th ed.). Englewood Cliffs, NJ: Prentice-Hall.

Kolb, D.A., S.K. Winter, and D.E. Berlew. 1968. Self-directed change: Two studies. *Journal of Applied Behavioral Sciences* 4: 453–72.

Komives, J.L. 1972. A preliminary study of the personal values of high technology entrepreneurs. In A. Cooper and J. Komives (eds.). *Technical entrepreneurship: A symposium.* Milwaukee, WI: Center for Venture Management.

Kotkin, J. 1984a. The new small business bankers. *Inc.*, May:112–14, 118–26.

Kotkin, J. 1984b. Why smart companies are saying no to venture capital. *Inc.*, August:65–75.

Kotkin, J. 1986. The "smart team" at Compaq Computer. *Inc.*, February:48–56.

Kroeger, C.V. 1976. Managerial development in the small firm. *California Management Review* 17(1):41–47.

Kuehn, R.R. 1986. Scanning habits of small business managers. Paper presented to the Academy of Management, Chicago.

Ladd, A., Jr., J. Kanter, and B. Wigan. 1980. When friends run the business. *Harvard Business Review,* July-August:87–102.

Lansberg, I. 1983. Managing human resources in family firms: The problem of institutional overlap. *Organizational Dynamics,* Summer:39–46.

Laventhol and Horwath. 1985. *The challenges to entrepreneurs: A survey among owners of privately-held businesses.* New York: Laventhol and Horwath.

Lawrence, P.R., and J.W. Lorsch. 1969. *Organization and environment.* Homewood, IL: Irwin.

Lawyer, K. 1963. *Small business success: Operating and executive characteristics.* School of Business, Western Reserve University, Cleveland, OH.

Leaving the company to start one. 1985. *Venture,* October:24.

Leonard, L.S. 1983. *The wounded woman.* Boston: Shambhala.

Lessem, R. 1983. The art of entrepreneurship. *Journal of General Management* 8(3):39–49.

Levenson, H. 1974. Activism and powerful others: Distinctions with the concept of internal-external control. *Journal of Personality Assessment* 38:377–83.

Levine, D.M., and G.A. Kuhlman. 1984. Successful entrepreneurs and the ego: Implications for career adaptation. Paper presented to the Academy of Management, Boston.

Levinson, H. 1971. Conflicts that plague family businesses. *Harvard Business Review,* March-April:90–98.

Lewis, J.L., C.H. Sewell, and C.L. Dickson. 1961. *Identification and evaluation of problems and needs of small manufacturing management.* Atlanta, GA: Industrial Development Branch, Engineering Experiment Station, Georgia Institute of Technology.

Likert, R. 1984. The nature of highly effective groups. In D.A. Kolb, I.M. Rubin, and J.M. McIntyre (eds.). *Organizational psychology: Readings on human behavior* (4th ed.:153–65). Englewood Cliffs, NJ: Prentice-Hall.

Liles, F. 1974. Who are the entrepreneurs? *MSU Business topics* (Winter) 22:5–14.

Linden, E. 1984. The role of the founder: Murphy's law. *Inc.,* July:90–100.

Lipper, A., III. 1985. Entrepreneurship education. *International Council for Small Business Newsletter* 22(3):9.

Little, B.L. 1986. The performance of personnel duties in small Louisiana firms: A research note. *Journal of Small Business Management,* October:66–69.

Litwin, G., and R. Stringer. 1968. *Motivation and organizational climate.* Boston: Harvard University Press.

Locke, E.A. 1968. Toward a theory of task motivation and incentives. *Organizational Behavior and Human Performance* 3:157–89.

Logan, W.G. 1986. Finding your angel. *Venture*, March:38–44.

Long, W., and W.E. McMullen. 1984. Mapping the new venture opportunity identification process. In J. Hornaday, F. Tarpley, J. Timmons, and K. Vesper (eds.). *Frontiers of entrepreneurship research 1984*. Wellesley, MA: Babson College.

Lublin, J.S. 1984. Running a firm from home gives women more flexibility. *The Wall Street Journal*, 31 December.

MacCrimmon, K.R., and D.A. Wehrung. 1986. *Taking risks: The management of uncertainty*. New York: Free Press.

Mace, M.L. 1986. *Directors: Myth and reality*. Boston, MA: Harvard Business School Press.

MacMillan, I.C. 1983. The politics of new venture management. *Harvard Business Review*, November-December:8,12,16.

MacMillan, I.C., R. Siegel, and P.N.S. Narasimha. 1985. Criteria used by venture capitalists to evaluate new venture proposals. *Journal of Business Venturing* 1:119–28.

MacRury, K. 1986. Between a rock and a hard place. *Inc.*, July:101–102.

Maddi, S.R. 1980. *Personality theories: A comparative analysis* (4th ed.). Homewood, IL: Dorsey.

Mahar, M. 1985. Corporate cast-offs. *Venture*, May:78–84.

Mahar, M. 1986. Who's sorry now? *Venture*, August:30–36.

Maier, N.R.F. 1984. Leadership principles for problem solving conferences. (Originally published 1970.) In D. Kolb, I. Rubin, and J. McIntyre. *Organizational psychology* (4th ed.). Englewood Cliffs, NJ: Prentice-Hall.

Mamis, R.A. 1984. New money. *Inc.*, April:93–100.

Mancuso, J.R. 1974. What it takes to be an entrepreneur: A questionnaire approach. *Journal of Small Business Management* 12(4):16–22.

Mangan, D. 1986. Leading a turnaround. *Venture*, December:52–54.

Manz, C.C., and C.A. Snyder. 1983. Systematic self-management . . .: How resourceful entrepreneurs meet business challenges . . . and survive. *Management Review*, October:68–73.

Martin, J., S. Sitkin, and M. Boehm. 1984. *Founders and the elusiveness of cultural legacy*. Unpublished manuscript, Stanford University Report No. 726.

Martin, M.J. 1984. *Managing technological innovation and entrepreneurship*. Reston, VA: Reston.

Mason, R., and I. Mitroff. 1981. *Challenging strategic planning assumptions.* New York: Wiley.

McBer and Company. 1986. *Entrepreneurship and small-enterprise development second annual report.* Washington, D.C.: The United States Agency for International Development.

McClelland, D.C. 1961. *The achieving society.* Princeton, NJ: D. Van Nostrand.

McClelland, D.C. 1965. Achievement motivation can be developed. *Harvard Business Review,* November-December:7–16,20–24.

McClelland, D.C. 1985. *Human motivation.* Glenview, IL: Scott, Foresman.

McClelland, D.C. 1987. Characteristics of successful entrepreneurs. *Journal of Creative Behavior* 21:219–33.

McClelland, D.C., and D.G. Winter. 1971. *Motivating economic achievement.* New York: Free Press.

McCullough, D. 1983. Mama's boys. *Psychology Today,* March:32–38.

McGhee, P.E., and V.C. Crandall. 1968. Beliefs in internal-external control of reinforcement and academic performance. *Child Development*:91–102.

McMullan, W.E. 1982. In the interest of equity: Distributing equity among new venture employees. In K. Vesper (ed.). *Frontiers of entrepreneurship research 1982.* Wellesley, MA: Babson College.

Meredith, G.G., R.E. Nelson, and P.A. Neck. 1982. *The practice of entrepreneurship.* Geneva: International Labour Office.

Middlebrook, P.N. 1980. *Social psychology and modern life* (2nd ed.). New York: Alfred Knopf.

Miles, R.E., and C.C. Snow. 1978. *Organizational strategy, structure, and process.* New York: McGraw-Hill.

Miles, R.H., and W.A. Randolph. 1980. Influence of organizational learning styles on early development. In J. Kimberly and R. Miles (eds.). *The organizational life cycle.* San Francisco: Jossey-Bass.

Miles, R.H., and W.D. Perreault, Jr. 1982. Organizational role conflict: Its antecedents and consequences. In D. Katz, R. Kahn, and J. Adams (eds.) *The study of organizations.* San Francisco: Jossey-Bass.

Miller, D. 1983. The correlates for entrepreneurship in three types of firms. *Management Science* 29(7):770–91.

Miller, D., M.F.R. Kets de Vries, and J. Toulouse. 1982. Top executive locus of control and its relationship to strategy-making, structure, and environment. *Academy of Management Journal,* 25:237–253.

Miller, D., and J. Toulouse. 1986. Strategy, structure, CEO personality and performance in small firms. *American Journal of Small Business,* Winter:47–62.

Miller, M. 1963. *The way of enterprise.* London: Deutsch.

Miner, A.S. 1986. Systematic serendipity: Ambiguity, uncertainty and idiosyncratic jobs. Working paper 7:86–23. Graduate School of Business, University of Wisconsin, Madison.

Mintzberg, H. 1973. *The nature of managerial work.* New York: Harper and Row.

Mintzberg, H., and J.A. Waters. 1982. Tracking strategy in an entrepreneurial firm. *Academy of Management Journal* 25:465–99.

Mirels, H.L. 1970. Dimensions of internal versus external control. *Journal of Consulting and Clinical Psychology* 34:226–28.

Miron, D., and D.C. McClelland. 1979. The impact of achievement motivation training on small businesses. *California Management Review,* Summer:13–28.

Mitton, D.G. 1982. The anatomy of a high leverage buyout: Roadmap for transition from manager to entrepreneur. In K. Vesper (ed.). *Frontiers of entrepreneurship research 1982.* Wellesley, MA: Babson College.

Montagno, R.V., D.F. Kuratko, and J.H. Scarcella. 1986. Perception of entrepreneurial success characteristics. *American Journal of Small Business,* Winter:25–32.

Neilsen, E.M. 1982. A developmental model of two person relationships and its implications for the management of relationships in careers. Unpublished paper, Case Western Reserve University.

Neiswander, D.K. 1985. Informal seed stage investors. In J. Hornaday, E. Shils, J. Timmons, and K. Vesper (eds.). *Frontiers of entrepreneurship research 1985.* Wellesley, MA: Babson College.

Neiswander, D.K., B.J. Bird, and P.L. Young. 1987. Entrepreneurial hiring and management of early stage start employees. In N. Churchill, J. Hornaday, B. Kirchhoff, O. Krasner, and K. Vesper (eds.). *Frontiers of entrepreneurship research 1987.* Wellesley, MA: Babson College.

Nelton, S. 1986. *In love and in business.* New York: Wiley.

Nicholson, N. 1984. A theory of work role transitions. *Administrative Science Quarterly* 29:172–91.

Norburn, D. 1984. Boardroom reform: An international perspective. Working paper 85.13. Cranfield School of Management, Cranfield Institute of Technology, Cranfield, Bedford, MK43, OAL, England.

Osgood, W.R., and W.E. Wetzsel. 1977. A systems approach to venture initiation. *Business Horizons* 20:42–53.

Perera, S.B. 1981. *Descent to the goddess: A way of initiation for women.* Toronto: Inner City Books.

Perkins, D.M. 1981. *The mind's best work.* Cambridge, MA: Harvard University Press.

Perry, C. 1984. Differences between intending and existing and between high-growth and low-growth entrepreneurs. *Management Forum* 10(3):147–55.

Persinos, J.F. 1986. The advice squad. *Inc.*, January:80–84.

Peters, T.J., and R.H. Waterman. 1982. *In search of excellence.* New York: Harper and Row.

Peterson, R. 1985. Creating context for new ventures in stagnating environments. In J. Hornaday, E. Shils, J. Timmons, and K. Vesper (eds.). *Frontiers of entrepreneurship research 1985.* Wellesley, MA: Babson College.

Pinchot, G., III. 1985. *Intrepreneuring.* New York: Harper and Row.

Piore, M., and C. Sabel. 1985. The second industrial revolution. *Inc.*, September:25–30,34–38,41,44–48.

Piore, M.J. 1986. Review of *Discovery of the capitalist process. Venture,* March:124.

Platt, H.D. 1985. *Why companies fail.* Lexington, MA: Lexington Books.

Porter, M.E. 1980. *Competitive strategy: Techniques for analyzing industries and competitors.* New York: The Free Press.

Posner, B.G. 1985. Strategic alliances. *Inc.*, June:74–80.

Posner, B.G. 1986. The first day on the job. *Inc.*, June:73–75.

Posner, B.G. 1987. All my sons. *Inc.*, January:68–72.

Poza, E.J. 1984. Family entrepreneuring or how to succeed without succession. Paper presented at the 30th anniversary conference of the Gestalt Institute of Cleveland.

Quinn, J.B. 1985. Managing innovation: Controlled chaos. *Harvard Business Review,* May-June:73–84.

Quinn, J.S. 1982. Managing strategies incrementally. *Omega* 10: 613–27.

Ray, G.H., and P.K. Hutchinson. 1983. *The financing and financial control of small enterprise development.* New York: Nichols.

Reglan, F. 1956. *The hero: A study in tradition, myth, and drama.* Westport, CT: Greenwood Press.

Reynolds, P.D. 1987. New firms: Societal contribution versus survival potential. *Journal of Business Venturing* 2:231–46.

Reynolds, P.D., and S. Freeman. 1987. *1986 Pennsylvania new firm study: Volume two: New firm contributions to Pennsylvania.* Wharton School, University of Pennsylvania.

Rhodes, L. 1984a. "Being dead is bad for business," *Inc.*, July: 79–88.

Rhodes, L. 1984b. The passion of Robert Swiggett. *Inc.*, April:121–26,131–34,139,140.

Rhodes, L. 1986. Kuolt's complex. *Inc.*, April:72–75,78–84.

Rhodes, L., and P. Amend. 1986. The turnaround. *Inc.*, August: 42–48.

Rich, S.R., and D. Gumpert. 1985. *Business plans that win $$$.* New York: Harper and Row.

Richardson, R. 1971. *Fair pay and work.* Carbondale, IL: Southern Illinois University Press.

Richman, L. 1984. Growing steady. *Inc.*, September:69–81.

Richman, R. 1985a. Assets and liabilities. *Inc.*, May:88–91.

Richman, T. 1985b. Personal business. *Inc.*, April:68–72.

Richman, T. 1985c. Who's in charge here? *Inc.*, June:92–94.

Richman, T. 1986a. The entrepreneur in the gray-flannel suit. *Inc.*, March:99–106.

Richman, T. 1986b. Love 'em and leave 'em. *Inc.*, May:124–30.

Rizzo, J.R., R.J. House, and S.I. Lirtzman. 1970. Role conflict and ambiguity in complex organizations. *Administrative Science Quarterly* 15:150–63.

Roberts, E.B., and H.A. Wainer. 1966. Some characteristics of technical entrepreneurs. Research program on management of science and technology. Working paper No. 195–66. Cambridge, MA: Massachusetts Institute of Technology.

Robinett, S. 1985. What schools can teach entrepreneurs. *Inc.*, February:50,54,58.

Robinson, R.B., and J.A. Pearce. 1984. Evolving strategy in the venture capital industry: An empirical analysis. In J. Pearce (ed.). *Academy of Management Proceedings '84.* Boston: Academy of Management.

Rockey, E.H. 1986. Envisioning new business: How entrepreneurs perceive the benefits of visualization. In R. Ronstadt, J. Hornaday, R. Peterson, and K. Vesper (eds.). *Frontiers of entrepreneurship research 1986.* Wellesley, MA: Babson College.

Rogers, C.R., and R.E. Farson. 1984. Active listening. In D. Kolb, I. Rubin, and J. McIntyre (eds.). *Organizational psychology: Readings on human behavior in organizations.* (124–52). Englewood Cliffs, NJ: Prentice-Hall.

Rogers, E.M., and F.F. Shoemaker. 1971. *Communication of innovations.* New York: Free Press.

Rogolsky, S. 1985. Symposium: Managing the continuity of family firms. Presented to the Academy of Management, San Diego.

Rokeach, M. 1960. *The open and closed mind: Investigations into the nature of belief systems and personality systems.* New York: Basic Books.

Rokeach, M. 1973. *The nature of human values.* New York: Free Press.

Ronstadt, R. 1984a. *Entrepreneurship: Text, cases and notes.* Dover, MA: Lord.

Ronstadt, R. 1984b. Ex-entrepreneurs and the decision to start an entrepreneurial career. In J. Hornaday, F. Tarpley, J. Timmons, and K. Vesper (eds.) *Frontiers of entrepreneurship research 1984.* Wellesley, MA: Babson College.

Ronstadt, R. 1985a. Every entrepreneur's nightmare: The decision to become an ex-entrepreneur and work for someone else. In J. Hornaday, E. Shils, J. Timmons, and K. Vesper (eds.). *Frontiers of entrepreneurship research 1985.* Wellesley, MA: Babson College.

Ronstadt, R. 1985b. The educated entrepreneurs: A new era of entrepreneurial education is beginning. *American Journal of Small Business,* Summer:7–23.

Ronstadt, R., J.A. Hornaday, R. Peterson, and K.H. Vesper. 1986. *Frontiers of entrepreneurship research 1986.* Wellesley, MA: Babson College.

Rosenblatt, P.C., L. de Mik, R.M. Anderson, and P.A. Johnson. 1985. *The family in business.* San Francisco: Jossey-Bass.

Rotter, J. 1966. Generalized expectancies for internal versus external control of reinforcement. *Psychological Monographs* (80)1, Whole No. 609.

Rotter, J. 1980. Interpersonal trust, trustworthiness, and gullibility. *American Psychologist* 35:1–7.

Russell, S. 1984. Life after Memorex. *Venture,* August:44–46.

Sandberg, W.R. 1986. *New venture performance: The role of strategy and industry structure.* Lexington, MA: Lexington Books.

Sanford, J.A. 1980. *The invisible partners.* New York: Paulist Press.

Saranson, S. 1972. *The creation of settings and the future societies.* San Francisco: Jossey-Bass.

Schein, E.H. 1977. Career anchors and career paths: A panel study of management school graduates. In J. Van Manne (ed.). *Organizational careers: Some new perspectives.* New York: Wiley.

Schein, E.H. 1983. The role of the founder in creating organizational culture. *Organizational Dynamics,* Summer:13–28.

Schere, J.L. 1982. Tolerance of ambiguity as a discriminating variable between entrepreneurs and managers. In K.H. Chung (ed.). *Academy of Management Proceedings '82.* New York: Academy of Management.

Schollhammer, H. 1982. Internal corporate entrepreneurship. In C. Kent, D. Sexton, and K. Vesper (eds.). *Encyclopedia of entrepreneurship.* Englewood Cliffs, NJ: Prentice-Hall.

Schon, D.A. 1967. *Technology and change.* New York: Delacorte Press.

Schrage, H. 1965. The R & D entrepreneur: Profile of success. *Harvard Business Review,* November-December:56–69.

Schumpeter, J.A. 1954. *History of economic analysis.* New York: Oxford University Press.

Schumpeter, J.A. 1961. *The theory of economic development.* New York: Oxford University Press. (Originally published 1934.)

Sexton, D.L. 1980. Characteristics and role demands of successful entrepreneurs. Paper presented to the Academy of Management, Detroit.

Sexton, D.L., and N.B. Bowman. 1984. The effects of preexisting psychological characteristics on new venture initiations. Paper presented to the Academy of Management, Boston.

Sexton, D.L., and N.B. Bowman. 1986. Validation of personality index: Comparative psychological characteristics analysis of female entrepreneurs, managers, entrepreneurship students and business students. In R. Ronstadt, J. Hornaday, R. Peterson, and K. Vesper (eds.). *Frontiers of entrepreneurship research 1986.* Wellesley, MA: Babson College.

Sexton, D.L., and C.A. Kent. 1981. Female executives and entrepreneurs: A preliminary comparison. Paper presented at the Babson College Entrepreneurship Research Conference.

Sexton, D.L., and P.M. Van Auken. 1982. Successful vs. unsuccessful entrepreneurs: A comparative study. Paper presented to the Southwest Division of the Academy of Management, Dallas, TX.

Shapero, A. 1972. The process of technical company formation in a local area. In A. Cooper and J. Kosives (eds.). *Technical entrepreneurship: A symposium.* Milwaukee, WI: Center for Venture Management.

Shapero, A. 1975. The displaced uncomfortable entrepreneur. *Psychology Today,* November:83–88,133.

Shapero, A. 1980. Are business schools teaching business? *Inc.,* January:13.

Shapero, A. 1981a. Entrepreneurship: Key to self-renewing economies. *Commentary,* April:19–23.

Shapero, A. 1981b. Numbers that lie. *Inc.,* May:16.

Shapero, A. 1982a. Inventors and entrepreneurs: Their roles in innovation. WPS 82–35. College of Administrative Science, Ohio State University.

Shapero, A. 1982b. Some dimensions of entrepreneurship. Author's draft, submitted to C. Kent, D. Sexton, and K. Vesper (eds.). *Encyclopedia of entrepreneurship.* Englewood Cliffs, NJ: Prentice-Hall.

Shapero, A., and J. Giglierano. 1982. Exits and entries: A study in yellow pages journalism. Working paper, College of Administrative Science, The Ohio State University, Columbus, OH 43210.

Silver, A.D. 1983. *The entrepreneurial life.* New York: Wiley.

Simon, M.A. undated. What we know about the creative process. Manuscript from the Department of Psychology, Carnegie-Mellon University.

Sinetar, M. 1985. Entrepreneurs, chaos, and creativity—Can creative people really survive large company structure? *Sloan Management Review,* Winter:57–62.

Singh, J.V., D.J. Tucker, and R.J. House. 1986. Organizational legitimacy and the liability of newness. *Administrative Science Quarterly* 31:171–93.

"Small business-dominated industries show lowest failure rates." 1986. *Journal of Accountancy,* February:26–27.

Smith, N.R. 1967. *The entrepreneur and his firm: The relationship between type of man and type of company.* Lansing, MI: Bureau of Business and Economic Research, Graduate School of Business Administration, Michigan State University.

Smith, N.R., and J.B. Miner. 1983. Type of entrepreneur, type of firm and managerial motivation: Implications for organizational life cycle theory. *Strategic Management Journal* 4:325–40.

Smith, N.R., and J.B. Miner. 1985. Motivational considerations in the success of technologically innovative entrepreneurs: Extended sample findings. In J. Hornaday, E. Shile, J. Timmons, and K. Vesper (eds.). *Frontiers of entrepreneurship research 1985.* Wellesley, MA: Babson College.

Stanworth, M.K.J., and J. Curran. 1976. Growth and the small firm—an alternative view. *The Journal of Management Studies,* May:95–110.

Star, A.D., and M.Z. Massle. 1981. Survival rates for retailers. *Journal of Retailing* 57(2):87–97.

Steele, F.I. 1979. The instrumental relationship. In W. Bennis, J. Van Mannen, E. Schein, and F. Steele (eds.). *Essays in interpersonal dynamics.* Homewood, IL: Dorsey.

Steinhoff, D. 1978. *Small business management fundamentals* (2nd ed.). New York: McGraw-Hill.

Stevenson, H.H. 1985. A new paradigm for entrepreneurial management. In J. Kao and H. Stevenson (eds.). *Entrepreneurship: What it is and how to teach it* (30–61). Cambridge, MA: Harvard Business School.

Stinchcombe, A.L. 1965. Social structure and organizations. In J. March (ed.). *Handbook of organizations.* Chicago: Rand McNally.

Sutton, D.P., and T. Post. 1986. The cost of going public. *Venture,* April:30–34,38–40.

Swayne, C., and W. Tucker. 1973. *The effective entrepreneur.* Morristown, NJ: General Learning Press.

Tate, C.E., L.C. Megginson, C.R. Scott, and L.R. Trueblood. 1978. *Successful small business management* (rev. ed.). Dallas: Business Publications.

Teach, R.D., F.A. Tarpley, and R.S. Schwartz. 1986. Software venture teams. In R. Ronstadt, J. Hornaday, R. Peterson, and K. Vesper (eds.). *Frontiers of entrepreneurship research 1986.* Wellesley, MA: Babson College.

The age of alliances. 1984. *Inc.,* February:68–69.

The bottom line: Unequal enterprise in America. 1978. Report on the president's interagency task force on women business owners. Washington, D.C.: U.S. Government Printing Office.

"The second industrial revolution." 1985. *Inc.,* September:25–30,34–38,41–44,48.

The venture index of venture capital activity. 1986. *Venture,* September:98.

"The word spreads." 1983. *The Economist,* December:66–69.

Thurston, P.H. 1986. When partners fall out. *Harvard Business Review,* November-December:24–26,30,32,34.

Timmons, J.A. 1971. Black is beautiful, is it bountiful? *Harvard Business Review,* November-December:81–94.

Timmons, J.A. 1975. The entrepreneurial team: An American dream or nightmare? Unpublished paper. Boston, MA: Northeastern University.

Timmons, J.A. 1976. Characteristics and role demands of entrepreneurship. *American Journal of Small Business* 3:5–17.

Timmons, J.A. 1982. Careful self-analysis and team assessment can aid entrepreneurs. In *Trials and rewards of the entrepreneur.* Boston, MA: Harvard Business Review.

Timmons, J.A. 1985. "The Valley," *Inc.,* July:53–58.

Timmons, J.A., D.F. Muzyka, H.H. Stevenson, and W.D. Bygrave. 1987. Venture capital and the search for potentially successful ventures: The characteristics of successful ventures. Paper presented at the Babson Entrepreneurship Research Conference, Malibu, CA.

Valentine, D. 1985. Peaks and valleys. *Inc.*, May:29–34,37–38,41–49.

Van de Ven, A.H. 1980. Early planning, implementation and performance of new organizations. In J. Kimberly and R. Miles (eds.). *The organizational life cycle.* San Francisco: Jossey-Bass.

Van Maanen, J. 1979. On the understanding of interpersonal relations. In W. Bennis, J. Van Maanen, E.H. Schein, and F.I. Steele (eds.). *Essays in interpersonal dynamics* (13–42). Homewood, IL: Dorsey.

Van Maanen, J., and E.H. Schein. 1977. Career development. In J. Hackman and J. Suttle (eds.). *Improving life at work* (30–95). Santa Monica, CA: Goodyear.

Vesper, K. 1980. *New venture strategies.* Englewood Cliffs, NJ: Prentice-Hall.

Vesper, K.H. 1986. New developments in entrepreneurship education. In D. Sexton and R. Smilor (eds.). *The art and science of entrepreneurship* (379–88). Cambridge, MA: Ballinger.

Virany, B., and M.L. Tushman. 1986. Executive succession: The changing characteristics of top management teams. In J. Pearce and R. Robinson (eds.). *Academy of Management Best Papers Proceedings 1986.* Chicago, IL: Academy of Management.

Wainer, H., and I.M. Rubin. 1969. Motivation of research and development entrepreneurs. *Journal of Applied Psychology* 53:178–84.

Ward, J.L. 1986. Family ownership, business strategy and performance: A look at the PIMS data base. Paper presented to the Academy of Management, Chicago.

Ward, J.L. 1986. *Keeping the family business healthy.* San Francisco: Jossey-Bass.

Weick, K.E. 1979. *The social psychology of organizing* (2nd ed.). Reading, MA: Addison-Wesley.

Welsh, J.A. 1975. The man at the head of the stairs. In J. Schreier, J. Susbauer, R. Baker, W. McCrea, A. Shapero, and J. Komives (eds.). *Entrepreneurship and enterprise development: A worldwide perspective.* Milwaukee, WI: Project ISEED, Center for Venture Management.

Welsh, J.A., and J.F. White. 1983. *The entrepreneur's master planning guide.* Englewood Cliffs, NJ: Prentice-Hall.

Whelan, E.P. 1983. Marty Alpert: The electronic renaissance man. *Cleveland,* May:64–68.

Whitehead, R. 1984. Planning for "the next economy." *Inc.,* June:44–53.

Wholey, D.R., and J.W. Brittain. 1986. Organizational ecology: Findings and implications. *Academy of Management Review* 11:513–33.

Willens, H. 1984. *The trimtab factor: How business executives can help solve the nuclear weapons crisis.* New York: Morrow.

Winter, S.K., J.C. Griffith, and D.A. Kolb. 1970. Capacity for self-direction. In M. Miles and W. Charters (eds.). *Learning in social settings* (458–67). Boston: Allyn & Bacon.

Wojahn, E. 1986a. Divorce entrepreneurial style. *Inc.*, March:55–64.

Wojahn, E. 1986b. Little big man. *Inc.*, June:77–85.

Wojahn, E. 1986c. Will the company *please* come to order. *Inc.*, March:78–80,83–86.

Wolfe, D.M., and D.A. Kolb. 1984. Career development, personal growth, and experiential learning. In D. Kolb, I. Rubin, and J. McIntyre (eds.). *Organizational psychology: Readings on human behavior in organizations* (124–52). Englewood Cliffs, NJ: Prentice-Hall.

Woodman, M. 1980. *The owl was a baker's daughter.* Toronto: Inner City Books.

Woodman, M. 1985. *The pregnant virgin: A process of psychological transformation.* Toronto: Inner City Books.

Woodworth, R.T., et al. 1969. *The entrepreneurial process and the role of accountants, bankers, and lawyers.* Seattle, WA: The School of Business, University of Washington.

Young, D.R. 1983. *If not for profit, for what?* Lexington, MA: Lexington Books.

Young, E.C., H.D. Welsch, and A.R. Triana. 1984. Comparison of Hispanic and non-Hispanic entrepreneurs on perceived problems and information sources utilized. Paper presented to the Academy of Management, Boston.

Zander, A. 1982. Resistance to change—its analysis and prevention. In M. Plvnick, R. Fry, and W. Burke (eds.). *Organization development.* Boston, MA: Little, Brown (193–96). (Originally published, 1950.)

Zaslow, J. 1986. 'New nepotism' calls for junior to earn stripes away from home. *The Wall Street Journal*, 14 January.

INDEX